MUSLIMS
IN
WESTERN
POLITICS

MUSLIMS
IN
WESTERN
POLITICS

Edited by Abdulkader H. Sinno

Indiana University Press
Bloomington and Indianapolis

This book is a publication of

Indiana University Press
601 North Morton Street
Bloomington, IN 47404-3797 USA

http://iupress.indiana.edu

Telephone orders	800-842-6796
Fax orders	812-855-7931
Orders by e-mail	iuporder@indiana.edu

The paper used in this publication meets the minimum requirements of American National Standard for Information Sciences—Permanence of Paper for
Printed Library Materials, ANSI Z39.48-1984.

Manufactured in the United States of America

Library of Congress Cataloging-in-Publication Data

Muslims in Western politics / edited by Abdulkader H. Sinno.
    p. cm.
  Includes bibliographical references and index.
  ISBN 978-0-253-35247-7 (cloth : alk. paper) — ISBN 978-0-253-22024-0
(pbk. : alk. paper) 1. Muslims—Western countries. 2. Muslims—Europe,
Western—Politics and government—Congresses. 3. Muslims—United
States—Politics and government—Congresses. 4. Muslims—Canada—
Politics and government—Congresses. 5. Muslims—Government
policy—Europe, Western—Congresses. 6. Muslims—Government
policy—United States—Congresses. 7. Muslims—Government policy—
Canada—Congresses. 8. Europe, Western—Politics and government—
1989—Congresses. 9. United States—Politics and government—
2001—Congresses. 10. Canada—Politics and government—
1980—Congresses. I. Sinno, Abdulkader H., date
  D842.42.M87M87 2008
  305.6'97091821—dc22

                                     2008019717

1 2 3 4 5 14 13 12 11 10 09

To those who speak truth to power
To those who suffer because of others' fears

Contents

Acknowledgments

This volume is based on the contributions to the "Muslims in Western Politics" conference that I convened at Indiana University on September 22–24, 2005. It would not have been possible without the strong support of IU unit heads, faculty, and administrators to bring some of the best researchers in the field to this conference.

This project owes much to wonderful visionary colleagues at IU. It began with a conversation and encouragement from Robert Rohrschneider, then director of the Center for West European Studies. Both he and Fritz Breithaupt, who succeeded him as director, provided me with the kind of necessary advice that only hard-earned experience would otherwise bring. Ted Carmines helped fund the conference and convince first-rate scholars to participate, and infused the process with his legendary bonhomie. I also acknowledge the support of two more superb colleagues for their participation and support, Jeff Isaac and Nazif Shahrani.

I acknowledge the generous sponsorship of the Center for the Study of Global Change, the Center for West European Studies (WEST), the Middle Eastern and Islamic Studies Program (MEISP), the Department of Political Science, the Office of the Dean of the College of Arts and Sciences, the Office of the Dean of Faculties, the Office of the Chancellor, the IU School of Law, the College Arts and Humanities Institute, the Barr Koon Fund, the Department of French and Italian, the Office of International Programs, the American Studies Program, the Center for Citizenship and Participation, and the Center for the Study of American Politics. These Indiana University units financed the conference and the research assistance that helped produce this book.

Among administrators, I acknowledge the indispensable and ever-outstanding staff of the Department of Political Science: Scott Feickert helped me navigate complicated financial logistics, James Russell provided first-rate technical support, and Margaret Anderson was of continuous assistance. Adam Jacobs assisted with logistics. Ahmed Khanani meticulously assisted with formatting this manuscript.

I thank all contributors to this volume for providing sophisticated essays in a timely fashion and for the pleasure of collaborating with them.

I finally recognize my editor at Indiana University Press, Dee Mortensen, and her staff for their helpfulness and patience.

Note on Transliteration

We generally employ the transliteration system suggested by the *International Journal of Middle Eastern Studies.* For names and terms that have come into regular English usage, we do not transliterate (e.g., Saudi Arabia instead of Saʿudi ʿArabia, Shia instead of Shiʿa). We also drop initial hamzas and ʿayns for well-known names, like Ali, for convenience. We do not add long vowel lines or the dots for velarized letters in the complete certainty that those familiar with Middle Eastern languages will be able to recognize the correct word from the transliteration, and that those not so familiar will be unaffected.

MUSLIMS
IN
WESTERN
POLITICS

I

An Institutional Approach to the Politics of Western Muslim Minorities

Abdulkader H. Sinno

This is a book about how Western institutions interact with each other and growing Western Muslim minorities to shape the way Muslim minorities in Western Europe and North America are perceived, represented, and treated. Its goal is to answer important policy-relevant research questions in comparative context to explain variation among different North American and European countries. For instance, why are there many more Muslim parliamentarians in Western Europe and Canada than in the United States? How does the Canadian state benefit from the cooperation and input of the Canadian Muslim population in law enforcement much more successfully than the American and the British? Why do Muslims in Britain receive more religious rights than in France? Why do social conflicts in France sometimes produce riots by minority youths but grievances in Canada and, more slowly, in the United States are redressed within established institutions? Such are some of the urgent and complicated questions collectively addressed by the contributors to this volume.

The theoretical thread that binds the chapters of *Muslims in Western Politics* is the use of an institutional approach to explain Muslim representation, attitudes, organizational development, civil rights, image, and political identification in West European and North American liberal democracies. Chapters in each of the volume's four parts address different institutional explanations of one or more such dimensions of Western Muslim existence in Europe and North America. They address the effect of Western historical institutional developments on the treatment of new Muslim minorities, issues of representation, public attitudes toward Muslim minorities and their civil rights, and the treatment of Muslim minorities in the legal sphere and law enforcement. Bringing them together allows us to understand how different institutions (governments, parliaments, courts, the media, political parties, churches, and law enforcement) interact to shape the lives of Western Muslims and the future of Western liberal democracies. But why should we care about this topic?

The Importance of Western Muslim Minorities

Contributors to this volume do not consider "Muslim" to necessarily mean a religious identity, but instead an identity that may have religious, racial, political, or cultural dimensions. It may be in flux and sometimes irrelevant, but it is hard to escape in the context of today's politics in Western Europe, the United States, and Canada (the "West" for short in this volume). Politicians who define themselves as "culturally Muslim" or even as "secular Muslim" find themselves dealing with "Muslim" issues and being considered as "Muslim" by their own political parties when they wish to emphasize their diversity, by minority constituents who feel connected to them or who do not trust them, by jealous rivals wishing to discredit them, by the media when they need "Muslim" voices, and by civil society's organizations. Even those who define themselves in opposition to the Islam of their families, such as the former Dutch parliamentarian Ayaan Hirsi Ali, end up being understood (and used) in the context of the broader politics of Western Muslim minorities. Non-religious members of Muslim minorities are defined as "Muslims" by the media, by Muslim organizations, by religious leaders, and in the speeches of many politicians. Nowadays non-Muslim European politicians talk of "Muslims" in their countries more than of "Pakistanis" or "Turks." And surveys (see Allen and Wike's contribution to this volume) have shown the consolidation of a "Muslim" identity among Western Muslims. Even if someone from a Muslim background wishes to do so, it is not easy to escape being a "Muslim" in the West anymore. To borrow from two eloquent contributors to this volume, Muslims and Islam have been racialized (Jamal) and "being Muslim is not just a matter of faith, but also a sociological fact" (Klausen).

The Muslim populations of west European and North American countries have grown dramatically since the 1970s, when their numbers were minuscule. Individuals who practice the religion or who belong to ethnic groups that are traditionally Muslim are now estimated to make up some 1–2 percent of the

North American population and 4 percent of the population of the European Union.[1] Absent dramatic changes like the accession of Turkey to the EU, which would make Muslims a sixth of the Union's population, or changes to immigration laws that would slow growth, these percentages are likely to double in the next twenty to thirty years because of immigration and relatively higher fertility rates among Western Muslims than among non-Muslims. In a few decades, it is quite possible that one of every four or five Frenchmen will be of Muslim background and that several European countries will have proportions of Muslims larger than the current proportions of blacks and Latinos in the United States. Of course, many Western Muslims may assimilate to the point of making Muslim identity irrelevant, but that does not seem likely in the short run in most Western countries. Muslims are now an integral part of the West and are here to stay. Yet, the interactions between Western Muslims and the institutions of their countries have been problematic in many ways.

American Muslims have been quite successful in the socioeconomic field but have been targeted extensively and discriminatorily in the legal and law enforcement spheres. Laws passed by Congress (the so-called Patriot Act) make it easy to target them and others. They have also been sidelined in the political process by powerful rivals such as the pro-Israel and evangelist lobbies. Some media outlets, such as Fox News and Christian religious programming, the American movie industry, and some Evangelical churches, have been promoting views and images of Muslims that encourage restrictions on their civil rights and liberties. On the bright side, legal challenges, grassroots social activism and coalition building, American Muslim activism, and the election of a Democratic Congress in 2006 are likely to redress some of the transgressions on the civil rights and liberties of Muslim Americans.[2]

European Muslims have suffered from different problems. Many are disenfranchised by being effectively blocked from gaining citizenship in spite of being longtime residents or even having been born in their country of residence (e.g., Germany, Austria, Spain, Italy, Greece). Mainstream politicians now find it acceptable and even advantageous to denigrate Muslim minorities in traditionally liberal countries such as Italy, France, the Netherlands, and Germany.[3] Overtly anti-Muslim political parties such as the Belgian Vlaams Belang and the French Front National have made considerable gains in local elections and now attract a substantial number of the national electorate. Racism and Islamophobia (prejudice against Muslims or those considered to be Muslims) have made it difficult for Muslims to integrate professionally and to move up the economic ladder in countries like France and Belgium, and have contributed to the development of minority ghettos mired in poverty and hopelessness.[4]

The most worrisome trend across Western countries is that Islam has become racialized and that Muslims have become an "other" to whom it is acceptable to apply exceptional, and otherwise unacceptable or even illegal, treatment. Despite the "humanist" European ideal referred to in the now dormant European constitution and the theoretical universality of the American Bill of Rights, Muslim individuals and communities regularly receive treatment that would not be acceptable if applied to other citizens of Western democracies. It is easy for people with German blood and Jews from the Commonwealth of Independent States to immigrate to Germany, for example, but millions of Muslim Turks who spent much or all of their lives in the country cannot become German citizens. The Bush administration held thousands of Muslim residents incommunicado and without legal rights for up to two years and deprived American Muslim citizens of basic constitutional rights through the designation of "enemy combatant" (Cole). It also effectively shut down Muslim charities after 9/11 by meting out heavy prison sentences, now allowed under post-9/11 legislation, to their officers. The convictions are on flimsy charges that have nothing to do with heavily publicized accusations by Bush administration officials that these charities or their officers have been supporting terrorism. The Bush administration and Canadian legislation (Roach) also stymied the emergence of new organized Muslim charities by threatening donors with prosecution for supporting terrorism if any of their charitable donations reached an organization that the governments disapprove of, even if the donors intended the donations to reach proper recipients.[5] Adding insult to injury, the Bush administration touted successful Muslim Americans overseas in a botched public relations campaign to influence the populations of Muslim countries to believe that it is friendly to Islam and Muslims.[6] Dutch politicians devised a formula of "not tolerating Muslim intolerance" to denigrate and isolate Dutch Muslims while pretending to continue to adhere to their traditionally tolerant liberalism. The flawed assumption underlying the formula is that all Muslims are intolerant, homophobic, and misogynistic—a particularly odd caricature of the vibrant and diverse Muslim communities of the Western world.

Members of Western Muslim minorities have reacted in a variety of ways. Most try to live normal lives away from the tumult of identity politics and confrontation. Some have tried to develop organizations such as the UK's Muslim Council of Britain and the Council on American-Islamic Relations in the United States to address grievances and civil rights transgressions and to engage state institutions. Some intellectuals such as the Swiss Tariq Ramadan and the American Khaled Abou El Fadl worked on new theological interpretations of Islamic text in the hope of reconciling minority Muslim citizenship in a liberal and democratic West with core Muslim beliefs, only to be attacked by extreme right pro-Israel activists who fear that effective Muslim integration would allow Muslim communities sympathetic to the plight of the Palestinians to become influential over their countries' foreign policies.[7] Some in Europe, like the organizations Hizb al-Tahrir and al-Muhajiroun in the United Kingdom and the Belgian activist Dyab Abou Jahjah, advocate different strands of brash self-empowerment that sometimes touch on separatism, confrontational political activism, and even the use of violence. They evoke in their language and behavior the American civil-rights-era organizations of Malcolm X and the Black Panthers. No such Muslim organizations exist in North America today. Yet others began to take advantage of openings in political institutions to join established political parties and run for political office.

Many Western Muslims, particularly Europeans, continue to feel that they live in the midst of Western societies without belonging to them (see Allen and Wike's essay on self-identification in this volume).[8] And clashes of cultures and violent attacks have made many in non-Muslim Western publics wary of Muslim minorities. Western states and their rapidly growing Muslim populations are adjusting to each other under the constant pressure of exogenous shocks such as transnational terrorism and wars in the Middle East that involve Western militaries or produce intense interest among Westerners, Muslims and non-Muslims. The way they manage the process will deeply affect the future of Western polities and their relations with the Muslim world, which constitutes a fifth of humanity.

A worst-case scenario for some European countries, such as France and Belgium, is of ghettoized, young, and embittered Muslims becoming an irreconcilable part of society with their own separate and parallel institutions. This may very well be a recipe for future civil wars. The frustrated Muslims of Europe would draw inspiration and support from Islamist states and organizations elsewhere and provide justification for those who wish to make the case that the West is inherently anti-Muslim.

A rosier scenario is of Western Muslims integrating effectively into their societies but feeling that their identity, lifestyle, and beliefs are welcomed and appreciated. They would enrich the cultures of their countries, consolidate their democratic institutions, help invigorate their economies, and stabilize declining European populations without engendering feelings of xenophobia or threat. They would also, by example and through their networks, help to promote genuine and stable liberal democracies in countries with Muslim majorities that would become durable trade and security partners. They would defang, by prospering in the midst of their own Western countries, any argument beyond their borders that the West is anti-Muslim.

Of course, all countries are ongoing ventures evolving through stages that can hardly be described as purely successful or solely grim. Western countries do indeed fall somewhere between the two extremes, with Canada being somewhat ahead, in spite of some glitches, of the United States and west European countries. Most Western countries do better in some areas than in others and can learn from other countries how to improve some institutional practices. It is therefore important to explore the institutional practices and policies that would produce more equitable and robust Western liberal democracies that preserve the dignity, security, and rights of their populations.

An Institutional Approach

Which institutions matter and how do they help explain variation in the treatment and the politics of Muslim minorities? Contributors to this volume assess the role of governments, parliaments, political parties, the courts, the media, churches, and law enforcement. They all matter, but they matter differently as they interact in many possible configurations over time and across countries. We explore some of these permutations in comparative context.

Contributions to part 1 both assess the influence of institutional legacy on the treatment of Muslim minorities in the West and provide introductions to the development of several Western Muslim communities. Yvonne Haddad and Robert Ricks (chapter 2) argue that the Muslim-American experience of integration fits a classic pattern of mutual adjustment between minorities and American institutions. The American myth and ideal of religious freedom has always had within it the potential to marginalize and penalize those viewed to be beyond an ever-expanding range of accepted cultures and religions. The Muslim-American community's leaders and organizations are adjusting to institutional pressures and opportunities as others did before them, albeit in the context of the challenging 9/11 legacy, and transforming these institutions in the process of their Sisyphean effort to join the mainstream. In the process of making their argument, Haddad and Ricks identify the numerous but important institutions and actors that are helping Muslims integrate and those that are trying to isolate this minority. The contest is close and the stakes are high because those who are trying to undermine American Muslims include some highly ideological and influential evangelical leaders and supporters of the Israeli right.

Christopher Soper and Joel S. Fetzer (chapter 3) argue that differences in historical state-church institutions explain the different ways Germany, Britain, and France treat their Muslim minorities. Such institutions may provide openings for Muslims to press for recognition and accommodation (Britain, where other religious minorities were accommodated before them with the support of the Church of England) or keep them from doing so (France's strict *laïcité*, or separation between state and church). Complex German institutions produce mixed results.

Jorgen Nielsen (chapter 4) critiques the use of macro-institutional taxonomies employed by Soper and Fetzer as well as others. He refers to developments in Britain and France, states that are considered to have distinct institutional arrangements in most typologies, to argue that what matters may be specific laws, the party in power, divisions within the Muslim communities in each country, the proportion of Muslims within immigrant populations, and the strengthening of EU institutions. He concludes that the macro-institutional typologies used by others are dated and irrelevant.

Part 2 deals with issues of Muslim representation in Western political institutions. Abdulkader Sinno (chapter 5) describes Muslim representation across parliaments in Western liberal democracies and argues that a majoritarian electoral system, as opposed to proportional representation, in conjunction with larger districts largely explains Muslim underrepresentation in American institutions. This is so because even moderate public hostility toward Muslim candidates would make it difficult for a Muslim candidate to be first past the post in a winner-takes-all contest, unless there are enough Muslim supporters in the district to counter public hostility. Large American electoral districts make it difficult for the small and diffuse Muslim minority to have the concentration necessary to accomplish this. Very few districts, mostly liberal ones like Minnesota's Fifth Congressional District, which elected Keith Ellison to Congress, and Indiana's Seventh, which elected André Carson, do not disadvantage Muslim candidates. He tests his argument in a nested study of electoral campaigns by American Muslims.

Jytte Klausen (chapter 6) interviews three hundred European Muslim leaders to better understand the group of people who represent the Muslim population in the public sphere. She finds that most of them were not born in Europe and feel that being Muslim is important to them. They are also a very diverse and engaged group that is developing a very European attitude toward civic engagement. Mosque leadership, however, is of poor quality and would benefit if European imams were trained to engage and assist the integration of Europe's Muslims. European Muslim representation is still hampered by the reliance of some European governments on ties with countries of emigration to manage their own Muslim citizens and residents, by government manipulation of Muslim organizations, and by organizational fragmentation within Europe's Muslim communities.

Abdulkader Sinno and Eren Tatari (chapter 7) explore the perceptions, experiences, and political behavior of British Muslim members of city councils, political parties, and parliamentary chambers to learn whether they perceive that their presence in these institutions helps members of minority communities. They find that British Muslim representation on the local level yields clear advantages for both the Muslim minority and the society at large but that the situation is more complicated for British Muslim parliamentarians. Muslim life peers can speak more freely on Muslim issues than other Muslim parliamentarians from the Labour and Conservative parties. Muslim members of Parliament (MPs) and members of the European Parliament (MEPs) from the two large parties are largely no different than non-Muslim ones, from the perspective of members of the Muslim minority. Party discipline generally prevents them, with few exceptions, from advocating on behalf of minority rights and positions on foreign policy, even if they wish to do so.

The third part of this volume addresses Western public opinion about Muslim minorities. Jodie Allen and Richard Wike (chapter 8) analyze survey data collected by the Pew Global Attitudes Project on the attitudes of Western publics toward Muslim minorities and vice versa. They generally find that Western Muslim minorities are less inclined to see a "clash of civilizations" than general European publics and to find no contradiction between being a devout Muslim and living in a modern society. European Muslims also tend to have more positive views of European Christians than the other way around and to be more concerned with their livelihood than with religious or cultural matters. They also find substantial differences among countries, with higher tolerance toward Muslims in France and Britain than in Germany and Spain.

Erik Nisbet, Ronald Ostman, and James Shanahan (chapter 9) dig deeper into the correlates of attitudes by the American public toward the Muslim-American minority. Their summary of a large number of surveys reveals disquieting rates of ignorance of basic facts about Islam and of negative attitudes toward the religion and its adherents. Nisbet and his colleagues also use data from a survey they conducted to unravel the correlates of attitudes toward Muslim Americans and support for restricting their civil liberties. They find that conservative political orientation, poor education, Christian media use, and reliance on television news and entertainment programming all drive negative opinions of Muslim Americans and the desire to restrict their civil liberties.

Amaney Jamal (chapter 10) argues that large sections of the American public are willing to restrict the civil liberties of Muslim Americans, a very un-American thing to do, because of a process of "racialization" of Muslim and Arab Americans as enemy "Other." She bases her argument on an analysis of survey data from a study of the Detroit-area population. She finds that Protestants and those who believe in a clash of civilizations are more likely to support restrictions on the civil liberties of Muslim Americans. Her findings are consistent with the national study by Nisbet, Ostman, and Shanahan because a large segment of the Protestant Evangelical population follows Christian media programming and tends to be conservative.

The last part of this volume focuses on the development of legal and law enforcement institutions across the Atlantic since 9/11. Three contributors (Kent Roach on Canada, David Cole on the United States, and Anja Dalgaard-Nielsen on the European Union) study how Western countries balance security needs with civil liberties in the courts, in immigration regulations, and in law enforcement. They present their narratives of this evolution in the context of contentious politics and complex institutions.

Kent Roach (chapter 11) argues that Canada's initial post-9/11 attempts to restrict civil liberties in the hope of increasing security have been partly replaced by a more balanced approach to policy making that includes sunset provisions for new policing powers, seeking input from members of the Muslim minority, and grievance procedures. The government, under pressure from civil rights and other groups, did amend its original anti-terrorism bill to provide safeguards for civil liberties. Abuses, including the case of Maher Arar, helped reassess practices and policies. The system, however, still includes loopholes that have allowed some abuses and that may allow further transgressions on civil liberties. They include the definition of terrorism under the law and the use of immigration laws to detain non-citizens for long periods of time without due process.

Anja Dalgaard-Nielsen (chapter 12) explains how European cooperation on intelligence gathering and anti-terrorism operations has advanced in the slow and bureaucratic way typical of EU institutions. She finds that, although successful in some areas, new institutions that facilitate policing and cooperation are still lacking and have become largely unaccountable by developing in the bureaucracy away from the moderating influences of the European Parliament and the European Court of Justice. Some practices, particularly dragnet measures, have indeed trampled on the civil rights of Muslim minorities who have little recourse to challenge such transgressions. Dalgaard-Nielsen makes recommendations to increase policing effectiveness while avoiding abuses against Europe's marginalized minorities.

David Cole (chapter 13) argues that powers claimed and used by the Bush administration in the wake of the 9/11 attacks have provided little protection to the American public, produced much abuse of Muslims in America, trampled on civil liberties, and weakened the rule of law. These dramatic changes include the adoption of a judicial doctrine of prevention that undermines the right to due process, the use of inhumane treatment against detainees, and the secretive incarceration of thousands of Muslims (including American citizens under the designation of "enemy combatant") on American soil without access to lawyers and the right to know and challenge evidence against them. Other practices facilitated by the Patriot Act include the monitoring of houses of worship and the obtaining of warrants to search and monitor individuals. The Bush administration had little to show for all these extraordinary measures when compared to other policing practices that respect constitutional rights and conform to international treaties. Legal challenges and the election of a Democratic Congress seem to have finally tempered some of the practices established by the Bush administration.

I conclude this book with policy recommendations for Western governments and Muslim organizations based on our comparative research and collective findings.

Notes

1. We have fairly precise numbers and proportions in Canada (2% in the 2001 census, and the percentage is expected to double or triple in twenty years), the UK (some 2.7% in 2001 census and some 8% in London), and some other European countries that ask for religion in their censuses. Estimates are much rougher in countries with censuses that do not break populations down by religion, such as the U.S. (anywhere between 0.8% and 2% of the population in 2007) or France (5–10%).

2. For more on these issues, see the chapters in this volume by Haddad and Ricks, Sinno, Nisbet et al., Jamal, and Cole.

3. They include, among many others, the former Italian prime minister Silvio Berlusconi, who claimed that Islamic civilization is inferior to Western civilization, and the now deceased Dutch politician Pim Fortuyn (assassinated by an animal-rights activist), who called Islam a "backward culture."

4. This is well documented in the case of France in reports by SOS Racism and other non-governmental organizations (NGOs). See, for example, *The Situation of Muslims in France,* a report by the Open Society Institute, online at http://www.eumap.org/reports/2002/eu/ international/sections/france/2002_m_france.pdf, and "French Muslims Face Job Discrimination," BBC News, November 2, 2005, online at http://news.bbc.co.uk/go/pr/fr/-/1/hi/world/ europe/4399748.stm (accessed April 16, 2007).

5. See, inter alia, "Muslim Charities and the War on Terror," OMB Watch, February 2002, online at http://www.ombwatch.org/pdfs/muslim_charities.pdf, accessed on April 16, 2007. Also see Haddad and Ricks in this volume.

6. For example, see "Islam: Muslim-Americans to Improve U.S. Image Abroad," Heather Maher, Radio Free Europe, Friday, June 16, 2006, online at http://www.rferl.org/featuresarticle/ 2006/06/b47f318d-dcef-4b59-ac09-9a9d33a70805.html, accessed on April 16, 2007. The British government of Tony Blair tried the same strategy by sending its Muslim parliamentarians to Muslim countries ("Muslim Parliamentarians on Goodwill Mission," *Muslim News,* August 1, 2002).

7. Such attacks on Tariq Ramadan and concerns that Western Muslims are a danger to Western Jews and support for Israel are peppered across right-wing pro-Israel websites. See, inter alia, a paper by Alvin Rosenfeld promoted by the American Jewish Committee that claims that anti-Semitism in Europe "has roots within Arab Muslim culture." Alvin Rosenfeld, "'Progressive' Jewish Thought and the New Anti-Semitism," online at http://www.ajc.org/atf/cf/ %7B42D75369-D582-4380-8395-D25925B85EAF%7D/PROGRESSIVE_JEWISH_THOUGHT .PDF (accessed on April 16, 2007).

8. American Muslims seem to be much better integrated and satisfied than European ones according to a May 22, 2007, Pew Survey Report, *Muslim Americans: Middle Class and Mostly Mainstream.* Available online at http://people-press.org/reports/display.php3?ReportID=329 (accessed on May 24, 2007).

PART ONE

WESTERN MUSLIMS AND
ESTABLISHED STATE-RELIGION
RELATIONS

2

Claiming Space in America's Pluralism: Muslims Enter the Political Maelstrom

Yvonne Yazbeck Haddad and Robert Stephen Ricks

In the aftermath of the September 11, 2001, attacks on the World Trade Center and the Pentagon, the George W. Bush administration has legislated policies that impact the Muslim population of the United States and threaten, in a more fundamental way, the guarantees of liberty and freedom of speech, thought, and religion enshrined in the U.S. Constitution.[1] While it is too early to assess whether American policies will have a permanent impact on the integration and assimilation of Muslims and Arabs into American culture, it is clear that the measures adopted by the government have had a profound impact on Muslims living in the United States. These measures have already disrupted the lives of thousands and left them in the grip of constant apprehension; they have also impeded the entry and full participation of the American Muslim community in the public square.

This disruption has occurred both through official means, such as the controversial PATRIOT (Providing Appropriate Tools Required to Intercept and Obstruct Terrorism) Act, and by more subtle pressures that infiltrate the internal discourse of the Muslim community and tend to reshape and redirect its interactions with the public sphere. For example, the U.S. government is currently attempting to play an important role in identifying, and in some fashion creating, a "moderate Islam" that is distinctly different from that espoused by al-Qaeda and the mujahideen—one that, ironically, rejects the same articulation of the faith encouraged by former American administrations and their allies during the Cold War, namely a fundamentalist Islam that would act as a firewall against the spread of socialism, Marxism, or communism in Muslim nations. As this brand of Islam is no longer useful, and has actually become an impediment to American interests and security, the Bush administration has launched several initiatives at home and abroad to foster, nurture, and empower "moderate" Muslims. At the same time it is acting to undermine those Muslims it has designated as "terrorists," "fundamentalists," "extremists," "jihadists," or "Islamists" (Haddad 2004). In response to harassment and discrimination, a few Muslims have been prompted to reexamine the theological and ideological constructs that define the contours of diasporic Islam. The policies have also propelled new claimants to the intellectual leadership of the Muslim community, fostering a more amiable—and less "threatening"—redefinition of Islam. At the same time, government policies appear to have subtly encouraged the attitudes of those intent on criticizing the religion of Islam and its teachings by failing to consistently condemn hate speech against Islam.[2] All of these factors have combined to pose a new and intense challenge to the identity, security, and autonomy of American Muslims and their communities. For Muslims, this is a key historical moment as they strive to overcome these challenges and become fully empowered as participants in civic and political life; likewise, this is a moment that compels Americans to once again examine their country's relation to the ideals of religious freedom and pluralism. It is as yet unclear in which direction these challenges will be resolved.

This study provides a brief historical overview of the American ideal of religious freedom and contrasts it with the more sobering reality of marginalized religious groups throughout its history. It focuses on Muslim attempts to fit into the American religious mosaic and gain recognition as legitimate actors within its political maelstrom, and on Muslim responses to both internal and external challenges faced by the Muslim community in the aftermath of 9/11. It also looks at the efforts of a few Muslim leaders to redefine the role of Islam in a pluralistic American society, and at the impact of the reality of 9/11 on the articulation of Islam in the American public square. Finally, it explores some of the initiatives that have been generated within the Muslim community to deal with these issues.

Religion and the American Public Square

In the International Religious Freedom Act, a 1998 bill that made advocacy of religious freedom abroad a tenet of American foreign policy, the following sketch of the history of religious freedom in the United States was presented:

The right to freedom of religion undergirds the very origin and existence of the United States. Many of our nation's founders fled religious persecution abroad, cherishing in their hearts and minds the ideal of religious freedom. They established in law, as a fundamental right and as a pillar of our Nation, the right to freedom of religion. From its birth to this day, the United States has prized this legacy of religious freedom and honored this heritage by standing for religious freedom and offering refuge to those suffering religious persecution. (Moore 2002, 27)

This language, unqualified and enshrined in official legislation, reflects the late-twentieth-century myth of the American republic as a bastion of religious freedom and, for all of its egregious simplifications, probably approximates popular understanding of this history. In the minds of most Americans, the United States has always represented a place of religious refuge and freedom: it is the original and most notable embodiment of this ideal, whose later adoption by other nations is a clear testament to its universal appeal and value. It is not that this myth has no basis in fact, simply that the truth is rather more problematic. On the one hand, the United States has managed to avoid devastating wars of religion and has become, in the early twenty-first century, the most religiously diverse nation on earth (Eck 2002).[3] Overall, the American model for religious pluralism—at least the current articulation of that model—has proved quite robust and successful. On the other hand, however, American history has seen its share of religious tension, prejudice, and injustice on both official and popular levels. To assert that from its inception to the present day the country has acted as a benign and open refuge to seekers of religious asylum is historically myopic. The history of religiously marginalized groups in the United States shows that rather than merely acting as a "refuge to those suffering religious persecution," the government has, both openly and in more subtle ways, acted out of fear, misunderstanding, and prejudice toward religious groups outside the mainstream. The general public ignorance of this history suggests that many do not recognize this persecution for what it is or actually support it in the name of national unity, morality, or security. The current situation of government scrutiny and popular apprehension of the American Muslim community is, despite its unique contours and context, not without historical precedent.

Perhaps it is not surprising that the history of religious freedom in the United States is marked by exceptions and setbacks to the ideal because there is some degree of deliberate ambiguity in the source texts of the American republic and a history of selective application of promised rights. For much of American history, supposedly universal rights have been reserved for white citizens insofar as federal policies codified racism, the enslavement of Africans, and the dispossession of indigenous peoples (Johnson 1998). Protection for the free practice of religion, another hallowed right, has likewise not been uniformly applied.

The words commonly interpreted as guaranteeing freedom of religious practice are found in the First Amendment, enjoying pride of place alongside such rights as freedom of speech, press, and assembly. The "free exercise" and "establishment" clauses of the First Amendment—those impinging on the right of religious freedom—represented an attempt of the Founding Fathers to reach a middle ground in relation to issues of liberty and religious establishment. The language of these clauses is strikingly brief: "Congress shall make no law respecting an establishment of religion, or prohibiting the free exercise thereof." Perhaps due to the concision of this language, it has proved remarkably amenable to contrasting interpretations. Hundreds of subsequent legal decisions have attempted to parse these words and apply them to cases in which religious freedom has intersected with other areas of the public sphere (Hamburger 2002; Hutchison 2004; Lambert 2003). In fact, throughout the nation's history, legal minds have debated the recurrent and difficult question of how the republic should define and position itself in relation to religious practice (Segers 2002). It seems clear that the Constitution espouses the notion of religious freedom, but is not clear just exactly what bounds this freedom implies and how it is to be translated into practice. For example, what role should religion play in the life of the polity, or in the formulation of policy? Is the United States a Christian nation or is it secular? Is it sufficient to ground the nation on a civil religion of shared values and morality that transcend any single religious tradition? Or, as the title of one book has it, "What's God got to do with the American experiment?" (Dionne and Dilulio 2000).

These questions were just as vexing and controversial in the past as they are today. Despite the language of the First Amendment's "establishment clause," it is clear that at the foundation of the Republic there was a de facto "establishment" of Protestantism: it was the dominant religion and Anglo conformity (understood as white and Protestant) was the accepted paradigm.[4] The popular narrative of religious history in the United States follows the expansion of this paradigm to include non-Protestant and even non-Christian religions under the umbrella of religious freedom. The chapters in this narrative appear to move quickly along the path toward an all-embracing religious pluralism, the lens that now filters, in hindsight, the official understanding of how the process unfolded. As substantial immigration changed America's cultural and demographic landscape, it became fashionable, by the turn of the twentieth century, to refer to the United States as a melting pot, a metaphor that appeared to create a space for the inevitable and seemingly benign cultural assimilation that was part of the American immigrant experience. By the middle of the twentieth century, the influential sociologist Will Herberg revised the paradigm and promoted the "triple melting pots" where identity is grounded in religious affiliation. He suggested that the three ways of being American were to be a Protestant, a Catholic, or a Jew (Herberg 1983). Members of these three groups were posited as equal constituents of the polity—this despite the reality that some "unmeltables" were present. With the opening of the gates of immigration in 1965, the American religious landscape changed as Buddhists, Jains, Hindus, Sikhs, and Muslims began to transplant their families and their faiths to American soil. Alternatives to the various assimilation models gave way in the 1980s and 1990s to multiculturalism, the notion that diversity itself is good and that various cultures and competing faiths can coexist in a democratic society that embraces pluralism, tolerance, and broadly defined notions of religious freedom.

This narrative is the kernel of truth at the heart of the religious freedom myth, and in many ways it is an inspiring and positive story. Jewish historian Jonathan Sarna (1987) argues that despite initial hostility toward non-Protestant faiths, American institutions have made room for other faiths to be practiced. Judaism, for example, was able to thrive precisely because of American tolerance of freedom of religion, religious pluralism, voluntarism (dependent on the voluntary support of a committed laity), coalitionism (the need to seek allies), and interfaith organizations. There are, however, other facets to the narrative of religious freedom in the United States—facets that are often overlooked or elided by the sheer momentum of the dominant plotline. Underlying the expansion of religious freedom were legal, theological, and demographic challenges to the dominant paradigm from other groups viewed as marginal (or potentially subversive) by the Protestant mainstream. While Muslims may complain that today Islam seems to have become the consummate "Other" in the eyes of many American citizens, American religious history demonstrates that there have been different religious Others that have been objects of criticism and discrimination. During the colonial period, Baptists and Quakers were deemed to be dangerous to the American nation. In the early national period, the protest was focused on Mormons and Adventists; in the nineteenth and early twentieth centuries it targeted Catholics and Jews; and in the 1970s its objects were the "Moonies" and the "Hare Krishnas" (Foster 1987, 192). Today, it appears that it is the Muslims' turn. The historical experience of these marginalized or "outlying" religious communities offers parallels to the Muslim experience and offers a corrective to the received narrative of how religious freedom has historically unfolded in the U.S. (Moore 1987).

America remains a religious nation, or perhaps more precisely, a nation of religious citizens (surveys continue to document the fact that the majority of Americans are religious in one way or another).[5] The fact that the Constitution banned the establishment of religion has not meant that Americans favor secularism. Americans like to imagine their country as hospitable to religion, but they do not like to see this as compromising in any way its "Americanness." Conformity to certain "American" values is expected to supersede any commitment to faith (or, conversely, only faiths that conform to such values have been historically acceptable). Accordingly, the United States, a nation of immigrants from all over the world, has developed strong Americanizing institutions that have molded several generations of newcomers into patriots willing to fight for the nation and its causes. These institutions have promoted America as a model of democracy and tolerance—a nation that welcomes all who choose to join in the American adventure and share in the American dream. They function to shape the children of the new immigrants into proper citizens, stripping them of the vestiges of their culture and honing their religion to conform to the expectations of American "civility." For several decades in the early twentieth century the public school system, for example, was geared toward eradicating differences among the children of immigrants and bringing forth new American citizens with a shared vision of what it means to be American. With the influx of the post–World War II immigrants, a new effort at tolerating pluralism and hyphenated identities became the vogue in some jurisdictions. Still, even hyphenated Americans were, at their core, American.

Other institutions besides public education have had a similar effect. Service in the United States armed forces, for example, has also proved an effective tool of Americanization. Service in the military has been (and continues to be) a traditional means of social advancement and integration for immigrant and minority groups.[6] Perhaps most important of all, participation in the democratic process itself tends to have a conforming, moderating effect. The grassroots efforts, coalition building, debate, and accommodation that are necessary for effective representation of political interests tend to drive the engine of integration and the adoption of civic values. The crucial issue for religious groups is whether they can maintain some values that appear counter to the general civic virtues. Does becoming American mean abandoning primary loyalty to one's faith? The historical record of religious outsiders shows that entry of religious groups into the public square most often comes at a specific cost: religious practice will be tolerated, but if this practice conflicts with government policy, law, or the "will of the people" as the government articulates it, the religious group must cede precedence to the authority of the government (Flake 2004). The American Muslim community is currently attempting to take that most "American" of steps—full-fledged entry into the public square—without sacrificing its identity and autonomy as Muslim. Based on historical precedent, it is unclear whether they will be able to take such a step unscathed.

American Muslims on the Eve of 9/11

The majority of American Muslims immigrated to the United States after 1965. They came to a nation in the midst of religious and civic turmoil. The U.S. religious community was grappling with how to respond to a variety of challenges to its establishment theology ranging from the "death of God" theology,[7] "feminist theology,"[8] "liberation theology,"[9] and the black theology influenced by the Black Power movement.[10] America had passed anti-segregation laws and was increasingly defining itself as a pluralist and diverse nation. In the midst of this cultural and religious ferment, Muslims set out to create a place for Islam in the American mainstream, establishing organizations that paralleled those of the other recognized religions. For example, while Muslims affirm that there is no recognized "clergy" in Islam, they emulated the American religious model of voluntary organized religion. They organized mosques led by lay executive committees. The affluent communities hired imams (mosque preachers) to administer mosques and provide religious leadership. They established Sunday schools, women's Qur'an study groups, and Boy Scout and Girl Scout troops.

Muslim immigrants had to decide whether and how to make an effective transition from their countries of origin to being full participants in American society. Early immigrants had no experience of being a minority, living in diaspora, and creating institutions or organizing religious communities, and no religious leaders to provide instruction. By and large, they came from nations in which Islam has long been the established religion, where religious institutions are supervised and administered by nationalist governments. Lacking local leadership, some communities began inviting religious leaders from the Indian subcontinent such as Abu al-A'la al-Mawdudi and Abu al-Hassan Ali Nadvi to provide guidance (Nadvi 1983, 111). Both lectured throughout the United States and Canada and addressed questions concerning the legitimacy of whether a Muslim can live in a non-Muslim environment and continue to be considered a believer. They warned Muslims about the potential loss of their faith in a tolerant, multicultural, non-Muslim environment. Other speakers urged Muslims to maintain separate isolated communities since mixing with the local inhabitants could lead to the loss of their Islamic identity.

By the 1980s, with the steady growth of labor migration from Muslim nations and the formation of the Institute for Minority Affairs in Jidda, Saudi Arabia, new Muslim ideas concerning life in the diaspora began to be voiced. Rashid al-Ghannushi of Tunisia and Hassan Turabi of Sudan addressed large Muslim gatherings at the annual conventions of the Islamic Society of North America and identified the West not as *bilad al-kuffar* (land of the disbeliever, according to the classical distinction drawn between the lands of Islam and those of non-believers), but as *bilad maftuha* (an open country) or *dar al-da'wa* (abode of propagation), ready for the Islamic message. Muslims were urged to participate in the public affairs of their adopted country by emphasizing the pluralistic nature of Islam and its amity with Christianity and Judaism. Ghannushi reminded Muslim audiences that the freedom they enjoyed in the West to reflect on Islam, to inform others and publish about the faith, far exceeds that given citizens in Muslim nations. While the new immigrants and the foreign "experts" continued to debate the legitimacy of living in a non-Muslim state, other Muslims had no qualms: they were American. They included those who had emigrated between 1870 and the 1950s, as well as converts who appeared to be comfortable and able to maintain the imperatives of Islamic life and practice in the United States. Efforts to create

Islamic enclaves were deemed by many as unnecessary due to the promise of "the hospitable American melting pot." They believed that America and its institutions have room for Muslims, "not only to survive but also to flourish in honor and dignity" (Abdul-Rauf 1983, 271–272).

By the middle of the 1980s, Muslims were no longer concerned with debating whether they could live in the United States and maintain their faith, or if it was imperative to return to live under the jurisdiction of an Islamic state. Their discussion shifted to the definition of Muslim life in the American context and the scope of their participation in American society.[11] They sought to create a space for Islam in the U.S. (and to update Herberg) by redefining America as a Protestant-Catholic-Jewish-Muslim nation. A few began to envision a cohesive Muslim community with civic and political clout equal to that of the Jewish community. Those who participated in interfaith activities promoted the idea of dialogue among members of the "Abrahamic faiths"—Islam, Christianity, and Judaism—in the process seeking parallel status and equal voice. Small pockets of Muslims who adhere to the teachings of the Tablighi Jamaat, Hizb al-Tahrir, or Wahhabi doctrines persist in teaching that the West is *bilad al-kuffar*. They insist that the Muslim community must nurture itself as an implant in a foreign body and not acculturate and be altered in an alien environment. Muslims must beware, they warn, of the possibility of contamination and maintain a barrier to ensure the separateness, difference, and distinction of Islam and Muslims. These voices, however, are distinctly in the minority.

The majority of Muslims (estimated between 70 and 80 percent) in the United States are not active participants in mosques or Islamic religious institutions. They have embraced the fact that they are part of American society and have little concern for what the compromise might cost. Many refer to their children as "real" Americans, not just citizens. They look with disdain at organized Islamic mosques and centers and believe that non-practicing Muslims are just as "good"—if not better—than those who attend regular mosque services. That has not spared them or their children the abuse that is often heaped on Islam and its adherents in post-9/11 America, nor have they been spared from being subjected to the same policies designed to ferret out the terrorists and the "sleeper cells" in the United States.

For many Muslims in the West, 1989 was a watershed year because intense media attention to the so-called "Rushdie affair" brought increased scrutiny of Muslim communities, renewing doubts about their loyalty to fundamental Western values such as freedom of speech. While in Britain, where the first anti-Rushdie protests erupted, there was some debate about whether Salman Rushdie's novel *The Satanic Verses* represented an infraction of the blasphemy laws designed to protect religion, in the United States the resounding consensus was that true commitment to freedom of speech could never condone censorship of Rushdie's fiction. The American loyalty to this freedom was projected as quite absolute. The reality is, naturally, more problematic. Freedom of speech is by no means boundless: certain types of anti-Semitic or anti-black speech, for example, are no longer countenanced in the American public square. American Muslims reacted to the Rushdie affair with discomfort, as they realized quite clearly that they did not enjoy the same protection from defamation as did blacks and Jews. In addition to this discomfort, however, was a renewed sense of solidarity as a community. There was a phenomenal growth in the number of Islamic Sunday schools, for example, as parents feared that their children would accept Western perceptions of Islam and abandon their Islamic identity.

After the Iraqi invasion of Kuwait in August 1990, American Muslims were increasingly frustrated with their lack of input to U.S. policy, foreign and domestic. In their view, not enough effort was made diplomatically to solve the Gulf crisis. Recognizing this as a weakness in need of long-term remedies, Muslim organizations began to focus their efforts on building permanent institutions, especially on the construction of mosques and Islamic centers funded domestically and independent of foreign money. There was also an emphasis on finding space for a Muslim voice in the secular public square. Mainstream Islamic organizations, such as the Islamic Society of North America (ISNA), had been since 1986 encouraging their memberships to engage with secular and religious American society. Others, such as the Muslim American Society (MAS) and the Islamic Circle of North America (ICNA), have, since 2002, opened up their conventions to non-Muslim speakers and engaged in interfaith dialogue. The Council on American-Islamic Relations (CAIR), a Muslim organization that has gained prominence since its establishment in 1994, has attempted to represent the concerns of the Muslim community to the United States government and American society at large. These and other organizations have advocated Islamic issues on a larger scale and with greater sophistication than what was done previously.[12]

Political involvement of Muslims has grown quickly in the past two decades. The 1988 Jesse Jackson presidential campaign included fifty Arab and Muslim delegates to the Democratic National Convention. By the 1990s Muslims embarked on a policy of engagement with American society that culminated in such new moves as joining forces with existing secular Arab organizations and becoming more actively involved in local and national political movements.[13] In the 2000 presidential campaign Muslim organizations for the first time publicly supported a specific candidate. They chose George W. Bush because, unlike Al Gore, Bush had met with the leadership of American Arab and Muslim organizations and listened to their concerns. During the presidential debates he questioned the fairness of profiling Muslims and Arabs as permitted by the Comprehensive Anti-Terrorism Act of 1995. It was the first time in American history that a candidate talked about Arab issues: secret evidence and airline profiling. It seemed that a new moment of relevance and influence for Muslim Americans had arrived. Maher Hathout, senior adviser of the Muslim Public Affairs Council, welcomed the process of incorporation of Arabs and Muslims into the democratic process: "This is a real new millennium, a new era, hopefully for American Muslims seeking freedom and peace. We are not asking to be included; we already got ourselves included. Did we make a difference? We don't know. Will we make a difference? God willing, definitely, we will."[14] These expectations would be frustrated when the Bush administration shied away from engaging with the Muslim community upon taking office and delayed setting up an appointment to meet with its leadership until September 11, 2001.

The Impact of 9/11 on the American Public

As Amaney Jamal and Erik C. Nisbet, Ronald Ostman, and James Shanahan quantitatively demonstrate in this volume, the attacks of 9/11 have generated a great deal of fear of Muslims and apprehension about Islam among a growing number of non-Muslims in the United States. The fear is aggravated with every security alert issued by the government warning of impending attacks, as well as by the propaganda generated to elicit support for the War on Terror in Afghanistan and Iraq. It appears to have tapped into a long history of American fear and subsequent demonization of Islam. Thus while the promoters of a civil society in the United States profess America's openness to immigration and support of pluralism as foundational principles of its polity, the country's heritage reveals a historical antipathy toward Islam and Muslims.

American society, having struggled during the twentieth century to rid itself of racism and anti-Semitism, thus appears to be reverting to an inherently anti-Saracen (anti-Arab, anti-Muslim) mindset. The Founding Fathers depicted Islam as a religion of despotism and the oppression of women, the antithesis of what they imagined that America was to become.[15] These themes were useful in fostering a concept of the Other opposed to the liberty understood to be the foundation of the American republic. As a result of the attacks of 9/11 many Americans appear to have given up any pretense of political correctness in regard to Islam and have engaged in diatribe against the religion, its scripture, its prophet, and its adherents. Some strident voices in the media engage in the demonization of Arabs, Islam, and Muslims as the monolithic "outsiders," the essential Other. Their beliefs, values, and customs are characterized as inferior, barbaric, sexist, irrational, and worthy of repeated condemnation.[16]

Muslims are viewed with more intense or particular suspicion than other religious groups, but they are not unique in being the victims of misunderstanding or prejudice: a Pew survey found that 31 percent of respondents said there are reasons they might not vote for a Muslim candidate. This compares to 14 percent for a Jewish candidate, 15 percent for a Catholic candidate, and 41 percent for an atheist

(Pew Forum on Religion & Public Life 2005). A recent CAIR survey, however, paints a bleaker picture: approximately one in four Americans believe that Islam is a "religion of violence and hatred" (Council on American-Islamic Relations 2006, 3). None of these numbers alone can capture, however, the extraordinary scrutiny to which Muslims are routinely subjected, nor the structural and cultural challenges to the Muslim community's participation in the public square—challenges which have only been exacerbated by the policies and the rhetoric of the past few years.

In the post-9/11 world, American policy makers and those in the administration have tended to depict the world in binary fashion with poles of good and evil, civilized and uncivilized, democratic and despotic. At the same time they have insisted on policies that in reality are the antithesis of the American ideals of democracy, tolerance, and civilization—the very ideals, ironically, that the American political elite claims the terrorists aim to destroy. Many political analysts believe that in the two decades since the collapse of the Soviet empire the U.S. has been searching for another evil to be vanquished. Now it appears that the enemy has been identified, and "terrorist Islam" rather than communism is portrayed as the enemy of freedom, godliness, civilization, and all that is good. Some seriously question whether such an enemy can be part of American civil society, even one that proclaims itself to be multicultural and/or pluralistic. Thus has begun the quest for moderate Islam.

President Bush spoke to the issue: "The faith of the terrorist is not the true faith of Islam. That's not what Islam is all about. Islam is peace. These terrorists don't represent peace; they represent evil and war. When we think of Islam, we think of a faith that brings comfort to a billion people around the world. Billions of people find comfort and solace and peace."[17] One can read this statement as a public affirmation of the faith of Islam in order to stem possible violence against Muslims as retribution for 9/11, or as an indirect ultimatum to Muslims in the United States to fashion an Islam that is compatible with whatever Bush has in mind. Such statements are highly ambiguous. Still at issue are such concerns as, What does "moderate" really mean (moderate in relation to whom and what)? Is "moderate" simply middle-of-the-road? What is the middle ground?

In the aftermath of the attacks of al-Qaeda on the World Trade Center and the Pentagon, President Bush addressed the world and announced: "[E]ither you are with us, or you are with the terrorists."[18] This binary division of the world into righteous victims and heinous enemies appears to leave no rhetorical room for a pluralism that celebrates difference or for a different take on reality. It allows for no alternate analysis of why the attack was perpetrated. Any suggestions that such violence might be related to American foreign policy have been interpreted as support for the enemies of America or as coming from apologists for terrorism.[19]

Officials and journalists increasingly began to identify the United States as a

Judeo-Christian nation—a new shorthand, perhaps, for the 1960s Herbergian formula of Protestant, Catholic, and Jew. For many, pluralism has become a questionable paradigm. American citizens, however, appear to be of two minds on this issue, reflecting major divisions in the nation. On the one hand, many feel that "Judeo-Christian" has a "nice ring" to it. A Pew Forum on Religion & Public Life survey (July 2003) found that 84 percent of Americans say that one can be a good American without believing in God even though 67 percent believe the United States to be a "Christian" nation. Representing the expansion of the covenant forged after the Second World War between mainline Protestant denominations and liberal Jews, the "Judeo-Christian" label seeks to integrate all citizens, regardless of their faith, into the American mainstream promoting a pluralistic, multicultural, multifaith society working for the public good. Openness to a more tolerant pluralism was promoted in mainline churches, synagogues, and public schools as part of the initial reaction to 9/11, which saw the outpouring of support for Muslims by concerned neighbors, rabbis, and ministers.

For others, however, more appealing than this kind of religious tolerance is a closed and exclusive Judeo-Christian identity that preaches a God of vengeance and war, a God of retribution and violence who does not tolerate other faiths, especially Islam. Among the most vociferous in expressing this perspective are prominent leaders of right-wing Evangelical Christianity such as Pat Robertson and Jerry Vine.[20] In an interview on NBC-TV, the Reverend Franklin Graham called Islam "a very wicked religion." In his book *The Name,* Graham wrote, "The God of Islam is not the God of the Christian faith," and that "the two are different as lightness and darkness" (Graham 2002, 2). In response, Ibrahim Hooper of CAIR observed that Franklin Graham obviously thinks that America *is* engaged in a war against Islam.[21] This kind of evangelical right-wing position is represented among such members of the Bush administration as General William Boykin and former attorney general John Ashcroft. They believe that God has charged them with combating evil, which they now see as manifest in Islam, or at least its extremist factions. As if hostility from policy makers were not enough, in the print and broadcast media Zionist provocateurs such as Daniel Pipes, Steve Emerson, and David Horowitz stalk and caricature Muslim organizations (such as CAIR) as extremist and label academics who are against Israeli policy as dangerous to America and its youth.[22]

The response to 9/11, then, has been ambivalent and at times double-edged—not uniformly positive or negative. The initial impact of 9/11 on the Muslim community was one of deep shock and fear of potential backlash. Muslims were surprised and pleased by the response of some in the Christian and Jewish communities who supported them. They were grateful to the rabbis and ministers who volunteered to stand guard at mosques, schools, bookstores, and Islamic institutions to keep avengers away. They were amazed at the number of American women who donned a scarf for a day in solidarity with Muslim women who veil. They were also touched by the little gestures of kindness such as neighbors' offers to act as escorts or purchase groceries for them. They were mostly pleased that Americans were finally interested in Islam and were reading about the religion and getting acquainted with the tenets of their faith.

Yet despite many encouraging demonstrations of openness and support on the individual and local level, Muslims and others were disconcerted by policies enacted on the federal level in the name of national security. For Muslims, the most distressing measure adopted by the Bush administration is HR 3162, commonly known as the USA Patriot Act of October 24, 2001. In essence it lifted legal protection of liberty for Muslims and Arabs (and others) in the United States. It sanctioned the monitoring of individuals, organizations, and institutions without cause and without judicial approval. Muslims noted that while the Anti-Terrorism Act had sanctioned the incarceration of Arabs and Muslims with secret evidence, the Patriot Act has sanctioned their incarceration with no evidence. The provisions of the Patriot Act have been protested by the American Bar Association, the American Civil Liberties Union, and the American Librarians Association. Several Arab and Muslim organizations in coalition with civil liberties groups sued the American government, insisting that this act is un-American.[23] In a certain sense the current controversy about the Patriot Act is simply the most recent incarnation of an old debate about how to balance security and civil liberty. It has deep roots in American history: the 1798 Alien and Sedition Acts, which sanctioned the deportation of foreigners and the suppression of "seditious" speech, have been seen by some as an eerie historical precedent for the Patriot Act. The Alien and Sedition Acts are almost universally regarded as a nadir in the history of liberty in America and a blemish on John Adams's presidency. History and future generations will one day judge whether the Patriot Act contradicts the freedoms vouchsafed in the Constitution.

The American Constitution guarantees freedom of speech, movement, and political expression; and freedom from illegal search and prejudice, discrimination, and persecution based on race, national origin, or religion. Muslims, however, increasingly feel that because of their ethnicity and/or religious affiliation they no longer have the luxury to publicly disagree with policies of the Bush administration. For Arabs and Muslims the freedom of speech guaranteed to all Americans now appears to be conditional upon certain shibboleths and litmus tests; non-citizens whose behavior does not conform risk being accused of being anti-American and deported or incarcerated. Increasingly they question whether government policies are designed to force a return migration of Muslims to their countries of origin or to "tame" Islam, making it more compliant to American and Israeli interests and sensitivities.

Government policies have curtailed political and religious speech domestically, often indirectly, by creating an atmosphere of intimidation in which American Muslims do not feel that they can speak freely on certain issues. Since mosques are under FBI surveillance, imams censor their own sermons, which are now restricted to devotional topics with few references to issues of social, economic, or political justice. Islamic literature that used to be available for free distribution has disappeared from many public places. Self-censorship has also extended to website content and recommended links.

Security measures adopted by the Bush administration have generally been viewed by Arabs and Muslims as being specifically anti-Muslim rather than generally anti-terrorist. These policies include direct challenge to an Islamic definition of the role of women in society. The American government has set up a bureaucracy in the Department of State specifically to help bring about the liberation of Muslim women. "To liberate them *from* what *to* what?" many Muslims wonder, suspecting that the liberation sought by the United States is really from Islam and its values. Islamic textbooks are monitored and censored by American embassies overseas for any anti-Western, anti-American, or anti-Israeli content. It appears to many that the only "Islam" that can now be taught is one that is vetted and sanctioned by the CIA in what amounts to a kind of new externally imposed *ijtihad,* that is, the process of independent interpretation of the religious text normally reserved to established Muslim scholars.

The atmosphere created by official rhetoric and monitoring has negatively impacted the Muslim community. Even more disconcerting, however, is the U.S. government's material and structural intrusion into the affairs of Muslim groups. These include the monitoring of non-governmental organizations (NGOs), as well as civic, charitable, and religious organizations, which risk the freezing of their assets if they are suspected of having unacceptable ties. In effect, the American government has assumed a veto power over one of the basic tenets of the Islamic faith by monitoring charities and organizations that support efforts to help the needy overseas out of fear that they might transfer funds to terrorist organizations.[24] Another visible change that may be the consequence of the government's close surveillance of Muslim institutions is the redirection of welfare efforts. While funds had been raised to ameliorate the conditions of poverty in homelands left behind, the focus of charity work moved to the United States. *Zakat* money that might have gone to purchase an ambulance for a remote village in Pakistan, for example, was allocated for such homeland projects as purchasing a school bus for an Indian reservation. Tithes that had been utilized to feed the hungry, educate the illiterate, and care for the orphans overseas are now redirected into local soup kitchens and free medical clinics in ghettos.[25]

The degree to which the Bush administration has shown itself willing to interfere structurally in the affairs of the Muslim community was manifest when the government raided the homes and offices of the national Muslim leadership in northern Virginia—leaders who had been vaulted into national prominence, ironically, by cooperating with the Clinton administration.[26] Many Muslims believe that the raids were part of the effort by the U.S. government to replace them with new leadership. The question being mulled over is, What sort of Islam will the American government now tolerate? The government has clearly articulated

its desire for a "moderate" Islam and has demonstrated that those who resist being co-opted risk being harassed and, potentially, marginalized.

Other profound changes are under way, the ramifications of which are still
unfolding. For the majority of Muslims who had emigrated with the idea that if
things did not work out they could always return home, the 9/11 attacks appear to
have settled the "myth of return": Muslims are here to stay. The question for them
is how to adjust to the intensified scrutiny by anti-immigration groups, government security agencies, Evangelical hate groups, and pro-Likud (Israeli right) organizations that demand repeated public demonstrations of patriotism and
allegiance to America and its policies. Many have had a hard time convincing their
fellow Americans that they also feel under attack. Their repeated denunciations of
terrorism as un-Islamic do not seem to be sufficient. Some have offered themselves
to the American government as a bridge to Muslim organizations overseas and to
various governments, others have volunteered to serve in the armed services, and
some claim that thousands have signed up to act as translators, of whom only a few
have been hired because of suspicions regarding their loyalty.

Also noticeable is the fact that the community has embarked on coalition
building with human-rights, religious-rights, and civil rights groups. For children
of the immigrant generation, relating to non-Muslims has become a priority: this
is reflected in greater numbers of interfaith contacts and occasions being initiated
by Muslims. As Mohammad Nimer of CAIR notes, "[A]s a result of interfaith and
civic encounters, Muslims have gained greater acquaintance with the public square
and engaged some of its players, managing to initiate dialogue with diverse groups
on issues of common interest" (Nimer 2004, 162–163). They are inviting members
of churches and synagogues to come and visit the mosques and engage in dialogue.
Muslims are increasingly joining national organizations that work for the promotion of justice against corporations and sweatshops, protection of the environment, and peaceful conflict resolution. Still, many feel that because of their ethnicity
or religious affiliation they no longer have the luxury of disagreeing with government policy. While freedom of thought is, in principle, a right for all Americans,
there seems to be an exception if one is Arab or Muslim. The policy of "you are
either with us or against us" appears to leave no room for an independent interpretation of what the Islamic faith has to say on the issue.

The Scramble for Muslim Space in American Pluralism

The attacks of 9/11 interrupted an ongoing process in which the Muslim community in America was experiencing what Dr. Agha Saeed has called a "complex
transition from outsiders to insiders" (Saeed 2002, 40). Historically, immigrant,
religious, and minority groups have passed through these transitions to become
(more or less) full participants in the public square. Due to these recent attacks

and their aftermath, American Muslims, unfortunately, no longer have the luxury of making that transition in a gradual and natural fashion. They have been thrust into the public eye in an abrupt and dramatic manner—a situation that has tested the Muslim community and its leaders in ways that would have been difficult to anticipate. The raids on homes and offices of Muslim leaders in Virginia was perceived as an effort by the United States government to undermine the existing leadership. A few individuals have stepped up and volunteered to "lead Muslims into moderation." Several individuals have been funded by various agencies of the U.S. government; their mission is to provide new reflections and interpretations of Islam. They have opened offices and are in the process of leading others into "right thinking." To date, they appear to have few followers since they are perceived as agents of the effort to undermine Islam.

While the current atmosphere has accelerated the search for leaders within the Muslim community and has focused public attention on issues of importance to the community, representation in the actual halls of power remains minuscule (see chapter 5, this volume). The events of September 11, 2001, had a decidedly negative impact on the number of Muslim candidates willing to run: in 2000, 700 Muslims were candidates for office at federal, state, and local levels; in 2004, that number was down to 100. As noted earlier, there was much optimism in the Muslim community about the 2000 elections. While speaking to Muslim leaders at a symposium in early 2001, Jim Moran, congressman from Virginia, said that "the American political system is open to everyone who wants to use it. The appropriate reaction is to learn and replicate from the Jewish experience and be a force within our electoral system. Get involved. Don't envy or hate."[27] Had the 9/11 attacks not occurred, perhaps American Muslims would have continued on their trajectory toward greater acceptance and representation. As it is, it may be many years before the setback of those attacks is overcome. Certainly the absence of Muslim elected officials is not the only obstacle to acceptance in the public square, but it is a telling one. Until the time that Muslim candidates run and succeed with greater frequency, American Muslims will have to hope for non-Muslim representatives who are sympathetic to their interests and issues. Some have tried to raise voices of optimism. Agha Saeed, for example, believes that the fact that any Muslim can be elected to public office given the current climate of hostility and apprehension is a positive sign.[28]

For the moment, then, the scramble to lead the American Muslim community is largely an internal one that is taking place on both the popular and the scholarly levels. Senior American Muslim scholars like Fathi Osman and Abdulaziz Sachedina have long advocated a pluralistic Islam grounded not in fear or isolation, but in engagement with American society and exploration of new models of leadership and public participation. Until recently this kind of interpretation had been eclipsed by more conservative ones. Recently, a small number of (mainly young) Muslim scholars have gained some prominence for their advocacy of what they dub "Progressive Islam."[29] They have published articles and set up websites devoted to discussions of an Islam based on concepts of justice, gender equality, and pluralism.[30] In *The Islamic Roots of Democratic Pluralism*, Abdulaziz Sachedina makes an eloquent case for the pluralistic strains of thought embedded within the Qur'an. The Islamic model is not only compatible with democratic pluralism, but can even further "interpersonal justice in society" (Sachedina 2001, 139). He provides a sensitive treatment of some of the issues involved in the encounter between Islam and modernity, and between Muslims and members of other faiths. On both the scholarly and popular levels, then, Muslims are attempting to engage the pressing issues of their communities in authentic fashion—by appeal to Islamic traditions and texts. This engagement is responding, naturally, to the exigencies of the current moment, but the intrusion of government rhetoric and policing into what is already a sensitive dialogue makes its outcome even more uncertain. The transition from "outsider" to "insider" in the American public square has never been an immediate or simple one; the obstacles are even greater when the internal autonomy of the community is threatened from without.

Conclusion

Muslim immigrants who came to America as adults in the 1960s with fully developed identities are now in the process of renegotiating those identities in what they experience as an increasingly hostile post-9/11 American environment. Their children, who know no other homeland, are working to formulate their own identities both as Muslims and as Americans. Part of the context for this process is the steady stream of questions challenging their religion coming from non-Muslim Americans since 9/11. Does Islam teach pluralism or hatred of others? Is all Islam militant? Are Muslims determined to convert America to Islam? Do Muslims want to impose sharia law in the United States? Do Muslims seek to establish a caliphate and rule the world? The American public, the American security apparatus, and the American government are increasingly demanding clear and unequivocal answers.

Muslim presence in the United States has not only challenged the Western image of itself as grounded in enlightened, democratic, rational, liberal, and tolerant traditions; it has put these same traditions to the test, especially after the events of 9/11. The Patriot Act as it is implemented has made it quite evident that the constitutional guarantees for freedom of speech, thought, and religion, embedded in the Bill of Rights, can no more provide a protective shield that insulates Muslims from profiling and entrapment, seizure and search, arrest, deportation, or incarceration. The events of 9/11 and their aftermath have jolted the Muslims of America out of their complacency and their expectation that they are on the way to being considered full constituents of American society. They came to realize that they have become American, and that while Islam as a religion is given a place in the American religious mosaic, their interpretation of it may require major rethinking to meet the increasing demands placed on its adherents to persistently and constantly prove their patriotism. This is a pattern with many historical precedents in American history. To gain full recognition in the public square, religious outliers have had to abandon heterodox practices and to demonstrate their loyalty and conformity to a degree that others have not. The attacks on Keith Ellison, the first Muslim to be elected to Congress, are a case in point (see chapter 5 of this volume).

The present moment is one of both vulnerability and opportunity for Muslims in America. It is also a moment for reflection. Muslims have become aware that despite their profound belief that America's foreign policies toward Muslim nations are unfair and unjust, if not hostile and destructive, America has been good to Muslims. It has provided them with a better standard of living. It has lived up to its promise by rewarding them with affluence as they lived by its values and work ethic. It has promised a better future for their children, who are guaranteed equal treatment under the law. It has also guaranteed freedom of religion, and the potential of their providing input into America's future. Will this potential be realized, or will it remain out of reach? Given the backlash to the events of 9/11, it is not clear at the moment whether Muslims in the United States will have the liberty to define what it means to be a Muslim. More important, it remains to be seen whether they will have a say in what it means to be an American.

Meanwhile, some Western authors and political leaders have continued to proclaim the "problem" of the presence of Muslims in the West as a potential threat not only to the "unique" Western cultural identity of liberalism, democracy, tolerance, and pluralism or multiculturalism, but also to the West as it has been fashioned over the centuries. The question remains: Will the democratic and pluralistic principles espoused by the West allow for a non-Judeo-Christian religion with a distinctive culture and different values to flourish in its midst? American Muslims are positing a challenge to America's vision of itself and its publicly professed values. They are demanding that America live up to its values of pluralism and freedom of speech and religion and make room for its Muslim citizens, allowing them to be fully American and fully Muslim, and to define their own religion without outside interference.

Notes

1. Cole and Dempsey (2002); Cole (2001). See also William Branigin, "Secret U.S. Evidence Entangles Immigrants; Rarely Used Law Now Falls Most Heavily on Arabs," *Washington Post,* October 19, 1997, sec. A3. See also Ronald Smothers, "U.S. Bars or Expels Suspect Immigrants on Suspect Evidence," *New York Times,* August 15, 1998, sec. A.

2. Consider, for example, the statement of former attorney general John Ashcroft that "Christianity is a faith in which God sends His son to die for you; Islam is a religion in which God requires your son to die for Him" (see Dan Eggen, "Ashcroft Disputes Report on Islam Views," *Washington Post,* February 12, 2002, sec. A). Also well publicized were the comments of Deputy Undersecretary of Defense for Intelligence Lt. Gen. William G. "Jerry" Boykin regarding

his encounter with a Somali Muslim: "I knew that my God was a real God, and his was an idol" and "[M]y God was bigger than his God" (see Bob Herbert, "Shopping for War," *New York Times*, December 27, 2004, sec. A).

3. Diana Eck is the director of the Pluralism Project at Harvard University.

4. In fact, the intent of the First Amendment was most likely to prohibit the federal government from interfering with the states' establishment of religion. Many of the states had established religions (which received preferential tax treatment, for example) at the time the Constitution was ratified, and Massachusetts, the last state with an established religion, did not eliminate it until the 1830s. There is, then, a technical sense in which Protestantism was the official religion of America. The "unofficial" Protestant hegemony lasted much longer—indeed, in some sense it may still be alive.

5. See, for example, a recent survey in the *Journal of Religion and Society* which notes that "the United States is the only prosperous first world nation to retain rates of religiosity otherwise limited to the second and third worlds" (Paul 2005). Currently there is a heated debate on how to accommodate diversity in religious practice, and whether and how that practice should interface with the public sphere. For example, about half of Americans are comfortable with the idea that churches should voice their opinion on political issues; fewer would be eager to hear these opinions from their individual clergy. See Pew Research Center for the People & the Press (2001).

6. See, for example, the website of the Association of Patriotic Arab Americans in Military: http://www.apaam.org (accessed February 4, 2008). On George Washington's interest in a national army as an Americanizing institution, see Ellis (2000).

7. Bent (1967), Murchland (1967), and Cobb (1970).

8. Russell (1977), Christ and Plaskow (1979), and Clark and Richardson (1977).

9. Brown (1978), Ogden (1979), Anderson and Stransky (1979).

10. Muse (1968), Wagstaff (1969), Greer (1971), Wilmore and Cone (1979).

11. Some Muslim thinkers have worked toward developing a "*fiqh* for minorities" such as the Muslim minorities in the United States and Europe. For instance, see Al-Alwani (2004).

12. See, for example, CAIR's 2003 "Islam in America" ad campaign: http://www.american muslims.info. CAIR's main website is http://www.cair.com (accessed February 4, 2008).

13. These include, among others, the American-Arab Anti-Discrimination Committee and the Arab American Institute, which serve both Christian and Muslim constituents from the Arab world.

14. Comments in a symposium, January 5, 2001.

15. Muslim pirates, or "corsairs," who plagued American (and European) shipping in the Mediterranean, were perhaps the first "Other" to be demonized in the American psyche. The offensives against the corsairs produced the first American heroes as well as much material for propaganda. See Allison (1995).

16. See, for example, the articles of www.danielpipes.org and www.frontpagemag.com. See also www.steveemerson.com and www.investigativeproject.org.

17. President George W. Bush, September 17, 2001, at the Islamic Center of Washington D.C.; http://www.cnn.com/2001/US/09/17/gen.bush.muslim.trans/ (accessed September 28, 2006).

18. This was said in a special address to a Joint Session of Congress on September 20, 2001. The text of Bush's speech can be found at http://www.whitehouse.gov/news/releases/2001/09/ 20010920-8.html. In later press conferences, Bush said, "[E]ither you're with us or you're against us in the fight against terror." See CNN's War on Terror coverage, "You Are Either with Us or against Us," November 6, 2001. Available at http://archives.cnn.com/2001/US/11/06/gen.attack .on.terror/ (accessed September 28, 2006).

19. See the interpretations offered by Daniel Pipes, David Horowitz, Steve Emerson, and others at their websites (listed above in note 16).

20. Muqtedar Khan, May 25, 2003, "The Public Face of Christian Evangelical Bigotry." Available at http://www.glocaleye.org/bigotry2.htm (accessed October 6, 2006).

21. Deborah Caldwell, "Poised and Ready," available at http://www.beliefnet.com/story/123/story_12365.html, and Mark O'Keefe, "Plans Under Way for Christianizing the Enemy," at http://www.newhouse.com/archive/okeefe032603.html (accessed October 6, 2006).

22. Most notorious are the efforts of Pipes and others on the www.campus-watch.org website and Horowitz's (2006) publication *The Professors*.

23. Former congresswoman Mary Rose Oakar, president of the American-Arab Anti-Discrimination Committee (ADC), said that it was "completely incompatible with basic civil liberties, most notably freedom from unreasonable search and seizure by the government guaranteed by the Fourth Amendment to the Constitution." See "Update on ADC's Challenge to the USA Patriot Act," November 3, 2003. Available at http://adc.org/index.php?id=2054 (accessed October 6, 2006). Other Arab-American and Islamic organizations that joined ADC in the brief include Muslim Community Association of Ann Arbor, Arab Community Center for Economic and Social Services, Bridge Refugee and Sponsorship Services, Council on American-Islamic Relations, Islamic Center of Portland, and Masjid as-Sabir of Portland, Oregon.

24. See, for example, an article at the website of the Muslim Public Affairs Council (MPAC): "American Muslim Charities: Easy Targets in the War on Terror," December 3, 2004. Available at http://www.mpac.org/article.php?id=355 (accessed October 6, 2006).

25. See CAIR Ohio, "Muslims to Feed Needy during Ramadan," September 20, 2005. Available at http://www.cair-net.org/default.asp?Page=articleView&id=1776&theType=NR (accessed October 6, 2006).

26. See Mustafa Abdel-Halim, "FBI Raids Islamic Institute in Virginia." Available at http://www.islamonline.net/English/News/2004-07/02/article06.shtml (accessed October 6, 2006). This describes a raid in July 2004. Similar raids on the offices of Muslim organizations and the homes of their leaders took place in March 2003. See Ayesha Ahmad and Neveen Salem, "Exclusive: Muslim Leaders, Victims Denounce Federal Raids on Homes, Businesses and Institutions." Available at http://www.islam-online.net/English/News/2002-03/22/article20.shtml (accessed October 6, 2006).

27. Jim Moran, symposium, January 5, 2001.

28. See Hazem Kira, "More Muslims Elected to Office in 2004" (no date). Available at http://www.amaweb.org/pView.asp?action=viewPDetails&pageId=11028&pCatName=&pGrpName=Articles (accessed October 6, 2006).

29. Safi (2003), Esack (1997), and Abdul Rauf (2004).

30. As an example of a progressive Muslim website, see Muslim WakeUp!: www.muslimwakeup.com (accessed October 6, 2006).

References

Abdul Rauf, Feisal. 2004. *What's Right with Islam: A New Vision for Muslims and the West.* New York: HarperSanFrancisco.

Abdul-Rauf, Muhammad. 1983. "The Future of the Islamic Tradition in North America." In *The Muslim Community in North America,* ed. E. H. Waugh, B. Abu-Laban, and R. B. Qureshi, 271–278. Edmonton: University of Alberta Press.

Al-Alwani, Taha J. 2004. "Toward a Fiqh for Minorities: Some Reflections." In *Muslims' Place in the American Public Square,* ed. Zahid H. Bukhari, Sulayman S. Nyang, Mumtaz Ahmad, and John L. Esposito, 3–37. Lanham, Md.: AltaMira Press.

Allison, Robert J. 1995. *The Crescent Obscured: The United States and the Muslim World, 1776–1815.* New York: Oxford University Press.

Anderson, Gerald H., and Thomas F. Stransky, eds. 1979. *Liberation Theologies in North America and Europe.* New York: Paulist Press.

Bellah, Robert N., and Frederick E. Greenspahn, eds. 1987. *Uncivil Religion: Interreligious Hostility in America.* New York: Crossroad.

Bent, Charles N. 1967. *The Death of God Movement: A Study of Gabriel Vahanian, William Hamilton, Paul Van Buren [and] Thomas J. J. Altizer.* Westminster, Md.: Paulist Press.

Brown, Robert McAfee. 1978. *Theology in a New Key: Responding to Liberation Themes.* Philadelphia, Pa.: Westminster John Knox Press.

Bukhari, Zahid H., Sulayman S. Nyang, Mumtaz Ahmad, and John L. Esposito, eds. 2004. *Muslims' Place in the American Public Square: Hopes, Fears, and Aspirations.* Lanham, Md.: AltaMira Press.

Carty, Thomas J. 2004. *A Catholic in the White House? Religion, Politics, and John F. Kennedy's Presidential Campaign.* New York: Palgrave Macmillan.

Christ, Carol P., and Judith Plaskow. 1979. *Womanspirit Rising: A Feminist Reader in Religion.* San Francisco: Harper and Row.

Clark, Elizabeth, and Herbert Richardson. 1977. *Women and Religion: A Feminist Sourcebook of Christian Thought.* New York: Harper and Row.

Cobb, John B., Jr. 1970. *The Theology of Altizer: Critique and Response.* Philadelphia, Pa.: Westminster Press.

Cole, David. 2001. "Secrecy, Guilt by Association, and the Terrorist Profile." *Journal of Law and Religion* 15, no. 1/2: 267–288.

Cole, David, and James X. Dempsey. 2002. *Terrorism and the Constitution: Sacrificing Civil Liberties in the Name of National Security.* New York: New Press.

Council on American-Islamic Relations [CAIR] Research Center. 2006. "American Public Opinion about Islam and Muslims 2006." Available at http://www.cair.com/cairsurvey analysis.pdf (accessed September 28, 2006).

Dionne, E. J., Jr., and John J. Dilulio, Jr., eds. 2000. *What's God Got to Do with the American Experiment?* Washington, D.C.: Brookings Institute.

Eck, Diana. 2002. *A New Religious America: How A "Christian Country" Has Now Become the World's Most Religiously Diverse Nation.* San Francisco: Harper.

Ellis, Joseph. 2000. *Founding Brothers: The Revolutionary Generation.* New York: Alfred A. Knopf.

Esack, Farid. 1997. *Qur'an, Liberation, and Pluralism: An Islamic Perspective of Interreligious Solidarity against Oppression.* Oxford, UK: Oneworld.

Flake, Kathleen. 2004. *The Politics of American Religious Identity: The Seating of Senator Reed Smoot, Mormon Apostle.* Chapel Hill: University of North Carolina Press.

Foster, Lawrence. 1987. "Cults in Conflict: New Religious Movements and the Mainstream Religious Tradition in America." In *Uncivil Religion: Interreligious Hostility in America,* ed. Robert N. Bellah and Frederick E. Greenspahn, 185–204. New York: Crossroad.

Graham, Franklin. 2002. *The Name.* Nashville, Tenn.: Thomas Nelson.

Greer, Edward. 1971. *Black Liberation Politics: A Reader.* Boston: Allyn and Bacon.

Haddad, Yvonne. 2004. "The Shaping of a Moderate North American Islam: Between 'Mufti' Bush and 'Ayatollah' Ashcroft." In *Islam and the West Post 9/11,* ed. Ron Geaves, Theodore Gabriel, Yvonne Haddad, and Jane I. Smith, 97–114. Burlington, Vt.: Ashgate.

Hamburger, Philip. 2002. *Separation of Church and State.* Cambridge, Mass.: Harvard University Press.

Herberg, Will. 1983. *Protestant, Catholic, Jew: An Essay in American Religious Sociology.* Chicago: University of Chicago Press.

Horowitz, David. 2006. *The Professors: The 101 Most Dangerous Academics in America.* Lanham, Md.: Regnery Publishers.

Hutchison, William R. 2004. *Religious Pluralism in America: The Contentious History of a Founding Ideal.* New Haven, Conn.: Yale University Press.

Johnson, Paul. 1998. *A History of the American People.* New York: HarperCollins.

Lambert, Frank. 2003. *The Founding Fathers and the Place of Religion in America.* Princeton, N.J.: Princeton University Press.

Moore, Kathleen. 2002. "The Politics of Transfiguration: Constitutive Aspects of the International Religious Freedom Act of 1998." In *Muslim Minorities in the West: Visible and Invisible,* ed. Yvonne Y. Haddad and Jane I. Smith, 25–38. Walnut Creek, Calif.: AltaMira Press.

Moore, Laurence R. 1987. *Religious Outsiders and the Making of Americans.* New York: Oxford University Press.

Murchland, Bernard, ed. 1967. *The Meaning of the Death of God: Protestant, Jewish and Catholic Scholars Explore Atheistic Theology.* New York: Random House.

Muse, Benjamin. 1968. *The American Negro Revolution: From Nonviolence to Black Power, 1963–1967.* Bloomington: Indiana University Press.

Nadvi, Syed A. Hassan Ali. 1983. *Muslims in the West: The Message and Mission.* Trans. Khurram Murad. London: New Era Publications.

Nimer, Mohammad. 2004. "Muslims in the American Body Politic." In *Muslims' Place in the American Public Square,* ed. Zahid H. Bukhari, Sulayman S. Nyang, Mumtaz Ahmad, and John L. Esposito, 145–164. Lanham, Md.: AltaMira Press.

Ogden, Schubert Miles. 1979. *Faith and Freedom: Toward a Theology of Liberation.* Nashville, Tenn.: Abingdon.

Paul, Gregory S. 2005. "Cross-National Correlations of Quantifiable Societal Health with Popular Religiosity and Secularism in the Prosperous Democracies." *Journal of Religion and Society* 7. Available at http://moses.creighton.edu/JRS/2005/2005-11.html (accessed December 7, 2006).

Pew Research Center for the People & the Press. April 10, 2001. "Survey Reports. Faith-Based Funding Backed, but Church-State Doubts Abound." Washington, D.C.: Pew Research Center. Available at http://people-press.org/reports/display.php3?ReportID=15 (accessed December 7, 2006).

Pew Forum on Religion & Public Life. July 24, 2003. "Growing Number of Americans Say Islam Encourages Violence among Followers: Religious Divides on Gay Marriage, Israeli-Palestinian Conflict." Washington, D.C.: Pew Research Center. Available at http://pewforum.org/press/index.php?ReleaseID=20 (accessed December 7, 2006).

Pew Forum on Religion & Public Life. July 26, 2005. "Views of Muslim-Americans Hold Steady after London Bombings: Fewer Say Islam Encourages Violence." Available at http://pewforum.org/docs/index.php?DocID=89 (accessed December 7, 2006).

Russell, Letty M., in cooperation with the National Council of Churches of Christ in the United States, Division of Education and Ministry, Task Force on Sexism in the Bible. 1977. *The Liberating Word: A Guide to Nonsexist Interpretation of the Bible.* Philadelphia, Pa.: Westminster Press.

Sachedina, Abdulaziz. 2001. *The Islamic Roots of Democratic Pluralism.* Oxford, UK: Oxford University Press.

Saeed, Agha. 2002. "The American Muslim Paradox." In *Muslim Minorities in the West: Visible and Invisible,* ed. Yvonne Y. Haddad and Jane I. Smith, 39–58. Walnut Creek, Calif.: AltaMira Press.

Safi, Omid, ed. 2003. *Progressive Muslims: On Justice, Gender, and Pluralism.* Oxford, UK: Oneworld.

Sarna, Jonathan D. 1987. "Jewish-Christian Hostility in the United States: Perceptions from a Jewish Point of View." In *Uncivil Religion: Interreligious Hostility in America,* ed. Robert N. Bellah and Frederick E. Greenspahn, 5–22. New York: Crossroad.

Segers, Mary C. 2002. "Religion and Liberal Democracy: An American Perspective." In *Piety, Politics, and Pluralism: Religion, the Courts, and the 2000 Election,* ed. Mary C. Segers, 1–15. Lanham, Md.: Rowman & Littlefield.

Wagstaff, Thomas. 1969. *Black Power: The Radical Response to White America.* Beverly Hills, Calif.: Glencoe Press.

Waugh, Earle H., Baha Abu-Laban, and Regula B. Qureshi, eds. 1983. *The Muslim Community in North America.* Edmonton: University of Alberta Press.

Wilmore, Gayraud S., and James S. Cone, eds. 1979. *Black Theology: A Documentary History, 1966–1979.* Maryknoll, N.Y.: Orbis Books.

3

The Practice of Their Faith: Muslims and the State in Britain, France, and Germany

J. Christopher Soper and Joel S. Fetzer

Muslims have become a part of this society. More than three million Muslims live in Germany permanently. They are not going to "go home." Their home is here.

—Nadeem Elyas (2001), chair of the Zentralrat der Muslime in Deutschland, Cologne, Germany

There is a realization that Muslims are here, that we are citizens, and that we have to be treated equally. We are not asking for special treatment; what we want is fair treatment. You apply the same rules to us as to anybody else.

—Yaqub Zaki (2001), executive director of the Muslim Institute Trust, London, England

Let no one be in any doubt—the rules of the game are changing. Coming to Britain is not a right. And even when people come here, staying here carries with it a duty.

—Tony Blair, then British prime minister, August 5, 2005

Do we want the river of Islam to enter the riverbed of [European] secularism?

—Jean-Pierre Raffarin, former French prime minister

State accommodation of Muslim religious practices is an increasingly important political issue across Western Europe. More than fifteen million Muslims currently live in Western Europe, which makes them the largest religious minority in the region. The number of Muslims in Europe has tripled in the last thirty years: Islam is the third-largest religion overall in Europe, and in most west European countries it is growing much faster than the historically dominant Catholic and Protestant congregations (Hollifield 1992; Masci 2004). Political controversy about the rights, status, and place of Muslims in west European nations has also escalated in recent years. This is partly because of the political efforts by Muslims to gain public recognition for their religious rights and practices as states have had to grapple with how far to go in accommodating Muslims. The renewed attention is also a function of attacks by Muslim extremists that have challenged the idea that Muslims will successfully integrate into the values of the West. Islam is a significant social and religious force in Western Europe.

The quotations above suggest two points that we intend to explore in this chapter. The comments by Yaqub Zaki and Nadeem Elyas imply that Muslims want the state to recognize their religious status and accommodate their religious practices justly and fairly. We show below, however, that west European states vary considerably in what they perceive to be equitable treatment for Muslim citizens and immigrants and what they consider to be reasonable and just accommodation of Muslim religious practices. In spite of similar challenges, their governments balance differently the recognition of the religious rights of Muslims with policies that promote their effective incorporation into the values of the host country.

The primary aim of this chapter is to explain how three European states, Britain, France, and Germany, have accommodated the religious needs of Muslims and to explore why there is such a difference in how they have done so. These countries are ideal for comparative purposes for two reasons. First, they have the largest Muslim populations in Europe. According to the most recent census, there were 1.6 million Muslims living in Britain in 2001; Muslims made up 3 percent of the total population of Britain and over half (52 percent) of the non-Christian religious population. Although French law forbids census takers from asking about one's religion or ethnicity, the Interior Ministry estimated the Muslim population at around five million in 2000 (ADRI 2000, 20–21); this represents nearly 8 percent of the French population. Finally, there are approximately 3.5 million Muslims living in Germany, which represents about 4 percent of the German population (Spuler-Stegemann 2002, 14).

A second reason that Britain, France, and Germany are particularly appropriate for this analysis is that they represent the three dominant patterns of religious politics found in the region. We have two distinctions in mind. The first is among Catholic-dominated countries (France), Protestant-dominated countries (Britain), and religiously mixed countries (Germany). The second distinction is among nations with a tradition of anti-clericalism and church-state separation

(France), those with a state church (Britain), and those where the state accommodates more than one religious tradition (Germany).

The quotations by Tony Blair and Jean-Pierre Raffarin, on the other hand, suggest a secondary purpose of this chapter: to explore whether the deadly attacks by Muslim extremists in Madrid, London, and the Netherlands over the past several years have had any impact on the political efforts by Muslims to gain public recognition for their religious practices. Political debate in every country has centered on the issue of whether states have been too accommodating to the religious rights of Muslims. Some European political leaders have argued that secularism is, or ought to be, the goal of public policy on matters of state accommodation of a group's religious practices. In asking for public recognition of their religious rights, therefore, Muslims pose a challenge to a secular mindset that wishes to divorce matters of "religion" from matters of "state." As we argue toward the end of the chapter, however, there remains a tension between Europe's increasingly secular political culture, on the one hand, and state policy that provides benefits to religious groups, on the other. We offer some ideas on how this tension might play itself out in the years ahead on the issue of public recognition for the religious rights of Muslims.

Background

Muslims began immigrating to Europe in large numbers following the Second World War. They were part of a great wave of immigration that brought workers from the poorer countries of the Mediterranean, Eastern Europe, and the former colonies to the industrialized states of the West that were enjoying an economic boom and trying to rebuild in the aftermath of World War II. Private employers and governments across Western Europe actively recruited foreign workers to provide the labor necessary to continue the economic expansion (Bade 1983, 59–95; Frémeaux 1991, 209–275).

In the face of the economic recession of the early 1970s, however, European states gradually closed their borders to low-skilled workers but allowed for the possibility of family reunion and political asylum. Host countries assumed that immigrants were temporary workers who would want to return to their country of origin, but many foreign-born residents had no interest in doing so. Ironically, this effort to restrict immigration had the unintended consequence of encouraging a "second wave" of immigration as family members and dependents of the original postwar economic migrants joined their families in Western Europe. This policy transformed the immigrant population from single migrants to families who wanted permanent settlement (Kettani 1996; Boyer 1997, 87–104; Nielsen 1999, 25–35). Since many of these immigrants were Muslims, the Muslim population in Western Europe expanded rapidly.

Family settlement also changed the political calculus; immigrants became concerned not simply with their political and economic rights as workers, but also with their cultural and religious needs as permanent residents or citizens. Vexing policy questions emerged regarding the religious rights of Muslim immigrants and citizens. Governments were suddenly confronted with such issues as how or whether to accommodate Muslim religious practices in state institutions such as schools, prisons, and hospitals, how or whether to help develop their communities, whether to pass laws specifically designed to protect Muslims against religious discrimination, and what efforts to make to stem native discrimination against them.[1] This produced intense political controversy.

There have been a number of fine studies of immigration into Western Europe.[2] These scholars have focused much-needed attention on a phenomenon that has, in the words of one analyst, "been more transformative in [its] effect" in Western Europe than any other since 1945 (Messina 1996, 134). These accounts, however, tend to focus on economic and citizenship issues and largely ignore questions of the religious identity and needs of Muslims. Social scientists, in short, have devoted very little attention to the religious aspect of Muslim policy demands, despite the fact that social and political tensions have mounted in recent years over a series of religious matters.

One reason for this silence on religious questions has been a perception among social scientists, often assumed rather than stated, that Western Europe is essentially secular and that issues of church and state are no longer relevant to public policy. According to this view, religious disputes were historically important in Europe, but those issues were largely settled, or at least minimized, in recent decades as the state became more secular and began to treat religious groups more or less equally. There is something to this thesis. Religion, which was at the center of political conflict in Europe a century ago, became less important politically in the middle decades of the twentieth century. However, the migration and settlement of large numbers of Muslims into Western Europe poses a new challenge to the existing church-state arrangements and has resurrected somewhat dormant religious disputes. Religious conflicts are once again the source of political controversy in Britain, France, and Germany. What remains to be explained is how each of these countries has responded to that debate.

Church-State Institutions and the Politics of Religious Recognition

The most important factor shaping how Britain, France, and Germany have accommodated the religious needs of Muslims is the inherited church-state institutions unique to each state. Those institutions have been important for the politics of religious recognition in two distinct ways. First, the preexisting church-state institutions have forged an ideological assumption about how or whether each state should recognize Muslim religious rights. Muslims have experienced those ideological predispositions either as an opportunity for their own political mobilization or as limiting their capacity to make a case for state accommodation of their religious practices. Second, Muslims inherited unique church-state public policies in each of the three states that shaped the politics and the outcome of their own political movement for religious recognition by the state. That British public policy recognized religious groups' claims meant that Muslims would logically press the state to accommodate their rights as well. On the other hand, the French commitment to a strict separation between church and state made it more difficult for French Muslims to gain public recognition for their religious practices. In order to examine how church-state institutions have fostered these disparate trajectories, we turn now to an examination of Muslim mobilization in the three countries.

Britain: The Established Church and Muslim Religious Practices

Britain has an established church, the Church of England, which enjoys certain benefits from the state. Clerics in the Church of England have guaranteed positions in the House of Lords; there are no formal membership provisions for leaders of any other religious tradition (Weller, Feldman, and Purdam 2001). The state's blasphemy law protects the Christian religion; attempts by Muslims to extend the law to cover Islam have failed (Commission for Racial Equality 1990). Nor do political leaders as a matter of course support extending the benefits of the religious establishment to minority faiths. One of the largest backbench rebellions since the 2001 Labour Party victory came on the House of Commons' debate on a provision of the government's Education Bill that called for extending public finance to more faith-based schools, including those of minority faiths.

The establishment of a particular religion might, therefore, have posed a barrier to Muslims as they negotiated with the state over contested religious practices. Because Islam was not the officially recognized religion, Muslims might have been left out of the policy mix of state benefits accorded to the Church of England. Contrary to these expectations, however, Britain's church-state model has served as an important institutional and ideological resource for Muslim activists. Part of the reason for this is that the established-church model has, at least for the past century, not been aggressively pursued to the disadvantage of other religious groups. Instead, the Church of England has come to see its role as working with Roman Catholics, Protestant nonconformists, and even Jews to promote consensual religious values (Medhurst and Moyser 1988; McClean 1996; Monsma and Soper 1997).

British policy makers have recently broadened the existing church-state model to incorporate Muslims and other minority faiths. When confronted with the issue of girls wearing the hijab in state-run schools, British educational authorities quickly reached a compromise that allowed girls to wear the headscarf so long as it conformed with the color requirements of the school uniform (Liederman 2000). After many years of trying to win state aid for Islamic schools under the same conditions that govern aid to Christian schools within the state system, the government in 1998 gave approval to two independent Islamic schools (Howe 1998). A 2005 government White Paper calls for even more government-aided religious schools (Great Britain 2005). The curriculum in required religious education classes includes an extensive treatment of not only Christianity, but also Judaism, Islam, and Sikhism (Keene and Keene 1997).

The presence of an established church and its close link with politics and public policy in Britain offer two advantages to Muslims. First, it encourages Muslims to press the state to recognize their religious practices in the same way that the state accommodates other religions. In discussing the government's recent decision to finance Islamic schools, one Muslim leader noted to us:

> The fact that there were no government funded Muslim schools was a ridiculous anomaly that had to go. The Anglicans had their schools, Roman Catholics had their schools, Jews had their schools. It was only right that we got our schools. (El-Essawy 2001)

Muslim activists, in short, make explicit reference to the religious-establishment model to legitimate a variety of public policy demands. These leaders also understand that the religious establishment and its close links to public policy make it more likely that they too will win state recognition.

Just as importantly, the religious establishment enables Muslim leaders to make the argument for a public, political role for religion. Far from arguing for the disestablishment of the Church of England, Muslims are very conscious that the Church is a significant resource for them (Modood 1994). One Muslim leader put the matter succinctly:

> [T]here is much good in keeping the religious establishment intact. The establishment makes possible a recognition of a person's right to put into action what he most sincerely believes in. It is a recognition of a person's most fundamental right, the right to practice their religion. Finally, the establishment provides a public role for religion, which is a very positive thing. (Amer 2001)

Muslims simply want the state to expand the church-state dynamic that already recognizes religious practices in a variety of ways. Given the state's commitment to such liberal political values as tolerance and equal treatment, it is no surprise that for the most part, the British state has, over time, accommodated Muslim religious practices as it does Christian and Jewish ones.

France: *Laïcité* and Muslim Religious Practices

French policy on state accommodation of religious practices is governed above all else by *laïcité,* or a certain version of separationism between religion and state. Today, a century after its enactment into French law, *laïcité* continues to structure public debate over the proper place of religion in French politics and society. Not only secularists but even most practicing Christians, Jews, and Muslims still justify their respective positions by appealing to some version of this particularly French concept (Cesari 2000). French constitutional and legal sources firmly require that no religion is to receive any legal establishment, that the state must be neutral in religious matters, and that churches are part of the private sector and may not receive any direct state funding. What is unique about these legal provisions is that they were accompanied by a head-on attack on the Roman Catholic Church (Basdevant-Gaudemet 1996).

This separation can be traced to the French Revolution, which pitted the state against the Catholic Church in a conflict in which both sides laid claim to ultimate control over the social and political order. The Church became identified with the traditional order and a revival of the ancien régime; it opposed the secularization, democratization, and political liberalism of the French Revolution. The state, on the other hand, became an implacable opponent of the Church and even tried to destroy it with a series of radical reforms in the early years of the revolution. This de-Christianization campaign failed, but the revolutionaries did establish a regime of church-state separation that helped to fuel a lasting animosity between the partisans of the Church and those of the revolution, culminating in the 1905 law on the separation of church and state. The law deprived the Church of its official status and ended all forms of state aid to the Catholic Church. Politics became an arena of conflict where the parties aggressively opposed or defended separatism, or *laïcité*.[3]

In France's political ideology, *laïcité* is a very powerful political reality. Elite and popular support for this separation of church and state has made it difficult for Muslims in France to argue that the state should accommodate their particular religious practices. In general, the state has been vigorously secular and opposed to the notion that public institutions should be made to assist the religious practices of Muslims (Kepel 1987; Peach and Glebe 1995; Ramadan 1999). France has followed the logic of *laïcité* by rejecting multiculturalism as an appropriate educational model. Aside from such short lessons on the "Muslim world" as those in the *cinquième* history and geography class, French secondary school students learn nothing about Islam (Marseille and Scheibling 1997). Even before the French legislature completely banned the hijab from state schools in 2004, some local school authorities had already been dismissing girls for wearing the headscarf.[4] French Muslim leaders estimate that between 1989 and the early 2000s, "hundreds" of Muslim young women had been expelled from public schools for refusing to remove the hijab (Kabtane 2001; Merroun 2001). French teachers' union leader Francis Bergin (2001) explains that in the public space the individual must "leave his or her religious concepts behind." This mindset, which is widely shared among policy makers, puts Muslims on the defensive when they enter the policy realm as Muslims.

In such an ideological and institutional climate, it has been impossible for Muslims to put on the policy agenda such things as support for separate Islamic schools or state aid for Muslim social service organizations. Muslims have tried to press for state aid to private Islamic schools under the same conditions that govern aid to Roman Catholic schools. In the 2002 presidential election, the Forum Citoyen Cultures Musulmanes, a coalition of French Muslim organizations, presented a policy platform which included a proposal for state funding of private Islamic schools. Advocates of a strict version of *laïcité* dismissed this recommendation out of hand, however, and metropolitan France currently contains no publicly recognized Islamic schools. As Strasbourg Muslim leader Fouad Douai (2001) correctly observed, "it is this conception of *laïcité* which makes it difficult [for Muslims]." As an ideological construct *laïcité* makes it difficult for Muslims to do much beyond fighting rearguard actions on symbolic, though significant, issues such as the wearing of the hijab. Opponents of state recognition of Muslim rights inevitably appeal to *laïcité* as a justification for their refusal to countenance state recognition for Muslim religious practices.

Germany: Multiple Establishment and Muslim Religious Practices

The institutional structure of religion and politics in Germany is a hybrid of the French and English models. The Basic Law affirms that there is to be a separation of church and state; the state may not favor or establish any particular religion. On the other hand, the constitution links the church and state in certain endeavors. The state levies a church tax (8–9% of income tax), or *Kirchensteuer*, on members of the recognized Catholic and *Evangelische* churches and of Jewish congregations that provides for a majority of the churches' budget and helps finance many of their social, health, and cultural activities (Robbers 1996). The Basic Law also requires that state schools provide formal religious instruction as a part of the core curriculum. The religious makeup and history of Germany go a long way toward explaining this unusual system.

Germany is a religiously mixed country and has been since the Peace of Westphalia affirmed the practice of *cuius regio, eius religio* (the religion of the ruler is the religion of the state). The unification of Germany under Bismarck in 1871 brought these disparate traditions together into one multiconfessional nation-state. The leadership of the new German state was conservative and overwhelmingly Protestant. The state allied itself with the Protestant *Evangelische* churches, and Bismarck launched his famous *Kulturkampf* to establish state supremacy over the Catholic Church, including control over primary education and suppression of the Church's political role (Kalyvas 1996). As in France, the political threat from the state led to the formation of a Catholic party of religious defense, the Zentrum, which lasted until the end of the Weimar Republic (Spotts 1973).

The end of the Second World War brought significant constitutional and political changes to the relations between church and state. First, Protestants and Catholics put aside their historical animosity and formed the interconfessional Christian Democratic Union. The party committed itself to promoting non-sectarian Christian values, although it quickly developed into a catchall conservative party advocating policies that benefited both churches. Second, the new West German Constitution adopted the principle of church-state separation (first articulated during the Weimar era), which means that the state may not favor any particular religion. On the other hand, the Basic Law formalized the church tax system and the requirement of religious instruction in the schools (Kommers 1997).

The German institutional arrangement created a policy legacy where church and state worked closely together for common purposes. As in Britain, the issue for German Muslims was not whether the state should accommodate religion in public institutions; it already did. The question, instead, was whether the state would be willing to expand its informal religious establishment and consider Islam a public corporation despite the fact that Muslims were not party to the original compromise. Much like the British church-state system, the German model legitimated Muslim demands for public recognition of their religious practices. The state has, for example, funded some Islamic social welfare and cultural organizations as well as an Islamic school in Berlin (Doomernik 1995). In the state of North Rhine–Westphalia, moreover, education authorities have mandated the teaching of Islam in required religion courses in public schools, and have even gone so far as to write the required textbook. The clear intent of this decision is to encourage Muslims to learn more about their faith in the public schools, and to ensure that the version of Islam they are taught is fully compatible with liberal democracy (Gebauer 1986 and 2001; Pfaff 2001).

This is not to suggest that Muslims have had an easy time gaining access to the system. To date, no *Land* government has recognized any Muslim group as a public corporation, which is a requirement for inclusion in the church tax system. German Muslims are quick to point out the impact of such differential treatment. The leader of one Muslim umbrella organization expressed it as follows:

> [W]e receive next to no government support for our institutions. The other religious groups receive 100 percent funding from the state for all of these social

> programs. But for us, even though we pay our taxes, out tax money goes to
> something else [than to Muslim-run social agencies]. (Totakhyl 2001)

That the state formally recognizes other churches and provides them with public money, however, is what makes possible this claim of a disparity in how Muslims are treated. The German institutional structure, in short, provides a model to which Muslims can point in arguing for state support for their religious practices.

The public incorporation of Muslims in Britain, France, and Germany can be interpreted as a path-dependent process shaped by the constitutional and legal patterns of church-state relations in each country as well as the history of country-specific arrangements that have been worked out over time between religious groups and the state. The result has been policy divergence, as states have responded to Muslim demands in light of their unique legal, historical, and constitutional structures. This is not to suggest that these patterns have preordained the outcome of these disputes; the persistent political controversy in Britain, France, and Germany around the public incorporation of Islam suggests that there is no inevitable outcome in the politics of religious recognition. However, inherited structures and practices have shaped the contours of the political debate in meaningful and important ways.

Secularism, the State, and the Future of European Muslims

An important factor that we have not discussed at length, but that promises to shape how states respond to Muslims in the years ahead, is European secularism. The chief social characteristics of this secularization are declining church membership and the retrenchment of religious belief into the private sphere (Davie 2000). In Germany, for example, the proportion of the population that has no religious affiliation is almost as large as the proportion of Protestants and Catholics. Germans are not highly religious—less than half of Germans consider themselves religious and only about 40 percent think that religion is an important feature of their nationality. Germany is not alone in experiencing this kind of secularism; it is widespread throughout Western Europe.

One possible consequence of this trend is that political elites, borrowing from the French model, will argue that secularism warrants the state's removing itself from the business of recognizing any churches and moving away from a system that has historically granted religious institutions important power in such policy areas as education and the provision of social welfare (Iverson 2004). Ironically, the immigration of Muslims into Europe might well hasten this secular trend, as political elites conclude that the increased political disputes around religion are simply not worth the cost of maintaining the inherited church-state links. Rather than extending state benefits to include Muslims and other religious newcomers, in short, it is possible that the future will hold increased political efforts to further secularize European church-state arrangements. With virtually no one attending church throughout the region, policy makers might decide that state aid to religious schools (Britain) or a system of church taxes (Germany) is an historical anomaly that deserves to become part of the dustbin of history.

A more secular public policy might also be attractive to those political elites who perceive Islam to be a danger to Western values. The attacks by Muslim extremists in Madrid, London, and Amsterdam over the past several years have raised questions about whether European Muslims have successfully integrated into the values of the West (Schneider 2005).[5] The violence itself is evidence that some Muslims have not. In short, those who have concluded that Islam is incompatible with liberal democratic values might prefer the secular ideal that would protect the private expression of religious beliefs but refuse to recognize religious differences in the public domain under the assumption that Muslims, along with other citizens, can and should adopt a French, British, or German identity and set of values that is separate from their religious makeup. To suggest, however, that religiously inspired political views or practices are out-of-bounds because they are public expressions of religious beliefs is profoundly anti-democratic and badly misunderstands the nature of religion. So long as Muslims are deeply religious, it is natural to expect that their faith will influence all areas of their life, including the political. European Muslims will inevitably experience this kind of secularism as an attack and will conclude that a public policy that forces a secular identity on them is hostile to their religion.

If the quotation by the former French prime minister Jean-Pierre Raffarin cited at the beginning of this chapter is indicative of the views of secularly minded rulers in Europe, Christian leaders would probably do well to recognize that secularism is potentially a greater threat to their religious identity than is Islam. After all, if the riverbed of Europe is secularism, as Raffarin suggests, it presumably leaves little room for a Muslim or Christian foundation. In response to the secular challenge, in short, it is equally possible that European Christians, Muslims, and Jews will form a most unusual political coalition to protect the very idea that religion has a legitimate public political role to play. European Muslims are more socially conservative than their non-Muslim counterparts, particularly on such issues as abortion and homosexuality, which further points to the possibility of a social and political coalition of orthodox religionists who wish to preserve a public space for religious expression.

There is some indication that Christian and Muslim leaders are beginning to recognize their shared political interests. Tariq Modood, a British Muslim, notes that "the real division of opinion is not between a conservative element in the Church of England versus the rest of the country, but between those who think religion has a place in secular public culture and those who think not" (Modood 1994, 72). Leslie Newbigin, a British Christian, asserts that "in our present situation in

Britain where Christians and Muslims share a common position as minority faiths in a society dominated by the naturalistic ideology, we share a common duty to challenge this ideology" (Newbigin 1998, 22). It is also important to note that the Christian churches have, on the whole, been an institutional ally for Muslims as they have sought recognition from the state. Some of this support was principled; Christian leaders have recognized the legitimacy of the claims made by Muslims and for the most part have sprung to their defense. Some of the aid from Christian leaders has been strategic; they have implicitly recognized that to deny public benefits to Muslims is to open the question of state aid to any church. It would be ironic, or possibly the work of a benign deity with a supremely active sense of humor if, after centuries of dispute, it was secularism, rather than religion, that drew Christians and Muslims together in a joint effort to retain a public role for religion.

In the long run, we believe that equitable public policy on the rights of religious believers is a good recipe for political stability and the successful social incorporation of European Muslims. States will have to work out those arrangements in the context of their own church-state history and institutional structure. The situation in Britain is far from perfect, but the bulk of British Muslims have embraced liberal values; the Muslim Council of Britain, the nation's largest Muslim membership organization, "utterly condemned" the London terrorist attacks in the summer of 2005. Preexisting church-state practices have both allowed Muslims to practice their religion freely and encouraged them gradually to adopt British social values (Cesari 2000).

Even if it wanted to, France cannot abandon its historical commitment to church-state separation: legal, historical, and constitutional patterns of church-state relations are the framework through which these issues are resolved. What we do argue, however, is that not all forms of *laïcité* are equal. A more benign reading of this tradition would be consistent both with French constitutional history and, more importantly, with the successful integration of Muslims into French society. According to this reading, *laïcité* requires government neutrality among religions. While it does prohibit governmental promotion of religion, it does not require the suppression of individual religious practice. Read in this light, *laïcité* would not force French schools to expel girls for wearing the hijab. This interpretation is far more compatible with the goal of producing a French Islam. Allowing Muslims to practice their religious faith not only would send the message that the state is not hostile to Islam, but would also encourage Muslims to put down roots and establish an indigenous vision of Islam.

In short, preexisting institutions are the context through which such arrangements will be worked out, but they need not be considered straitjackets that preordain political outcomes. European Muslims are only going to become more numerous in the decades ahead, and it is critical that they be able, like religious newcomers that have preceded them, to maintain their religious values and practices if they wish, while fully embracing the values of their respective countries as well.

Notes

Portions of this chapter are from Joel S. Fetzer and J. Christopher Soper, *Muslims and the State in Britain, France, and Germany* (New York: Cambridge University Press, 2005), and are used with permission.

1. Morsy (1992); Cesari (1997); Nielsen (1999, 36–46); Özdemir (1999, 244–259).
2. Collinson (1993); Soysal (1994); Joppke (1999); Money (1999).
3. Frigulietti (1991); Gibson (1991); Meyer and Corvisier (1991); Baubérot (2000).
4. Adam Sage, "Headscarf Ban Is Judged Success as Hostility Fades," *The Times* (London), September 5, 2005, p. 31.
5. See also Jeffrey Fleishman, Ralph Frammolino, and Sebastian Rotella, "Outraged Europeans Take Dimmer View of Diversity," *Los Angeles Times,* September 5, 2005, sec. A4.

References

Agence pour le Développement des Relations Interculturelles (ADRI). 2000. *L'Islam en France.* Paris: La Documentation Française.

Amer, Dr. Fatma (Head of Education and Interfaith Relations, Islamic Cultural Centre, London Central Mosque). April 16, 2001. Interview with J. Christopher Soper, London.

Bade, Klaus J. 1983. *Vom Auswanderungsland zum Einwanderungsland? Deutschland 1880–1980.* Berlin: Colloquium Verlag.

Baubérot, Jean. 2000. *Histoire de la Laïcité Française.* Paris: Presses Universitaires de France.

Basdevant-Gaudemet, Brigitte. 1996. "State and Church in France." In *State and Church in the European Union,* ed. Gerhard Robbers, 119–146. Baden-Baden: Nomos Verlagsgesellschaft.

Bergin, Francis (Syndicat National des Enseignements de Second Degré). July 5, 2001. Interview with Joel Fetzer, Paris.

Boyer, Alain. 1997. *L'Islam en France.* Paris: Presses Universitaires de France.

Cesari, Jocelyn. 1997. *Faut-il Avoir Peur de L'Islam?* Paris: Presses de Sciences Po.

———. 2000. "Muslims in the West: Ambassadors of Democratic Pluralism." *Middle East Affairs Journal* 6 (Fall): 217–228.

Collinson, Sarah. 1993. *Beyond Borders: West European Migration Policy Towards the Twenty-first Century.* London: Royal Institute of International Affairs.

Commission for Racial Equality. 1990. *Law, Blasphemy, and the Multi-Faith Society.* London: Elliot House.

Davie, Grace. 2000. *Religion in Modern Europe: A Memory Mutates.* Oxford: Oxford University Press.

Doomernik, Jeveon. 1995. "The Institutionalization of Turkish Islam in Germany and the Netherlands: A Comparison." *Ethnic and Racial Studies* 18 (January): 46–63.

Douai, Fouad (Gérant, Société Civile Immobilière, Grande Mosquée de Strasbourg). July 10, 2001. Interview with Joel Fetzer, Strasbourg.

El-Essawy, Hesham (Director, Islamic Society for the Promotion of Religious Tolerance). April 10, 2001. Interview with J. Christopher Soper and Joel Fetzer, London.

Elyas, Nadeem (Chair, Zentralrat der Muslime in Deutschland). February 15, 2001. Interview with Joel Fetzer, Cologne.

Fetzer, Joel S., and J. Christopher Soper. 2005. *Muslims and the State in Britain, France, and Germany.* New York: Cambridge University Press.

Forum Citoyen, Cultures Musulmanes. 2002. *Pour une France juste: 89 propositions du F.C.C.M. aux Candidats.* Paris: La Médina Édition.

Frémeaux, Jacques. 1991. *La France et L'Islam Depuis 1789.* Paris: Presses Universitaires de France.

Frigulietti, James. 1991. "Gilbert Romme and the Making of the French Republican Calendar." In *The French Revolution in Culture and Society,* ed. David G. Troyansky, Alfred Cismaru, and Norwood Andrews, 13–22. Westport, Conn.: Greenwood Press.

Gebauer, Klaus, ed. 1986. *Religiöse Unterweisung für Schüler islamischen Glaubens: 24 Unterrichtseinheiten für die Grundschule.* Soest, W. Germany: Landesinstitut für Schule und Weiterbildung.

Gebauer, Klaus (Leiter des Referates Sozialwissenschaften, Geschichte, Religionslehre, Erdkunde; Landesinstitut für Schule und Weiterbildung). April 23, 2001. Interview with Joel Fetzer, Soest, Germany.

Gibson, Ralph. 1991. "Why Republicans and Catholics Couldn't Stand Each Other in the Nineteenth Century." In *Religion, Society, and Politics in France Since 1789,* ed. Frank Tallet and Nickolas Atkin, 107–120. London: Hambledon Press.

Great Britain. Department for Education and Skills. 2005. *Higher Standards, Better Schools for All: More Choice for Parents and Pupils.* London: Crown Copyright.

Hollifield, James F. 1992. *Immigrants, Markets, and States: The Political Economy of Postwar Europe.* Cambridge, Mass.: Harvard University Press.

Howe, Darcus. 1998. "State Funding for Muslim Schools Is a Victory against Islamophobia and for Common Sense." *New Statesman* 11 (487): 48.

Iverson, Hans R. 2004. "Religion in the 21st Century." *Dialog: A Journal of Theology* 43 (1): 28–33.

Joppke, Christian. 1999. *Immigration and the Nation-State: The United States, Germany, and Great Britain.* Oxford: Oxford University Press.

Kabtane, Kamel (Director, Grande Mosquée de Lyon). May 30, 2001. Interview with Joel Fetzer, Lyon.

Kalyvas, Stathis N. 1996. *The Rise of Christian Democracy in Europe.* Ithaca, N.Y.: Cornell University Press.

Keene, Michael, and Jan Keene. 1997. *Junior Steps in Religious Education, Year 4.* Cheltenham, UK: Stanley Thornes Publishers.

Kepel, Gilles. 1987. *Les Banlieues de L'Islam: Naissance d'une Religion en France.* Paris: Éditions du Seuil.

Kettani, M. Ali. 1996. "Challenges to the Organization of Muslim Communities in Western Europe: The Political Dimension." In *Political Participation and Identities of Muslims in Non-Muslim States,* ed. A. R. Shadid and P. S. Van Koningsfeld, 14–35. Kampen, the Netherlands: Kok Pharos Publishing House.

Kommers, Donald P. 1997. *The Constitutional Jurisprudence of the Federal Republic of Germany.* 2nd ed. Durham, N.C.: Duke University Press.

Liederman, Lina Molokotus. 2000. "Pluralism in Education: The Display of Islamic Affiliation in French and British Schools." *Islam and Christian Muslim Relations* 11 (1): 105–117.

Marseille, Jacques, and Jacques Scheibling. 1997. *Histoire-Géographie 5ᵉ: Programme 1997.* Paris: Nathan.

Masci, David. 2004. "An Uncertain Road: Muslims and the Future of Europe." Washington, D.C.: Pew Forum on Religion & Public Life.

McClean, David. 1996. "State and Church in the United Kingdom." In *State and Church in the European Union,* ed. Gerhard Robbers, 307–322. Baden-Baden: Nomos Verlagsgesellschaft.

Medhurst, Kenneth, and George Moyser. 1988. *Church and Politics in a Secular Age.* Oxford, UK: Clarendon Press.

Merroun, Khalil (Imam, Évry mosque). June 29, 2001. Interview with Joel Fetzer, Évry, France.

Messina, Anthony M. 1996. "Not So Silent Migration: Postwar Migration to Western Europe." *World Politics* 49 (1): 130–154.

Meyer, Jean, and André Corvisier. 1991. *La Révolution Française.* Paris: Presses Universitaires de France.

Modood, Tariq. 1994. "Establishment, Multiculturalism and British Citizenship." *The Political Quarterly* 65 (1): 53–73.

Money, Jeannette. 1999. *Fences and Neighbors: The Political Geography of Immigration Control.* Ithaca, N.Y.: Cornell University Press.

Monsma, Stephen V., and J. Christopher Soper. 1997. *The Challenge of Pluralism: Church and State in Five Western Democracies.* Lanham, Md.: Rowman & Littlefield.

Morsy, Magali. 1992. "Rester Musulman en Société Etrangère." *Pouvoirs* 62: 119–133.

Newbigin, Leslie. 1998. "Conclusion: Coercion and the Cross." In *Faith and Power: Christianity and Islam in "Secular" Britain,* ed. Leslie Newbigin, Lamin Sanneh, and Jenny Taylor, 20–24. London: SPCK.

Nielsen, Jorgen S. 1999. *Toward a European Islam: Migration, Minorities, and Citizenship.* London: Macmillan.

Özdemir, Cem. 1999. *Currywurst und Doner: Integration in Deutschland.* Bergisch Gladbach, Germany: Gustav Lübbe Verlag.

Peach, Ceri, and Günther Glebe. 1995. "Muslim Minorities in Western Europe." *Ethnic and Racial Studies* 18 (1): 26–45.

Pfaff, Ulrich (Ministerialrat, Ministerium für Schule, Wissenschaft und Forschung des Landes Nordrhein-Westfalen). March 23, 2001. Interview with Joel Fetzer, Düsseldorf.

Ramadan, Tariq. 1999. *Muslims in France: The Way towards Coexistence.* Leicester, UK: The Islamic Foundation.

Robbers, Gerhard. 1996. "State and Church in Germany." In *State and Church in the European Union,* ed. Gerhard Robbers, 323–333. Baden-Baden: Nomos Verlagsgesellschaft.

Schneider, Peter. 2005. "The New Berlin Wall." *New York Times Sunday Magazine,* December 4, p. 66.

Soysal, Yasemin Nugoglu. 1994. *Limits of Citizenship: Migrants and Postnational Membership in Europe.* Chicago: University of Chicago Press.

Spotts, Frederick. 1973. *The Churches and Politics in Germany.* Middletown, Conn.: Wesleyan University Press.

Spuler-Stegemann, Ursula. 2002. *Muslime in Deutschland: Informationen und Klärungen?* Freiburg: Herder.

Totakhyl, Ghulam Dastagir (General Secretary, Islamrat für die Bundesrepublik Deutschland). February 5, 2001. Interview with Joel Fetzer, Bonn.

Weller, Paul, Alice Feldman, and Kingsley Purdam. 2001. *Religious Discrimination in England and Wales.* London: Home Office Research Study.

Zaki, Yaqub (Executive Director, The Muslim Institute Trust). April 10, 2001. Interview with J. Christopher Soper and Joel Fetzer, London.

4

Religion, Muslims, and the State in Britain and France: From Westphalia to 9/11

Jorgen S. Nielsen

Britain and France have been offered by many social and political scientists as two distinct models of how a west European democratic nation-state should set about absorbing recently immigrated ethnic and religious minority communities. France has been portrayed as representing an "assimilationist" model in which the individual is integrated directly into a secular republic as a citizen, while the United Kingdom is said to represent an "integrationist" model in which communities are absorbed—or an individualist versus a communalist approach (e.g., Kepel 1997). I investigate these claims with specific reference to Islam and show that the distinctions between the two countries are more of form than of substance, and that under the impact of changing environments, particularly in the political field, they were converging even before the impact of developments that followed the terrorist attacks of September 11, 2001.

Church-State Relations

Fetzer and Soper (2005; see also their chapter in this volume) have recently argued that the various church-state relations inherited by contemporary European states have been a factor underrated by scholars in their discussions of the processes of local accommodation of the growing Muslim presence. They refer to existing discussions of church-state relations which traditionally identify three types:[1]

1. Countries where the relationship is governed by a concordat, such as has traditionally been the case in Italy, Spain, and Portugal. Some scholars would include, at least partially, Germany in this category.
2. Countries with a state church, such as Denmark, Finland, Norway, and, until quite recently, Sweden. England might also be included, as could Greece.
3. Countries with separation between church and state such as France, the Republic of Ireland, Belgium, and Holland.

This particular typology works if viewed from a constitutional perspective with a Catholic bias. Seen from a north European angle and a Protestant bias, a slightly different typology might make better sense (e.g., Vetvik 1992):

1. There is a laicist type with a sharp separation between church and state, as in France and the Irish Republic. Over the last several decades the Netherlands has moved in this direction.
2. The concordat type that follows the Napoleonic precedent includes countries like Italy, Spain, and Portugal, even though legislation has in some cases moved beyond this.[2]
3. Countries with some form of domestically arranged "establishment." These can be subdivided into two types:
   a. Countries where churches, and occasionally other religions, function within the legal framework of some kind of recognition, whose privileges usually extend equally to all recognized churches. They include Austria, Germany, the Alsace-Moselle region of France, Wales and Scotland, and the "free churches" in England.
   b. Countries that have churches which are somehow incorporated, in varying degrees, within the state structures. Denmark is probably the purest example of this, and England would fall into this category as well, at least as regards the Church of England.

Recently, a major critique of such traditional typologies has been suggested by Silvio Ferrari (2003). He argues that, while they may describe the constitutional positions, they are of little use in analyzing the situation on the ground, and that they attribute excessive importance to legal and constitutional arrangements which are often, in fact, fossils with little practical impact. One might give as an example the sharp contrast in realities between France and the Irish

Republic, both of which have a regime of separation or *laïcité*. Building on the work of François-Georges Dreyfus (1993), Ferrari suggests that it is much more useful to talk of a European model in which differences among the various countries should be considered along three dimensions:

1. The protection of individual rights of religious freedom, a tradition that has grown out of European history since the eighteenth century and is currently expressed in article 9 of the European Convention on Human Rights.
2. The degree of withdrawal of the competence of the state in religious matters and the autonomy of religious confessions.
3. Selective collaboration between the state and religious confessions.

The proponents of this approach are explicit that this model is a west European one, one which arises out of the history of medieval Catholic Christendom, and that it therefore does not transpose readily to Orthodox Eastern Europe, or by implication to the Muslim world. One can quickly raise pernicious questions about this model. Were the traditional Scandinavian Lutheran state churches not as Constantinian in terms of church-nation relations as are the Orthodox churches? Or is this to read a modern understanding of nation into an Orthodox tradition where it meant something significantly different, at least until Western concepts of nation were absorbed by the peoples of Orthodox Europe?

There are apparent contradictions between the analysis of Ferrari, on the one hand, and Fetzer and Soper, on the other, but they can be attributed to the different scholarly disciplines out of which they come. For the lawyer, the legal situation is the most important, and Ferrari's argument is essentially that, in this regard, there are other developing dimensions of the law that are actually more influential than the traditional constitutional positions. For Fetzer and Soper it is the public assumptions of what is "right," and the channels of accommodation which such assumptions allow, that are most influential in the sociopolitical process of integration.

The major challenge to traditional models is, of course, the new Muslim presence within the countries that are heir to Western Christendom. The rest of this chapter tests these models against the realities of the growing presence of Islam and Muslim communities and their organizations. To do this with reference to Britain and France is a particularly good test of the models because the two countries are often given as examples of markedly different types. Comparing the two countries should be even more interesting because they have been cited by many commentators as representing two distinct paradigms, sometimes mutually exclusive, in their approaches to the integration (or is it assimilation?) of Muslim settlers (see Kepel 1994).

The Historical Background

The point at which the French and British histories of the relationship between the emerging nation-state and religion diverged can symbolically be located in the Reformation, or more specifically in Henry VIII's decision to withdraw England from the authority of Rome. But this is to oversimplify a divergence that had roots in significant social changes, particularly in England, where economic and social power was increasingly moving away from the court and the landed aristocracy to the independent rural gentry and increasingly assertive urban merchant interests and their corporations. While French royal absolutism reached its peak in the seventeenth century, these new socioeconomic interests founded the short-lived Cromwellian Commonwealth. The growing urban and rural middle classes were a fertile ground for the appearance of various "nonconformist" or "dissident" Protestant movements, including the conglomeration of the so-called Puritans who were the core of the parliamentary revolt against Charles I and the establishment of the Commonwealth in 1649. The loss of English royal predominance was confirmed in the "revolution" of 1688–89. By this time England already had to come to terms with a de facto religious pluralism. The crackdown that followed the failed Gunpowder Plot in 1605 had succeeded in imposing Anglicanism and effectively condemning Catholics to two centuries of exclusion.

Similar economic developments were taking place in France, but the surviving feudal hierarchies allowed the monarchy to assert its enormous power, reaching its peak under Louis XIV, by co-opting the aristocracy to stifle independent urban mercantile development. State monopolies were given a much greater role than they ever received in pre-twentieth-century Britain. In these circumstances, the religious pluralism which had continued to exist in France since the Treaty of Nantes became increasingly precarious. The final step of divergence between the two countries in this domain came when, in 1685, the supremacy of the Catholic Church was asserted with the revocation of the Treaty of Nantes and the exile of the Huguenots, much to the economic benefit of Britain and other neighboring countries.

From a European perspective, it was increasingly Britain that was out of step in its attitude to public religion. The 1648 Treaty of Westphalia, with its principle of *cuius regio, eius religio,* had confirmed the single-religion state as the norm. With the acceptance that it was for the ruling prince to determine what that religion should be, Westphalia also represented a historic retreat in the powers and aspirations of the papacy to interfere in the politics of Western Europe. So while the rest of the continent established a pattern where one particular church essentially had a monopoly position backed by the political power, England executed its king a year later and embarked on a road that became increasingly plural.

The tensions between the status quo and the changing economic and social circumstances, combined with the growing pressure of ideas associated with these changes, contributed to the explosion of the French Revolution in 1789. The stubborn defense of its powers by the Catholic Church and its allies through the nineteenth century led to a degree of polarization which was hardly known in Britain. Indeed, the pluralism of churches in Britain generated a situation where specific churches could work with different social and political trends. So while significant parts of the hierarchy in the Church of England were long-time supporters of conservative forces, other churches supported the burgeoning movement for workers' rights and trade unions: it was not a contradiction in terms to be socialist and Christian. In France, on the other hand, the one official church had to carry within itself the tensions which in Britain could be dissipated among different denominations. Major sections of the socialist and republican movements became anticlerical, sometimes viciously so, while the conservative establishment was defended by the Catholic hierarchy, often to the extreme discomfort of parts of the clergy and the flock.

One result of this historical process is that on one point Britain and France do share a distinction from much of the rest of Western Europe. Neither country has a general legal regime for the recognition of religion such as applies, for example, in countries like Austria, Belgium, or Germany. In neither country is it possible to admit a religion or religious denomination to a preexisting "recognized" status from which predictable consequences flow. Specific British denominations have been accorded their own legal status at various points in the past. This has impacted the status of the various Protestant Free Churches, the Jews, and the Roman Catholic Church. The privileges associated with such status differ according to denomination and according to which part of the United Kingdom one is dealing with. Thus, the Church of England is the only one in which the priest acts as marriage registrar, while all other religions, whether or not they are governed by special legislation, may apply to have an officer recognized as registrar. Another consequence is that when such denominations wish to make changes of substance to their constitutions they may very well need new legislation. The most notable recent occasion on which this happened was when the Presbyterian and Congregationalist churches in England and Wales wished to merge into the United Reformed Church, for which they needed a new act of Parliament. Acts of Parliament have also been required to legalize the decisions of the Church of England to ordain women priests.

In France, the link between state and religion was severed in 1905. The process leading to this was not without bitterness, and the law's general acceptance must, in part, be attributed to the moderation of the socialist leader Jean Jaurès, who faced down the hard-line demands of the antisecularist trends within his movement. In fact, the law did not implement a complete divorce between state and church in that the state retained residual financial responsibilities for the upkeep of buildings in existence at the time of separation. In addition, the law only had a domestic function, so the extensive interests of the French state in international church affairs continue to this day. Treaties between the Vatican and France continued to fall under the responsibility of the Religious Affairs Department of the Foreign Ministry, as did French ecclesiastical possessions abroad, some of which were church buildings. The

French region Alsace-Moselle enjoys a different status because it was under German rule in 1905, and it retained the church-state arrangement that had developed in the period between 1870 and when it returned to French sovereignty at the end of the First World War. In Alsace-Moselle the state subsidizes the Roman Catholic Church, the Lutheran Church, the Calvinist Church, and the Jewish religion as well as public education in those religions. This applies to the three *départements* of Moselle and Upper and Lower Rhine (Basdevant-Gaudemet 2004).

In both France and Britain religious groups, which did not have legal status as such, functioned under the laws regarding association, and those varied over time. But by this time Muslims had begun to arrive and settle, and further discussion has to take this new dimension into account.

Early Moves and the Beginning of Labor Migration

In both countries, the arrival of people of Muslim background was directly associated with the spread of imperial power.[3] Britain's presence around the coast of Africa and in the Indian subcontinent had brought natives of those regions to the imperial center. It is difficult to describe this process in general terms. Some of the people who came were from the social elites, such as chieftainly families in West Africa, or sons of Indian princes, themselves using the imperial sea routes to do their own bit of exploring. Often they came as partners in commercial deals. Some were traders taking advantage of the long-distance opportunities that imperial communications opened up. Many were from the opposite end of society, people who signed on for some of the most uncomfortable jobs on ships. Many were only temporary visitors, but inevitably some settled where they had landed in Britain.

The watershed in this story was the opening in 1869 of the Suez Canal. The British sea route to India very quickly moved from going around the Cape of Good Hope to passing through the Red Sea. Britain established a coaling station in Aden on the Yemeni coast.[4] There was extensive traffic of both goods and people across the narrow stretch of sea between Arabia and Somalia on the other side. Soon British ships were picking up cheap Yemeni and Somali labor, who boarded in Aden and often stayed in Britain when they were signed off at the end of the trip. Cardiff and South Shields, near Newcastle, soon had noticeable settlements of Yemenis and Somalis. Liverpool had already started to build up a population of West Africans, while people from all over the world could be found in London.

The leadership of the various small communities affected their visibility. The Yemeni and Somali communities brought with them a particular Sufi order, namely the North African 'Alawiyyah. The community evolved around the practices and networks of this order. It was not a wealthy community, and it had very little access to any form of leadership which could mediate with the host society. So they tended to be found in small converted premises where they worshipped and taught their children. Some began to move inland to the industrial cities—the first recorded Muslim place of worship in Birmingham was a house converted in the early 1940s. By contrast, London and Liverpool saw the first formal mosque developments. At the initiative of a small group of Indian and British aristocrats, the Shahjehan Mosque opened in 1889 in the southwest London suburb of Woking. The Woking Muslim Mission had strong Ahmadi connections. It was only later, as the rift between the Ahmadiyya and mainstream Sunnism expanded, that the Woking mosque became marginal to developments in London.[5] At the same time, in Liverpool, an English convert known as Abdullah Quilliam pulled together people and resources to convert a row of terraced houses into a mosque and Islamic center. Quilliam had traveled around the Mediterranean, and a few years before the outbreak of the First World War was made sheikh al-Islam of Great Britain by the Ottoman sultan.

The outbreak of war diverted attentions elsewhere. The Liverpool center closed and Woking became marginal, but plans were started by a group of Indian and Arab notables to establish a central mosque for London. By the 1940s this plan had gained support in government circles, and a plot of land was set aside for the project by King George VI on the edge of Regent's Park. Delays and changes of sponsorship meant that the project was not completed until the mid-1970s.

The Muslim presence in France is equally the product of empire, specifically the Algerian experience, which was always much more troubled than Britain's relationship with India. France took control of Algeria over the period from 1830 until 1847 against determined resistance led, in the name of Islam, by 'Abd al-Qadir al-Jaza'iri. Over the following decades France engaged in an active policy of colonizing the region with French settlers, at times in a close partnership with a Catholic hierarchy that had its own aggressive missionary policy. These inauspicious beginnings set a tone that is still a significant factor in North African Muslims' perceptions of France.

The first immigrants into France from North Africa found employment partly in the olive oil industry of the south and partly in the mining industry of the northeast. While some of the migration was voluntary, there was always an element of indentured labor. This was particularly the case during the two world wars, in the second of which, for example, the Vichy French authorities provided Algerian labor for the Germans to build the Atlantic Wall. Another dimension was the use of colonial troops in the trenches of World War I. It was in recognition of the contribution to the war effort of both troops and requisitioned laborers from North Africa, some 200,000 in all, that the French government, soon after the end of the war, decided to support the building of the Paris Mosque. Run by trustees representing Tunisia, Algeria, Morocco, and Senegal, the building was opened in 1926, ironically in the year that the 1905 separation of state and church came of age (Boyer 1992).

But France not only attracted—or requisitioned—labor migration. Starting in the early nineteenth century, France, especially Paris, was regarded across the Mediterranean as an intellectual and cultural center of some importance, much more so than Britain. Muhammad Ali sent student missions to Europe, and above all to Paris, to learn language and modern technology as part of his project to build up the autonomous power of Egypt. Of course, they brought back much more, making a significant contribution to Arab cultural renewal, especially in the Middle East.[6] As Britain's power grew in the region toward the end of the century, Paris also became a popular resort for individuals whom the British exiled from Egypt. The great Muslim reformers Jamal al-Din al-Afghani and Muhammad ʿAbduh, for example, jointly founded their journal *Al-ʿUrwa al-Wuthqa* while exiled in Paris.

Labor migration to France continued to develop steadily during the interwar period and, again, after the Second World War. Until the outbreak of the Algerian War of Independence, most of this immigration was Algerian; many Algerians were already beginning to bring their families. Although Algeria was legally constituted as part of metropolitan France, Muslims were subject to restrictions that effectively gave them a kind of second-class citizenship. These Algerian communities in France played a major role in financing and organizing the Algerian independence movement, and the French authorities cracked down hard on them. During 1957 alone, forty thousand were imprisoned.

It was only during the 1960s that labor migration into France began to spread significantly beyond Algeria, first incorporating large numbers from Tunisia and Morocco and then from parts of French West Africa, above all Senegal. By the end of the 1980s, statistics indicated that Moroccans had almost caught up with Algerians. Following an agreement with Turkey signed in 1966, Turkish immigration also became important, especially in the north and east.

Britain was experiencing its first major period of immigration from Muslim countries at roughly the same time. Once the economy picked up, after the end of the war, the main sources of labor from outside the British Isles were the Caribbean and then India: the Pakistanis only started arriving in large numbers at the end of the 1950s. At regular intervals thereafter the empire returned to haunt the now diminished former metropolis: Cypriots leaving the uncertainties of ethnic strife on the island, East African Asians expelled from Kenya and Uganda, and Somalis seeking better alternatives to their impoverished existence at home.

Islam Arrives

Apart from the few highly profiled initiatives mentioned earlier, there were few outward signs that these newly settling populations were Muslim. The imposition of restrictions on labor immigration, in 1962 in Britain and a decade later elsewhere, created the conditions that increased the profile of Islam. The continuing ease with which wives and children entered, even when economic migration had been severely restricted, meant that a much broader area of everyday culture and custom was imported into Europe with the process of family reunification. In particular, it was the ritual and educational needs of the young Muslim families that initially spurred the formation of Muslim organizations, and thence the intrusion of Islam into the public space. The conversion of property into mosque use (to be followed by the building of new mosques), usually associated with various forms of Islamic instruction, took off quite markedly almost immediately after the gates of labor migration were closed. The establishment of mosques and associated institutions was soon followed by the appearance of special-interest organizations, which often reflected social and political ones in the countries of origin.

One effect of this development was that Muslim groups soon had to find their way into the organizational patterns of the new environment. In France this was, for many years, not easy. The formation of voluntary associations was governed by a law of 1901 which essentially confirms the free right to organize subject to a simple procedure of registration that protects the organization against official interference except in very limited and specific circumstances. However, during the 1930s the government had responded to the rise of fascist movements inspired by Italy and Germany by imposing tight restrictions on the right of foreign residents to form associations under the law of 1901. The procedure included, in the case of Muslim organizations, a process of vetting by the Religious Affairs Department of the Foreign Ministry. In 1989 the restrictions imposed on foreigners associating were abolished; there was immediately an explosion in the number of Muslim associations. At the same time, the 1905 law separating church and state allowed for the creation of associations with a cultural purpose with the significant advantage of being entitled to tax relief.

Superficially, Britain's approach to the formation of voluntary associations appears to be very different. There is no law of association that requires registration; rather there are a variety of laws under which an association can function if it wishes to. If it is merely a matter of having a bank account, no more is required than three signatures authorized by a resolution of the association. If an association wishes to "trade" (i.e., to receive money from grant-giving bodies, private or public, or through public fund-raising, and to spend such income), the law does become involved, usually in the form of a requirement to register under the Companies Act. If the association wants tax privileges it has to register as a charity with the charity commissioners, who over the last two decades have become increasingly proactive in exercising their duty of oversight as regards both activities and proper financial accounts. But, in essence, although the legal and administrative regimes show marked differences, one must conclude that these are essentially differences of form rather than of substance. The freedom to associate, also for religious purposes, is fundamentally permissive.

Religious interests in the educational system have often been a central dimension of the expression of Islam in the public space. There is undoubtedly a significant difference between the two countries in this area.[7] Given the nature of the 1905 settlement in France, the state cannot provide funding for schools managed by religious organizations. The Catholic Church manages an extensive network of "free schools," and a few attempts have been made to establish similar, privately funded Muslim schools. In England, the 1944 Education Act represented a deal between state and church whereby the churches retained some control over their schools and religious education in return for handing over general responsibility to the state. Subsequent education acts have not substantially altered this compromise even though new legal forms have been introduced. In principle, publicly funded Muslim schools were permissible under this legislation although political opposition meant that it was only in 1998 that the first two were authorized.

Testing the Bounds

Throughout this period of settlement, there was a general belief that while the two countries were facing a new phenomenon it was not something of major significance, and that it could be integrated comparatively painlessly with only minor adjustments to make space for the occasional peculiarity. In Britain, in fact, the public and political debate throughout this period was expressed in terms of race relations. Home Secretary Roy Jenkins's famous statement defining multiculturalism was made precisely in the context of a race relations discourse, not a religious one: "cultural diversity, coupled with equal opportunity, in an atmosphere of mutual tolerance."[8] The French discourse remained overwhelmingly that of the *république laïque* with the expectation of assimilation into an open and liberal understanding of "Frenchness." During the 1980s it was the Catholic Church, not Islam, that was the main source of challenge to this consensus in the context of proposals that the state should contribute to the financing of the "free schools."

The year 1989 was a watershed with the "Rushdie affair" breaking out in Britain at the beginning of the year and the "headscarves affair" in France in September.[9] In both countries, the main immediate pressure was demography: the children of the immigrants had grown up in Europe, usually had citizenship, and had expectations of economic and political participation, and they were frustrated. In Britain it was the six-to-fifteen-year-old age group of Pakistani origin that was the largest ten-year group recorded in the 1981 Census (Office of Population Censuses and Surveys 1981). That group was by 1989 in its teens and early twenties. A similar demography applied in France. In both countries, unemployment among the ethnic minorities was higher than the national average, and young people coming into the labor market were often experiencing blatant racial discrimination. In France the affair coincided with the bicentenary of the French Revolution, an event which, as it celebrated republican aspects of French identity, left other parts of France, such as the Catholic tradition, ambivalent and, in the case of Muslims, feeling excluded. The challenge of the campaign against Salman Rushdie in Britain was to the liberal establishment, and of the headscarves in France to the republican establishment.

In both countries there were parallels in the responses. Public debate suddenly discovered Islam as a domestic cultural factor. Despite the subsequent cries of "Islamophobia," the debate was not monolithic. Secularist politicians and intellectuals in both countries condemned the activation of an Islamic dimension, and some launched an all-out attack on Islam as such, calling to mind both medieval and modern caricatures and stereotypes. Others were clearly unhappy with developments but were more circumspect in their public expression. It was noted that Roy Jenkins wondered aloud about the wisdom of his earlier advocacy of multiculturalism. But there were also many who claimed to see hypocrisy and double standards in the way Muslim citizens were being attacked for asserting their right to voice an opinion in public. Many also argued that Muslims were only asking for rights and considerations which others took for granted (see Research Papers 1989 and Ahsan and Kidwai 1991).

Perhaps the most important consequence of the affairs was, however, that Muslims had effectively claimed their right to a place in the public space. Publishers and media outlets began to take Muslim sensitivities into account in a way they had not done before. A Danish national newspaper editor, for example, introduced a policy for reporting on Muslim affairs that she called the "Jew test." It required that anyone writing about Islam and Muslims should test the appropriateness of what they were writing by replacing "Muslim" with "Jew." Similarly, the media in France and Britain, possibly more in the latter than in the former, were beginning to adopt the sensitivity toward Muslims that had previously become a habit in relation to Jews.

The response at the official level was even more remarkable, although its character was obviously influenced by the different public structures and processes in the two countries. It could be argued that the French government was initially more forthcoming than the British. Already in early 1990s, the minister of the interior established the Conseil de Réflexion sur l'Islam en France (CORIF). For the two years it functioned, it considered practical issues such as dates for Ramadan, and public provision for Muslims, such as access to burial and food and chaplaincy provision in prisons and the armed forces (Basdevant-Gaudemet 2000). A change of minister led to a change of policy toward the creation of a unified representative Muslim council led by the Paris Mosque and Islamic Institute. It was clear that one dimension of this French policy was to encourage the creation of a "moderate" integrated Islam, and the authorities therefore welcomed the issue in December 1994 of the *Charte du culte Musulman en France*.[10] The trouble with this approach was that the leadership of the Paris Mosque and its director were never accepted broadly by the various parts of the Muslim community; opposition collected around the Union des Organisations Islamiques de France (UOIF) and the Fédération Nationale des Musulmans de France (FNMF), both of which had a growing following of young people. Any attempt to pull these various trends together was blocked by the outbreak of the Algerian civil war following the aborted elections of 1992. For the French government and for much of the French public, Islam now became an issue of security, especially following several fatal bomb attacks in Paris in the mid-1990s which were attributed to Algerian Islamist underground organizations that resented French support for the Algerian junta. In the meanwhile, a number of school directors continued to ban headscarves; the resulting cases ended up in the Conseil d'État, which usually, though not always, threw out the ban. At the beginning of the 1994–95 school year the government issued a directive authorizing school directors to ban wearing religious symbols ostentatious enough to constitute proselytism. This was followed by a series of bans, some of which were upheld and others not.[11]

Official response in Britain to Muslim assertiveness in the public and political spheres was much more gradual. This was no doubt related to the fact that there was no single issue, such as the wearing of headscarves, which became the symbolic focal point of the whole debate. It is rather ironic that the headscarf did not become such an issue because Britain is the only west European country with a school uniform tradition. School uniforms had been an issue during the 1970s when the first great influx into schools of the children of immigrants took place. The school population was diverse, and school dress issues were dissipated in various directions: dress requirements of Asian girls (with or without headscarf), turbans for Sikh boys, and hairstyles for both sexes and various ethnic groups.[12] By the mid-1980s most local education authorities, which at that time was where such decisions were made, had adopted flexible uniform policies allowing for cultural variations governed by common color rather than design codes.

During the first part of the 1990s the Conservative government was, in many ways, the main obstacle to the greater involvement of Muslims in the political sphere. This government reluctance to respond was one reason for the various headline-grabbing Muslim initiatives of the early years of the decade. In 1992 the Muslim Parliament of Great Britain was established at about the same time that a group of mostly British converts established the Islamic Party of Britain. These groups enjoyed considerable attention from the media but failed to attract support from Muslim communities. More successful in the long term was the UK Action Committee on Islamic Affairs (UKACIA), an alliance of various existing Muslim organizations initially established to coordinate the anti-Rushdie campaign. It was out of this alliance that, after careful preparation, a new Muslim Council of Britain (MCB) appeared in 1997.

Informal meetings began to take place between selected Muslim representatives and Foreign Office officials during the last years of the Conservative government, but the main issue of Muslim interest in education was blocked on the question of recognition of Muslim schools within the publicly funded system (Radcliffe 2004). Muslim organizations had by 1994–95 begun to realize that while their attention was concentrated on the Rushdie question, major changes had been taking place in the education system, starting with the Education Reform Act of 1988 and followed by the implementation of England's first national curriculum. They now began to put on pressure for public funding for Muslim schools, gaining the support of local authorities and the ministry but ultimately running against the political decision of the Conservative secretary of state. The New Labour government brought in a much friendlier attitude. In January 1998 the first two Muslim schools gained recognition. A series of meetings took place between the Home Office and the MCB, with other ministries becoming involved. A habit of cooperation was established that gave Muslims concrete results: amendments to bills in Parliament, consular support during the pilgrimage to Mecca and Medina, Muslim chaplains in hospitals, a Muslim adviser in the Prison Service, and so forth.

Such cooperation also meant that both "sides" were dealing with each other in a much more differentiated manner than had been the case a decade earlier. Both government and media were careful not to equate incidents of actual or planned violence by Muslims with the Muslim community as a whole or Islam as such. Likewise, Muslim organizations and spokespersons were careful to keep the bridges to government open when they disagreed with specific government policies and decisions.

The 1990s introduced security concerns. The Algerian civil war quickly spilled over into France, especially after explosions on the Paris metro in the middle of the decade. Slightly later, the British authorities began to review their policy toward Islamist radicals, particularly those given asylum in the country, with an eye on their potential impact on young British-born Muslims. France had long had a much more aggressive approach to the balance between civil and religious rights and the needs of internal security than had Britain, and Britain's alleged "softness" toward, in particular, radical Islamist asylum seekers was behind French caricatures about "Londonistan" during the 1990s. After the dissident IRA bombing of Omagh in Northern Ireland, Parliament passed new anti-terrorism legislation which was later widely seen by Muslims as being in part targeted at them.[13] The terrorist attacks of September 11, 2001, moved the UK authorities into an even more aggressive attitude, and by the time of the attacks on London in July 2005, British government ministers were holding French attitudes up as a model.

Exaggerated Contrasts?

It has become common, as I intimated briefly at the beginning of this chapter, to cite Britain and France as having adopted contrasting approaches to the new ethnic and religious pluralism. France follows the republican ideals of liberty and the individual rights of the *citoyen,* and it is as such that the newcomer is expected to integrate. The settlement of 1905 created a demarcated private space for religion. Opponents of the "French way" have accused it of being assimilationist, and certainly some of the petty harassment to which people are exposed could be cited to support the accusation. The headscarves of Muslim women and the big beards of Muslim men are cited, including by officials dealing with citizenship applications, as evidence of refusal or reluctance to accept the principles of the Republic.[14] But French politics and government administration are also driven by at least some of the pragmatism that is often cited as the British characteristic.[15] The reality of the situation in the aftermath of the 1989 headscarves affair was that some remedy had to be found to calm tempers. The Conseil d'État helped, partly by not being predictable. The Ministry of the Interior sought to influence circumstances by engaging in negotiations with Muslim organizations and specifically by sponsoring the establishment of favored ones, with only a modicum of success. But the active involvement of the government, as well as competition between the interior and the foreign ministries at certain points, while far from meeting the wishes of significant sectors of the Muslim population, did send the message that official France could also engage in the "communalist" approach which was supposed to be the British prerogative. When the Algerian war then threatened to take priority over all other considerations, different parts of the Muslim population were prepared to respond. By the end of the 1990s several of the key individuals on the Muslim side, including some associated with groups like the UOIF and the FNMF, were ready to participate in a working group with the Ligue des Enseignants (the teachers had always been among the strongest institutional defenders of *laïcité* and the 1905 settlement) discussing Islam and laicism.[16]

Through the 1980s and the early 1990s Britain, on the other hand, was only to a limited extent living up to the "communitarian" stereotype. With a few exceptions, the central government refused to deal with the Muslim community in any kind of collective form. Some local governments, however, did develop experience in such collective dealings during this period (Nielsen 1994). It was only with the Labour accession to power in 1997 that this approach impacted seriously on central government. But at the same time, the individual rights approach, which had never been the strongest dimension of British public life, received a boost with the introduction into UK law of the European Convention on Human Rights through the Human Rights Act 1998 (it came into effect in 2000). British judges also have greater discretion to take cultural peculiarities into account than their continental counterparts, especially when dealing with family relations, because of the strong common-law tradition in Britain. One could argue that such a flexible approach is, in fact, more "individualistic" than the "same-rule-fits-everyone" approach common to the Napoleonic legal systems of mainland Europe.[17]

The traditional typologies at the beginning of this chapter are not particularly valuable for comparing France and Britain; at minimum they are certainly no longer helpful. They did reflect the sharp distinctions which appertained until the beginning of the twentieth century, even though it was only with the 1905 settlement in France that the paths reached the full extent of their divergence. Since 1945, however, those paths have not so much reconverged as become irrelevant.

The individual rights of religious freedom laid down in the European Convention now have equal standing in both countries. They may administer them differently, but this does not change the substance. In fact, both countries arguably face the same challenges in this field, namely the boundary between the collective rights of the state and its inhabitants as a whole on the one hand, and the individual right to religious freedom on the other. This has to do with definitions of what constitutes religion and the debate over the function and place of religion in the public space, not to mention where one draws the line between the private and public spaces. These are questions which all of Europe and North America have to deal with, and an obvious conclusion is not yet in sight.

Both countries clearly accept and generally function on the principle that the state has only limited competence in religious matters and only limited right to interfere in the autonomy of religious confessions. In Britain, some of that state competence continues to be laid down in law, especially in relation to the older, mainstream churches. But in France there is also legislation, including that of 1905, that specifies areas of state competence.

More important is probably the acceptance that, informally, the state has a legitimate interest in religious affairs. In some ways this may mark the strongest contrast between the past and the present, while at the same time highlighting that the two states are currently at the point of closest policy convergence in their histories. Essentially, in both cases the state has retreated from its claim to dominance in religious affairs. This was the claim that was so vigorously opposed in England in the seventeenth and eighteenth centuries, including by those who laid the foundations for the United States of America. The contest was more polarized and lasted longer in a less religiously plural France.

Perhaps the major contrast between the two countries today has much less to do with religion than with ethnic pluralism and race, and their interaction with religious pluralism. In France, the numerical predominance of Islam among immigrants and ethnic minorities has tended to create a situation where public perceptions easily equate ethnic minority and Islam: the race question becomes inseparable from the issue of Islam. In Britain the much more notable presence of other religions, such as Sikhism and Hinduism, and, above all, the prevalence of Christianity in many different forms among Afro-Caribbean immigrants, make for a much more complex situation. Race is not nearly so simply equated with one particular religion, and the ethnic mix makes it more difficult to identify Islam with one ethnic minority group. This contributes to a much more fluid public perception and debate as well as leaving space for individuals and groups to develop a broader range of identity options in the public space (Bauman 1996). However, the focus on security since September 11, 2001, has introduced a further factor toward convergence, but this is discussed in greater detail in part 4 of this volume.

Notes

1. See, for example, European Consortium for Church-State Research (1994) and Robbers (1996).

2. Spain in particular has moved since the restoration of the monarchy; see De la Hera and de Codes (1998).

3. It should be noted that it did not start with empire; see Matar (1998).

4. A brief survey of this history can be found in Nielsen (2004, 4–6 and 177–191). A more detailed account is in Ansari (2004).

5. The Ahmadi movement, founded in northern India in the late 1800s, was from the beginning attacked for heresy, an accusation which gathered strength through the twentieth century until many Muslim countries during the 1970s declared it to be non-Muslim.

6. See the early chapters in Hourani (1962).

7. Accommodation to Muslims in the educational sphere is the main test used by Fetzer and Soper in their comparison of Britain, France, and Germany (2005; see especially pp. 130–145).

8. Quoted by Kenan Malik, "The Trouble with Multiculturalism," *Spiked-politics,* December 18, 2001; available at http://www.spiked-online.com/Articles/00000002D35E.htm (accessed October 27, 2006).

9. An early, but still worthwhile, account of particularly the Bradford environment out of which the Rushdie affair first sprang is Lewis (1994). A useful summary of the issues behind the "headscarves affair" is Barrett (1996).

10. For an English translation see "Charter of the Muslim Community in France," *CSIC Papers: Europe,* no. 17, 1996.

11. A comparative discussion of Muslims and European education systems can be found in Maréchal (2003).

12. It is probably not unreasonable to suggest that the path to tolerating Muslim girls wearing headscarves had been pioneered by Sikh men demanding the right to wear turbans: Sikh regiments had been among the elite of the British Indian army—and they were men.

13. See *British Muslims Monthly Survey,* September 1998, p. 1, available at http://artsweb .bham.ac.uk/bmms/1998/09September98.html (accessed October 27, 2006).

14. The group of consultants working on Religious and Cultural Aspects of Equality of Opportunities for Immigrants for the Council of Europe, which I chaired, was shown copies of such letters during its fact-finding visit to Paris in October 1995. The group's report was published in January 1996 as Council of Europe doc. MG-S-REL (95) final.

15. Rouland talks of "firmness in principle, and flexibility in practice" (1998, 531).

16. As debate sharpened in the late 1990s, the Ligue des Enseignants withdrew its sponsorship of the working group, which continued to meet independently, holding a series of seminars recently published by Gresh and Islam et Laïcité (2005).

17. According to Foblets (2003), increasing cultural pluralism may be inducing "Napoleonic" courts to resurrect elements of common-law approaches.

References

Ahsan, M. M., and A. R. Kidwai, eds. 1991. *Sacrilege versus Civility: Muslim Perspectives on "The Satanic Verses" Affair.* Leicester, UK: The Islamic Foundation.

Ansari, Humayun. 2004. *The Infidel Within: Muslims in Britain since 1800.* London: Hurst & Co.

Barrett, Chris. 1996. "Confrontation at Creil: Secularism, Multi-culturalism and the 'Headscarves Affair' in France," *Case Studies for Politics,* no. 25. University of York, Department of Politics (available at http://www.york.ac.uk/depts/poli/research/csp/25.htm; accessed October 26, 2006).

Basdevant-Gaudemet, Brigitte. 2000. "The Legal Status of Islam in France." In *Islam and European Legal Systems,* ed. S. Ferrari and A. Bradney, 97–124. Aldershot, UK: Ashgate.

———. 2004. "Islam in France." In *The Legal Treatment of Islamic Minorities in Europe,* ed. R. Aluffi Beck-Peccoz and G. Zincone, 59–82. Leuven, Belgium: Peeters.

Baumann, Gerd. 1996. *Contesting Cultures: Discourses of Identity in Multi-ethnic London.* Cambridge: Cambridge University Press.

Boyer, Alain. 1992. *L'Institut Musulman de la Mosquée de Paris.* Paris: CHEAM.

Conseil Representatif des Musulmans de France—Charters, and the Centre for the Study of Islam and Christian-Muslim Relations. 1996. "Charter of the Muslim Community in France." Translated by Michael Walpole. *CSIC Papers, Europe,* no. 17 (1996).

De la Hera, Alberto, and Rosa M. Martínez de Codes, eds. 1998. *Spanish Legislation on Religious Affairs.* Madrid: Ministerio de Justícia, Centro de Publicaciones.

Dreyfus, François-Georges. 1993. "Le protestantisme contre l'Europe." In *Religions et transformations de l'Europe,* ed. Gilbert Vincent and Jean-Paul Willaime, 127–141. Strasbourg: Presses Universitaires de Strasbourg.

European Consortium for Church-State Research. 1994. *The Legal Status of Religious Minorities in the Countries of the European Union.* Milan: Giuffrè.

Ferrari, Silvio. 2003. "The Legal Dimension." In *Muslims in the Enlarged Europe: Religion and Society,* 2nd ed., ed. Brigitte Maréchal, Stefano Allievi, Felice Dassetto, and Jorgen Nielsen, 219–254. Leiden: Brill Academic Publishers.

Fetzer, Joel S., and J. Christopher Soper. 2005. *Muslims and the State in Britain, France, and Germany.* New York: Cambridge University Press.

Foblets, M. C. 2003. "Muslim Family Laws before the Courts in Europe: A Conditional Recognition." In *Muslims in the Enlarged Europe: Religion and Society,* ed. Brigitte Maréchal, Stefano Allievi, Felice Dassetto, and Jorgen Nielsen, 255–284. Leiden: Brill Academic Publishers.

Gresh, Alain, and Islam et Laïcité, eds. 2005. *Islam de France, Islams d'Europe.* Paris: L'Harmattan.

Hourani, Albert. 1962. *Arabic Thought in the Liberal Age, 1798–1939.* London: Oxford University Press.

Kepel, Gilles. 1994. *A l'ouest d'Allah.* Paris: Seuil.

———. 1997. *Allah in the West: Islamic Movements in America and Europe.* Translated by Susan Milner. Stanford, Calif.: Stanford University Press.

Lewis, Philip. 1994. *Islamic Britain: Religion, Politics and Identity among British Muslims; Bradford in the 1990s.* London: I. B. Tauris.

Maréchal, Brigitte. 2003. "Modalities of Islamic Instruction." In *Muslims in the Enlarged Europe: Religion and Society,* 2nd ed., ed. Brigitte Maréchal, Stefano Allievi, Felice Dassetto, and Jorgen Nielsen, 19–77. Leiden: Brill Academic Publishers.

Matar, Nabil. 1998. *Islam in Britain, 1558–1685.* Cambridge: Cambridge University Press.

Nielsen, Jorgen S., ed. 1989. *The "Rushdie Affair": A Documentation.* Centre for the Study of Islam and Christian-Muslim Relations, no. 42. Birmingham, UK: Selly Oak College.

Nielsen, Jorgen S. 1994. "Islam, Musulmani e Governo Britannico Locale e Centrale: Fluidità Strutturale." In *Musulmani Nella Societa Europea,* ed. Jean Jacques Waardenburg, 143–156. Turin: Fondazione Giovanni Agnelli. English version in idem, 1999. *Towards a European Islam,* 36–46. London: Palgrave Macmillan.

———. 2001. "Muslims, the State and the Public Domain in Britain." In *Religion and Politics in Britain and Germany,* ed. R. Bonney, F. Bosbach, and T. Brockmann, 145–154. Munich: K.G. Saur.

———. 2004. *Muslims in Western Europe.* 3rd ed. Edinburgh: Edinburgh University Press.

———. 2005. "L'Islam en Grande-Bretagne." In *Islam de France, Islams de'Europe,* ed. Alain Gresh and Islam et Laïcité, 59–64. Paris: L'Harmattan.

Office of Population Censuses and Surveys. 1981. *Census 1981: Country of Birth, Great Britain.* London: Her Majesty's Stationery Office.

Radcliffe, Liat. 2004. "A Muslim Lobby at Whitehall? Examining the Role of the Muslim Minority in British Foreign Policy Making." *Islam and Christian-Muslim Relations* 15 (3): 365–386.

Research Papers. 1989. "The 'Rushdie Affair': A Documentation." *Research Papers: Muslims in Europe,* no. 42 (June).

Robbers, Gerhard, ed. 1996. *State and Church in the European Union.* Baden-Baden: Nomos Verlagsgesellschaft.

Rouland, Norbert. 1998. "Les politiques juridiques de la France dans la domaine linguistique." *Revue Française de Droit Constitutionnel* 35: 517–562.

Vetvik, Einar. 1992. "Religion and State from a Western Christian Perspective." In *Religion and Citizenship in Europe and the Arab World,* ed. Jorgen S. Nielsen, 7–24. London: Grey Seal.

PART TWO

WESTERN MUSLIMS AND
POLITICAL INSTITUTIONS

5

Muslim Underrepresentation in American Politics

Abdulkader H. Sinno

Up to 2 percent of the American population is Muslim or of Muslim background, and American Muslims are, on average, more educated and affluent than the average American. Yet, there is only one Muslim congressman, Keith Ellison, who was elected in 2006 from Minnesota's Fifth Congressional District, no state governors or lieutenant governors, only four state legislators, and very few federal appointed officials, such as National Institutes of Health director Elias Zerhouni, and ambassadors Zalmay Khalilzad and Shirin Tahir-Kheli.[1] There is extreme underrepresentation in political appointments even at lower levels, such as on the staff of members of Congress and to advisory committees. In contrast, other Western countries such as Canada, the United Kingdom, Belgium, and the Netherlands have much higher proportions of parliamentarians who either are Muslim by faith or have parents from traditionally Muslim immigrant groups. In this chapter, I broadly describe Muslim representation in Western parliaments and attempt to explain American Muslim underrepresentation in comparative context.

I do not assume or imply that American Muslims have consistent collective political interests, form a cohesive community, or feel that they can only be adequately represented by someone who is their co-religionist—even though these may very well be, or could become, reasonable generalizations. I also do not necessarily imply that a Muslim is better represented by a Muslim than a non-Muslim or that an American Muslim elected official represents his district any differently than a non-Muslim one. I simply attempt to solve the puzzle of American Muslim underrepresentation, almost complete absence, in elected and appointed positions. This underrepresentation is particularly puzzling because attitudes toward Muslims are more positive in the United States than in many European countries with higher levels of representation and because American Muslims, unlike European Muslims, have the socioeconomic advantages (advanced education, high incomes) that normally encourage incorporation into state elites.

Some of the explanations I explore are American Muslims' reluctance to participate and compete, poor understanding of the political process, the incentives of the electoral system, district size, the influence of aggressively pro-Israel and Evangelical organizations, and general public hostility toward Muslims. I argue that while electoral systems and popular hostility toward Muslims alone do not explain much, the combination of large majoritarian districts with even a moderate level of popular hostility toward members of the geographically diffuse minority is sufficient to explain American Muslim underrepresentation.

Muslim Identity and American Muslim Numbers

Like other authors in this volume, I do not consider "Muslim" to necessarily indicate a religious identity, but an identity that may have religious, racial, political, or cultural dimensions. This is particularly useful in studying the dynamics of political representation. The politicized identities of elected representatives, perhaps more so than the rest of us, shift with circumstances and expectations. Even those who define themselves as "culturally Muslim" or even as "secular Muslim" find themselves dealing with "Muslim" issues and being considered a "Muslim" by their own political parties when they wish to appear diverse, by minority constituents who feel connected to them or who do not trust them, by jealous rivals wishing to discredit them, by the media when they need "Muslim" voices, and by civil society's organizations. For example, Said el-Khadraoui, Belgium's secular and very European-looking member of the European Parliament, who was born to a mixed Moroccan-Flemish couple, was celebrated as a member of an "ethnic minority" by his colleagues on the Parliament's newly formed Anti-Racism and Diversity Intergroup.[2] A broader, more inclusive, definition of who is a Muslim is useful to understand the broad range of dynamics that affect Muslim representation. I therefore consider a parliamentarian to be Muslim if he or she is Muslim by faith or has at least one parent who is Muslim by faith or belongs to a group that is traditionally Muslim.

The number of Muslims in the United States is both difficult to estimate and subject to highly politicized debates. It is difficult to estimate the number of Muslims because survey methods are not particularly effective for counting unevenly distributed and hard-to-define small populations and because of fear of divulging identity by members of a vulnerable minority, differences in self-identification among those who belong to ethnic groups that are traditionally Muslim, and inflation of attendance numbers by mosque officials. Polls conducted since 2001 produced estimates that vary between 1.5 million and 7 million.[3] In addition, organizations that want to empower American Muslims and some among those who wish to keep them from influencing U.S. foreign policy in the Middle East have engaged in public squabbles over those numbers in the belief that perceived numbers translate into political influence.[4]

Phone surveys tend to produce the lowest estimates of Muslim Americans, between 1.5 million and 2.5 million, perhaps because members of this group are less inclined to give out personal information to a stranger over the phone than other Americans. Estimates based on mosque attendance tend to be the highest, in the 6–7 million range, perhaps because mosque leaders exaggerate the size of their constituencies or because the multiplier that researchers use to extrapolate the size of the community from mosque attendance is inflated. It is likely that the rapidly growing population of Americans who are Muslims by faith or descend from traditionally Muslim immigrant groups falls between the two ranges of estimates, at some 4–5 million, around 1.5 percent of the U.S. population.

Counting Muslims in Canada and some European countries is less difficult. Canada and the United Kingdom ask residents to choose a religion in their censuses, even if they do not practice. The 2001 censuses found that the Muslim Canadian proportion of the population doubled in a decade to 2 percent of the total and that the UK Muslim population is at some 3 percent of the total. Estimating the number of Muslims in most other European countries does pose serious methodological difficulties but is more manageable than in the United States because of the strong association between national immigrant groups and religion, regional concentration, and the smaller size and populations of European countries (Brown 2000). As of 2007, some twenty-two million Muslims live in the West, an estimated three percent of the combined populations of the United States, Canada, Western Europe, Australia, and New Zealand (around 740 million residents).

Are Muslims Poorly Represented in American Politics?

Table 5.1 lists the names of Muslim members of Western legislatures as of December 2006, the number of parliamentarians in these legislatures, estimates of the proportion of Muslims in those countries and in the legislatures, and the ratio of

Table 5.1. Muslim Members of Western Parliaments as of December 2006

Country or Entity	Chamber	Total Members	Muslim Members	Percent Muslims		Ratio
				Population	Parliament	Parliament/Population
United States	House (2006–2008)	435	1. Keith Ellison (Democrat)	1.5%	0.2%	0.13
	Senate (current)	100	—		0%	0
Belgium	La Chambre/de Kamer (2003–)	150	1. Talbia Belhouari (PS) 2. Mohammed Boukourna (PS) 3. Cemal Cavdarli (SP.A) 4. Dalila Douifi (SP.A) 5. Nahima Lanjri (CD&V) 6. Anissa Tamsamani (PS)	4%	4%	1
	Senat (2003–2007)	71	7. Jihane Annane (MR) 8. Sfia Bouarfa (PS) 9. Mimount Bousakla (SP.A) 10. Fatma Pehlivan (SP.A) 11. Amina Sbai (PS) 12. Fauzaya Talhaoui (SP.A)	4%	8.45%	2.1
Canada	House of Commons (2006–)	308	1. Rahim Jaffer (Conservative) 2. Wajid Khan (Liberal) 3. Yasmin Ratansi (Liberal) 4. Omar Alghabra (Liberal)	2%	1.3%	0.65
	Senate	105	5. Mobina Jaffer (Liberal)	2%	0.95%	0.48
Denmark	Folketing (2005–)	179	1. Huseyin Arac (SDP) 2. Naser Khader (SLP) 3. Kamal Qureshi (SF)	3.7%	1.68%	0.45

Country	Institution		Members			
EU	European Parliament (2004–2009)	France 78	1. Kader Arif (Socialist) 2. Tokia Saifi (UMP)	8%	2.56%	0.32
		Belgium 24	3. Saïd el-Khadraoui (SPA)	4%	4.2%	1.05
		Germany 99	4. Cem Ozdemir (Green) 5. Vural Oger (Socialist)	4%	2.02%	0.51
		UK 78	6. Syed Kamall (Conservative) 7. Sajjad Karim (LDP)	3.3%	2.56%	0.78
		Netherlands 27	8. Emine Bozkurt (Soc)	5%	3.70%	0.74
		732	TOTAL MEP	3.3%	1.09%	0.33
France	Assemblée Nationale (2002–)	577	1. Mansour Kamardine (Mayotte, UMP)	8%	0.17%	0.02
	Sénat	331	2. Alima Boumedienne-Thiery (Soc) 3. Ibrahim Soibahaddine (Mayotte, UMP) 4. Bariza Khiari (Socialist) 5. Eliane Assassi (Communist)	8%	1.21%	0.15
Germany	Bundestag (2005–)	614	1. Lale Akgun (SPD) 2. Ekin Deligoz (Green) 3. Huseyin Kenan Aydin (WASG) 4. Sevim Dagdelen (Die Linke) 5. Hakki Keskin (Die Linke)	4%	0.81%	0.20
Greece	Hellenic Parliament (2004–)	300	1. Ahmed Ilhan	3.5%	0.33%	0.09

(continued)

Table 5.1. (*continued*)

Country or Entity	Chamber	Total Members	Muslim Members	Population	Parliament	Parliament/ Population
				Percent Muslims		Ratio
Netherlands	Tweede Kamer (2006–)	150	1. Khadija Arib (PvdA) 2. Naima Azough (GL) 3. Samira Bouchibti(PvdA) 4. Coskun Coruz (CDA) 5. Tofik Dibi (GL) 6. Sadet Karabulut (SP) 7. Fatma Koser Kaya (D66)	5.8%	4.67%	0.81
New Zealand	House of Representatives (2005–)	121	1. Ashraf Choudhary (Labor)	.9%	0.83%	0.92
Norway	Storting (2005–)	169	1. Saera Khan (Labor)	1.7%	0.59%	0.35
Sweden	Riksdag (2006–)	349	1. Reza Khelili Dylami (Moderate) 2. Mehmet Kaplan (Green) 3. Ameer Sachet (SD) 4. Maryam Yazdanfar (SD)	3.9%	1.15%	0.29
United Kingdom	House of Commons (2005–)	646	1. Sadiq Khan (Labour) 2. Khalid Mahmood (Labour) 3. Shahid Malik (Labour) 4. Mohammad Sarwar (Labour)	3.3%	0.62%	0.19

| United Kingdom | House of Lords | 721 | 5. Nazir Ahmed (Labour)
6. Waheed Alli (Labour)
7. Kishwer Falkner (LDP)
8. Pola Manzila Uddin (Labour)
9. Adam Hafegee Patel (Labour)
10. Amirali Alibhai Bhatia (crossbench)
11. Mohamed Iltaf Sheikh (Conservative) | 3.3% | 0.97% | 0.29 |

these proportions. Twelve Western countries, as well as the European Union, have Muslim parliamentarians, some in more than one chamber. Nine other Western countries where Muslims make up more than 0.5 percent of the population do not currently have Muslim parliamentarians (Australia, Austria, Finland, Ireland, Italy, Luxembourg, Malta, Spain, and Switzerland).[5] I estimate that there are 64 Muslims out of a total of 8,815 parliamentarians in the 21 Western countries where Muslims number more than 0.5 percent of the population. This amounts to a ratio of 0.73 percent or roughly a fourth of the proportion of Muslims in these countries (22 million out of 740 million, or 3 percent). They serve in seventeen chambers.

As of December 2006, Belgium and the United Kingdom had the largest number of Muslim parliamentarians (thirteen each). They served in the three chambers of both countries—the upper and lower chambers and the European Parliament. They were followed by the Netherlands with eight; France and Germany with seven each; Canada with five; Sweden with four; Denmark with three; and New Zealand, Norway, Greece, and the United States with one each.

Twenty-nine of the sixty-four are women (45%), a much higher proportion than the overall ratio of women in OSCE (the fifty-five states of the Organization for Security and Cooperation in Europe) legislatures (19.6% according to data compiled by the Inter-Parliamentary Union as of June 30, 2007).[6] Women are almost twice as well represented among Muslim parliamentarians in appointed and proportionally elected legislatures (49% of Muslim parliamentarians) than in majoritarian legislatures (27%). This is most likely because party leaders in proportional representation (PR) systems have much discretion over the selection of minority members of their list and are likely to choose liberal Muslim women who conform to their visions of Muslim assimilation. Muslim parliamentarians, however, are also more likely to be women than non-Muslim parliamentarians in majoritarian systems (the U.S., Canada, and the UK).

Figure 5.1 plots the percentage of Muslim parliamentarians versus the percentage of the Muslim population in the legislatures of the twenty-one Western countries as of December 2006. The parity line (one-to-one ratio) functions as a visual aid.

The only Western country where the proportion of Muslim parliamentarians exceeds the proportion of Muslims in the population is Belgium, and they do so in all three chambers. During its 2003–2006 session, the Dutch Tweede Kamer (lower chamber) also had more Muslim parliamentarians than parity, but this changed with the 2006 election that brought down the number of Muslims from 10 to 7 out of 150. The 2007 Belgian election also brought down the number of Belgian senators from 6 (a staggering 8.45%) to 1. Canada's House of Commons, the Dutch and British EU delegations, the Dutch Kamer, and New Zealand's House of Representatives are all within two-thirds of parity in regards to Muslim representation. Other countries and chambers have lower rates.

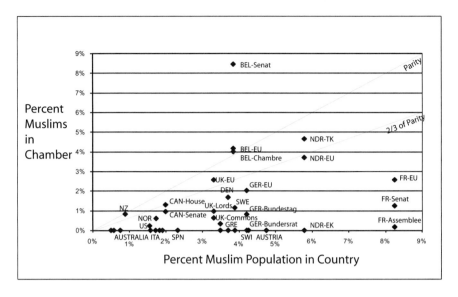

FIGURE 5.1.
Percentage Western Muslim Parliamentarians versus Percentage
Size of Muslim Minorities (December 2006)

The larger European countries generally have low rates of Muslim representation. Germany has only 5 Muslim parliamentarians among the 614 members of the Bundestag and none in its upper chamber. The proportion of Muslim German members of the Bundestag is a fifth of the proportion of Muslims in Germany. Underrepresentation in Germany can be explained at least in part by the daunting naturalization process—some estimate that before the latest reforms in citizenship laws, only a sixth of the Muslims in Germany were citizens.[7] The French parliament has only three female Muslim senators of North African descent (one is of mixed parentage), in addition to two parliamentarians from the mostly Muslim overseas territory of Mayotte, which is guaranteed representation in both chambers, out of a total of 908 parliamentarians. Underrepresentation is underscored by the estimated proportion of the Muslim population of France, the highest in the West, at some 8 percent. Muslim representation in the United Kingdom is also a fraction of what population numbers would predict, a fifth as much in the Commons and a third as much in the Lords.[8]

Muslim members of the European Parliament (MEPs) from France (2.56% Muslim), Germany (2.02%), and the UK (2.56%) reflect the numbers of Muslims in their society better than Muslim members of the national parliaments. The one Belgian and one Dutch Muslim MEP reflect adequately the proportion of Muslims in both countries. Overall the eight Muslim MEPs constitute just over 1

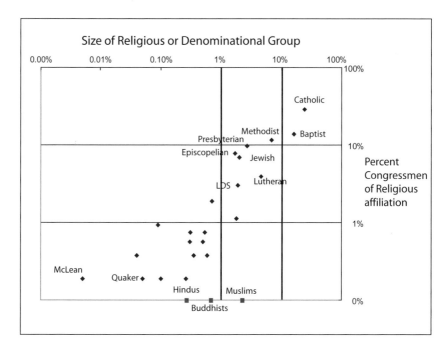

FIGURE 5.2.

Percentage U.S. Congressmen versus Percentage of Their Religious or
Denominational Communities (109th Congress, logarithmic scale)

percent of the legislature, a third of the percentage of Muslims in the European
Union.

American Muslim representation is among the lowest for Western Muslims.
It compares with the rates of representation of the historically disadvantaged
Greek and French Muslims. But how do American Muslims perform compared to
members of other American religious and ethnic groups?

Figure 5.2 plots on a logarithmic scale the percentage of members of the
109th Congress (2005–2006) who disclose their religion or denomination versus
the proportion of adherents of the religion or denomination in American society.[9]
I use a logarithmic scale to disaggregate the smaller religious groups or denominations. Thirty-two congressmen do not claim to belong to a particular religion
or denomination. There were no Muslim, Hindu, or Buddhist members of the
109th Congress. Except for Muslims, and perhaps Buddhists if you consider the
higher estimates of their numbers, all organized religions whose adherents number more than 1 percent of the American population were represented in Congress. The 110th Congress, elected in November 2006, was the first to include one
Muslim and two Buddhists.

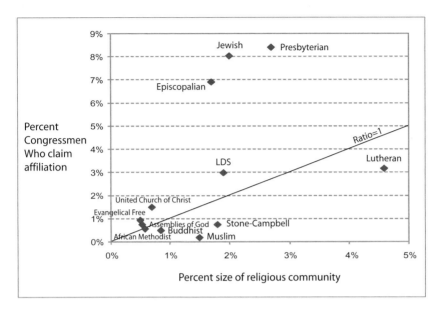

FIGURE 5.3.

Percentage Congressmen versus Percentage Religious Group Size (Groups between 0.5 and 5 percent of U.S. population, 110th Congress)

Congress generally reflects the religious composition of Judeo-Christian religious groups in society quite well for denominations with 1 percent or more of the population. Some members of the House and Senate even belong to tiny groups like the Quakers, Foursquare Gospel, and Nazarenes. Some groups, such as the Methodists, Presbyterians, Latter-day Saints (Mormons), Christian Scientists, Episcopalians, and Jews, are overrepresented, but no Christian religious denomination is grossly underrepresented. Religious and denominational affiliation do not seem to affect the electoral opportunities of candidates for Congress from the Judeo-Christian tradition today, thus producing a distribution of congressmen's religious backgrounds that roughly reflects the proportions of these religious groups and denominations in society. This seems to even apply to groups that were once marginalized, such as Mormons, who also benefit from their concentration in the state of Utah and districts of other states.[10]

For a more fine-tuned look at the election of congressmen from groups that are comparable in size to the Muslim community, in Figure 5.3 I plot the same two variables for all religious groups whose members form between 0.5 and 5 percent of the U.S. population (110th Congress).

Seven out of eleven religious groups or denominations whose adherents number between 0.5 and 5 percent of the U.S. population are, and have been consistently in the last few decades, strongly overrepresented in Congress. There are three to four times as many Presbyterian, Episcopalian, and Jewish members of Congress than a random draw from the population would predict. United Church of Christ or Congregationalist congressmen are twice as numerous as their numbers in American society would suggest. Members of the Churches of Latter-day Saints, Assemblies of God, and Free Evangelicals are overrepresented by roughly 50 percent. African Methodists are near parity.

Lutherans are underrepresented by a third and Stone-Campbell churches are underrepresented by half. Buddhists are underrepresented by one-half to two-thirds, depending on how their numbers are estimated. Muslims are the most underrepresented of all groups that number between 0.5 and 5 percent of the population both in the 110th Congress and in congressional history. All else being equal, one would expect to find five to ten times more Muslims serving in Congress.

The extreme underrepresentation of American Muslims in American politics is even more astonishing because at least the immigrant portion of the American Muslim population enjoys some of the advantages in education and income that likely facilitate the overrepresentation of Presbyterians, Episcopalians, and Jews in Congress. While the Muslims of Europe tend to lag behind the rest of the population in education and economic performance, American and Canadian Muslims are overachievers professionally, educationally, and economically. Two Zogby polls (2001 and 2004) found that American Muslims have a higher median household income than Americans as a whole (above $50,000 a year) and that 58–59 percent have completed their college education, more than twice the national rate.[11] All else being equal, we should see a higher rate of American Muslims running for office and getting elected than in society at large, but this is obviously not the case.

Muslims are also underrepresented among congressional staffers. There are only about fifteen Muslim congressional staffers out of some 9,000, about 0.17 percent of the total, or about a tenth of their proportion of American society.[12] Ten of the fifteen Muslim congressional staffers attend Friday prayers at a designated room in the Capitol, and some, like Jameel Aalim-Johnson, the previous, African-American chief of staff for Representative Gregory Meeks of New York, are quite assertive about their religious beliefs and identity.

American Muslims are also underrepresented in state politics. Not a single U.S. governor or lieutenant governor is American Muslim. Only five members of elected state legislatures were Muslim in 2007. They are North Carolina state senator Larry Shaw (Democrat), Missouri state assemblymen Yaphett El-Amin and Rodney Hubbard (Democrats), Maryland house of delegates member Saqib Ali (Democrat), and New Hampshire house member (one of four hundred) Saghir Tahir (Republican). Three of the five are African Americans and two (Ali and Tahir) are Americans with family roots in India and Pakistan. The five Muslim state legislators fill 0.067 percent of the 7,382 state senate and assembly seats in the fifty states, or roughly one-fifteenth to one-thirtieth the proportion of Muslims in

American society. States where the proportion of American Muslims is higher than the national average (California, New York, New Jersey, Michigan, Ohio, Illinois, and Indiana) do not have a single elected American Muslim in their legislatures.

It is puzzling that the United States, a country whose political culture emphasizes diversity and immigrant roots, produces so few elected Muslim officials while the populations of several European nation-states with disadvantaged and marginalized Muslim populations elect Muslims to their national parliaments and to the European Parliament at rates that sometimes approximate, or even exceed, their proportion in the general population.

Explaining American Muslim Underrepresentation

Some apparently intuitive explanations for the lack of American Muslim representation are misleading. Some have argued that American Muslims might be reluctant to participate and compete in American politics, perhaps for ideological reasons. While caustic debates on the merits and desirability of political participation among American Muslims were frequent up until the 1990s, the increase in the size of the American Muslim community, the realization that Muslims are here to stay, and increased infringements on civil liberties after the 9/11 attacks have all but ended these debates. Recent polls (Zogby 2001 and 2004) of American Muslims have found that 79–82 percent of them are registered to vote, with 85–88 percent of the registered voters very likely or somewhat likely to vote.[13] The Zogby poll (2004, 18) also reports that 86 percent of American Muslims claim that it is either very important (53%) or somewhat important (33%) for them to participate in politics. The Mosque in America study (Bagby, Perl, and Froehle 2001, 31) reports that 77 percent of interviewed mosque representatives strongly agreed with the statement "Muslims should be involved in American institutions" and that another 19 percent somewhat agreed with the statement. Only 4 percent of respondents disagreed in this group of interviewees, who are more likely to be ideologically or theologically biased against participation than the general American Muslim population. Muslim conventions often include speakers and organizers to educate Muslims about how to lobby, how to organize political action committees, and how to become politically active in other ways. Muslim political organizations are becoming more active and vocal, and the United States does not have anti-establishment and anti-participation Muslim organizations such as the British Hizb al-Tahrir. There is also little reason to believe that American Muslims have a poor understanding of the political process and the opportunities it provides because of their higher levels of education and income and the rapid growth of American Muslim organizations. In the American Muslim community the debate on whether to participate in the political process is over.

Legal status or rates of citizenship also do not explain American Muslim underrepresentation. If 79–82 percent are registered to vote, then at least that many are American citizens. Even though candidates for office are required to have been citizens for a number of years, there were still millions of talented, educated, accomplished, and ambitious American Muslims who were eligible to run for office in 2006. A third or so of American Muslims—African-American Muslims and converts from all backgrounds—also grew up in the shadow of American institutions and are as likely to be interested in politics as other Americans.[14] And a much higher proportion of Muslims in the United States are citizens than in European countries, particularly Germany, that still manage to elect some of them to national legislatures and to the European Parliament.

The ethnic fragmentation of American Muslims may hinder their electoral and political prospects in comparison to highly organized ethnic or religious communities such as American Mormons or Jews or Canadian Ismaili Muslims, but not enough to explain extreme underrepresentation. Some have argued that African-American and immigrant Muslims have different priorities that impede collaboration: African Americans are mostly concerned with civil rights and social welfare, and immigrants are more interested in foreign policy issues. Such generalizations, while not completely unfounded, are both exaggerations and becoming less relevant after the defining shock of 9/11 and the domestic reactions that followed it. The attacks of 9/11 made African-American Muslims more aware of the effect of world politics on their lives, and immigrant Muslims more sensitive to issues of social equity, civil rights, and civil liberties.

Data from the Pew Research Center survey of Muslim Americans (2007) suggests that there is convergence.[15] When asked, "In your own words, what do you think are the most important problems facing Muslims living in the United States today?" both immigrant and native African-American Muslims most frequently provided similar answers. All top answers had to do with perceptions of Islam and Muslims: "discrimination, racism, and prejudice" was given by 17.1 percent of immigrant respondents and 15.6 percent of African Americans; "viewed as terrorists" by 13.5 percent and 15.5 percent, respectively; "ignorance/misconceptions of Islam," 9.8 percent and 30.9 percent; "stereotyping/generalizing about all Muslims," 7.4 percent and 22.3 percent. Those who answered "war" or "U.S. foreign policy" were statistically insignificant.

When Keith Ellison, an African-American Muslim, was running for the seat in Minnesota's Fifth Congressional District in 2006, he received volunteer support from Somali immigrants in his district and financial backing from Muslims of immigrant background from across the country.[16] Federal Election Commission records of contributions to Ellison's campaign reveal that most contributors with Muslim-sounding names, a quarter to a third of the total, have typically South Asian- and Arab-sounding first names or family names. Several immigrant Muslim businessmen and organizations arranged fund-raisers for Ellison as well.[17] He also received a donation from a newly registered Muslim political action committee (PAC) with diverse membership, the Indiana Muslim Political Action Committee Taskforce, which promotes Muslim representation and assists candidates who are supportive of civil rights and liberties. African-American Muslim candidates in local races across the country have also received substantial contributions from immigrant Muslims. Ethnic divides may be significant in some areas of Muslim-American life, but they seem not to inhibit Muslims from supporting serious Muslim candidates with different ethnic backgrounds.

Increased convergence in the attitudes of American Muslims is facilitated and encouraged by the proliferation of multi-ethnic mosques, the formation of multi-ethnic Muslim organizations that produce an overarching American Muslim political discourse, and the readiness of community groups and governing institutions in a very religious country to accept the development of a meaningful American Muslim identity. Ninety percent of all American mosques have at least some Arabs among their members, and 87 percent have at least some African-American and South Asian members.[18] This means that no more than 13 percent of American mosques are mono-ethnic, but the percentage is probably even smaller. Mosques are also social and political spheres, and they tend, by their mere existence, to define a community of believers in the eyes of participants and outsiders.

A broader American Muslim political agenda is also being forged by emerging organizations like the Council on American-Islamic Relations (CAIR), the American Muslim Alliance (AMA), the Muslim Public Affairs Council (MPAC), the Muslim American Society (MAS), and the Islamic Society of North America (ISNA) that have adopted an increasingly hegemonic discourse of Muslim rights, influence, votes, and identity that is oblivious to ethnic differences or to ethnic political interests within the Muslim population. American and Canadian Muslim organizations tend to cooperate much more to achieve collective goals than the fragmented and rival Muslim organizations one finds in France or Germany, probably because in North America intra-Muslim dynamics are not distorted by promises of state patronage and recognition.[19] Louis Farrakhan's Nation of Islam and some ethnic immigrant organizations like the Pakistani American Congress try to maintain separate or parallel ethnic agendas, but they are less consequential and have less appeal than non-ethnic Muslim organizations.[20] And finally, the federal, state, and local governments as well as non-governmental organizations, journalists, and academics have accepted the emerging American Muslim identity and discourse. Religious identity has stuck better than ethnic identities, because the mosque is a more visible symbol of distinctiveness than any ethnic institution, because the emerging discourse from the so-called "war on terror" brings attention to the "Muslim" within, and because the United States is a very religious country where people are inclined to imagine communities centered on religious institutions. Acknowledgments of the Muslim presence by the White

House (Eid celebrations at the end of Ramadan and presidential visits to mosques) and Congress (opening sessions with Muslim prayers) also increase the perception among those with a link to Islam that, at least in the political sphere, being an American Muslim is more significant and meaningful than being Turkish-, Bosnian-, Pakistani-, or Arab-American.[21]

The majoritarian (first-past-the-post) American electoral system alone does not explain American Muslim underrepresentation in Congress. Across Western liberal democracies (the twenty-one countries listed above), Muslims are underrepresented at the same rate (roughly one-fifth) in chambers elected by majoritarian and proportional systems. (The ratio of the percentage of representatives to the percentage of the Muslim population is 0.2 in majoritarian systems and 0.23 in electoral systems relying on proportional representation.) The aggregate numbers, however, mask very interesting differences and dynamics.

Muslims are either much better represented in proportional representation systems than in majoritarian systems or not represented at all. The ratio is 0.57 in the eleven Western chambers elected through proportional representation that have any Muslim members. Fourteen other such chambers in Western countries that have a Muslim population of more than 0.5 percent (Austria, Switzerland, Italy, Spain, Luxembourg, and Finland) do not have any Muslim representatives at all. It could be that a tipping point of party competition for Muslim (or, more broadly, immigrant) votes moves all parties from avoiding recruiting Muslim candidates to doing so actively. The tipping point is reached if one party achieves electoral gains by recruiting a Muslim candidate. The first to adopt this tactic and succeed gives an incentive to all others, except far-right parties, to do the same. Once parties begin to compete for the Muslim vote, Muslims become well represented because proportional representation systems produce more parties than majoritarian systems, and most parties include a well-positioned Muslim candidate on their list to attract, or not completely lose, the minority vote. Many of these candidates therefore make it to parliament. The ten Dutch Muslims in the Tweede Kamer of the 2003–2006 session belonged to six different parties, and one of them formed his own one-person group. Their seven successors who were elected in 2006 belonged to five different parties. The six Belgian Muslim legislators in the lower house belong to three different parties.

Differences in Muslim representation are also stark among the five Western chambers elected through a majoritarian system. The French Assemblée (the only Muslim is from Mayotte) and the U.S. Senate have no Muslims, but the Canadian House of Commons has a Muslim representation ratio of 0.65, the British House of Commons a ratio of 0.19, and the U.S. House a ratio of 0.13. The details of the processes of selection and election of Muslim candidates in Western majoritarian systems suggest an explanation of American Muslim underrepresentation.

The majoritarian American system alone does not explain poor Muslim representation in Congress. Canada's majoritarian House of Commons has one of the best rates of Muslim representation in the West, only trailing Belgian and Dutch chambers among Western countries whose population is more than 1 percent Muslim. Geographic dispersion in combination with a majoritarian system also does not completely solve the puzzle of Muslim near absence in Congress—it does not affect the electoral odds of members of other small, dispersed American denominations and religions such as American Jews.

By itself, public hostility toward Muslims does not explain the minority's underrepresentation either. Data from a comparative 2005 Pew study that gauged, among other things, public attitudes toward Muslims in seven Western countries indicate that there is no clear relationship between public opinion and rates of representation.[22] The countries with the highest (UK, 72%) and lowest (Germany, 40%) levels of favorable opinion toward Muslims (sum of respondents having very or somewhat favorable opinion of Muslims) have the same levels of representation (0.19 ratio) in their elected lower chambers. The U.S. and Canada have almost the same levels of favorable opinion (Canada at 60% and the U.S. at 57%), but the rate of Muslim representation is five times higher in Canada's House of Commons than in the U.S. House of Representatives (Canada at 0.65 and U.S. at 0.13). The Netherlands, which has the highest rate of Muslim representation among the seven surveyed Western countries in its lower chamber, also has, along with Germany, one of the highest rates of negative opinion toward Muslims in the West (45% favorable opinion).[23] The French have the second-highest rate of favorable opinion toward Muslims at 64% and minuscule rates of representation. Institutions and other factors mediate the effect of public opinion toward Muslims in explaining rates of Muslim representation.

The exceptionally low Muslim representation in Congress is better explained by the *combined effect* of a majoritarian system, large districts, and hostility toward Muslim candidates by more than a quarter of the American voting public.

Popular hostility toward Muslim candidates is stoked by individuals and organizations that support the American-Israeli Public Affairs Committee's (AIPAC) mission to preserve a pro-Israel Congress, by Evangelical churches led by theologians who consider themselves to be in an epic and Manichaean battle with Islam, and by ultraconservatives who consider Islam to represent a geopolitical threat to the United States.[24] Their attacks on Muslim candidates or those who support American Muslim views deter Muslims from running for public office and discourage parties from recruiting Muslim candidates. The exceptional election of Keith Ellison confirms the rule: Minnesota's Fifth Congressional District is a predominantly liberal one where the influence of groups connected to AIPAC and Evangelical churches has little effect on elections. The district's relatively small population of those who would never vote for a Muslim was effectively counterbalanced by an American Muslim community that was energized to support a credible Muslim candidate who was attacked because of his religion. Attacks on Ellison were also not likely to sway enough voters to make a difference in this heavily Democratic district.

The negative public attitudes toward Muslim Americans that are documented by Nisbet et al. and by Jamal (chapters 9 and 10 in this volume) affect the electoral chances of Muslim candidates. Polls conducted between 1999 and 2007 by Gallup, Fox News, the *Los Angeles Times*, Rasmussen, and Pew find that between 31 and 61 percent of their respondents claim that they would not vote for a Muslim candidate for president.[25] Those rates are generally 2–5 times the rates for Catholics or Jews, slightly worse than the proportion of those who wouldn't vote for a Mormon, but a little better than the proportion of those who wouldn't vote for an "atheist." This reluctance to vote for a Muslim presidential candidate extends to other electoral contests. A 2003 Pew survey reports that 31 percent of the general public have reasons not to vote for "a well-qualified candidate" who is Muslim when the office is not specified.[26] The numbers, however, may be misleading because some biased voters could reconsider their opposition when deciding on an actual Muslim candidate who challenges their perceptions of Muslims. This is likely because those who know little about Islam or do not know any Muslims tend to have more negative opinions of Muslims than those who do.[27] Biased voters may also opt to vote based on policies instead of background if the stakes are high and they agree with the policy positions of the Muslim candidate. Still, hostility toward Muslim candidates is very real.

Hostility toward Muslim candidates is not only expressed in the privacy of the voting booth. It often translates into harassment and attacks on the candidate's religion, or even suspected religion, of a type and intensity that are simply not used against congressional candidates from other faith groups anymore. Syed Mahmood, a Muslim Pakistani American, ran in 2002 as a Republican candidate for California's Thirteenth Congressional District. He attempted to challenge sixteen-term incumbent Democrat Pete Stark. Mahmood was not likely to win in the heavily Democratic district and raised a tenth as much money as Stark; even Muslim organizations like the American Muslim Alliance chose to back Stark over Mahmood because of Stark's strong positions in defense of civil liberties.[28] In spite of being a long-shot candidate, Mahmood was targeted in a vicious hate campaign: his campaign signs were defaced, and his office received hate calls and e-mails that included slurs commonly used against Muslims or Arabs. This was not a campaign directed by Mahmood's opponent—they came together after the election to speak against the war in Iraq and the Bush administration's policy. Muslim candidates as diverse as Palestinian-American Maad Abu Ghazalah, who ran for Congress in California's Twelfth Congressional District as a Libertarian; Maryland state representative Saqib Ali; Prospect Park (New Jersey) mayor Mohamed Khairullah; and Anaheim (California) city council candidate Bill Dalati also faced harassment, threats, religious pigeonholing, and racial slurs.[29]

Right-wing commentators have found it expedient to attack Barack Obama's superficial connections to Islam (his paternal grandfather was a Muslim and his middle name is Hussein), even though he is a practicing member of the Trinity

United Church of Christ.[30] And in a bizarre plot, a conservative web magazine claimed that the presidential campaign staff of Hillary Clinton unearthed evidence that Obama "was a Muslim, but concealed it," and that he attended a fundamentalist "madrassa" for four years as a child in Indonesia.[31] Fox News, the *Washington Post,* and Glenn Beck's Headline News program on CNN referenced the misleading article before a CNN investigation found out that Obama in fact attended a mixed, multireligious public school in Indonesia.[32] The authors of the article must have hoped to discredit both Democratic campaigns by claiming that the Clinton campaign uses unsavory tactics and that Obama has Muslim roots. The assumption underlying the scheme is that being linked to Islam taints a political career.

Keith Ellison, in spite of the overwhelming odds in his favor before the election and his landslide victory, still had to contend with demeaning attacks because of his religion from his Republican rival, media figures, pro-AIPAC and conservative websites, and fellow congressmen.

Ellison's Republican opponent, Alan Fine, made clear his distaste for Ellison's faith, even if he sometimes couched his attacks in accusations of anti-Semitism. He mockingly referred to Muslim-sounding pseudonyms that Ellison used in college, condemned his association with American Muslim organizations, and said, "I'm personally offended as a Jew that we have a candidate like this running for U.S. Congress."[33] In one debate, Fine responded to a statement by Ellison about the universality of pain and anger by saying, "That's what Hitler said."[34]

When Ellison declared his intention to carry a Qur'an to his swearing-in ceremony, conservative pundit Dennis Prager called it "an act of hubris . . . that undermines American civilization." In a web column, the talk-show host said, "Insofar as a member of Congress taking an oath to serve America and uphold its values is concerned, America is interested in only one book, the Bible. If you are incapable of taking an oath on that book, don't serve in Congress."[35] Another conservative media figure, CNN host Glenn Beck, asked Ellison after his election to "prove to me that you are not working with our enemies."[36]

The most stunning attack by a fellow congressman came from Representative Virgil H. Goode Jr., a Republican who represents a district in south-central Virginia, who wrote in a letter to constituents: "I fear that in the next century we will have many more Muslims in the United States if we do not adopt the strict immigration policies that I believe are necessary to preserve the values and beliefs traditional to the United States of America." Goode also wrote, in reference to "the Muslim Representative from Minnesota," that "if American citizens don't wake up and adopt the Virgil Goode position on immigration there will likely be many more Muslims elected to office and demanding the use of the Koran."[37] In spite of the hostility, Ellison used a copy of the Qur'an that was once owned by Thomas Jefferson and loaned from the Library of Congress in his swearing-in ceremony. In another remarkable statement by a congressional colleague, Republican representative from Idaho Bill Sali said in an interview that Ellison's election was "not what was envisioned by the Founding Fathers," but apologized later for his choice of words.[38]

On the more tolerant side, congressional colleagues from both parties stood by Ellison during these episodes. The National Jewish Democratic Council supported Ellison and called on Alan Fine, the Minnesota Republican Party, and other Republican organizations "to end their unbalanced and irrational attacks on Minnesota Democratic candidate for Congress Keith Ellison."[39] He was also backed by many Jewish community groups in his district. The fact remains, however, that no candidate for Congress in recent memory had to put up with as many attacks on his faith as Keith Ellison did.

Potential Muslim candidates are also discouraged by the resources that AIPAC and its allies direct against congressional candidates who are sympathetic to the Palestinians. In the logic of ethnic politics, those who are committed to supporting Israel in the context of American politics do so because of ethnic and religious identification and would therefore expect Muslim candidates to have similar attitudes toward Palestinians. Such groups have targeted pro-Palestinian candidates for Congress in the past, such as Georgia's Cynthia McKinney and Alabama's Earl Hilliard. And while the effect of the donations given to McKinney's and Hilliard's opponents might be overstated, representatives of Jewish organizations did not shy away from claiming credit for once defeating McKinney.[40] More worrisome, a number of aggressive pro-AIPAC activists attacked McKinney, because she received money from American Muslim individuals and organizations, in an effort to both intimidate Muslim Americans and to leverage perceived popular hostility toward them.[41]

An early example of Jewish groups trying to impede Muslim-American representation was a successful attempt by the Zionist Organization of America (ZOA) and the Conference of Presidents of Major American Jewish Organizations, which counts the Anti-Defamation League and AIPAC among its members, to convince Democrat Richard Gephardt, then the House minority leader, to withdraw the nomination of an American Muslim to serve on a federal counterterrorism commission.[42] Salam Al-Marayati, the Iraqi-American director of the Muslim Public Affairs Council, was appointed to serve on the National Commission on Counterterrorism in 1999 and was unceremoniously deselected based on the excuse that his security clearance might take too long to be processed. The deselecting of Al-Marayati discouraged many Muslim-American community leaders from seeking to serve the public through government institutions and convinced many that powerful American Jewish organizations are dedicated to disenfranchising Muslim Americans and shutting them out of the American political system.[43]

Pro-Israel organizations may not target future Muslim candidates, but potential Muslim candidates probably factor the possibility of such attacks into their decisions to run for office. They may also suspect that some of the Islamophobic attacks on Ellison, Mahmood, and others probably emanated from individuals influenced by Evangelical and AIPAC-allied groups.

One indication that potential Muslim candidates fear insurmountable electoral hostility toward them is that the number of American Muslims running in elections at all levels dropped dramatically between the 2000 and subsequent elections. According to the American Muslim Alliance, it dropped from 700 (of whom 153 were elected, for a 22% success rate) in the 2000 elections to 60 (17%) in the 2002 elections and 150 (50%) in the 2004 elections.[44] The reason for the drop is, of course, the attacks of 9/11. Many of those who ran in 2002 and 2004 were incumbents who already had the trust of their constituents and were therefore more likely to be elected, but the drastic reduction in the number of candidates in the wake of 9/11 implies that an unfavorable electoral environment deterred potential first-time candidates from running.

The effect of popular hostility on Muslim representation increases with the size of electoral districts because the larger the district, and the smaller and more dispersed the Muslim population in the country, the less likely that the Muslim minority will be large enough in any district to counterbalance the portion of the population that would never vote for a Muslim. It also becomes more difficult for Muslim voters to influence the party selection process.

Electoral districts in the UK and Canada are about a sixth the size of American congressional districts, and as of 2001, Muslims made up more than 10 percent of the populations of 39 UK constituencies and 5–10 percent of the population of 60 more constituencies, out of a total of 646.[45] Muslim Canadians constitute more than 10 percent of the populations of 6 ridings and 5–10 percent of the populations of 30 more ridings, out of a total of 308.[46] American Muslims probably exceed 5 percent of the population in very few congressional districts, if any.

Seven of the eight Muslim parliamentarians in the lower chambers of the UK and Canada were in fact elected in districts with sizable Muslim populations. Among British Muslim parliamentarians, Khalid Mahmood's Birmingham Perry Barr constituency has an estimated 15.9 percent Muslim population, Mohammad Sarwar's Glasgow Govan (the first district he represented before redistricting) was 9.3 percent Muslim, and Sadiq Khan's Tooting 7 percent. In one British district with an estimated 16.5 percent Muslim population, Dewsbury, the two major opponents in the 2005 election were Muslims (Labour's Shahid Malik defeated the Conservative Sayeeda Warsi). Among Canadian Muslim parliamentarians, Yasmin Ratansi's riding of Don Valley East has the second-largest Muslim concentration in the country at 12.5 percent, Omar Alghabra's Mississauga-Erindale 6.8 percent, and Wajid Khan's Mississauga-Streetsville 5.7 percent. Canada's Conservative Rahim Jaffer seems to be the exception to the rule. His riding of Edmonton-Strathcona has few Muslims.

If properly motivated and mobilized, a Muslim population that makes up as little as 5 percent of a district's residents could boost a Muslim candidate's chances in the primaries. Once the candidate is his party's official choice, party loyalty in the broader electorate increases his odds in the general elections. Sinno and Tatari (chapter 7) provide examples of Muslim bloc votes in British primaries that helped the advancement of Muslim candidates. Keith Ellison also strongly benefited from the mobilization of Somali Americans and other Muslim voters in his district to beat six other rivals in the fragmented Democratic primary race of September 2006.[47] After he won the Democratic primary, Ellison was all but guaranteed to win the largely Democratic district.

The exceptionally low Muslim representation in Congress is probably best explained by an unfavorable mix of a majoritarian first-past-the-post system, large districts, and hostility from the Evangelical, pro-AIPAC, and ultraconservative sections of the American voting public that deters Muslims from running for elected office and discourages the two large parties from recruiting them. But what would the politics of Muslim candidates be like if more Muslim Americans manage to get elected to Congress in spite of those formidable hurdles?

The Future of Muslim Participation in Politics

Currently, the politics of the American Muslims are the politics of self-preservation in the face of encroachments on their civil rights and liberties, of developing credibility as equal participants in the face of religious and cultural hostility, of defending themselves against suspicions of double loyalty, of protecting labor rights from institutional ignorance or malice, and of attempting to support the rare sympathetic political candidate in the face of the formidable AIPAC-Evangelical alliance.

Changes in American society and American politics, however, could help increase American Muslim representation over time. The Muslim-American population is growing quickly, it is becoming more established, it is getting organized, it is developing a common identity because of societal pressures and its own inner dynamics, and it is growing into one of the more socioeconomically accomplished religious communities in the country. A new, more assertive generation of U.S.-born Muslims, including the children of the large cohort that immigrated in the 1980s and 1990s, will become professionally and, potentially, politically active in the coming two decades. Outreach efforts and political engagement by American Muslims might win over some of their detractors. A peaceful solution to Arab-Israeli conflicts and a U.S. withdrawal from Iraq might diffuse the motives behind the aggressive Evangelical and pro-AIPAC attitude toward American Muslims, their organizations, and public personalities. The increased assertiveness of Jewish peace activists and critics of AIPAC tactics, including academics and public figures such as President Jimmy Carter, might provide an opening. Until the day comes, however, when being a Muslim does not affect the electoral prospects of a candidate, only heavily liberal districts such as Minnesota's Fifth Congressional and Indiana's Seventh will allow a Muslim candidate a reasonable chance to get elected.

Attacks on Keith Ellison based on his religion are unusual in American politics today. They do, however, reflect a historical pattern of attacks (perhaps with different motivations) on early elected representatives from once marginalized groups. President John F. Kennedy, of course, faced questions regarding his Catholic religion and religiosity before the 1960 presidential election (Carty 2004). In the first decade of the twentieth century, Senator Reed Smoot, a Mormon, faced a congressional inquiry before he was allowed to take his seat (Flake 2004). Such discriminatory and disparaging behavior normally abates after the public, leaders of dominant groups, and other elected officials adjust to the idea that members of the minority can serve their constituencies well.

If the Muslim elected officials of Canada and the UK (the other two countries with majoritarian systems) are any indication, future Muslim-American congressmen are more likely to be left of center than conservative. Those who will be elected from predominantly white conservative districts (like Rahim Jaffer in Canada) will likely be strongly in favor of cultural assimilation, and those who will be elected from districts with large minority populations will be supportive of minority rights (for instance, Sadiq Khan in the UK). Like representatives from other minorities who preceded them, over time their religion will become less significant in defining their positions, attitudes, support, and image. Still, they may hold stronger views than other elected officials on matters of civil rights and foreign policy toward Muslim countries. They may also play a role in conflict resolution within the United States and abroad.[48]

The United States will only be catching up with other Western countries when more Muslims serve in Congress. Muslim Americans are an integral part of American society, but their ongoing underrepresentation and the exceptionally hostile treatment of Muslim candidates are a sign that American democracy is falling short of its own standards of equity. The ways to redress Muslim-American underrepresentation are not simple. Political leaders have to clearly support the recruitment of American Muslims into the two large parties and condemn attempts to exclude them by entrenched interest groups. American Muslims themselves must continue to organize and attempt to become active within the parties. Unfortunately, the forces arrayed against increased Muslim-American representation are formidable. The stakes, however, are high for both American Muslims and for the country as a whole. The Muslim minority will need strong dedicated voices in elected office to defend its civil rights and liberties if infringements increase. American society as a whole would benefit from increased representation that would consolidate the sense of ownership and belonging of this vulnerable minority and improve perceptions of the United States in the Muslim world.

Notes

I acknowledge the valuable research assistance of Ahmed Khanani and Eren Tatari. They helped compile the information about Western parliamentarians. This chapter shares preliminary findings from a broader research project on the characteristics of Muslim representation.

1. André Carson, who is also Muslim, was elected in a March 11, 2008, special election to represent Indiana's Seventh District in Congress. He replaced the late six-term congresswoman Julia Carson, who also happened to be his grandmother.

2. "Fighting Racism, for Diversity," *The Parliament Magazine,* December 2004.

3. The Pew Research Center (2007) estimates that there are 2.35 million Muslims in America; CAIR and other Muslim organizations believe that there are six to seven million Muslims, relying on a study based on interviewing mosque leaders (Bagby et al. 2001). Smith (2002) argues that most estimates of the numbers of American Muslims are inflated. For a more detailed overview of research on the topic, see Pew Research Center 2007, 9–14.

4. Four Muslim organizations sponsored the Mosque in America project (Bagby et. al. 2001) that produced the higher estimates. The American Jewish Committee financially supported and promoted research by Smith (2002) that argues that estimates of the numbers of American Muslims are inflated. See, for example, the press release titled "U.S. Muslim Population Figures Examined," available online at http://www.ajc.org/site/apps/nl/content2.asp?c=ijITI2PHKoG&b =837277&ct=867209 (accessed July 1, 2007).

5. Ireland had a Muslim parliamentarian, Dr. Moosajee Bhamjee, in the 1990s. The remaining eight countries have never had one.

6. Statistics available online at http://www.ipu.org/wmn-e/world.htm (accessed July 7, 2007).

7. See Klausen 2005, 20–22, for more on citizenship rules in west European countries.

8. See Sinno and Tatari (chapter 7, this volume) for additional details on British Muslim representation.

9. I compiled numbers by checking the websites of congressmen and drawing on the article by Jonathan Tilove, "New Congress Brings with It Religious Firsts," *Religion News Service,* December 11, 2006, which includes a count by Albert Menendez.

10. Still, some Americans do not seem ready to accept a Mormon president as of 2007. See, for example, Adam Nagourney and Laurie Goodstein, "Mormon Candidate Braces for Religion as Issue," *New York Times,* February 8, 2007.

11. http://www.projectmaps.com/PMReport.htm,and http://www.projectmaps.com/ AMP2004report.pdf. The less methodologically reliable Mosque in America (Bagby et al. 2001, 15) survey reports that mosque leaders claim on average that 48 percent of mosque participants have completed their college education. The Pew Research Center's survey (2007, 18) finds Muslim Americans to be very similar in these areas to the general American population: 10 percent have engaged in graduate studies (9 percent for the general public) and an additional 14 percent have college degrees (16 percent for the general public).

12. Pauline Jelinek, "Muslim Congressional Aides Taking Stand," Associated Press, June 2, 2006.

13. The more recent Pew survey (Pew Research Center 2007, 47) finds more modest rates of registration (63 percent for Muslims versus 76 percent for the general public).

14. The Pew Research Center (2007, 1) finds that African Americans make up 20 percent of the American Muslim population. Another 15 percent of their interviewees over eighteen years old are native-born, including non-African-American converts and a small population of adult children of immigrants.

15. I recognize the Pew Research Center for providing the breakdown of the data while the data set was still embargoed. The number of immigrant respondents was 752 and native African-American respondents 145.

16. Somalis are estimated to number 30,000 in Minnesota's Fifth Congressional District.

Neil MacFarquhar, "Democrat Poised to Become First Muslim in Congress," *New York Times,* October 8, 2006. Peter Skerry, "The New Muslim-Liberal Coalition," *Time,* November 11, 2006.

17. "Muslims Rally around Congressional Candidate," Associated Press, September 22, 2006.

18. Bagby et al. 2001, 17.

19. See different country descriptions in Hunter (2002) for accounts of how interaction with European states aggravates rivalries among Muslim organizations. See also Klausen, chapter 6 in this volume.

20. Members of the Nation of Islam number between 30,000 and 100,000. They are a small fraction of the total African-American Muslim population, which is estimated at 500,000 to 1,500,000.

21. Imam Siraj Wahhaj delivered the first Islamic invocation in the House of Representatives in 1991 and Imam Warith D. Mohammed the first invocation before the Senate in 1992.

22. PEW Global Attitudes Project, "17-Nation Pew Global Attitude Survey," July 14, 2005, 11–17. Online as "Islamic Extremism: Support for Terror Wanes among Muslim Publics," at http://pewglobal.org/reports/display.php?ReportID=248 (accessed April 6, 2008).

23. For a review of surveys on the particularly negative views the Dutch hold toward Muslims, see Froukje Demant, Marcel Maussen, and Jan Rath, "The Netherlands: Muslims in the EU," Open Society Institute EU Monitoring and Advocacy Program 2007, 38–41. Available online at http://www.eumap.org/topics/minority/reports/eumuslims/background_reports/download/netherlands/netherlands.pdf (accessed April 6, 2008).

24. A Pew survey (Pew Forum 2003, 11) reports that 42% of Evangelical Protestants say they have reasons not to vote for someone who is Muslim as opposed to 31% of the general public (28% for mainline Protestants and Catholics, 30% for blacks, 31% for Hispanics, and 24% for secular Americans). The same report also documents higher rates of hostility toward Muslims among Evangelicals.

25. The reported percentages of Americans who would be less likely to vote for a Muslim candidate for president are as follows: Gallup 1999: 38% won't vote a Muslim into White House; Fox News, January 2003: 49% would hold a Muslim presidential candidate's religious beliefs against him and would be less likely to vote for him; Pew Research Center, June 2003: 38% of Americans would not vote for a Muslim candidate for president, even if nominated by their own political party; Pew 2005: 31% would not vote for a Muslim candidate for president; *Los Angeles Times,* June 2006: 54% said no to the prospect of a Muslim in the White House; *Rasmussen Report,* November 2006: 61% of likely voters say they would never consider voting for a Muslim presidential candidate; Gallup poll, December 2006: 45% less likely to vote for a Muslim candidate for U.S. president because of his religion; Fox News/Opinion Dynamics, December 2006: 45% would be less likely to vote for a candidate for president who is Muslim. Pew poll, February 2007: 46% less likely to vote for a presidential candidate who is Muslim.

26. Pew Forum 2003, 10.

27. CAIR Research Center, "American Public Opinion about Islam and Muslims 2006," 8–9. Available online at http://www.cair.com/cairsurveyanalysis.pdf (accessed July 12, 2007).

28. Putsata Reang, "AMPCC Supports Incumbent Pete Stark against Syed Mahmood," *San Jose Mercury News,* November 2, 2002.

29. See, for example, Deborah Kong, "Muslim Candidates Preserve Their Faith in U.S., Politics," *Seattle Times,* December 7, 2003; Michelle Boorstein, "More Muslims Gaining Political Ground: Although Md. Delegate-Elect Doesn't Trumpet Faith, His Win Signals New Surge," *Washington Post,* November 30, 2006, p. A01; Dave McKibben, "GOP Leader Says Anaheim Council Candidate Backs Extremist Groups: Syrian-born Bill Dalati focuses on America's enemies, Web note says. Dalati says his faith and heritage are being questioned," *Los Angeles Times,* October 9, 2006; Jill Lawrence, "American Muslims Gaining a Foothold in Politics," *USA Today,* March 23, 2006, available online at http://www.usatoday.com/news/washington/2006-03-23-american-muslims-cover_x.htm (accessed July 8, 2007).

30. See, for example, Debbie Schlussel, "Barack Hussein Obama: Once a Muslim, Always a Muslim," December 18, 2006, online at http://www.debbieschlussel.com/archives/2006/12/barack_hussein.html (accessed July 7, 2007). MSNBC's Chris Matthews noted on November 7, 2006, that Obama's "middle name is Hussein" and suggested that it would "be interesting down the road." During the November 28 edition of MSNBC's Hardball, Republican strategist Ed Rogers referred to "Barack Hussein Obama." On the December 11 edition of CNN's *Situation Room,* correspondent Jeanne Moos noted that "[o]nly one little consonant differentiates" Obama and Osama. She then added, "[A]s if that similarity weren't enough. How about sharing the name of a former dictator? You know his middle name, Hussein." On the December 11 edition of *The Situation Room,* CNN senior political analyst Jeff Greenfield compared Obama's "business casual" clothing to Iranian President Mahmoud Ahmadinejad's "jacket-and-no-tie look." Greenfield concluded the segment by saying: "Now, it is one thing to have a last name that sounds like Osama and a middle name, Hussein, that is probably less than helpful. But an outfit that reminds people of a charter member of the axis of evil, why, this could leave his presidential hopes hanging by a thread." He later explained on the CNN website that he was making "a joke." These examples are extracted from a broader compilation by mediamatters.com at http://mediamatters.org/items/200612200005 (accessed July 7, 2007).

31. "Hillary's Team Has Questions about Obama's Muslim Background," January 17, 2007, available online at http://www.insightmag.com/Media/MediaManager/Obama_2.htm (accessed March 3, 2007).

32. "CNN Debunks False Report about Obama," CNN, January 23, 2007, available online at http://www.cnn.com/2007/POLITICS/01/22/obama.madrassa/index.html (accessed July 6, 2007).

33. Neil MacFarquhar, "Democrat Poised to Become First Muslim in Congress," *New York Times,* October 8, 2006.

34. Rochelle Olson, "Fifth District Hopefuls Get a Bit Edgy," *Minneapolis Star-Tribune,* November 6, 2006.

35. Dennis Prager, "America, Not Keith Ellison, Decides What Book a Congressman Takes His Oath On," November 28, 2006, available at http://www.townhall.com/Columnists/Dennis Prager/2006/11/28/america,_not_keith_ellison,_decides_what_book_a_congressman_takes_his _oath_on (accessed July 8, 2007).

36. Mediamatters.org, "CNN's Beck to First-ever Muslim Congressman: '[W]hat I Feel Like Saying Is, 'Sir, Prove to Me That You Are Not Working with Our Enemies,'" November 15, 2006, available at http://mediamatters.org/items/200611150004 (accessed July 3, 2007).

37. "Lawmaker Won't Apologize for 'Islamophobic' Letter," CNN, December 21, 2006, available at http://www.cnn.com/2006/POLITICS/12/20/lawmaker.koran/ (accessed July 11, 2007).

38. Erika Bolstad, "Idaho Lawmaker Apologizes to Muslim Congressman," *McClatchy Newspapers,* August 17, 2007, available at http://www.mcclatchydc.com/homepage/v-print/story/19000.html (accessed July 7, 2007).

39. "NJDC Calls on Alan Fine and Republicans to Apologize for Hate-Filled Attacks on Keith Ellison," September 21, 2006, available at http://njdc.typepad.com/njdcs_blog/2006/09/njdc_calls_on_a.html (accessed July 7, 2007). Jennifer Siegel, "Jewish Dems Defend Muslim Candidate," *Jewish Daily Forward,* September 29, 2006, online at http://www.forward.com/articles/jewish-dems-defend-muslim-candidate/ (accessed July 7, 2007).

40. See, for example, Nathan Guttman, "Lobbying for the Pro-Israel Candidates," *Haaretz,* May 7, 2004, and Mathew Berger, "Cynthia McKinney, Critic of Israel, Wins Democratic Primary in Georgia," *Jewish Telegraph Agency,* July 21, 2004.

41. For example, Daniel Pipes Weblog, "Cynthia McKinney's Arab and Islamist Donors," July 9, 2004, where he writes: "Georgia holds its primary on July 20; should McKinney win it, as seems likely, radical Arab and Muslim causes will have achieved their first significant electoral victory in the United States." Available at http://www.danielpipes.org/blog/290 (accessed July 4, 2007).

42. John Kruger, "Arab-Americans Charge Bias on Capitol Hill," *The Hill Newspaper,* July 14, 1999.

43. Dean Murphy, "For Muslim Americans, Influence in Politics Still Hard to Come By," *New York Times,* October 27, 2000.

44. The American Muslim Alliance could not reproduce upon request the lists on which it bases its numbers.

45. Census, 2001. Available online at http://www.statistics.gov.uk/census2001/profiles/rank/ewmuslim.asp (accessed July 12, 2007).

46. See compilation by the Canadian Islamic Congress based on census data. Available online at http://www.canadianislamiccongress.com/election2006/grading_table.php (accessed July 12, 2007).

47. Neil MacFarquhar, "Democrat Poised to Become First Muslim in Congress," *New York Times,* October 8, 2006. Andrew Haeg, "Muslims Learning Politics in 5th District Race," Minnesota Public Radio, October 13, 2006, available at minnesota.publicradio.org/display/web/2006/10/13/muslimvoters/ (accessed July 7, 2007).

48. See Sinno and Tatari (chapter 7 in this volume) for examples from the UK.

References

Bagby, Ihsan, Paul Perl, and Bryan Froehle. 2001. "The Mosque in America: A National Portrait," available online at http://www.cair.com/Portals/0/pdf/The_Mosque_in_America_A_National_Portrait.pdf (accessed February 13, 2008).

Brown, Mark. 2000. "Quantifying the Muslim Population in Europe: Conceptual and Data Issues." *International Journal of Social Research Methodology* 3: 87–101.

Carty, Thomas J. 2004. *A Catholic in the White House? Religion, Politics, and John F. Kennedy's Presidential Campaign.* New York: Palgrave Macmillan.

Flake, Kathleen. 2004. *The Politics of American Religious Identity: The Seating of Senator Reed Smoot, Mormon Apostle.* Chapel Hill: University of North Carolina Press.

Hunter, Shireen, ed. 2002. *Islam, Europe's Second Religion: The New Social, Cultural, and Political Landscape.* Westport, Conn.: Praeger.

Klausen, Jytte. 2005. *The Islamic Challenge: Politics and Religion in Western Europe.* New York: Oxford University Press.

Pew Forum, "Religion and Politics: Contention and Consensus," July 24, 2003, available online at http://pewforum.org/publications/surveys/religion-politics.pdf (accessed July 7, 2007).

Pew Research Center. 2007. "Muslim Americans: Middle Class and Mostly Mainstream." Available online at http://pewresearch.org/assets/pdf/muslim-americans.pdf (accessed July 12, 2007).

Smith, Tom. 2002. "The Polls-Review: The Muslim Population of the United States: The Methodology of Estimates." *Public Opinion Quarterly* 66 (3): 404–417.

Zogby International and Project MAPS. December 14, 2001. "Report on Muslims in the American Marketplace." Zogby International, Utica, N.Y. Available at http:/www.zogby.com/americanmuslims2001.pdf (accessed April 6, 2008).

———. October 2004. "Muslims in the Public Square." Zogby International, Utica, N.Y. Available at http://www.zogby.com/americanmuslims2004.pdf (accessed April 6, 2008).

6

Muslims Representing Muslims in Europe: Parties and Associations after 9/11

Jytte Klausen

Hostility against Muslims among European publics and elites, as well as the shrill voices of Islamic radicals, has caused controversy and division but not deterred increasing civic engagement and more traditional forms of political participation. One unexpected consequence of the acrimony is that governments increasingly look for Muslims to act as interlocutors, and many Muslim leaders inevitably find themselves involved. Religious pluralism is an unintended consequence of unwanted immigration. It has raised difficult questions about the requirements of religious toleration, which Europeans are reluctant to face. The Madrid train bombing on March 11, 2003, and the July 2005 bombings of the London tube system reinforced the perception that Islam and Islamism are threats to the European social and political system. Paradoxically, the two events also induced governments and politicians to reconsider the importance of government involvement in promoting integration.

Muslim Civic Engagement Before and After 9/11

Civic engagement among Europe's Muslims started increasing in the 1990s. A wave of mosque construction initiated after 1985 signified a new desire to build permanent roots and intergenerational religious communities. Scholars have described the collective cognitive shift among Muslim immigrants as the end of "the myth of return" and the emergence of new hybrid identities such as British Muslims or French Arabs (Ballard 1994; Werbner 2002). Others have gone further and argued that the shift signaled the constitution of Muslims as an ethnic minority or a "parallel society" (Modood 2005; Heitmeyer, Müller, and Schröder 1997).

The crystallization of new varieties of political imagination and modes of representation picked up speed after 9/11. The pressure to organize increased as governments and politicians looked for "responsible" interlocutors. Rising hostility toward Muslims also motivated them to organize and represent themselves as who they "really are." In Britain, in particular, anger against foreign policy has engendered an unprecedented increase in Muslim political participation and led to record-high participation in the 2005 election. In the immediate aftermath of 9/11, the creation of broadly inclusive and moderate national Muslim associations giving new voice to Muslims' hopes and aspirations for integration appeared to be an unexpected, but welcome, outcome.

The picture today is significantly more complicated. The increased participation and demand for representation that we can observe has produced fragmentation rather than consolidation. The good news is that it is not possible to impute a shared political identity—the "fifth column" scenario of a cohesive dangerous Muslim presence—to European Muslims (Warner and Wenner 2006). The bad news is that in the resulting confusion governments and the media can find new reasons to refuse to extend recognition to Muslims as "partners" in the negotiation of solutions to the problems of integration. The cacophony of voices claiming to speak for Muslims notwithstanding, the underlying trend is one of increased participation and political integration. This is most clearly observed in the realm of electoral politics, where every election brings in new elected representatives of Muslim background and the presence of Muslim voters is increasingly felt in contested local elections and within the community organizations of the political parties.

Between 2002 and 2005, I interviewed three hundred European Muslim civic and political leaders who are part of what I describe as the new Muslim political elite (Klausen 2005). My questions aimed to discover how important faith is to the Muslim political leaders, and what consequences—if any—they drew from their faith and identity for public policy. I considered as "elite" anyone of Muslim faith or background who held elected or appointed office in political or civic organizations at the national, regional, or metropolitan level in one of six European countries—the United Kingdom, France, Germany, the Netherlands, Sweden, and Denmark. I interviewed parliamentarians, city councillors, leaders, and spokespeople from civic associations, advocacy groups, and local and national umbrella organizations of mosque councils and interfaith groups, and also some of Europe's leading imams and Islamic scholars.

Why study the elite? Elites are a sociological fact. Democracies adapt in part by encapsulating and integrating new social groups and their political and civic leaders. The prospects for a future accommodation with Islam in Europe rest, to a large extent, on the ability of a Muslim elite to obtain influence and gain recognition as representative voices in debates on policies having to do with the position of Islam and Muslims within national institutions. Political scientists often study politics through the lens of elite identity and preferences; it is common to focus on established elites such as parliamentarians or trade union leaders. In this case, the approach enabled me to focus on what the conflict looks like from the European Muslim side.

Islam is today the largest minority religious denomination in Europe. There are more Muslims than Catholics in the Protestant north, and more Muslims than Protestants in the predominantly Roman Catholic countries. There are about fifteen million Muslims in Western Europe, but only a few dozen Muslims have been elected to European parliaments. In the United Kingdom, it is estimated that about one million Muslims were eligible to vote in the May 2005 election. The 2001 census, now a bit outdated, told us that there were 1.6 million Muslims in the country, just shy of 3 percent of the population.

In France, there are perhaps five to six million Muslims, but we really do not know because no reliable statistics exist. Some demographers argue that 2.6 million is the more accurate number. No one knows how many Muslims can vote, but it appears that few do. The Netherlands has one of the highest concentrations of Muslims relative to the population: 5 percent of Dutch residents are Muslims; about half can vote. By contrast, there are an estimated three million Muslims in Germany, of whom only about half a million can vote. In Italy, Muslims, like other immigrants, are overwhelmingly illegal: only an estimated 50,000 of Italy's two million Muslims can vote. With the exception of the few countries where the census asks people what their religion is, estimates are derived from immigration statistics and estimates of fertility rates among different population groups. The lack of accurate statistics invites speculation, and wildly exaggerated predictions of a Muslim "population takeover" circulate.

Ethnicity and national origin also vary greatly from country to country. Most European Muslims are from South Asia or Turkey. Arabs are a minority estimated at around 20 percent of all European Muslims, but are predominant in France. An increasing number are Africans. National origin matters because Islamic practices vary widely across countries of origin. Nonetheless, ethnic diversity is also muted by shared experience. It is at least in part because of this extraordinary diversity that Muslims speak the national languages of Europe when they meet in political or civic organizations.

Diversity has increased in recent years, in part because of increased immigration of political refugees from new areas of conflict and in part because of the growing presence of native-born Muslims, who prefer to speak the language they have grown up with. The early waves of immigrants to Europe held on to the "myth of return," the idea that their exile was temporary, and they organized in transnational networks with the primary aim of retaining contact with the "home" country.

In the 1990s the émigré associations of the past gave way to new national associations. These were often modeled on organizations created for other faiths. Both the Muslim Council of Britain (MCB, formed in 1997) and the Council of Muslims in Germany, Zentralrat der Muslime in Deutschland (ZMD, formed in 1995) imitate their Jewish counterparts in organization and objectives. The French Council for the Islamic Faith, Conseil Français du Culte Musulman (CFCM), finally set up by the government in 2002 after several false starts, was based upon the model of the Consistoire for Jews created in 1808. With the notable exception of terrorists and radical clerics, European Muslims' political engagement and expectations have, since the 1990s, increasingly become framed in national European idioms.

Who are the Muslim leaders? There were several surprises. We tend to assume that the current generation of Muslim leaders, and other immigrant-origin groups, are generally the educated and integrated descendants of earlier waves of migrants. Many of the people I interviewed referred to themselves as "typically second-generation." The term, it turned out, was used metaphorically to describe a political outlook focused on integration and acceptance of European norms and expectations. In actuality most of the current generation of leaders are not native-born but immigrant.

The numbers varied among the six countries in the study, but few of the leaders I interviewed were born in Europe. Most had arrived as young adults, either as political refugees or as students. Some said that they had come at a time when the rules were not yet so restrictive and that they had migrated because they were threatened as student activists by the security services of their home countries. About a handful of the parliamentarians in the study had come as political refugees, obtained citizenship, and stood for election in the span of a decade. Most of the leaders had completed secondary education prior to coming and were from middle-class families with histories of learning and political engagement. The share of native-born leaders was higher in Great Britain and the Netherlands than elsewhere, undoubtedly a reflection of the earlier onset of mass migration to those countries.

Elected office aside, citizenship is not a legal prerequisite for civic and political engagement, but it matters greatly in practice. A minority of the leaders are native-born (one or two out of five in my study), but most are citizens (Klausen 2005, 23). The non-naturalized leaders, between one-tenth and one-quarter of the respondents, were not elected officials but participated in civic associations. In Denmark and Germany, both countries with particularly restrictive naturalization laws, between one-tenth and one-quarter of the political leaders I identified did not have citizenship. One out of ten of the French participants were not citizens, a figure that puts France below Britain, Sweden, and the Netherlands in terms of legal assimilation.

Sources of Political Imagination and Differentiation

Fouad Ajami and Neil Ferguson have both argued that European Muslims have brought their political agendas with them from their countries of origin. They argue that Europe's Muslim associations are "Trojan horses" for organizations banned in Islamic countries, and that Muslim political activism in Europe is driving a wedge between the U.S. and Europe on important foreign policy issues. At first blush, my findings seem to support this thesis in two ways. First, the present generation of leaders consists mostly of recent immigrants, who were politically active before coming to Europe. And second, being Muslim "matters." Increasingly, political issues and preferences are shaped by a growing sense of faith or ethno-religious origin and background. It does not follow, however, that the political agenda is that of the banned Islamist organizations. They are a source of political inspiration for some individuals, but so are human rights, democracy, the antiwar movement, feminism, and faith itself. But because restrictive access to naturalization acts as a barrier to immigrant participation in mainstream political organizations, Muslims are frequently pushed to organize in "Muslim-only" organizations.

Some of the most notorious clerics active in Europe were granted political refugee status in Europe in the mid-1980s, including Omar Bakri Mohammad, the founder of al-Muhajiroun, a British radical group associated with known terrorists, and Abu Hamza al-Masri of Finsbury Park Mosque fame. Abu Laban, the Danish imam who was responsible for sending off a delegation with a folder of Danish cartoons to Cairo and Damascus, is also a political refugee who was unable to travel to Egypt because of his past. They are, in different ways, representatives of extremists who have found political freedom in Europe to continue their projects. But so is Ayaan Hirsi Ali, the Dutch-Somali politician who gained fame for her criticism of Islam.

The political refugees, who came in the 1980s when European policies were lenient, adhered to many different ideologies, and many more of them were liberals than Islamists. Many of the interviewees described themselves as, in a way, fighting the same battle now that they had fought before. Only four or five out of the three hundred people in the study said that their objective was an Islamic state. For others it was human rights, the fight against fundamentalism, or, in some cases, freedom from religious compulsion of any sort.

To be a "Muslim" is both a religious and an ethnic description of self. Islam is the name of the religion. A Muslim, or in the case of women, a *Muslima*, is a person who practices Islam. Strict adherence to these definitions would make the label "secular Muslim" a contradiction in terms. We do not readily speak of a "secular Christian." Yet such are the real-life complexities of taxonomies that people readily accept: being Muslim is not just a matter of faith, but also a sociological fact. "Muslim" is an ethnic category and a description of origin, as well as a faith. Muslims are Europe's new religious *and* ethnic minority. Individuals balance what matters most in different ways. For some, faith is the only source of identity, but for many others faith takes a backseat to country of origin, particularly in the context of increasing hostility toward Muslims and their characterization as "others."

The label "Muslim" is, so to speak, "in play." As stereotypes of who Muslims are and what they want, or do not want, are propagated in the media and by xenophobic politicians, Muslims react to the perceived bias and appropriate the label as a source of countermobilization. Muslims describe the "culture war" as Islamophobia. The term connotes an irrational fear of Islam, which they believe drives the biased and preconceived depictions in the papers and politicians' speeches. Non-practicing Muslims self-identify as Muslims and say they are victimized by Islamophobes who discriminate against them because of preconceived stereotypes of all Muslims as fanatics. Believers feel singled out and misrepresented because people have the wrong idea about Islam. Both groups respond by asserting their identity. Needless to say, the radicals do so as well; they weave the experience of bias into a conspiratorial tale about injustice and persecution and propose a political Islamist utopia as a solution.

It is common among observers of European politics to assume that the "integrated" Muslims, who participate in political life, have also left their faith behind. The German term *Kultur-Muslime,* "culturally Muslim," is often used to describe individuals who do not put their faith on display. But it is a fallacy to presume that religiosity is incompatible with civic competence and, conversely, to assume that the integrated Muslims are apostates. In my interviews, I found that faith matters greatly to most Muslims and that religiosity does not predict political affiliations. Most of the leaders in my study said that Islam was important to them personally. Three out of five said their faith was very important, one out of five that it is sometimes important, and only one out of five said that it was not important.

Among the very religious, most said they belonged to the political center or left. The single largest subgroup in my study consisted of personally religious self-described centrists. Non-believers, in contrast, belonged mostly to the far left or to the secular conservative parties. Many religious Muslims indicated that ideally they would support the Christian Democratic parties. In the Netherlands, Muslims have joined the Christian Democratic Appeal (CDA) in large numbers, and two Muslims were elected to the parliament from the CDA. The German Christian Democratic Party has chosen instead to reemphasize Christianity as a prerequisite for being German, and many German Muslims regretfully concluded that they could not support the party and turned instead to the Greens. Europe's Christian Democratic parties have long used the term "secularly Christian" to describe their distinctive objectives, and only the Dutch CDA has responded to the presence of non-Christian conservative voters by developing an Abrahamic approach to the representation of the interests of believers.[1]

Abortion, gay rights, and bioethics are some of the issue areas where religious Muslims find common ground with other religious associations and lobbies. The MCB has steadfastly maintained that homosexuality is a sin and has joined the Anglican and the Roman Catholic churches in opposing gay adoption rights. When the organization's secretary-general, Iqbal Sacranie (who was replaced in 2006 by Dr. Muhammad Abdul Bari), was criticized for saying that same-sex relationships risked "damaging the foundations of society," the MCB pointed to the split in the Anglican Church over gays and declared that Muslims would not be "bullied" into speaking against scripture.[2]

Nonetheless, many religious Muslims regard "value conservatism" as less salient than other issues that are generally important for the left, in particular anti-discrimination enforcement and social protection. Centrist Muslims often migrate to the Green parties, because of the parties' emphasis upon human rights. The preponderance of centrists among the more religious leaders may also reflect a deliberate decision on the part of the national Muslim civic associations to avoid becoming identified with, and being taken for granted by, the social democratic or labor parties that historically have been able to count on immigrant voters.

Party choice is contingent on values, but also on what is offered by the political parties. French Muslims complained bitterly about the Socialist Party's intolerance of religious expression, and tended to remark that one had to be committed to "the holy principle of *laïcité*" to succeed in the party.

There was greater agreement on practical policy. When I asked what should be done about the integration of Islam, consensus was that ties to Islamic countries must be severed and that ways must be found to educate imams at European universities and to normalize the legal situation of mosque communities according to national laws. There were disagreements about how far to push for equity with Christian churches. Some mentioned what they saw as government pressures to "Christianize" Islam, yet agreed that European Muslims must sever ties with the Islamic world. Many leaders argued that governments should provide "help for self-help," but otherwise leave Muslims to build their faith institutions as they pleased. Others argued for straightforward legal and institutional parity: "[W]hat goes for the pastor goes for the imam," said a Danish city councilor. The consensus was that European Islam must be detached from Islamic countries, and that European governments must help.

One of the main characteristics of the development of Islam over the past two hundred years is the collapse of religious authority. In Europe, migration has allowed Islam to develop in the absence of clerical control. One consequence is a return to the "book." Many young people told me that they were learning Arabic and reading the Qur'an to "make up their own mind" about its meaning. It is, of course, illusory to think that the text is accessible in the absence of theory or interpretation, and while some of Europe's Muslims celebrate the freedom to interpret the Qur'an independently, others battle to protect orthodoxy against assimilation.

Religious Life and Civic Participation

Mosque communities have become an important building block for Muslim civic and political engagement in Europe. The large national associations in France, Germany, and Britain all in one way or another have mosque communities as the basic unit of organization. Mosque communities are also building blocks for other types of self-help groups and for civic involvement in local politics and interfaith dialogue. Much is said about the unfortunate role of politicized clerics in shaping the political consciousness of European Muslims, but in reality it is the mosque managers and mosque councils that are the more important civic actors—they hire the imams and run the affairs of the mosque. There may be about eight thousand mosques in Western Europe, not including the many small and informal prayer rooms that exist in community centers and storefronts. This is not a large number considering the size of European Muslim communities (some fifteen million people). The building momentum and the demand for educated and professional imams are likely to continue as Muslims benefit from integration and increased prosperity. Nonetheless, serious questions remain about how to provide the resources necessary to sustain the institutionalization of Islam in Europe.

It is estimated that Abu Hamza al-Masri preached his Islamist vision in over one hundred British mosques in 1999 alone. Today, radical clerics are reduced to preaching outside mosques or in private apartments to closed groups of adherents. Still, the focus on what is said in the mosques remains an issue of contention. One frequently voiced concern is that conservative or uneducated imams fail to provide new generations of European Muslims with adequate religious instruction, and therefore help fuel alienation and push young people into the arms of radicals. Another complaint is that the imams are an obstacle to the "modernization" of Islam, particularly on issues such as academic achievement and women's rights. It should be noted that Muslims are often among the first to voice these complaints.

We know very little about who the imams are. Herein lies another reason why national security policy and integration policy overlap. Most Western European governments have no knowledge of the exact number of mosques, who preaches in them, or where the imams come from. Many are so-called backyard mosques, a category that is a big concern for European Muslim political and civic leaders and security agencies as well. Increasingly, it is also becoming the concern of governments that find themselves caught in a Catch-22 between a belief that Muslims need to assume the burden of adaptation and the reality that lack of transparency in the Muslim community has much to do with their own willful neglect of the community.

A French security agency conducted a census of French imams, which identified over a thousand imams, about half working full-time. Only 45 percent are paid regularly and the rest are paid in kind or unpaid. Of those who are paid, Turkey supports sixty, Algeria eighty, and Morocco only two. Saudi Arabia pays the salaries of about a dozen imams who have graduated from Saudi Islamic universities but are not Saudis. Less than 20 percent of the imams are of French nationality, and the ones who have citizenship are mostly naturalized. Very few are French-born. Half of the imams are either of Moroccan or Algerian origin.

Imams are mostly recruited by local mosque councils through kinship networks in the country of origin. One common complaint among the Muslims I spoke with was that the imams are out of touch with the values of the European-born and younger generations of Muslims, and that they do not speak the language. The French study largely confirmed these complaints. Over half of the imams were over fifty years old. One-third were found to speak French with ease, another third to speak it with some difficulty, and the rest not to speak it at all.

A similar census would probably yield comparable results in any west European country with respect to employment conditions, educational background, language competency, and legal status. We know that most British imams are trained abroad and recruited by local mosque councils. Fewer than 10 percent of the two thousand British imams have been trained in the UK. So long as a mosque council guarantees that it will provide an income for the imam, work permits have not usually been a problem. But Muslim community elders tend to recruit from the villages that they came from. Imams recruited in this way have often been educated in *madrassas* (traditional Muslim schools). One newly formed association of mosques, the British Muslim Forum, is strongly supportive of the idea that the government needs to provide help to upgrade the skills of imams and mosque managers.

There are an estimated 2,500 mosques and prayer houses in Germany. The Turkish government is the single largest source of imams in northern Europe, except in Britain. There are about eight hundred Turkish imams in northern Europe, mostly in Germany. When Turkish labor migrants—who were then called "guest workers"—began to appear in large numbers in Scandinavia, Germany, and the Netherlands, the governments of those countries entered into contracts with Turkey to supply pastoral care. The imams are paid by the Turkish government while abroad, and are granted temporary visas, usually for up to four years, by the national governments. The Turkish imams do not preach "political nonsense," my interviewees told me, but they are nonetheless not a solution for Muslims who want Islam to have a self-sustaining European base.

Public policy at the time aimed to facilitate the maintenance of ties between the migrants and the "home countries." The "host" states preferred things this way, because it helped sustain the fiction that the migrant laborers were a temporary solution to overheated labor markets. Host governments and "sender" governments had a joint interest in preventing immigration; both wanted the migrants to return when they got old. Today, everyone wants integration.

Extremism, Counterterrorism, and Community Action

The fight for control over the political imagination of European Muslims has intensified in recent years. Extremist groups have benefited from the growing sense that Muslims are subjected to global victimization and are attracting members in prisons and in schools. We have also witnessed the increased involvement of "offshore" political actors, including states and non-state organizations. The widespread protests in February 2006 against a Danish newspaper's publication of twelve caricatures of the Prophet Muhammad revealed the new importance of "offshore" political actors in shaping the agendas of Muslim political organizations in Europe.

The cartoons were published in Denmark on September 28, 2005, and were met with instant protests from Danish Muslims. Danish Muslim leaders were preoccupied with the intended insult to their community and not with the questions of blasphemy or matters of Qur'anic interpretation that subsequently have dominated the debate. The protests were against the increasingly hostile rhetoric dominating the Danish media, which the government was seen to endorse. The international demonstrations did not begin until five months later, in response to efforts coordinated by the Egyptian government working through the Arab League and the Organization of the Islamic Conference. Demonstrations in London and Paris in early February 2006 were organized by some of the large Muslim associations in those countries, and were fueled by a sermon on Qatar TV on Friday, February 3, 2006, by Sheikh Yusuf al-Qaradawi, an increasingly important actor in European Muslim politics, who said:

> The *ummah* [nation] must rage in anger. It is told that Imam Al-Shafi'i said: "Whoever was angered and did not rage is a jackass." We are not a nation of jackasses. We are not jackasses for riding, but lions that roar. We are lions that zealously protect their dens, and avenge affronts to their sanctities. We are not a nation of jackasses. We are a nation that should rage for the sake of Allah, His Prophet, and His book. We are the nation of Muhammad, and we must never accept the degradation of our religion.

The sermon was transmitted by Al Jazeera and also transcribed on IslamOnline.net, a website created by al-Qaradawi in 1997. The use of the term *"ummah"* to describe the religious community of all Muslims is standard on the site. Al-Qaradawi linked the protests against the cartoons to a criticism of "our feeble governments," meaning the Islamic countries' governments, which he accused of toeing the U.S.'s line, and warned them to not "split from their peoples." A second warning was directed against the Western governments—by implication the Danish but also the British government—for being silent about "crimes" offending the Prophet. Al-Qaradawi accused Western governments of causing terrorism because Muslims feel they must take the defense of the Prophet in their own hands.

There can be no doubt that al-Qaradawi's incitement to anger resonated with many European Muslims who felt injured by the implied description of the Prophet as a man of bloodshed and violence. But many Muslim leaders and Islamic organizations were unhappy with al-Qaradawi's role. The Organization of the Islamic Conference (OIC) and various governments distanced themselves from him and stressed the religious obligation to refrain from violence. The MCB's involvement also subsequently became a source of dissent and disengagement among British Muslims.

The MCB, alone among all the European Muslim associations, has for the past five years had observer status at the OIC. The former MCB secretary-general, Sir Iqbal Sacranie, attended the summit meeting of the OIC held in Saudi Arabia on December 6, 2005, at which the organization discussed and coordinated the response to the Danish cartoons. (As al-Qaradawi's involvement shows, the OIC was one among many actors involved in the mobilization of protests.) The affiliation has been a source of pride for the MCB, but has also become a source of criticism. Charging that the MCB had become "influenced by Saudi Arabia" and "Arab-dominated," a coalition of some 600 mosques and 250 local organizations mostly located in northern England formed their own organization, the British Muslim Forum (BMF), in March 2006. At the launch, Lord Nazir Ahmed, a Muslim member of the House of Lords, spoke of how "many organizations represent Muslims but not all of them are represented," an obvious dig at the MCB, and claimed that BMF was now the largest network of Muslim organizations. The charge of "Arab domination" appears to be an ethnic complaint, but is in fact a political one. The leadership of the MCB is predominantly South Asian and the position of secretary-general, by custom, rotates among individuals of Bangladeshi and Pakistani origin. Controversy has also erupted over Muslim leaders' involvement with Islamic countries and the OIC in France.

The MCB has increasingly found itself marginalized in consultation processes with the government. Following the July 2005 attacks, the British government launched a new community-based approach to counterterrorism. Described as a "partnership against extremism," the initiative signaled a shift in security policy away from traditional counterintelligence operations to an emphasis on prevention. The government sought consultation with Muslim community representatives about how to work with mosques and Muslim communities to prevent extremism. The recommendations were published in October in a report titled

Preventing Extremism Together (Home Office 2005). Suggestions ranged from proposals to improve community-police relations to policies for imam education and accreditation procedures for mosques.

Only some of the recommendations had been carried out a year later, and at the time of this writing participants in the consultation process were increasingly complaining about the lack of follow-up. Ruth Kelly, a junior Home Office minister in charge of community affairs, launched the Commission on Integration and Cohesion in August 2006, once again seemingly tagging policy initiative to bad news about Muslim terrorists: two weeks earlier, on August 10, the government had announced that it had uncovered a plot to blow up transatlantic airliners involving as many as twenty-five British Muslims from a London suburb. The commission was remarkably lacking in membership from the organizations and groups described as "partners" in the fight against extremism a year earlier.

Mosque management and imam training was another area of concern brought to the fore in the consultation process after the July 2005 bombings. Aiming to forestall government-sponsored monitoring, four Muslim associations announced on June 27, 2006, that a voluntary body had been created. The new organization, the Mosques and Imams National Advisory Board (MINAB), aims to promote "best practices in the country's 1600 mosques," the inaugural statement said. The board will, among other things, produce guidelines for training imams, and members have suggested that an academy for educating imams in Britain may be set up. The board includes groups that do not normally like to sit at the same table, the Muslim Association of Britain (MAB), which is linked to the Muslim Brotherhood, the MCB, the BMF, and the al-Khoei Foundation, which represents the interests of Shia Muslims.

The MCB's leadership defines the organization's goal as becoming the Muslim parallel to the Board of Deputies of British Jews—the recognized umbrella group for the representation of British Muslims' civic, political, and religious interests. The MCB's measured response to the events of 9/11 suggested that it might become such an organization, but the combined pressures of the government's unwillingness to allow the MCB to assume primacy, the proliferation of competing groups also claiming to represent Muslim interests, and the organization's increased stridency on issues of homosexuality and its refusal to participate in Holocaust Memorial Day events have undermined its position. In a recent interview with IslamOnline.net, al-Qaradawi's public relations website, the MCB's secretary-general, Muhammad Abdul Bari, complained that the government was trying to divide the British Muslim community along ethnic and sectarian lines and that it was shunning the MCB—the most representative Muslim organization. He continued, "So the government now is talking to something called Sufi Muslim Council founded a month ago."[3] Rival Muslim organizations accuse the MCB of dividing Muslims along ethnic and sectarian lines as well.

In France, competition and disagreement among Muslim associations have wreaked havoc with the government's desire to create a unified "French" Islam (Bowen 2004). Protracted negotiations between representatives of various Muslim constituencies and the government produced a complicated formula for indirect elections to the Conseil Français du Culte Musulman (CFCM), the first of which took place in 2004. The CFCM was from the start dominated by three associations: the Union des Organisations Islamiques de France (UOIF), which is linked to Yusuf al-Qaradawi and the Muslim Brotherhood; the Fédération Nationale des Musulmans de France (FNMF), which is linked to Morocco; and the Paris Grande Mosque (PGM) and various associated groups, including the Grande Mosque in Lyon, which are associated with Algeria.

Mohamed Bechari, the FNMF's general secretary, created a stir in April 2005 when he was appointed to the OIC's Fiqh Council, an organization charged with pronouncing on matters of compatibility between Islamic religious law and current issues. The OIC is usually considered in the Saudi Arabian "interest zone." The appointment was controversial for this reason, but also because Bechari has been seen as "a moderate" and his new position suggested a turning away from the idea of a "French" Islam. The French press has long argued that UOIF did not belong in "French" Islam because of the group's unseemly ties to the Muslim Brotherhood, a banned organization in many Islamic countries. In actuality, uncomfortable questions about the "Frenchness" of the CFCM's leaders were first raised by Dalil Boubakeur, the rector of the Paris Mosque and the government's chosen representative for French Islam, who was appointed president of the CFCM in 2003 despite weak support in the electoral process created by the government. Boubakeur is an employee of the Algerian government, as was his father, from whom he inherited the office. The Tabligh, a conservative missionary movement, and the association of Turkish mosques and imams, as well as a few independents, were also represented.

The CFCM was intended to help the government regulate matters of special interest to Muslims, such as procedures for halal certification (for food produced following religious law), oversight of Islamic cemeteries and abattoirs, and, most importantly, the creation of a French imam education. The CFCM quickly became bogged down in internal conflict over which association should control what office. The sense of futility grew when the French government in 2004 banned Muslim girls from wearing headscarves in public schools. When the CFCM finally produced a proposal for how to educate French imams, all it could do was to suggest the creation of two new schools: one run by Algeria and the other by Morocco. Imams-in-training would start their studies in France and then complete them at Islamic universities in the two countries.

After several postponements, the second elections to the CFCM took place in June 2005. They led to an unexpected victory for the FNMF, which won a plurality (nineteen) of the seats. The PGM and its associated organizations controlled ten seats and the UOIF another ten. The remaining four went to the association of Turkish mosques and imams and various independent regional groups. The executive board became paralyzed, and in January 2006, the FNFM forced a reshuffle and Bechari replaced Boubakeur as president. Opponents of Bechari accused him of violating the rules and, worse, embezzlement. Bechari was removed from his post as president of the CFCM in April 2006 by the judge overseeing the civil trial, but was cleared of criminal charges in June 2006.[4] At the same time, some of the other members of the CFCM, led by Kamel Kabtane, the popular rector of the Grand Mosque in Lyon, formed a new group—Rassemblement des Musulmans de France (RMF)—which they declared will "complement" the CFCM, and Kabtane and others boycotted the scheduled July 2006 meeting of the CFCM. The civil trial against Bechari was dismissed and the warring factions within the FNFM have ceased overt hostilities. The Executive Bureau of the CFCM met again, with much delay, in December 2006 under the leadership of Dalil Boubakeur. The primary topic of discussion was support for French Muslims going on the Hajj in Saudi Arabia and the creation of more abattoirs for the Feast of the Sacrifice, Eid al-Adha, which took place later the same month.

The many disagreements among the associations have stymied the French government's plan to use the CFCM as a tool to manage the integration process. The French government aimed to create a "French" Islam, but the procedures it created encouraged parochialism and cut short efforts by unaffiliated Muslim associations and leaders to build French Islam from the bottom up. Nicolas Sarkozy, who was then minister of the interior, who deliberately modeled the CFCM on the Consistoire and the Council of French Jewish Institutions (Conseil Représentatif des Institutions juives de France, CRIF), allowed the governments of Morocco and Algeria to influence the process by showing favoritism to the preexisting transnational organizations whose leaders depended upon those governments for their livelihoods and power. In the end, the CFCM became a vehicle for the Islamic countries' ambitions for control over European Muslims.

An early warning of the built-in contradictions of the project to build "French" Islam upon transnational organization came from an anthropology professor, Dounia Bouzar, who was appointed to the CFCM in 2003 as an independent (and the only woman), but resigned in 2005. She complained that as long as the CFCM was allowed to be dominated by people with one foot in France and the other in their country of origin, French Muslims would remain alienated from the council.[5] When I met Lhaj Thami Breze, the president of the UOIF, in December 2006, he complained bitterly about foreign governments' manipulations of their representatives in the CFCM. "It is not the 'Council of Foreign Muslims in France' [le Conseil Étranger des Musulmans de France]. We are supposed to be representatives of French Muslims." He blamed Dominique de Villepin for the ability of "sponsor" governments to control the CFCM because he preferred, as minister of the interior between April 2004 and June 2005, to delegate to the governments of Algeria and Morocco rather than support "the work of independent French Muslims."[6] Breze spares Sarkozy, who served as minister of the interior before and after Villepin, from such criticism. The UOIF also has international connections, but the Muslim Brotherhood is banned in most Islamic countries. The Moroccan and Algerian governments are as disinclined to work with the Brotherhood in France as they are at home.

It is still possible that the CFCM may become a functioning interlocutor between Muslims and the government and a force for integration, but it will not happen until the associational map created by the constitutional foundations for the CFCM has been modified though a difficult process of division and realignment. Interestingly, the past reluctance of the German government to recognize a "German" Islam may in the end produce more incorporation and compromise than state planning in the tradition of French *dirigisme*.

Over the next two or three years, representatives for German Muslims and the government will meet in a biannual Islamic conference, Islam Konferenz, to hammer out an agreement that will allow German Muslims to receive official recognition and the benefits currently given to three recognized faiths: the Protestant Church, the Roman Catholic Church, and the German Jewish community. Wolfgang Schäuble, the Christian Democratic interior minister, will preside. It is an unexpected turn of events because Schäuble, a Protestant, has in the past endorsed the idea that European "basic values" are fundamentally Christian. He also said that since the Roman Catholic Church had stopped using Latin in religious services, German Muslims could reasonably be expected to use only German in mosques. Recognition entails significant benefits, including a check-off option on tax returns, which would allow Muslims to have a share of their taxes channeled to the Muslim community. The tax is obligatory, and apart from paying to the two Christian denominations or the Jewish community, the only option currently available to Muslims is to choose civic charities. Another objective is to create an Islamic chaplaincy education, popularly known as "imam schools."

The participating associations include the ZMD, as well as the two Turkish associations, DITIB (Türkisch-Islamische der Anstalt für Religion) and the Islamrat, which have refused to collaborate in the past. The former represents the imams and mosque communities supported by the Turkish Directorate for Religious Affairs, the "state system," and the latter, mosques associated with Milli Görüs, an organization that has historically been associated with the banned Refah party in Turkey. The German Agency for the Protection of the Constitution continues to blacklist Milli Görüs because of its Islamist tendencies, which past German governments have chosen to regard as a violation of the German constitution. The controversial decision to include the Milli Görüs associations reflects the fact that some of Germany's most thriving mosque communities belong to this tendency. Two other associations are represented, one for the Alevites, a group whose Muslim credentials have been challenged by other Muslims because they do not think of the Qur'an as the revealed word of God, and VIKZ, an association of mosques and educational institutions often linked to the Muslim Brotherhood.

The Turkish government has played an important role behind the scenes to enable joint negotiations. Prime Minister Recep Tayyip Erdogan's party (AK Partisi or AKP) used to be aligned with Milli Görüs against the state-sponsored system. Today, the state system is headed by its former opponent. When the AKP government decided to go ahead with negotiations to join the European Union, it also decided that Turks living abroad would be of more help if they gained citizenship and became politically involved in their host countries. The government also reversed a long-standing policy of insisting that religious instruction of Turkish-origin students in Germany should take place in Turkish. The change in policy affected DITIB, which was told to find ways to work with other associations. In October 2005 the Turkish government also invited the president of the ZMD, Nadeem Elyas, a mild-mannered physician of Egyptian background who was often criticized for alleged ties to the Muslim Brotherhood (which he denies), and his deputy, Ayyub Axel Köhler, to Ankara for a meeting. A press release subsequently described the agenda for the meeting as a discussion of "the political importance of Muslim unity and prospects for a uniform structure."[7] Köhler, a convert originally from East Germany, replaced Elyas as president of the ZMD in March 2006.

It is difficult not to use the events of September 11, 2001, and July 7, 2005, as milestones to explain the shifting approaches of European governments toward Muslims. These are milestones set by events and perceptions that are, initially at least, extraneous to the pace of integration set by generational change and the gradual acquisition of social capital and material income in immigrant communities. If 9/11 brought on the realization that there was a problem with Islamic radicalism growing in Europe, 7/7 drove home the lesson that the problem could not be addressed in the absence of collaboration with Muslim leaders and communities, and that berating Muslims for not integrating was not a sufficient response. The invitation to "belong" was a welcome change for the absolute majority of European Muslims who have no interest in radical agendas and who are simply interested in integrating, socially and politically. But the hostility of large segments of European voters also meant that governments felt obliged to escalate the denunciation of "value relativism," even as they opened the door to a normalization of Muslims' position in European society. The result is that integration increasingly looks like assimilation to those Muslims who, like their Christian counterparts, worry about protecting the integrity of their faith, family values, and religious practices.

Notes

1. The term "Abrahamic religions" is used to describe a presumed commonality between the three monotheistic faiths, Christianity, Islam, and Judaism, based upon their roots in Abraham.

2. Ruth Gledhil, "Islam and Gays," *The Times,* January 5, 2006. Available at http://timescolumns.typepad.com/gledhill/2006/01/islam_and_gays.html#more (accessed December 16, 2006).

3. Amina Satour, "UK Shuns Main Muslim Bodies: MCB Leader," September 11, 2006. Available at http://www.islamonline.net/English/News/2006-09/11/02.shtml (accessed December 16, 2006).

4. See "L'Islam de France et la Justice," April 4, 2006. Available at http://nouvel-islam.org/spip.php?article57 (accessed February 14, 2008).

5. Bruce Crumley, "Going Her Own Way: Dounia Bouzar Is Showing Political and Religious Leaders How French Muslims Can Balance the Demands of Their Country with Those of Their Faith," *Time,* October 10, 2005. Available at http://www.time.com/time/europe/hero2005/bouzar .html (accessed December 16, 2006).

6. Personal interview, La Courneuve, December 12, 2006.

7. Zentralrat der Muslime in Deutschland e.V., October 27, 2005. "Zentralrat der Muslime in Deutschland (ZMD) bei Staatsminister Aydin und Diyanet-Präsident Bardakoglu in Ankara." Available at http://www.islam.de/3953.php (accessed December 16, 2006).

References

Ballard, Roger, ed. 1994. *Desh Pradesh: South Asian Experience in Britain.* London: C. Hurst & Co.

Bowen, John R. 2004. "Does French Islam Have Borders? Dilemmas of Domestication in a Global Religious Field." *American Anthropologist* 106 (1): 43–55.

Heitmeyer, Wilhelm, Joachim Müller, and Helmut Schröder. 1997. *Verlockender Fundamentalismus: Türkische Jugendliche in Deutschland.* Frankfurt: Suhrkamp.

Home Office. October 6, 2005. *Preventing Extremism Together: Places of Worship.* Available at http://www.homeoffice.gov.uk/documents/cons-prev-extreme/cons-prev-extreme?view= Binary (accessed December 16, 2006).

Klausen, Jytte. 2005. *The Islamic Challenge: Politics and Religion in Western Europe.* Oxford: Oxford University Press.

Modood, Tariq. 2005. *Multicultural Politics: Racism, Ethnicity, and Muslims in Britain.* Minneapolis: University of Minnesota Press.

Schmidt, Helmut. 2004. *Die Mächte der Zukunft: Gewinner und Verlierer in der Welt von morgen.* Munich: Siedler.

Warner, Carolyn M., and Manfred W. Wenner. 2006. "Religion and the Political Organization of Muslims in Europe." *Perspectives on Politics* 4 (3): 457–479.

Werbner, Pnina. 2002. *Imagined Diasporas among Manchester Muslims: The Public Performance of Pakistani Transnational Identity Politics.* Oxford, UK: James Currey.

7

Muslims in UK Institutions: Effective Representation or Tokenism?

Abdulkader H. Sinno and Eren Tatari

Muslim representation in political parties, local government, and legislatures in Britain has been on the rise in the last decade. In this chapter we explore the perceptions, experiences, and political behavior of British Muslim members of city councils, political parties, and parliamentary chambers to understand whether they perceive that their presence in these institutions helps members of minority communities. We gauge whether they think of themselves as representing Muslims and whether they feel that current British Muslim representation is effective, provides services to a disadvantaged minority, or functions as a tool for conflict resolution in the context of rising tensions and misperceptions. We also use our findings to speak to key theoretical and policy debates on minority representation.

Our research consists of forty in-depth interviews with elected British Muslim officials (city councillors, members of the House of Commons [MPs], members of the European Parliament [MEPs], and Lords), activists, unsuccessful candidates, party officials, and organizational leaders in London during the spring of 2006.

Like other authors in this volume, we do not consider "Muslim" to necessarily mean a religious identity, but an identity that may have religious, racial, political, or cultural dimensions (chapter 1). This chapter is, in part, about what British institutions and Muslim politicians, in all their diversity, make of this sociological reality. We therefore consider as "Muslim" someone who considers herself or himself to be Muslim or who has at least one parent from a Muslim background, unless he or she claims to adhere to another religion.

Until recently, minority issues in the UK have been discussed in racial terms (see chapter 4), but the religious identity of British Muslims has become more important to them, has attracted the interest of politicians, and has become an important part of the public discourse. Several studies confirm that "Muslim" identity has taken precedence over ethnic and other minority allegiances.[1] The 2001 riots in northern England, measures taken by the British government that threaten civil rights, and the 2003 antiwar protests against the involvement of British forces in Afghanistan and Iraq have catalyzed solidarity among British Muslims across ethnic lines. Since then, the attacks in London, police action, and other tense episodes must have further consolidated both identity and perceptions of British Muslims (chapter 8).

Despite the emergence of a prevalent Muslim identity, there are only few studies on political participation and representation of British Muslims. These studies focus on political representation of Muslims at the local level (Purdam 1996, 1998, 2000, 2001; Eade 1989). Others focus on the politics of mostly Muslim ethnic groups but not British Muslims in general (Anwar 1996, Eade 1989). The scholarship on representation still has to catch up with the transformation of minority identities in the UK, and this study addresses the old debates in the framework of a new salient minority identity, British Islam.[2] Does Muslim representation in political parties and elected office benefit the disadvantaged Muslim minority and society at large? Do British parties actively promote Muslim candidates or slow their promotion? In the case of British Muslims today, the answers hardly fall on one side or the other.

Trends in British Muslim Representation

British Muslim representation is increasing considerably on all levels. As of 2007, there are 13 British parliamentarians who are Muslim or come from a Muslim background—4 MPs out of 646, 7 life peers (Lords) out of more than 740, and 2 MEPs out of 78 British MEPs.[3]

The first Muslim MP, Mohammad Sarwar, was elected in the 1997 general elections from Govan, Glasgow. He was reelected in 2001 along with Khalid Mahmood (Birmingham Perry Barr). The number of Muslim MPs doubled again in the 2005 elections: Sadiq Khan and Shahid Malik joined Mahmood and Sarwar, who were reelected. They are all members of the Labour Party. Sarwar and Mahmood were born outside the UK whereas Khan and Malik were born in the UK.

The first Muslim MEP (out of 87 British MEPs at the time) was Bashir Khanbhai, who was elected in 1999 from the Eastern Region as a Conservative Party candidate. Khanbhai did not get reelected after he was accused by the Conservative Party of misusing travel funds, accusations he ascribes to retaliation for speaking on minority issues and to racism.[4] Syed Kamall (Conservative) and Sajjad Karim (Liberal Democrat) became Britain's two Muslim MEPs in 2004. Khanbhai was born in Tanzania, but Kamall and Karim were both born in the UK.

The first contemporary Muslim Lord, Nazir Ahmed (Labor), was elevated to the peerage in 1998. The other six Muslim Lords are Kishwer Falkner (Liberal Democrat), Iltaf Mohamed Sheikh (Conservative), Amirali Alibhai Bhatia (crossbench), Waheed Alli, Pola Manzila Uddin, and Adam Hafejee Patel (all Labour).[5] They are all of South Asian background (six of the seven are foreign-born), though Alli is of mixed background (Hindu mother) and Bhatia was born in Tanzania. Otherwise, they are quite diverse: two are women, they come from all three parties, some are socially conservative (Patel) while others are liberal (Falkner and Alli), some actively take leadership on Muslim minority issues (e.g., Ahmed) while some have a thin connection to Islam as either culture, religion, or identity (e.g., Alli).

All British Muslim parliamentarians have a long history of service as party activists before being nominated for their seats, put on their party's EU list, or introduced to the House of Lords.[6] Most of them served as local councillors prior to becoming parliamentarians. Most have college or graduate degrees, and others are successful businesspeople.

There is little precise research on the numbers, attitudes, and characteristics of Muslim councillors because of the previous scholarly and policy focus on the ethnic, instead of religious, dimensions of minority politics.[7]

Purdam (2000) estimates that there were 160 Muslim councillors in Britain (153 Labour, six Liberal Democrat, and one Conservative) in May 1996. They were overwhelmingly South Asian men, and many more self-identified as "Muslim" or "British Muslim" than as "British" or by referring to their ethnic identity. They were mostly professionals and self-employed businessmen, 21 percent were unemployed, 12 percent were retired, and less than 5 percent were manual laborers. Almost all councillors spoke English well and have been in Britain for over thirty years. The London-based *The Muslim News* estimates that a total of 217 Muslim councillors were elected in Britain, including 63 in London boroughs, in the May 2000 local elections.[8] We estimate that some 130 Muslim councillors have been elected to 32 London boroughs in the May 2006 elections based on a count of Muslim-sounding names. In one London borough, Tower Hamlets, where Bengalis make up a third or so of the population, 30 of 51 councillors are Muslim (25 Labour and 5 Liberal Democrat).

Muslim representation at the local level is now fairly close to parity in London. We estimate that almost 7 percent of councillors are Muslims; 8.2 percent of the city's population is Muslim according to the 2001 census. But does their presence on councils matter?

Does Local Muslim Political Representation Matter?

We interviewed 17 Muslim city councillors across London boroughs during the summer of 2006. We selected the councillors randomly based on their Muslim-sounding names. We conducted in-depth semistructured interviews that generally lasted between one and two hours to collect biographical information and to explore their perceptions, experiences, and political behavior as serving or retired city councillors.

The majority of the Muslim councillors we interviewed are first-generation immigrants. Eight are of Pakistani origin, 2 of Turkish origin, 3 of Indian origin, 3 of Bengali origin, and 1 of mixed background (Bengali and white British). Fourteen out of 17 were above 50 years old and the other three were 37 or 38 years old. Only 3 were born in England, and only 4 out of 17 councillors are female. Their educational backgrounds vary considerably: one ended his education at middle school, 2 finished high school, 5 had some form of training beyond high school but not a formal bachelor's degree, 4 finished college, 2 had master's-level education, and 2 had formal education beyond a master's degree. While the majority of the Muslim councillors (11) were from the Labour Party, the group also included 2 Conservatives, 3 Liberal Democrats, and 1 Labour member who defected to the Respect Party. Eleven said that they are Sunni Muslims, 4 said they are "Muslim" without specifying a sect, and 2 said they are Ahmadi. Eleven out of 17 responded positively when asked if they consider themselves to be religious. Those who identified themselves as non-religious Muslims indicated that Islam is more of a cultural identity and that their ethnic minority identity is more important to them than being "Muslim." One councillor described herself as a "cultural Muslim."

The Muslim councillors we interviewed tend to believe that they can offer Muslim constituents the kind of attention and assistance that they would otherwise not receive from elected officials. In all cases, councillors indicated that they get approached by Muslims from many ethnicities to take up their casework. Some even get approached by Muslims from other wards (constituents of other councillors) who feel more comfortable dealing with them than with their own councillors.

When asked why some Muslims approach them instead of other councillors, their most frequent answers were cultural affinity, language, understanding their particular needs, and trust. One councillor, for example, told us:

Because you are from the same background, when a family speaks about a large family living in a house, I would understand why. Some people do not understand why. It is the young child being raised by grandparents. They don't have to explain to me the reasons, which may be social or economic reasons. Or they simply want to live near an Islamic Center. I may suggest to them different avenues.

Some Muslim councillors believe that their intervention at key junctures averted discrimination against projects that were meant to serve the needs of the Muslim community. In one such case, after not being able to get a positive response from the council for five years, Yusuf Islam (a philanthropist who was known as the singer Cat Stevens before converting to Islam) contacted the only Muslim councillor in the Borough of Brent at the time for help in obtaining planning permission to establish an Islamic school. The councillor told us that the council committee blocking progress on the project granted permission to proceed after he intervened.

Another way in which Muslim councillors help Muslim constituents is by showing them how to effectively present their cases and lobby for their issues. This involves explaining to them the rules of the council, teaching them the proper specialized vocabulary, and coaching them in making their case. One councillor from the Borough of Walthamstow, for example, explained how he helped constituents obtain planning permission for a local mosque after their application was rejected based on technicalities.

Several Muslim councillors also served on advisory boards and committees that deal with minority issues and helped ease social tension and conflict between the police and the Muslim community. Most also mentioned that they hoped that their own service and activities will encourage civic involvement among Muslim youth. A few even stated that they actively work to get minority youth involved in the democratic process in the hope of developing a sense of belonging and decreasing feelings of marginalization and frustration. It is too early to tell and we have little research on the matter, but their example may mitigate the draw of extremists who attempt to recruit marginalized youth.

Councillors' responses indicated a high degree of professionalism and political socialization. Both those who identified themselves as religious and those who did not expressed interest in Muslim issues and have worked to help Muslim constituents in one way or another. However, they all made sure to explain that they are dedicated to assisting all their constituents and to ensure fairness and equality for all. All councillors emphasized that they represent all their constituents equally, and do not engage in favoritism. Some even emphasized that they want to make sure to avoid giving the impression that they engage in ethnic favoritism. One first-term Muslim councillor was very uncomfortable with Muslims approaching him instead of more senior (hence more experienced) councillors at a joint surgery (office hours). He even got into an argument with a Somali Muslim family who insisted on speaking to him instead of the other two councillors from his ward.

The councillors generally seemed comfortable dealing with non-Muslim colleagues and party activists. They all spoke highly of non-Muslim colleagues with whom they shared their party's electoral list in their ward. Some spoke of early tensions with party activists who resisted the entry of minority candidates, but indicated that this has changed over time.[9] Almost all expressed pride in representing ethnically mixed wards. One Muslim councillor, the one-time Hackney mayor Shuja Shaikh, for example, was particularly pleased with his strong and enduring relationship with the conservative Jews who make up the majority of his ward's population. He has been representing them effectively since 1974 in a mutually supportive relationship that helped him provide a government-funded housing agency for Muslims and an Islamic community center for the borough's growing Muslim population.

Still, there were some limitations. One devout Muslim councilwoman felt alienated because her non-Muslim colleagues gathered in pubs after council and committee meetings. She felt that her colleagues would bond and make important decisions in an informal environment that is not welcoming for her. Some also mentioned discrimination in important committees when it comes to issuing permits to build mosques or Islamic schools in contrast to Christian or Jewish ones.

In almost all cases, Muslim councillors mentioned that they collaborate on an ad hoc basis with other Muslim councillors across ethnic and party lines regarding Muslim issues. The one exception is a female councillor with mixed background (South Asian and white) who felt that Pakistani male colleagues did not consider her as one of their own and did not wish to collaborate with her. There is, however, no strong sense of solidarity or an organized effort to foster collaboration and learning among councillors. Some have mentioned that they talk with other Muslim councillors during meetings of the Pakistan Welfare Association or the Muslim Council of Britain (MCB). Only a few voiced a need or desire to have an organization for British Muslim councillors (one such organization unraveled several years ago). Most councillors get socialized into their roles by non-Muslim fellow elected officials from their party.

Almost all were proud to be minority elected officials. Most voluntarily shared with us experiences and memories that they felt were particularly significant in the context of minority representation: participating in decision making, having access to once opaque institutions, having met with the queen as mayors of their borough as few have done, and being able to help their communities. Several mentioned quite proudly how discourse and language in council and committee meetings have become much more respectful of minorities since they were elected. Their presence on the council decreases racist attitudes and language and increases awareness among other elected officials of the existence and needs of Muslim citizens. As one councilman told us:

> The very presence of a Muslim either as a councillor, or any other representative, makes a difference in the sense that the other people, the non-Muslims, become conscious of the Muslim representative's presence and also of the Muslim community. It has two effects. One is that the non-Muslims come to know about the requirements, needs, and demands of Muslims. Also, it deters them from being racist or anti-Muslim . . . they would not express in the open their prejudices, it deters them. And the other element is that gradual contact with the Muslim representative helps them to maintain continuous contact with the Muslim community and know more and more about it. It is a venue, an opportunity to learn more about Muslims. But it depends on the Muslim representative herself or himself. If the Muslim elected representative is positive, then he or she will receive a positive response from councillors and others.

Most are conscious of being perceived as a "Muslim" city councillor, and some expressed their desire to be able to redress negative stereotypes of Muslims in society by being good and fair at what they do. They also tend to be critical of the Muslim community: when asked to identify barriers to increased Muslim political representation, they mostly identified shortcomings within the Muslim community, rather than the system itself. Overall, these councillors came across as optimistic individuals who believe that Britain has much to offer to a new generation of Muslims with the right attitude.

Does Muslim Representation in British Parties and Legislatures Matter?

We interviewed 14 parliamentarians and party activists (4 MPs and MEPs, 4 Lords, and 6 party activists who unsuccessfully ran for seats in the Commons). We also interviewed leaders and officers of several Muslim organizations to get their input on the benefits of Muslim representation. We conducted in-depth semistructured interviews that generally lasted between forty-five and ninety minutes to collect biographical information and to explore their perceptions, experiences, and political behavior. We compared our interview findings with public records of the elected officials and other publicly available information. While the small number of Muslim parliamentarians and activists makes it difficult to make broad generalizations, the in-depth interviews did provide us with meaningful insights into the challenges and opportunities they face and the choices they make.

To gauge whether Muslim parliamentarians reflect the preferences and concerns of most British Muslims, we used as a reference the official positions of major Muslim organizations and answers from interviews with Muslim community leaders. British Muslims are particularly concerned with the protection of civil rights and liberties; support for economic, educational, and political opportunities for minorities; equitable legislation against hate speech and discrimination; and a just and balanced foreign policy toward Muslim countries and populations, including Iraq, Afghanistan, Kashmir, and the Palestinians.

The key for British politicians to be elected to the House of Commons is to be selected by their party for a safe, closely contested, or even marginal district. This is also where the pressures to conform begin to be applied to Labour and Conservative candidates. The selection process is the product of the interaction between party power brokers at the constituency and national levels and differs in its details among parties (Geddes 1998). The prospective Muslim (and other minority) candidate generally has to convince both levels of party governance that he has the potential to be a suitable winning candidate to have a chance to compete for a safe seat. He needs to first convince the national party administration that he should be put on the national lists of those eligible to compete (a much more centralized process for the Tories than others) and to pass muster with the local constituency. Bias against Muslim candidates can operate at different stages: their access to information and understanding of the selection process, discrimination in the appointment to the lists, and hostility within constituencies. Still, all large parties have recently made some headway to address bias in their national lists. In the 2005 election, the Liberal Democrats fielded 23 Muslim candidates, the Conservatives fielded 15, Labour 13, and Respect 10. The total of 51 from the three large parties is an improvement over the 27 from 2001. In the case of Conservatives and, oddly at first blush, the Liberal Democrats, bias is greatest at the level of the constituency, with little effort by the party's leadership to counterbalance it. This is probably because of the existence of strongly anti-immigration Conservative bastions and, until recently, the Liberal Democrat reliance on mostly white voters and activists. This may explain why all of their Muslim candidates competed for unwinnable seats and why they field a large number of candidates (to counterbalance the perception that they do not discriminate against them). An alternative explanation is that they are sincerely launching a pool of Muslim candidates on a trajectory that will ultimately lead a number of them to become MPs after "they cut their teeth on unwinnable then marginal seats," as one Conservative activist told us. The Labour Party's more complex selection system and its strong desire to keep the loyalty of the minority vote, on the other hand, has allowed serious Muslim Labour candidates to be put forth in a few winnable constituencies. Sizable Muslim involvement in Labour is also older than in the other two parties, which makes it more likely that strong Muslim candidates with knowledge of inner party workings would emerge. Labour might very well have had more Muslim MPs if it had not suffered in the 2005 election because of Tony Blair's unpopular support for the American invasion of Iraq.

The candidates, parliamentarians, and activists we interviewed had several explanations for why none of the many Tory and Liberal Democrat Muslim candidates were put forth in winnable districts. The first is that they still had to "pay their dues" to the party as political activists and candidates in unsafe districts before being given the chance to compete for safe ones. One senior Muslim Liberal Democrat activist blamed Muslim candidates from the same party for failing to apply for competitive seats early enough to have a chance to represent these constituencies. Off the record, others spoke of bastions of anti-Muslim attitudes within their own parties that hinder advancement.[10] One interviewee argued that those who speak forcefully on minority issues are ignored for important committee appointments in the Liberal Democrat party. Within Labour, some interviewees suspect that attacks during the first election of Mohammad Sarwar had anti-Muslim motivations.[11] Some have argued that the failed attempt at electoral fraud in the Labour Party election that was meant to keep Yasmin Qureshi from representing the party in the race for the Brent East constituency was one such instance of anti-Muslim racism.[12] A Labour Party investigation found that her rival's supporters disqualified some of her valid votes and ultimately awarded her the nomination. Others mentioned the advantage of the incumbency in slowing the recruitment of Muslims—incumbents are more likely to be reselected for safe seats, thus providing too few choice seats for a new cohort that includes Muslims. It may very well be that all these factors matter and that increased acceptance of Muslims and the development of an eligible pool of Muslim candidates in all parties will lead to increased Muslim representation in coming years. The only way to gauge the sincerity of Liberal Democrat and Conservative party leaders on the local and national levels is to see whether a good number of the Muslim candidates who ran in marginal seats to gain experience and serve the party will be accepted as candidates in winnable or safe seats in coming elections.[13]

The strenuous multistep selection processes also explain in part why MPs have little discretion. For a Muslim to be among the first to make it to Parliament, he has to show repeatedly, perhaps in different election cycles, that he is not a candidate who would cause the party to lose votes or who would breach party discipline. Party faithful who conform to the leadership's views, who please all the local and national veto players, are more likely to make it to Parliament. For example, two Conservative Party activists told us off the record that they felt "their future in the party would be over," as one of them told us, if their views on the Arab-Israeli conflict were to be known because of the entrenched influence of a pro-Israel group within the party leadership. Labour MP Khalid Mahmood describes incentives as follows:

> We are not representatives of Muslims, we represent our constituency. . . . We are here as British parliamentarians supporting our electorate. That's what we are here for and we can't forget that because those are the people who vote for us. . . . It is also true we work within our party because that is the party we get elected by. If I stand as Khalid Mahmood tomorrow, I'll be lucky if I get 2,000 votes. I get those votes because I am a member of the Labour Party, because I

stand on a Labour Party ticket, because all the support behind me comes from that.

Still, the parties do strategically give some leeway to candidates in close races in which dissent from party policy could allow the candidate to win. They may also not be able to monitor positions closely during hectic elections. One case in point was the 2005 race in Brent East in which Labour fielded an antiwar female Muslim candidate, barrister Yasmin Qureshi, in the hope of regaining the district lost to the Liberal Democrat Sarah Teather in a 2003 by-election in which Iraq loomed large. Qureshi explains her opposition to her party's policies as follows:

> Nobody has tried to stop me. A candidate for the war would have not had a chance of winning. I supported the Labour Party on all issues. It was on just two issues, all I said is that it was my personal views that the war was wrong and that the anti-terror laws were not workable . . . the more laws you make that are repressive the worse the situation gets. The element of control by the national party is exaggerated. There were 635 election campaigns. They didn't have time to sit there and guide people, to interfere in all of them.

Our interviews with activists from all three parties also suggest that they allow Muslim candidates in unwinnable and marginal districts to speak their mind and contradict party platforms in the hope of shoring up party support in those districts with large minority populations. The parties achieve local gains and incur no commitment costs because the candidates are not likely to get elected.

It may be unrealistic to expect much from most Muslim MPs—they are mostly backbenchers with little influence over policy making. Still, there is evidence that they are restricted by party control over committee appointments and promotions from playing an active role in conflict resolution or from expressing minority viewpoints in decisive policy debates on salient issues that deeply affect British Muslims, like terror laws and the war on Iraq. Several interviewees had little doubt that the quick advancement of the mild-spoken Shahid Malik—who was appointed to the powerful Home Affairs Select Committee and as parliamentary private secretary, in effect the first step on the government promotion ladder—when compared to the more assertive and critical Sadiq Khan is a case in point.[14] Sadiq Khan, a civil rights lawyer by vocation, broke vocally with Labour on the issue of anti-terrorism laws that would have allowed the government to detain people without charges (presumably Muslims under the current circumstances) for ninety days. The remaining three Muslim MPs supported Tony Blair on this issue. Since then, however, Sadiq Khan has been appointed to the Public Accounts Select Committee and as parliamentary private secretary to Jack Straw.

An interesting example of the ability—which is, however, not absolute—of the Labour Party to constrain its Muslim MPs can be found in their positions on the war with Iraq. The war was unpopular in Britain and particularly unpopular among British Muslims and their organizations. In late January 2003, every Muslim MP and Lord at the time spoke against the war.[15] They were MPs Mohammad Sarwar and Khalid Mahmood, Lords Ahmed and Patel, and Baroness Uddin. Sarwar, the most established Muslim MP, who constantly wins by wide margins, voted against authorizing the war, but Khalid Mahmood abstained from voting. The Lords and Sarwar continued their vocal opposition to the war.

In spite of restrictions, the Muslim parliamentarians we interviewed feel they make government institutions more minority-friendly in some basic areas, particularly when it comes to constituency casework. They may also have a certain degree of indirect influence by interacting on a regular basis with more senior parliamentarians and government ministers in the halls of power. The four Muslim MPs, for example, met with Tony Blair in the wake of the July 2005 attacks in London to discuss concerns of a backlash against Muslims in Britain.[16] And some reduce the incidence of Islamophobia and racism in Parliament by their mere presence or by speaking against it with their party's support. Shahid Malik, when he was a member of Labour's National Executive Committee and before he became an MP, spoke strongly against statements by Labour MP Ann Cryer that many believed verged on racism.[17] In a speech he made after his election victory, he said, "Yes I am Muslim. For those who said it was not possible, then here I am. But, of course, I am also British, English, born in Lancashire and now an honorary Yorkshireman."[18] He also criticized the racist British National Party (BNP) and vowed to help bring different communities in his constituency closer together. Muslim MPs also lend legitimacy to British Muslim organizations by joining them in voicing Muslim concerns in the media.[19] They also feel that they understand Muslim issues better, can have empathy for fellow Muslims, and can break the language barrier with immigrant Muslim communities when needed.

Party control is also strong for British MEPs, but the selection process is less daunting on the regional level for Muslim candidates who are supported by their parties. This explains in part the election of Conservative and Liberal Democrat MEPs in the last election. Their attitudes toward minority affairs are strikingly different. Syed Kamall, the Conservative MEP, is very restrained while the Liberal Democrat Sajjad Karim is quite outspoken. Of course, Sajjad Karim's views on minority rights and on Tony Blair's support for American wars in the Middle East are consistent with those of his own party. Yet, he also speaks strongly on Muslim issues across the EU, including criticizing the French ban on headscarves in schools.[20]

While the two MEPs self-identify as Muslims, they view their missions as Muslim representatives quite differently. The Liberal Democrat Karim finds it natural to speak forcefully on Muslim issues:

> As equal citizens we first have a responsibility to make sure that we are properly representing Europe, the UK and our region and, secondly, that if I have

particular knowledge of a subject, that I display this particular knowledge. When it comes to the Islamic communities, I have such knowledge. It is my duty that I share that with other parliamentarians because that allows them to make more informed decisions. . . . At the moment I have real concerns about how some European governments are treating their Muslims, and if that means I am a lone voice, I will raise it. Otherwise they have nobody to do it.

Conversely, the Conservative Kamall does not feel that it is the place of a minority MEP to represent minority interests:

I don't feel that I represent Muslims anymore than I represent any other community. I feel I represent Muslims in that I give a positive impression of Muslims, in that I dispel stereotypes about Muslims. . . . As a Conservative, I'll make more of an effort to say that I represent everyone. I don't think this is necessarily the case for Labour and the Lib Dem people. I think they wave a flag. I am not a flag waver. I don't wear a badge that says I'm a Muslim. . . . It is very easy to get pigeonholed. . . . It doesn't do any good for Muslims in the long term . . . this is the case of Labour MPs and it's a shame because later on if they want to go higher in their career, people will pigeonhole them as Muslims only talking about Muslim issues. If you want to build bridges you have to talk about issues that concern everyone.

The first Muslim British MEP, Bashir Khanbhai, was an outspoken Conservative, but his treatment by his party may prove to some that such behavior would not be tolerated. After serving a term in the European Parliament, Khanbhai was sacked from the party list based on allegations that he had overcharged the European institution for his travel expenses. He insisted that he made an unintentional mistake and agreed to refund the equivalent of $15,000, and the Conservative Party agreed with him after an internal investigation. Michael Howard, the Conservative leader, declared the matter "closed."[21] Later, grassroots pressure from within the Conservative Party and criticism from Labour caused Howard to reverse course and pull Khanbhai from the list. Khanbhai alleged that he was the victim of a racist campaign from within his party to oust him from politics.[22] His detractors insisted that they were acting to stamp out corruption. Regardless of whether the Conservative rank and file attacked Khanbhai because of his views or religion, his ejection may prove a deterrent for Conservative Muslim activists and elected officials who want to speak strongly on Muslim issues.

From the perspective of members of the Muslim minority, in other words, Muslim MPs and MEPs from the two large parties are largely no different than non-Muslim ones. Party discipline, peer pressure, and the threat of retaliation generally prevent them, with few exceptions, from advocating on behalf of minority rights and positions on foreign policy, even if they wish to do so. Indeed, many non-Muslim Liberal Democrats and the one Respect parliamentarian are far more outspoken on issues of Muslim civil rights and the British misadventure in Iraq than most Muslim MPs and MEPs.

The situation is different for Muslim life peers. Their life tenure provides them with the opportunity to defend minority interests if they choose to do so. Not all opt to do so actively, however, for a number of reasons. Some engage in self-censorship out of loyalty to their party—most are, after all, longtime party activists and loyalists. Some, like Lord Patel, a devout Muslim whose main focus is to manage British hajj operations by chairing the British Hajj Delegation, are not activists by nature and prefer to focus on causes dear to them instead of being outspoken on a broad range of issues. Some working peers may not want to speak against party policies if they are interested in appointments to significant committees.

All Lords with Muslim heritage (except for Lord Alli and a Church of England cleric of Pakistani Shia ancestry) clearly self-identify as Muslim. It seems that being "a Muslim" or an advocate on Muslim issues has become more significant for the life peers across the board because of the way societal and state relations with the Muslim minority have evolved. Baroness Falkner explains:

> I am not a particularly practicing Muslim. . . . I am a cultural Muslim . . . it changed over time . . . once I was politically active and engaged in issues to do with social justice and had a closer look at the Muslim community, it raised my awareness not only of the Muslim community but of all ethnic minorities, so I started defining myself as a member of an ethnic minority and, over time, as a Muslim. It particularly changed when I came here [the House of Lords] where I was much clearer about my identity as a Muslim because I saw so much legislation that was deleterious to the interests of Muslims. . . . It was important to have a voice to advance the interests of my community or to defend their interests.

Baroness Falkner does, however, more so than others, clearly specify that she cares about all other minority matters and general societal interests. Lords in general seem to accept a specialized minority role more than MPs and MEPs. Life peers across parties feel comfortable advocating on behalf of Muslim minorities, often, in the case of Labour, speaking against their party's policies. As Lord Patel puts it:

> Here [in the House of Lords], we are totally independent. We are not going to be elected by anybody. We are here for our lifetime. Over there [the House of Commons], their term is five years, they have strong whips, the whips may tell their constituencies not to select them. Still, during the preparation for the Iraq war, 140 Labour MPs opposed the war. They are not 100% politicians. . . . [On the terrorism law,] I told them [Labour leaders], as a matter of conscience, I'm not going to vote with you, and they agreed. We've got a completely different scenario in this House . . . even though we belong to a party, we vote our con-

science. We are those who scrutinize. We check their legislation word by word, sentence by sentence, and assess what is good for everybody, the nation, the community. . . . It wasn't, so I didn't vote for them.

Lord Nazir Ahmed has similar thoughts:

If I agreed like my Muslim colleagues in the other place [chamber] who have been supporting the government on terror laws, ID card laws, and asylum, immigration, and nationality laws, then I may have gotten into the government but it is important to live with my conscience. . . . If you can't make a contribution to the debate you shouldn't be here.

Lord Ahmed is one of the most active and outspoken of the Muslim peers. Much of his activism before being elevated to the peerage was also focused on Muslim and South Asian causes. These include founding the now defunct British Muslim Councillors Forum and assisting several Muslim professional associations. He is often called upon by the media and others to speak on issues relevant to the Muslim minority. As a Lord, he started an interfaith organization, led the first British Hajj Delegation—a position later filled by Lord Patel—and started an ambitious program to train imams in Britain and place them in prisons and the military as well as in mosques.

Similarly, Baroness Pola Manzila Uddin openly criticizes her party's policies and attitude toward British Muslims.[23] The Conservative life peer Mohamed Iltaf Sheikh, who was appointed in 2006, stated that he intends to be assertive on Muslim issues. He is also dedicated to grooming other Muslims to help them get elected or get appointed to meaningful positions.[24] The Liberal Democrat Baroness Kishwer Falkner also became more outspoken on Muslim issues after these issues became salient.

Most Muslim Lords generally coordinate among each other on issues of importance to Muslims, even though Lord Ahmed reports diminishing coordination recently. There is some distance between Lord Patel and Baroness Falkner on issues of religion. Muslim Lords often seek and get the support of Lord Alli based on common heritage, even though he does not consider himself a believer. Lord Sheikh had just been raised to the peerage at the time of the interviews so it was not clear whether he would cooperate with colleagues to the left on such issues. Lords find it difficult to cooperate with Muslim MPs because of the strictures on the MPs' behavior that we discuss above.

Muslim Lords also clearly believe that they have a certain ability to influence decision makers on critical policies. Lord Patel, who generally shuns the media, says:

We don't get enough time to speak in the chamber, so instead we go to different committees, we ask for meetings to speak with cabinet ministers and other ministers, to voice our concerns and we try to convince them to change the policy.

Baroness Falkner also feels that her intervention matters:

We all knew that [the terrorism bill] will affect Muslims more than anyone else. It was an almost Muslim-specific law. I spent a lot of time in the chamber arguing, meeting people on the government side, using lobbying techniques and personal conversations to convince them not to do it. Speaking to people on the joint committee on human rights . . . I did a lot of behind-the-scene work, including with Labour, Conservatives, and crossbenchers, to help them see the point of view why this legislation is so bad.

But Lord Ahmed is clearly conscious of the limitations:

I'm not a member of government, I'm a backbencher. I can only raise questions. I can say things but I cannot deliver . . . when there are raids like Forest Gate [violent police raids that targeted innocent British Muslims], I can raise concerns. I completely support the police, but they have to be professional.

Muslim Lords feel that they help the Muslim minority on immigration issues by writing letters of support, and by helping its members understand the benefits of engaging the parties and state institutions. They also use their posts and experience to advise Muslim organizations on how to function more effectively. Lord Patel, for example, was advising the Muslim Council of Britain to establish grassroots civic organizations that would strengthen Muslim involvement on the local level and make this minority more important for parties and politicians. Some, like Baroness Falkner, do not hesitate to use their public position to criticize shortcomings within the Muslim community and to push for harmonization of attitudes with the rest of society:

One of our duties is to say the difficult things to our communities . . . it is easier to hear things from our own, from within the *Ummah* (Islamdom). . . . Western Muslims are here and are here to stay and we are becoming more assertive, as we should. So far, so good. If we want to be assertive, we must be equal citizens. For me the best way to achieve this is to share core values. Core values are above all a respect for democracy and institutional liberalism. That includes human rights. That includes the rights of gays and gay Muslims, which I support. We have to be evenhanded in our respect for human rights across the board.

She does not, however, consider herself to have enough support and legitimacy within the British Muslim community to induce change.

Lord Ahmed is both vocal in addressing shortcomings within the Muslim community, with an eye on remedying them, and is perceived to be a genuine representative of the community by several mainstream organizational leaders. He is highly critical of "preachers of hate" as well as of high rates of involvement in crime and underachievement. He believes, however, that Muslim parliamentarians can bridge differences and help the Muslim minority better than others under the right circumstances:

> A Muslim member of Parliament understands the community's problem . . . only women can understand women's issues. Only Muslims understand feelings in the community, what turns them [British Muslims] on and off, what annoys them, how they need to be respected. . . . There are non-Muslim MPs who support Muslims and there are Muslim MPs who have not supported the Muslim community because of their own careers but they lose the respect of the community, they must be balanced.

Consequences for Academic Debates and Policy

The literature on British ethnic minority political participation is highly divided on the benefits of such participation for members of the minorities and society at large. Some (Kepel 1997; Sikand 1998) argue that the political mobilization of minorities based on ethnic ties and kinship networks furthers segregation by reinforcing ethnic and religious identities. It therefore impedes the integration of immigrants and harms both minorities and British society at large by furthering social fragmentation, particularly in the case of European Muslims. Koopmans and Statham (1999, 679) also argue that ethnic minority political participation seeks to further minority interests at the exclusion of broader societal interests, particularly in the case of Muslims.[25] In contrast, others, like Anwar (1986) and Adolino (1997), argue that effective ethnic minority political participation facilitates the integration process for immigrants by making them feel part of the system.

It seems to us, based on the interviews we conducted and on our broader research, that Muslim minority representation in British parties and elected office benefits British society, even if it triggers Islamophobic impulses within parties and society at first. Muslim elected officials can better assist an alienated segment of society and, in the process, alleviate bottled-up resentment. They also reduce counterproductive racism and discrimination in government institutions and mediate effectively when tensions rise between members of the Muslim minority and government agencies. They assist members of the minority who do not know how to deal effectively with government institutions. They also encourage civic involvement among Muslim youth and may even provide alternative role models rather than extremists who shun democratic institutions. They themselves become socialized into their profession and develop a strong ethos of fairness and service to all their constituents, Muslim or not. They build multi-ethnic coalitions within the electorate, within their parties, and within legislatures and city councils. By serving, they develop a sense of institutional ownership. There is little doubt that Britain benefits from developing a class of Muslim professionals with a sense of ownership and belonging that helps reduce societal tension. British parties may want to increase recruitment of Muslims at all levels of government. But to reach its full potential for the minority, Muslim representation needs to be more effective.

We find mixed evidence in the debate between demographic theorists and new social representation theorists. The former believe that "what matters is not just the policy outcome but who takes the decisions. By this standard, a Parliament which does not 'look like Britain', no matter how much it claims to speak on behalf of its constituents, remains fundamentally unrepresentative" (Norris and Lovenduski 1997, 186). Critics of this approach argue that strong emphasis on descriptive representation runs the risk of substituting tokenism or symbolic representation to more meaningful, substantive, or effective representation. Demographic theorists respond by asserting that descriptive representation naturally brings with it substantive representation, more or less, because women represent women better and blacks represent blacks better.[26]

Muslim minority representation benefits British Muslims, but in complicated and mixed ways. The benefits on the local level are clear. In the House of Lords, Muslim life peers have the autonomy and the platform to speak in defense of minority rights on critical issues of policy. In the House of Commons and the European Parliament, however, things are more complex. Muslim MPs and MEPs from the two large parties are largely no different than non-Muslim ones from the perspective of members of the Muslim minority. Party discipline generally prevents them, with few exceptions, from advocating on behalf of minority rights and positions on foreign policy, even if they wish to do so. The one MEP from the less restrictive Liberal Democrat party is more autonomous and expressive on such issues. The strictures of the Labour and Conservative parties are such that the majority Muslim population of a Tower Hamlets constituency voted for George Galloway from the Respect Party over two minority rivals (including a Muslim) in 2005 because they recognized that the outspoken Scot would represent them more effectively. Of course, Muslim MPs could become more outspoken as they consolidate electoral support, develop strong networks within their parties, assume government and party leadership positions, and increase in numbers.

To sum up, Muslim representation in the Labour or the Conservative parties currently does not help Muslim minorities much. The leaders of Labour and the Conservatives may want to provide their Muslim MPs with more autonomy if they wish to attract the Muslim vote and have their Muslim candidates gain greater legitimacy among minority constituencies. They do not need to look far for an example of the electoral benefits this would bring: Lord Nazir Ahmed, who developed such legitimacy by speaking forcefully on issues of interest for the Muslim minority, actively recruits Muslims for Labour. They may also wish to empower them to effectively institutionalize conflict resolution at the national level. Britain would benefit if Muslim Labour and Conservative MPs and MEPs become as effective at the national level as Muslim councillors are at the local level.

Most British Muslim elected officials are still from Labour, but other parties are catching up.[27] Official programs to recruit Muslim politicians to the Conservative and Liberal Democrat parties still have to bear fruit but might very well produce able politicians who will be allowed to compete for safe seats. All three parties now have wings dedicated to attract Muslims: Muslim Friends of Labour, the Conservative Muslim Forum, and a Muslim forum within the Ethnic Minority Liberal Democrats (EMLD) group. Parties that cater to minority needs like Respect also threaten to woo critical swing voters from Labour and the Liberal Democrats. The stakes are high because Muslims made up more than 10 percent of the electorate in forty highly competitive constituencies in 2005 and will become even more important in future elections as their proportion of the population increases. The three larger parties cannot afford to, and do not, ignore the Muslim minority anymore.

Integrating the Muslim minority in post-9/11 Britain is critical for security and to address its needs and vulnerability. The terrorist attacks of July 7, 2005, and other similar attempts by disenfranchised youth desperate and angry enough to find meaning in suicide attacks on civilians highlight the security risks. Their anger and desperation are rooted in the stagnation and discrimination that affect large swaths of the British Muslim population. Two and a half times more Pakistani and Bengali men are unemployed than whites. Muslim men earn on average 68 percent of what white men earn. Muslims make up 7 percent of the prison population.[28] The British Muslim community has also become more vulnerable to popular and institutionalized discrimination. Enhanced power given to law enforcement by the terrorism laws, increased arrests of South Asians, discrimination in immigration procedures against Muslim non-citizens, statements against Muslim attire by Labour officials such as Jack Straw, and local electoral successes by the Islamophobic British National Party all feed an environment of fear and vulnerability. This is the time to devise effective ways to reduce tensions, consolidate the role of British institutions, and institutionalize conflict resolution.

Increased and more autonomous British Muslim representation would play a major role in conflict resolution in post-7/7 Britain. Muslims are strongly underrepresented in the House of Commons, which would need to have nineteen to twenty-four Muslim MPs to reflect their current proportion in British society. Both Tories and Labour should allow Muslim and other minority MPs and MEPs more independence on issues of relevance to minority populations such as civil rights and liberties, religious freedom, religious schools, and foreign policy in the Muslim world. This would give them legitimacy among British Muslims in comparison to other community leaders who shun the democratic process. It would also institutionalize conflict resolution and avert arbitrary or poorly constructed policies that would stoke resentment and trigger cycles of violence and restrictions on minority rights.

Notes

Abdulkader Sinno acknowledges the support of the Center for West European Studies at Indiana University for funding the research trip to London where the interviews were conducted. Eren Tatari recognizes the support of the Indiana University Office of International Programs for providing the travel grant that funded her research trip to London. We thank the elected officials and others we interviewed for taking time from their busy schedules to meet with us.

1. Michael (2004) argues that second- and third-generation British Asians from predominately Muslim countries self-identify mostly as British Muslim, while Purdam (2000, 55) reports that more Muslim councillors self-identify as Muslim than Pakistani or British. Werbner (2002, 51) also argues that Muslim identity has solidified particularly after the Rushdie affair and the Gulf War protests.

2. Recent examples of studies of Muslim minority politics include Purdam 1996, 2000, 2001; Radcliffe 2004; Werbner 2000; Kahani-Hopkins and Hopkins 2002.

3. There were apparently two British Muslim parliamentarians in earlier times: the nineteenth-century peer Lord Stanley of Adderley and Lord Headley, who converted to Islam in 1913.

4. Nicholas Watt, May 13, 2004, "Embarrassment for Howard as Party Jettisons Candidate," *The Guardian*. Available at http://politics.guardian.co.uk/conservatives/story/0,9061, 1215471,00.html (accessed April 20, 2007).

5. Many organizations and scholars do not count Lord Alli in their lists of Muslim parliamentarians because only one of his parents is Muslim and because of his openly gay lifestyle. He does say, however, that Islam is important to his identity because some of his family members, including a brother, are Muslims.

6. This is generally true of most parliamentarians. See Geddes 1998 for more details.

7. Messina (1989, 174) reports that the number of non-white councillors in London boroughs increased from 35 in 1978 to 79 in 1984 to over 130 in 1986. Le Lohé (1998, 86–87) estimates that in the late 1990s, 215 out of 1,917 London city councillors (11.2%) were from ethnic minorities—144 South Asians, 66 Afro-Caribbeans, and 5 other (Vietnamese, Lebanese, Turkish Cypriots); of the 215, 194 were Labour, 15 Conservative, and 6 Liberal Democrat. Le Lohé also finds high rates of success among Labour Asian candidates: 130 out of 179 Asian candidates succeeded, a rate of 72.6% that compares favorably with Labour's overall success rate of 54.5%. Conservative and Liberal Democrat Asian candidates did less well. Eleven of 93 Conservative Asian candidates succeeded, an 11.8% success rate compared to an overall success rate of 29.1%. For Liberal Democrats, the Asian success rate was 7% whereas their overall success rate was 20%. Overall in the UK, there appear to have been some 350 ethnic minority councillors in the late 1990s, a rate of some 1.6% (Geddes 1998, 153; and Adolino 1998, 175). For research on early British Pakistani candidates, see Anwar 1996, chapter 8. See Garbaye (2005) on the growth in the number of minority representatives.

8. Hamed Chapman and Ahmed Versi, "Over 200 Muslim Local Councillors," *Muslim News,* May 25, 2001 (issue 145). Available through http://www.muslimnews.co.uk/ (accessed April 22, 2007).

9. Things seem to have improved considerably for minority candidates, at least in London, since Purdam (2001, 147) found that "there are also incumbent problems of discrimination,

exclusion and stereotyping. This research suggests that there is a general feeling among Muslim councilors that Muslims have been unfairly accused of illegal practices of recruitment and have been treated unfairly within their local parties to an extent that goes beyond simple party and candidate competition."

10. See Geddes 1998 for a discussion of earlier instances of discrimination toward minorities in the selection process.

11. See also Anne McElvoy, "Ethnic Entryism," *Spectator,* May 31, 1997; Stephen Goodwin, "Parliament: Muslim Community Welcomes the Rehabilitation of Sarwar," *Independent,* March 27, 1999; Ron McKay, *"It's Cost Him £400,000 to Clear His Name, Now Sarwar's Out for Revenge,"* *Sunday Herald,* March 28, 1999.

12. Ben Leapman, "My Sin to Be the First Asian Woman MP," *Evening Standard,* February 27, 2004, p. 24.

13. The most popular model to analyze the recruitment of minorities into British politics focuses on supply (from within the minority) and demand (from the parties). Researchers generally agree that both supply-side (talent, education, resources, etc.) and demand-side factors (discrimination, lack of openings, etc.) affect the recruitment of minorities. See, inter alia, Jewson and Mason 1986; Lovenduski and Norris 1989, 1994; Geddes 1998. Both types of factors seem to be relevant in the case of British Muslims.

14. Neil Hudson, "Blair Gives Job on Top Committee," *Yorkshire Evening Post,* July 30, 2005.

15. Jeevan Vasagar and Vikram Dodd, "Threat of War: Muslim Labour Peers and MPs against War," *Guardian Home Pages,* January 30, 2003, p. 4.

16. Catherine MacLeod, "Blair's Plea to Win Hearts of UK Muslims," *The Herald* (Glasgow), July 14, 2005, p. 2.

17. Pat Hurst and Alistair Keely, "Race Row as MP Warns of 'Asian Ghettos Rife with Drug Dealing,'" *Press Association News,* July 6, 2002. Incidentally, Baroness Uddin also criticized Cryer in the House of Lords for wanting to restrict marriage by UK Asians with non–English speakers from the subcontinent. Andrew Evans, "Minister Backs MP after Asians Comment," *Press Association News,* July 19, 2001.

18. Neil Hudson, "Shahid's Historic Night," *Yorkshire Evening Post,* May 6, 2005.

19. See, for example, "British Muslim Groups Have Written to the Prime Minister Calling for 'Urgent' Changes to UK Foreign Policy," *BBC News,* August 12, 2006, online at http://news.bbc.co.uk/2/hi/uk_news/4786159.stm (accessed May 10, 2007).

20. "MEP Hits Out over French Hijab Ban," UK Newsquest Regional Press, *This Is Lancashire,* September 25, 2004.

21. "Howard under Fire over Eastern Region Tory MEP's Expenses Fiddle," *Telegraph,* May 11, 2004.

22. Geoff Meade, "Ex-Tory MEP Claimed 'Undue' Travel Expenses," Press Association, November 23, 2004.

23. "The Kiss of Death," *Economist,* August 14, 2004, vol. 372, no. 8388.

24. Elham Asaad Buaras, "Tories Get First Muslim Parliamentarian," *Muslim News,* May 26, 2006, p. 14.

25. Similarly, Duyvene de Wit and Koopmans (2005, 71) state that "too much emphasis on, and facilitation of, cultural difference may be detrimental to integration."

26. See Norris (1997, 6–7) for a more detailed discussion of this debate.

27. *The Guardian* reports on May 31, 2004, that Muslim support for Labour dropped from 75% to 38% and that the Liberal Democrats increased their support from 15% to 36% since the 2001 election because of the Iraq War. "Muslims Told Not to Vote for Labour," *Guardian,* May 31, 2004. A July 2005 ICM poll of British Muslims found that 26% of them were inclined to vote for Labour, 19% for the Liberal Democrats, and 5% for the Conservatives. ICM, "Muslim Poll," July 2005. Available at http://image.guardian.co.uk/sys-files/Politics/documents/2005/07/26/Muslim-Poll.pdf (accessed April 22, 2007).

28. For a summary of those and other such statistics, see *The Guardian,* "Muslim Britain: The Statistics," June 17, 2002. Available at http://www.guardian.co.uk/religion/Story/0,2763 ,738875,00.html (accessed April 22, 2007). A series of ICM/*Guardian* surveys document increased perceptions of threat and discrimination by British Muslims (Polling the Nations).

References

Adolino, Jessica R. 1997. *Ethnic Minorities, Electoral Politics and Political Integration in Britain.* London: Pinter Press.

———. 1998. "Integration within the British Political Parties: Perceptions of Ethnic Minority Councilors." In *Race and British Electoral Politics,* ed. Shamit Saggar. London: UCL Press.

Anwar, Muhammad. 1986. *Race and Politics: Ethnic Minorities and the British Political System.* London: Tavistock Publications.

———. 1996. *British Pakistanis: Demographic, Social and Economic Position.* Coventry, UK: Centre for Research in Ethnic Relations, University of Warwick.

Duyvene de Wit, Thom, and R. Koopmans. 2005. "The Integration of Ethnic Minorities into Political Culture: The Netherlands, Germany and Great Britain Compared." *Acta Politica* 40: 50–73.

Eade, John. 1989. *The Politics of Community: The Bangladeshi Community in East London.* Aldershot, UK: Avebury.

Garbaye, Romain. 2005. *Getting into Local Power: The Politics of Ethnic Minorities in British and French Cities.* Oxford, UK: Blackwell.

Geddes, Andrew. 1993. "Asian and Afro-Caribbean Representation in Elected Local Government in England and Wales." *New Community* 20 (1): 43–57.

———. 1998. "Inequality, Political Opportunity and Ethnic Minority Parliamentary Candidacy." In *Race and British Electoral Politics,* ed. S. Saggar. London: UCL Press.

Jewson, Nick, and David Mason. 1986. "Modes of Discrimination in the Recruitment Process: Formalization, Fairness and Efficiency." *Sociology* 20: 307–334.

Kahani-Hopkins, Vered, and Nick Hopkins. 2002. "'Representing' British Muslims: The Strategic Dimension to Identity Construction." *Ethnic and Racial Studies* 25 (2): 288–309.

Kepel, Gilles. 1997. *Allah in the West: Islamic Movements in America and Europe.* Stanford, Calif.: Stanford University Press.

Koopmans, Ruud, and Paul Statham. 1999. "Challenging the Liberal Nation-State? Postnationalism, Multiculturalism, and the Collective Claims Making of Migrants and Ethnic Minorities in Britain and Germany." *American Journal of Sociology* 105 (3): 652–696.

Le Lohé, Michel. 1998. "Ethnic Minority Participation and Representation in the British Electoral System." In *Race and British Electoral Politics,* ed. S. Saggar. London: UCL Press.

Lovenduski, Joni, and Pippa Norris. 1989. "Selecting Women Candidates: Obstacles to the Feminization of the House of Commons." *European Journal of Political Research* 17: 533–562.

———. 1994. *Political Recruitment: Gender, Race, Class in the British Parliament.* Cambridge: Cambridge University Press.

Messina, Anthony. 1989. *Race and Party Competition in Britain.* New York: Clarendon Press.

Michael, Lucy. 2004. "Leadership in Transition? Issues of Representation and Youth in British Muslim Communities." ESRC/ODPM Postgraduate Research Programme, Working Paper 12.

Norris, Pippa, ed. 1997. *Passages to Power: Legislative Recruitment in Advanced Democracies.* Cambridge: Cambridge University Press.

Norris, Pippa, and Joni Lovenduski. 1997. "United Kingdom." In *Passages to Power: Legislative Recruitment in Advanced Democracies,* ed. P. Norris. Cambridge: Cambridge University Press.

Purdam, Kingsley. 1996. "Settler Political Participation: Muslim Local Councillors." In *Political Participation and Identities of Muslims in Non-Muslim States,* ed. W. Shadid and P. van Koningsveld. Kampen, the Netherlands: Kok Pharos.

———. 1998. "The Impacts of Democracy on Identity." Ph.D. diss., Manchester University.

———. 2000. "The Political Identities of Muslim Local Councillors in Britain." *Local Government Studies* 26 (1): 47–64.

———. 2001. "Democracy in Practice: Muslims and the Labour Party at the Local Level." *Politics* 21 (3): 147–157.

Radcliffe, Liat. 2004. "A Muslim Lobby at Whitehall? Examining the Role of the Muslim Minority in British Foreign Policy Making." *Islam and Christian-Muslim Relations* 15 (3): 365–386.

Sikand, Yoginder. 1998. "The Origins and Growth of the Tablighi Jamaat in Britain." *Islam and Christian-Muslim Relations* 9 (2): 171–192.

Skellington, Richard, and P. Morris. 1996. *'Race' in Britain Today.* London: Sage Publications.

Werbner, Pnina. 2000. "Divided Loyalties, Empowered Citizenship? Muslims in Britain." *Citizenship Studies* 4 (3): 307–324.

———. 2002. *Imagined Diasporas among Manchester Muslims.* Oxford, UK: James Currey.

PART THREE

INSTITUTIONAL UNDERPINNINGS
OF PERCEPTIONS
OF WESTERN MUSLIMS

8

How Europe and Its Muslim Populations See Each Other

Jodie T. Allen and Richard Wike

The general European populations and European Muslim minorities view each other and the larger conflicts between Western and Muslim countries quite differently. Most striking is the finding from polls conducted by the Pew Global Attitudes Project (GAP) in the spring of 2006 that, in many ways, the views of Europe's Muslims occupy a middle ground between the opinions that Western publics and Middle Eastern and Asian Muslim publics hold with respect to each other.[1] For example, while Europe's Muslim minorities are as likely as Muslims elsewhere to see relations between Westerners and Muslims as generally bad, they are considerably more likely to associate positive attributes with Westerners—including tolerance, generosity, and respect for women.[2] Moreover, not only are Muslims in Europe somewhat less inclined to see a "clash of civilizations" than are those living in predominantly Muslim countries, they are also considerably less likely to see such a conflict than are some of the general publics in Europe. While solid majorities of the overall populations in Germany and Spain see a natural conflict between being a devout Muslim and living in a modern society, most Muslims in both of those countries disagree. And in France, the scene of riots in heavily Muslim areas in the fall of 2005, large percentages of both the general public *and* the Muslim minority population see no conflict between being a devout Muslim and living in a modern society.

We first examine what polls tell us about how Europeans in Great Britain, France, Germany, and Spain (the four countries where Pew's 2006 polls included oversampling of Muslim minorities) generally view their resident Muslim populations, their attitudes toward Islam more broadly, and how those opinions differ among the countries surveyed. Next we discuss the general attitudes of European Muslims toward their countries, their religion, democracy, and other issues. Finally we focus on some important differences among the Muslim communities in two of the four countries, Great Britain and France, in which the Muslim oversamples were drawn.[3]

How Europe Views Its Muslim Populations

It's true that relations are bad, but to go from there to saying who's wrong? I think everyone bears some responsibility. On the Muslim side, it's too much religion, religion, religion, and they don't want to open up to others.

—Jeannine Pilé, 33, French housewife and mother[4]

Attempts at integrating Muslims in Germany have been inadequate. There is insufficient support for integration. In some ways, some Muslims remain susceptible to propaganda and fundamentalism. Another reason is what happened in Spain and the U.K. The terrorists were homegrown. It is very worrying.

—Andreas von Radetzky, 50, taxi driver, houseman, and teacher, Berlin

The Muslim community here is very isolated, so they don't understand the rest of Spain, and Spaniards don't understand them. Perceptions are based mostly on stereotypes.

—Zaida Díaz, 33, accountant, Madrid

Some people in Spain want to forget that we were a Muslim country for nearly 800 years. But you cannot deny your roots, and we all have Islamic roots.

—Manuela Aparicio, 58, publishing executive, Madrid

No clear European point of view emerges with regard to the Muslim experience, either among the majority populations or among Muslims living there. True, concern about the rise of Islamic extremism is ubiquitous (93% of Germans, 89% of the French, 84% of the British, and 77% of Spaniards say they are very or somewhat concerned). Also, as in the United States, solid majorities, ranging from 70% in Germany and 61% in both Spain and Great Britain, see relations between Muslims and Westerners as "generally bad." But there is little agreement over who is to blame for that estrangement: while 47% of the French public points the finger at Muslims, only 32% in Spain and 25% in Britain do the same.

Attitudes toward Muslims in general also vary widely across Europe. Overall, Germans and Spaniards express far more negative views of both Muslims and Arabs than do the French, British, or Americans. While 65% of the French public and 63% of the British express a "favorable view" of Muslims, only 36% in Germany and 29% in Spain share that positive opinion.

When non-Muslim Europeans were asked whether they associate specific characteristics with Muslims, the most frequently mentioned in every country was "devout." Substantial majorities in France also cited "generous" (63%) and "honest" (64%), with slightly more than half of the British and German publics agreeing that honesty (but not generosity) is a prevalent Muslim trait.

Spain and Germany also stand apart when asked about negative traits associated with Muslims. Roughly eight in ten Spaniards (83%) and Germans (78%) say they associate Muslims with being fanatical. But that view is less prevalent in France (50%), Great Britain (48%), and the United States (43%). Majorities in Spain (60%) and Germany (52%) saw Muslims as "violent," but only 41% of the French and 32% of the British agreed.

The general publics in Germany and Spain also tend to see a natural conflict between being a devout Muslim and living in a modern society; most Muslims in both of those countries disagree. And in France, the scene of recent riots in heavily Muslim areas, large percentages of both the general public *and* the Muslim minority population see no conflict between being a devout Muslim and living in a modern society.

Sizable majorities in Western Europe, as in the United States, continue to believe that Muslims in their country have a very or fairly strong sense of Islamic identity. As to whether that sense of Islamic identity is increasing, strong majorities in Great Britain (69%), France (68%), and Germany (72%—up from 66% in 2005) say that it is. In Spain, however, only a 46% plurality sees an intensifying Islamic identity.

No Apparent Backlash

There is little evidence of a widespread backlash against Muslim immigrants among Europeans generally. Majorities continue to express concerns about rising Islamic identity and extremism, but in most of the countries surveyed those worries did not intensify over the twelve months between the 2005 and 2006 Pew Global Attitudes surveys, a turbulent period that included the London subway bombings, the French riots, and the Danish cartoon controversy. Solid majorities in Spain (62%), France (58%), and Great Britain (57%) deem immigration from the Middle East and North Africa a "good thing." Only in Germany does a majority (59%) call such immigration a "bad thing."

Most notably, France shows no signs of a backlash in response to 2005's civil disturbances. In fact, a countertrend seems to have emerged with slightly more

Table 8.1. No Evidence of Backlash against Muslim Immigrants

| | Immigration from Middle East and North Africa is a . . . | | |
General public in . . .	Good thing %	Bad thing %	Don't know %
Spain	**62**	**33**	**5**
May 2005	*67*	*26*	*7*
France	**58**	**41**	**1**
May 2005	*53*	*45*	*2*
Nov. 2002	*44*	*53*	*3*
Great Britain	**57**	**32**	**11**
May 2005	*61*	*30*	*10*
Nov. 2002	*53*	*40*	*7*
Germany	**34**	**59**	**7**
May 2005	*34*	*57*	*9*

French people saying that immigration from the Middle East and North Africa is a good thing than did so in 2005. Nor do German and British publics express any increase in negative views of immigrants, although, unlike the French, they are not more positive toward immigrants in 2006. Among the four countries, only the Spanish public has hardened somewhat in its attitude toward immigrants.

Across-the-board attitudes toward Muslim immigrants are similar to views about immigrants from Eastern Europe. In Germany and Spain, as in Great Britain and France, the numbers among the general public calling immigration from Eastern Europe a good thing are virtually identical to those expressing approval of immigrants from the Middle East and North Africa. These levels of acceptance are essentially unchanged from those recorded a year earlier.

Still, irrespective of whether they welcome new immigrants or not, most Europeans doubt that Muslims coming into their countries want to adopt their national customs and way of life. Substantial majorities in Germany (76%), Great Britain (64%), and Spain (67%) say that Muslims in their country want to remain distinct from the larger society.

Fewer French, but still a majority (53%), agree. However, the percentage of the general public in France that believes newly arrived Muslims want to blend into the French way of life increased between 2005 and 2006. In 2005, Pew found only 36% of the French public saying that Muslims want to adopt the French way of life while 59% said they want to remain distinct; a year later 46% said adopt, 53% said remain distinct.

Concerns about Islamic Extremism

Sizable majorities among all the European general publics surveyed express concern about Islamic extremism in their countries. Germans are the most concerned on this score with 82% of the general public saying they are very (40%) or somewhat (42%) concerned. However, concern was nearly as high a year ago, when 78% of Germans expressed such concern, including 35% who then said they were very concerned.

In France, worry about Islamic extremism has remained essentially stable over the last year (76% of the public is at least somewhat concerned including 30% who are very concerned). And in Spain, such concerns have declined considerably. By contrast, British worries about Islamic extremism are especially intense and mounting. Among the general British public, 42% say they are very concerned, a marked increase from the 34% who said so a year earlier, in 2005. Worries about Islamic extremism *within* the British Muslim community are also greater than among Muslims in France, Germany, and Spain.

Still, few Europeans, non-Muslim or Muslim, believe that extremist groups like al-Qaeda command large followings in their countries. The striking exception here is Spain. Nearly as many among the Spanish public (41%) say that most or many of Spain's Muslims support such groups as say that just some or very few do so (46%).

Riots, Cartoons, and Controversy

Awareness of the 2005 riots in France is relatively high among both the general publics and Muslim minorities in Western Europe, ranging among the general population from 91% in Germany to 78% in Spain, and among Muslims from 86% in Germany to 63% in Britain. Irrespective of their views about the riots per se, by and large European Muslims say they are sympathetic to the youths from immigrant and working-class suburbs in France who felt frustrated by their place in the larger society. However, European general publics are divided on this issue. In Germany, more among the general public (64%) than among the predominantly Turkish Muslims in that country (53%) say they sympathize with the frustrations of French youth. By contrast, only 37% of the Spanish public is in sympathy, and despite more positive French views on many related issues in 2006, only 46% of the French general public takes the side of the country's alienated Muslim youth.

Non-Muslim Western Europeans present a more united front on the question of the controversy over the publication by a Danish newspaper of cartoons depicting the Prophet Muhammad. By wide margins, Europeans, like Americans, who had heard of the controversy believe that Muslim intolerance, not Western disrespect, was principally to blame for the controversy. On this issue, unlike many others, Europe's Muslim minorities share the perspective of their co-religionists in Muslim nations. Among those who are aware of the dispute, more than seven in ten Muslims in Spain (80%), France (79%), Great Britain (73%), and Germany (71%) say that Western disrespect for Islam spurred the conflict.

Western and Muslim publics agree that Muslim nations should be doing better in economic terms, but they differ as to the causes of that retarded prosperity. Germans most often blame Islamic fundamentalism (53%), while a plurality

Table 8.2. Where European Muslims and General Publics Agree and Disagree

	Muslims in . . .				General publics in . . .			
	Gr. Brit.	France	Ger.	Spain	Gr. Brit	France	Ger.	Spain
How many Europeans hostile toward Muslims								
Most	24	18	22	10	15	19	18	26
Many	18	21	29	21	25	37	45	34
Just some	34	32	22	32	38	28	27	27
Very few	18	28	21	32	18	17	7	8
Don't know/Refused	6	1	7	6	4	—	3	5
Muslims in your country want to:								
Adopt local customs	41	78	30	53	22	46	17	21
Remain distinct	35	21	52	27	64	53	76	67
Both (VOL.)	12	1	9	16	6	—	4	7
Don't know/Refused	12	1	10	5	7	1	3	4
Islamic identity among Muslims in this country								
Very strong	28	17	18	24	31	14	39	35
Fairly strong	44	58	28	40	48	62	45	44
Not too or not at all strong	25	25	49	32	14	23	12	11
Don't know/Refused	3	1	5	4	2	1	3	2
Rise of Islamic extremism								
Very or somewhat concerned	69	59	53	46	77	76	82	66
Not too or not at all concerned	29	41	44	49	22	24	17	32
Don't know/Refused	3	0	3	6	1	0	1	2

Mideast sympathies								
Israel	3	6	14	2	24	38	37	9
Palestinians	75	78	50	75	29	38	18	32
Both (VOL.)	4	8	4	7	5	9	4	16
Neither (VOL.)	8	7	22	11	22	12	31	34
Don't know/Refused	10	2	10	4	19	4	11	9
U.S. war on terrorism								
Favor	13	21	31	12	49	43	47	19
Oppose	77	78	62	83	42	57	50	76
Don't know/Refused	10	1	7	5	10	1	3	5
Rating of U.S.								
Favorable	23	30	24	19	56	39	37	23
Unfavorable	65	69	67	76	33	60	60	73
Don't know/Refused	14	1	10	5	11	1	3	5
Hamas victory*								
Good for Palestinians	56	44	32	57	32	24	11	28
Bad for Palestinians	18	46	37	22	34	69	71	47
Don't know/Refused	26	10	32	21	34	7	17	25
Iranian nuclear weapons**								
Favor	40	29	14	—	5	7	3	—
Oppose	41	71	78	—	89	92	97	—
Don't know/Refused	19	1	9	—	6	—	1	—
Rating of Iran								
Favorable	71	48	40	68	34	22	12	23
Unfavorable	10	51	44	24	39	77	82	66
Don't know/Refused	20	1	15	7	28	—	6	11

* Asked only of those who have heard about the Hamas victory.

** Not asked in Spain.

of French (48%) cite the lack of democracy in the Muslim world as the primary culprit. A narrow majority in Great Britain (51%) also sees Muslim government corruption as largely responsible for Muslim nations' poor economic fortunes—an assessment shared by solid majorities of Muslims in Spain, Great Britain, and France. German Muslims, however, point to a lack of education as the primary cause.

Finally, with respect to the central Middle East conflict between Israel and the Palestinians, European publics again show disparate views. In the past, Europeans have been considerably less inclined to share the U.S. public's strong pro-Israel stance. But a change was seen in the 2006 GAP survey (which was carried out prior to the Israel-Hezbollah conflict in Lebanon). Germans, in particular, were found to have become much more sympathetic to Israel in its dispute with the Palestinians.

Nearly four in ten Germans (37%) say they sympathize with Israel in the Mideast conflict compared with 18% who sympathize with the Palestinians. In March 2004, Germans' sympathies were evenly divided (24% Israel, 24% Palestinians). The French have also become more sympathetic to Israel. Four years ago, French respondents sympathized with Palestinians over Israel by roughly two to one (36% to 19%). Today, identical percentages sympathize with each side. The British remain split (24% favor Israel, 29% favor the Palestinians), roughly the same division recorded in 2004. In Spain, a 34% plurality favors neither side, but those who make a choice lopsidedly favor the Palestinians over Israel by a margin of 32% to 9%.

As seen in Table 8.2, just as the views of Europe's general publics toward their Muslim minorities vary across the four nations surveyed, so too do the views of Muslims in those countries. And in many cases, the views of the resident Muslim populations do not differ substantially from those taken by the general publics of those countries, as we describe in greater detail below.

How European Muslims View the West

Being a Muslim and a Westerner are not necessarily mutually exclusive. The problem is: we need more middle-class Muslims in the West. . . . The negative, inaccurate stereotypes of Islam overwhelm the positive opinions other Westerners should be forming about their everyday Muslim neighbors, like the other parents at the kindergarten, the local banker, policeman or shopkeeper.

—Cem Ozdemir, 40, member of European Parliament for Germany's Green Party

Islam is so close to Christianity as a religion that from the beginning the Church has been worried that it could draw away some of its faithful. So the Church campaigned against Islam because it presented a threat to the Church. And they still haven't done much to reverse that. Because of this, people in the West do not understand Islam. People in the West grab the little parts that do not fit with their view of the world, and they focus on them as proof that Islam and the West don't go together.

—Ahmed el Abdellaoui, 40, a translator who lives in Madrid but is originally from Morocco

In many ways, the views of Europe's Muslims are distinct from those of both Western publics and Muslims in the Middle East and Asia. Most European Muslims, for example, express favorable opinions of Christians, far more than do Muslims living in predominantly Muslim countries. Indeed, in Spain and Germany, Muslims feel much more favorably toward Christians than the majority populations feel toward Muslims. Fully 82% of Spanish Muslims express positive views of Christians, but just 29% of the general public in Spain expresses positive opinions of Muslims. In Germany, the gap is also sizable, though somewhat smaller (69% versus 36%).

And while European Muslims' views of Jews are less positive than those of Western publics generally, they are far more positive than those of publics in predominantly Muslim countries such as Jordan, Egypt, or Pakistan, where Pew polls find negligible numbers holding favorable views of Jews. Most notably, as shown in Table 8.3, a large majority of French Muslims (71%) say they have favorable opinions of Jews.

Moreover, while publics in largely Muslim countries generally view Westerners as violent and immoral, this view is not nearly so prevalent among Muslims in France, Spain, and Germany. British Muslims however, are the most critical of the four minority publics studied, and they come closer to views of Muslims around the world in their opinions of Westerners. To be sure, Muslims in Europe, especially in Great Britain, worry about their future, but their concern is more economic than religious or cultural. In fact, the 2006 GAP survey finds that Muslims are generally positive about conditions in their host nation—indeed, more positive than the general publics in all four European countries.

And while there are some signs of tension between Europe's majority populations and its Muslim minorities, Muslims do not generally believe that other

Table 8.3. Rating Jews and Christians

	Jews	Christians
Rating by . . .	%	%
French Muslims	71	91
German Muslims	38	69
British Muslims	32	71
Spanish Muslims	28	82
% with a favorable opinion.		

Europeans are hostile toward people of their faith. Still, 51% of Muslims in Germany and 42% of those in Britain see Europeans as hostile, and more than a third of Muslims in France and one in four of those in Spain say they have had a bad experience as a result of their religion or ethnicity.

Top Concerns Are Economic, Not Religious or Cultural

Although most European Muslims are satisfied with the general direction of their countries, large majorities still worry about their future. British Muslims are the most apprehensive: eight in ten are at least somewhat concerned, including about half (49%) who are very concerned. French Muslims follow closely behind in their anxiety, with 72% saying they are either very (38%) or somewhat (34%) concerned. Numbers expressing deep concern are somewhat lower in Germany (28%) and Spain (30%), although substantial majorities in both countries say they are at least somewhat worried as they look ahead.

Of the issues tested in the survey, unemployment emerges as the top concern of European Muslims, with majorities in the mid-50% range in France, Germany, and Spain and a 46% plurality in Britain saying they are very worried about joblessness. In addition, between a quarter and a third of the remaining Muslim samples express at least some concern on this issue.

European Muslims share the general publics' concerns about extremism among Muslim minorities in Europe. This is especially so in Great Britain, where as many express strong concern about extremism (44%) as about unemployment. Extremism is of somewhat less concern in France (30% very worried), Germany (23%), and Spain (22%); although in all these countries more than four in ten Muslims say they are at least somewhat concerned.

Table 8.4. Muslims More Concerned about Unemployment than Religious and Cultural Issues

| | Muslims in | | | |
	Great Britain	France	Germany	Spain
% very worried about . . .	%	%	%	%
Unemployment	46	52	56	55
Islamic extremism	44	30	23	22
Decline of religion	45	21	18	18
Influence of pop culture	44	17	18	17
Modern roles for women	22	16	9	10

Muslims in Britain emerge as the most worried on every other issue tested, with 45% very worried about the decline of the importance of religion among their co-religionists, 44% very concerned about the influence of the secular culture (movies, music, and television) on their youth, and 22% very concerned about the adoption of modern roles in society by Muslim women. Elsewhere in Europe these issues, especially the role of women, produce intense concern among relatively few Muslims.

In fact, not only is the adoption by women of modern roles of little or no concern to most European Muslims, it is apparently welcomed by many. About six in ten British and French Muslims, and about half of German and Spanish Muslims, believe the quality of life is better for women in the European country where they now reside than in most Muslim countries. In all four countries, the share of Muslims saying women there are worse off is less than 20%. Muslim women in Europe are slightly more likely than men—and in Spain, considerably more likely—to see the quality of life there as better for women than in most Muslim countries.

Nor do most Muslims fault Westerners for a lack of respect toward women. Large majorities of Muslims in Spain (82%), France (77%), and Germany (73%) think that Westerners are "respectful of women," although only about half of British Muslims (49%) agree. Little difference is seen between the responses of Muslim men and women in the samples. The general publics in these countries do not, however, reciprocate. Asked if Muslims are respectful of women, 83% of the Spanish public, 80% of the German, 77% of the French, and 59% of the British say no.

Blending In

As noted above, most Europeans doubt that Muslims coming into their countries want to adopt their national customs and way of life. By and large, Muslims living in Europe do not agree. In France, Great Britain, and Spain, Muslims are notably more likely than general publics to say that they want to adopt the customs and way of life of their countries of residence. Indeed, nearly eight in ten French Muslims (78%) believe this. Germany, however, is the exception: only 30% of German Muslims think Muslims coming into that country today want to assimilate—most say they want to be separate, and most Germans agree.

Despite this desire to assimilate, large percentages of Muslims in Europe say they think of themselves first as Muslims rather than as citizens of their country. The tendency is strongest in Great Britain, where 81% in the Muslim oversample self-identify as Muslim rather than as British, while in Spain 69% do so and in Germany 66%. In sharp contrast, Muslims living in France are far less likely to identify first with their faith rather than their nationality. While a 46% plurality identifies first as Muslim, a nearly equal 42% see themselves as primarily French, while an additional 10% say both equally. By contrast, Christians in European countries overwhelmingly self-identify with their respective nationalities rather than with their faith.

The levels of primary Muslim self-identification seen in Britain, Spain, and Germany are comparable to those found in most of the predominantly Muslim countries surveyed in 2006. In Pakistan, 87% primarily identify as Muslims; in Jordan 67% do so. In Nigeria, 71% of Muslims see themselves as Muslims first, whereas a smaller 53% majority of Christians primarily identify with their faith.

Asked whether Muslims living in Europe retain a very or fairly strong sense of Islamic identity, the views of Muslim minorities largely match those of the general public: in Great Britain, France, and Spain large majorities of both groups agree that they do. Again, Germany is the exception. While 84% of the German public sees Muslims having a strong Islamic identity, only 46% of Muslims living in Germany agree.

As to whether that sense of Islamic identity is increasing, strong majorities among the general publics in Great Britain (69%), France (68%), and Germany (72%, up from 66% in 2005) say that it is. In Spain, however, only a 46% plurality sees an intensifying Islamic identity, a view shared by similar numbers of Muslims in that country. Muslims in Great Britain are the most likely of all groups sampled to see a strengthening of Islamic identity, with fully 77% agreeing. In France and Germany, by contrast, the proportion of Muslims who see Islamic identity intensifying (58% and 54%, respectively) is smaller than among the general public.

But the general publics of Europe and their Muslim minorities part company on the question of whether an intensified Islamic identity is a desirable phenomenon. Those European Muslims who think Islamic identity is growing tend to consider it a good thing. This is especially so in Great Britain, where 86% applaud the perceived intensifying trend, and Spain where 75% agree. For their part, most non-Muslim Europeans strongly disagree. Among those in France who see Islamic identity on the rise, 87% call it a bad thing; in Germany, 83% say so; in Spain, 82%.

For those in Western Europe who look with disfavor upon growing Islamic identity, the primary concern cited is that it may lead to violence. However, many are also worried that it may keep Muslims from integrating into the larger society. For Muslims in Germany who see growing Islamic identity as worrisome, concern about retarding integration is paramount for 58%, while fewer than one in five worry about violence. Among French Muslims, concerns are split between violence (40%) and integration (45%).[5]

Islam, Modernity, and Terrorism

The prevailing view among non-Muslims in Europe is that being a devout Muslim poses a conflict with living in a modern society. But Muslims generally, especially those who live in major European countries, disagree. These contrasting views are particularly noteworthy in Germany and Spain. Fully 70% of the general public in Germany sees a conflict between being a devout Muslim and living in a modern society; 57% of German Muslims see no such conflict. In Spain, 58% of the general public says devout faith in Islam is incompatible with modern life; an even higher percentage of Spain's Muslims (71%) disagree. In France, however, comparably large majorities of the general public (74%) and French Muslims (72%) say there is no conflict between being a devout Muslim and living in a modern society.

European Muslims are not, however, insensitive to the struggle between Islamic fundamentalists and moderates. Among Muslims, majorities or pluralities in Britain (58%), France (56%), and Germany (49%) see such a struggle as ongoing in their respective countries. Again, Spanish Muslims differ from their European counterparts, with a majority (65%) saying they do not see fundamentalists and moderates in Spain as locked in conflict. However, in all four European countries, and especially in France, those who do see a struggle side heavily with the moderates.

This same tendency toward moderation is seen in European Muslim attitudes toward terrorism. In the predominantly Muslim countries surveyed by Pew in 2006, the belief that suicide bombing and other forms of violence against civilians are justifiable in the defense of Islam, while diminishing, still has considerable support. Among Nigeria's Muslim population, for instance, nearly half (46%) feel that such suicide bombings can be justified often or sometimes, while another 23% say these attacks can "rarely" be justified. By contrast, Europe's Muslim minorities overwhelmingly reject such a belief, with 70% of British Muslims, 64% of French Muslims, 83% of German and 69% of Spanish Muslims saying such tactics are never justifiable. Still, terrorism retains pockets of support in all four countries, with non-trivial minorities (7–16%) suggesting that suicide bombings against civilian targets can be justified to defend Islam against its enemies in at least some circumstances.

Table 8.5. Support for Suicide Bombing

Violence against civilian targets in order to defend Islam can be justified . . .

	Often/ Sometimes	Rarely	Never	Don't Know
	%	%	%	%
French Muslims	16	19	64	1
Spanish Muslims	16	9	69	7
British Muslims	15	9	70	6
German Muslims	7	6	83	3

On the other hand, many of Europe's Muslims, like many Muslims elsewhere, refuse to believe that groups of Arabs carried out the September 11, 2001, attacks on the World Trade Center and the Pentagon. This is especially true in Britain, where disbelievers outnumber believers 56% to 17%. By contrast, believers and disbelievers are about equally divided in France (48% to 46%) and in Spain (33% to 35%). In none of the Muslim populations surveyed, either in Europe or elsewhere, does a majority say that Arabs carried out these attacks.

The U.S.-led "Global War on Terror" is no longer popular among most European general publics, but is still less popular among their Muslim minorities. While, for example, 57% of the French general public now opposes the U.S.-led war, 78% of French Muslims do. In Germany the comparable numbers are 50% and 62%; in Britain 42% and 77%. Only in Spain does dislike of the U.S. War on Terror approach the same level in the general population (76%) as it does among the Muslim minority (83%).

Fully 93% of French Muslims, 83% of German Muslims, 75% of Spanish Muslims, and 68% of British Muslims say they have little or no confidence in Osama bin Laden to do the right thing in world affairs. Only in Spain (16%) and Great Britain (14%) does the percentage of Muslims saying they have a lot of some confidence in the al-Qaeda leader exceed single digits. (The number of Muslims offering no response to the question ranged from 18% in Britain down to 2% in France.) Nor do many European Muslims believe that extremist groups like al-Qaeda garner support among Muslims in their countries. In all four countries sampled, only about one in ten Muslims see any substantial level of support for terrorist groups among their countrymen. Most European general publics agree, with one notable exception. Nearly as many Spaniards say that most or many of Spain's Muslims support such groups as say that Islamic extremists draw support from just some or very few (41% vs. 46%). By comparison, just 12% of Muslims in Spain see their co-religionists there as supportive of al-Qaeda and similar groups.

Suspended between Islam and Europe

On some issues, Euro-Muslims are in accord with the views of Muslims in predominantly Muslim countries. A prime example is the ongoing dispute between Israel and the Palestinians. European Muslims heavily support the Palestinians over Israel by margins of 75% to 4% in Great Britain, 78% to 6% in France, 50% to 14% in Germany and 75% to 2% in Spain. On the question of whether the victory by Hamas in the 2006 election will be good or bad for the Palestinian people, however, Muslims in Europe are far less certain. Majorities of Muslims in Britain (56%) and Spain (57%) say that it will, but in both France and Germany opinion splits about evenly between those predicting good and bad outcomes.

The French Difference

Relations between Muslims and Westerners may be bad between governments;
I don't actually think they are bad between people. But the people don't really
get a chance to get to know each other. . . . I think the mass media has played
a big role in this. It's not objective on either side, and that leads to false
stereotypes.

—M'hand Chabbi, 29, of Moroccan origin, who sells Moroccan specialties in a central
   Paris market

When you see your Muslim friends on a daily basis you don't think that relations
with Muslims are bad. But if all you do is watch television, most of what you see
are extreme examples of Islam. Islam is not the religion of terror. But people are
afraid of terrorism and too often religion is mixed up in the debate.

—Pierre-Etienne Issoulie, 22, architect, Paris

When Muslim youth rioted in the suburbs of France in late 2005, commentators
were quick to fault the French "color-blind" assimilation model. "The unrest in
France's cities shows that social and policing policy has failed, as well as integration," read the title on an article in the *Economist*.[6]

Some, like Stéphanie Giry, disagree. She notes that French sociologists "agree
that the integration of Muslims into French society has proceeded fairly well"
(2006, 88). To the degree that the French model has failed in its implementation,
Giry argues, the fault lies with general economic stagnation and the failure of
French elites to recognize or address the real problems faced by Muslims as well
as others in France. Findings from the 2006 GAP survey suggest, as Giry main-
tains, that the French model can claim some success, however mixed. Some aspects of that relative success are especially striking when compared with the
attitudes and experiences of Muslims in Great Britain.

France is home to the largest Muslim population in Europe, an estimated five
million people primarily of Algerian and Moroccan heritage (no official estimate
is available because religion is not tabulated in France's census). As we note above,
French Muslims share many opinions with their co-religionists in neighboring
countries. Primary among them is concern about joblessness. More than half of
French Muslims (52%) say they are very worried about unemployment among
Muslims, the primary complaint of last fall's rioters, and an additional 32% say
they are somewhat concerned. These levels are comparable to those expressed by
Spanish, German and, to a slightly lesser degree, British Muslims. Curiously,
among French Muslims, only 48% of those under age thirty-five say they are very
worried about unemployment compared with 59% of their elders.

Jonathan Laurence and Justin Vaisse observe that "the riots, however, were
anything but religious in nature." Not only were many of the participants not

from Muslim backgrounds, but "they had no religious agenda, and, even more telling, no political agenda" (2006, 2).

While French Muslims do worry about their future in general terms, they are significantly less concerned than British Muslims. A majority (57%) is also at least somewhat concerned about the declining importance of religion among their co-religionists in France, though again, British Muslims are more troubled about declining religiosity among Muslims residing in Britain, with 73% sharing the worry. In this, as in other questions in the survey, no significant difference is seen among the responses of French Muslims of Algerian, Moroccan, or any other ethnicity.

Not surprisingly, a majority of French Muslims (63%) sympathize with the youthful rioters, but not much more so than do Muslims in Spain and Germany. Interestingly, British Muslims are significantly more tolerant of the French demonstrators, with fully 75% offering their sympathy.

French Muslims also share the view, prevalent elsewhere in Europe and in predominantly Muslim countries, that relations between Muslims and Westerners are bad. But while 58% of French Muslims view relations with Westerners as bad, far more (41%) view these relations as good than among British or German Muslims.

Additional points of similarity between French and other European Muslims include generally unfavorable opinions of the United States, of its "War on Terror" and, to a lesser degree, of its citizens. Also, like those of the great majority of Muslims in Great Britain and Spain, French Muslim sympathies in the Middle East lie with the Palestinians rather than with Israel. However, nearly two in three French Muslims (65%) worry about extremism among Muslims. And, like Muslims elsewhere in Europe, only a small minority among French Muslims (16%) say that suicide bombings and other violence against civilian targets in defense of Islam can often or sometimes be justified.

Voici la Différence

While the majority of Muslims in all four European countries surveyed say they have little or no confidence in Osama bin Laden, French Muslims are virtually unanimous (93%) in their disdain. Moreover, like German Muslims, French Muslims are heavily opposed (71%) to the acquisition of nuclear weapons by Iran. British Muslims, in contrast, are evenly split on the subject.

Most striking, however, is the difference between the views that French Muslims hold about people of other faiths and those held by Muslims elsewhere in Europe and in predominantly Muslim countries. With regard to Christians, French Muslims top even the general publics in the United States and France in favorable ratings (91% of French Muslims, versus 88% of Americans and 87% of the French, take that view). But what most distinguishes French Muslims from their co-religionists, not only in the Muslim world but in Europe, is their attitude toward Jews. Fully 71% of French Muslims express a positive view of people of the Jewish faith, compared with only 38% of German Muslims, 32% of British Muslims, 28% of Spanish Muslims, and still lower numbers in the predominantly Muslim countries surveyed. In this, Muslims reflect the view of the larger French public, among whom fully 86% express a favorable opinion of Jews, a higher proportion even than among the American public.

At Home in France?

There are a lot of Muslims who are much more open, who don't pray regularly. . . . There are some who are super-cool, who are not practicing, who are very open to France, and others who are less.

—Wahid Chekhar, 34, actor

Most Muslims in France feel very French—but they feel that the French don't see them that way, because they may look Arab or black. . . . Surveys suggest that Muslims are generally more conservative for example on issues such as sexuality and marriage . . . [But] the fraction of Muslims actively practicing their religion in France is only 10 percent, which is very similar to that of practicing Catholics.

—Catherine Wihtol de Wenden, immigration specialist and research director, Center for International Studies and Research, Paris

By and large Muslims in France do not seem to see themselves as surrounded by hostile natives. Just 39% say they think many or most Europeans are hostile toward Muslims, a considerably lower percentage than the 56% among the general French population who take that view. In Germany, where most Muslims are of Turkish descent, roughly half (51%) see Europeans as unwelcoming, a view shared by 63% of the larger German public.

This perception of welcome persists despite the fact that French Muslims are somewhat more likely than those in other European countries to report that they have had a bad experience attributable to their race, ethnicity, or religion. Nearly four in ten Muslims (37%) in France report such incidents, compared with 28% in Britain, 25% in Spain, and 19% in Germany. Younger French Muslims are more likely to report a bad experience—40% of those under age 35 compared with 31% of those age 35 or older.

A key distinction that emerges in the data is the self-perception of French Muslims when compared with their co-religionists elsewhere in Europe. Few Muslims living in France see a natural conflict between being a devout Muslim and living in a modern society. Seven in ten French Muslims (72%) perceive no such conflict, a view shared by a virtually identical 74% share of the French general public. In Great Britain, however, Muslims split evenly (47% see a conflict,

49% do not) while only 35% of the British general public see no inherent conflict between devotion to Islam and adaptation to a modern society.

Giry (2006) points to surveys and studies done by French scholars and polling organizations in support of the assimilationist tendencies of French Muslims. In particular she cites a 2004 survey by the French polling institute CSA in which more than 90% of Muslims in the sample said that "gender equality and other French republican values were important to them," as well as another recent poll in which more than seven in ten Muslims thought the controversy over the banning of headscarves in French schools was getting too much attention.

Moreover, when asked whether they consider themselves as national citizens first, or as Muslims first, French Muslims split relatively evenly (42% versus 46%) on the issue. Not only is this remarkably different from Muslims elsewhere in Europe (fully 81% of British Muslims self-identify with their religion rather than their nationality, for example), it is remarkably close to the responses given by American Christians when asked whether they identify first as national citizens or as Christians (48% versus 42%). Perhaps in this, as in other things, Muslims living in France are indeed absorbing the secular ways of their countrymen, among whom fully 83% self-identify with their nationality, rather than their religion.

On this one question, however, some evidence of a growing Islamic identity among younger French Muslims appears. Among those under age 35, many of them French by birth, only 40% self-identify primarily as French while 51% self-identify first as Muslim, and 7% say both equally. Among those 35 and older, 45% self-identify with their nationality, 36% as Muslims, and 16% as both equally.

However, no such age differential appears on the question of whether Muslims in France want either to be distinct from the larger culture or to adopt its customs. Nearly eight in ten French Muslims (78%) say most Muslims want to adopt French customs. The rates are similar for those 35 and older and those under 35. This high preference for assimilation compares with that expressed by 53% of Muslims in Spain, 41% in Britain, and 30% in Germany.

All in all, one might conclude that, despite their problems—prime among them joblessness among youth generally, not just Muslim youth—the French need take no integrationist lessons from their European neighbors, including those across the English Channel on whom we focus next.

British Muslims' More Skeptical View of the West

It's hard to pin the blame on anyone. The problem with the Muslims in Britain, certainly the South Asian community, is they came from very low social backgrounds, from villages in Pakistan. . . . These people had no other option but to ghettoize and that's what happened.

—Ali Abbas, a Pakistani economist from Lahore who is completing a doctorate at
  Hertford College, Oxford University

Relations are bad, for two reasons, one political, one spiritual. The political one is all about oil. The East has the oil and the West hasn't. They want it. Our countries are very weak. Iraq has made a big difference to opinion, particularly in Britain.

—Hojjat Ramzy, born in Iran but resident in the UK for twenty-seven years. Oxford-based, he acts as a Muslim chaplain for immigrants and for the Thames Valley Police and helps organize interfaith events with Christians and Jews in Oxford.

The July 7, 2005, London bombings, carried out by a "homegrown" terrorist cell of British Muslims, drew international attention to the issue of integration in Britain. Following the attacks, in which fifty-two people were killed and approximately seven hundred injured, a growing chorus of critics questioned the British model of multiculturalism. Stephen Schwartz declared in the *Weekly Standard* (2006) that "Britain has a problem with Islam."[7] Francis Fukuyama said that Europeans must "recognize that the old multicultural model was a failure in such countries as the Netherlands and Britain" (2006, 21). Other commentators, sounding a more alarmist note, have portrayed Britain's Muslim community as a hotbed for radicalism, raising fears about "Londonistan" and suggesting that extremist views are accepted by many British Muslims. Moreover, many of these critics allege, such extremism is often legitimized by non-Muslim elites who place misguided faith in multiculturalism.

The Pew survey data suggest that while the alarmists may exaggerate the challenges of integration in Britain, on many measures the British Muslim population does differ from others in Europe. Britain's approximately 1.8 million Muslims, who are largely of South Asian ancestry, are more skeptical of Westerners, and they are worried about a broader array of concerns than are Muslims elsewhere in Europe.[8] Moreover, they, along with the British general public, express a great deal of anxiety about Islamic extremism in their country.

A More Negative View of Secularism, the West, and Modernity

Religious identity is particularly strong among Britain's Muslims—eight in ten (81%) say they primarily think of themselves first as Muslim rather than as British, a higher level of Muslim identity than is found in Germany or Spain, and a much higher level than in relatively secular France. Indeed, British Muslims are more likely to identify with Islam than are their co-religionists throughout much of the Islamic world. Indonesian, Turkish, Egyptian, Jordanian, and Nigerian Muslims are all more likely to self-identify with their nationality than are British Muslims. Only Pakistani Muslims, at 87%, show a higher level of religious identity.

In their views of Westerners, British Muslims often resemble their co-religionists in predominantly Islamic countries more than they do their fellow Muslims in Europe. They are more likely than Muslims in Germany, Spain, or France to associate negative characteristics with Westerners; most see Westerners as selfish, arrogant, violent, greedy, and immoral. And while solid majorities of Spanish, French, and German Muslims believe that Westerners are generally respectful of women, British Muslims are divided on this question, with 49% saying they are respectful and 44% saying they are not. Their views are often even more negative than the views of their co-religionists living in Muslim countries. For instance, 64% of Muslims in Britain say Westerners are arrogant, compared with 53% of those in Pakistan, 49% in Egypt, and 48% in Jordan (48% of German Muslims see Westerners as arrogant, 45% of French Muslims, and 43% of Muslims in Spain. For more on the characteristics European Muslims associate with Westerners, see Wike and Grim 2007).

They are also more inclined to see a conflict between modernity and Islam. Indeed, Muslims in Britain, along with those in Pakistan, are the most likely to see a conflict between being a devout Muslim and living in a modern society—47% of both British and Pakistani Muslims see such a conflict, compared with only 25% of Spanish Muslims and 28% of those in Egypt.

Although, like Muslims elsewhere in Europe, most British Muslims are satisfied with the general direction of the country they now live in, they are the most concerned among Europe's Muslim minorities about the future of Muslims in their country. Eight in ten British Muslims (80%) express at least some degree of concern, and about half (49%) say they are very concerned.

Anxieties about religious decline and the influence of modern culture are also higher in Britain. British Muslims are more than twice as likely as followers of Islam elsewhere in Europe to say they are very worried about the decline of religion among Muslims in their country (45% are very worried). They are also more concerned about the influence of music, movies, and television on Muslim youth (44% very worried). And while only 22% are very worried about Muslim women taking on modern roles in society, this is nonetheless the highest level of concern among the four European Muslim populations included in the survey. Moreover, a poll conducted in March and April 2006 by the UK polling firm GfK NOP for Britain's Channel 4 found that a slim majority of Muslims in Britain, including 51% of British Muslim women, take a very unmodern view of gender roles, saying that wives should obey their husbands (GfK NOP 2006, 47).

When dealing with religious issues and other concerns, British Muslims often turn to their local mosque for direction. A full 42% say that, when seeking guidance on religious matters, they place the greatest trust in their local imam or sheikh. French (26%), Spanish (26%), and German (18%) Muslims are considerably less likely to look for such guidance. A significant minority (28%) of British Muslims look to imams and institutions outside of Britain, while relatively few rely on national religious leaders (4%) or religious figures on television (4%).

Relations with the Majority Population

The relatively negative feelings British Muslims have about the West do not appear to be driven by experiences with discrimination. Although many Muslims in Britain (28%) say they have had a bad personal experience because of their religion or ethnicity, and even more (42%) think many or most Europeans are hostile toward Muslims, these figures are similar to those found in other European Muslim communities. And the British general public has a relatively positive view of Muslims—63% say they have a favorable opinion, slightly below the 65% found in France, but considerably higher than in Germany (36% favorable) or Spain (only 29% favorable).

Still, there is a sense among British Muslims that tensions between their community and the majority population have increased since the London bombings. In April 2006 GfK NOP found that 63% believed hostility toward Muslims has increased since the attacks. And in a February 2006 poll of British Muslims by ICM for the *Sunday Telegraph,* 50% said relations between Muslims and white British people are getting worse, 19% said they are getting better, and 29% felt they are staying about the same. This poll also highlighted the extent to which these tensions are having a negative impact on the British Muslim community—60% said that Muslims have recently become more alienated from British and Western society, and 46% said that Muslims have become more radical in their views about society.[9]

Views on Extremism

Pew data underscore the fact that extremism is a major concern among Britain's Muslim population. More than four in ten (43%) are very concerned about Islamic extremism in their country, a considerably higher percentage, as noted earlier, than in France, Germany, or Spain. On this question, British Muslims agree with their country's general public, 42% of whom say they are very concerned about Islamic extremism.

As in other European Muslim communities, a relatively small, but still troubling, minority of British Muslims shows support for acts of terrorism. The overwhelming majority of British Muslims (70%) say suicide bombing and other forms of violence against civilians in defense of Islam can never be justified, but 15% believe these attacks can often or sometimes be justified, while another 9% say there is rarely justification for such violence. GfK NOP asked a question more specifically about the July 7 attacks and found that 22% thought the bombings were justified because of British support for the War on Terror (2006, 34).

Positive Signs

Despite the negative findings regarding the attitudes of Muslims in Britain, there are also many signs that the situation is not so dire. For instance, 51% of British Muslims say they are satisfied with the direction of their country, notably higher than levels of satisfaction among French Muslims (33%) and significantly higher than among the British general public (35%).

There are also signs of respect for the religious beliefs of the broader population—71% of British Muslims say they have a favorable view of Christians.

Moreover, despite the misgivings many Muslims have about certain aspects of the Western style of modernity, a solid majority says Muslim women have a higher quality of life in the West than in most Muslim countries. And while many in the Muslim community are concerned about radicalism, only 12% believe many or most of their fellow British Muslims support Islamic extremists like al-Qaeda.

Conclusions

Findings from recent polling suggest that, at least in the case of Muslims in Europe and the general publics among whom they reside, familiarity leads not to contempt but to at least some measure of mutual understanding. While there are important disagreements between Muslims and non-Muslims in Europe, it is also true that on many issues European Muslims occupy a middle ground, taking a more moderate stance than their co-religionists in countries where Islam is the dominant faith.

Despite the tumultuous events of the preceding year (riots, bombings, and so forth), attitudes among the four European publics surveyed in the spring of 2006 do not seem to have hardened against their Muslim minorities. Indeed, evidence of a reverse backlash can be found in France, where expressed positive views of immigrants from North Africa actually increased in the wake of the fall rioting by Muslim youth. There is, however, no predominantly shared view across countries: in particular, the publics of France and Great Britain are considerably more positive in their opinions than are those in Germany and Spain. And large majorities in all four countries, most notably in Britain, express concern about the rise of Islamic extremism as well as doubts about the degree to which Muslim immigrants wish to assimilate into the larger culture.

Given the diversity in their backgrounds and in the countries of their origin or ancestry, it is not surprising that attitudes and opinions held by European Muslims also vary greatly. As Martin Walker writes, in alarmist discussions about the impact of Muslim immigration into Europe, "the first myth is that there is any such phenomenon as European Islam" (2006, 18). The special oversamples drawn for the Pew 2006 GAP surveys reflect that diversity. Britain's Muslims in the sample are predominantly of Pakistani ancestry or origin, with smaller numbers from India and Bangladesh. By contrast, France's Muslims are primarily drawn from North Africa (Algeria and Morocco), while German Muslims are heavily of Turkish ancestry or origin. But ethnic origins do not account for all the differences observed: for example, as noted earlier, Spanish Muslims differ substantially in certain views from French Muslims although they too have predominantly North African backgrounds. The institutions of European countries and the attitudes of their non-Muslim populations probably matter just as much in shaping Euro-Muslim opinions.

Still, it is evident that, by and large, Muslims living in Europe have far more positive attitudes toward Westerners than do Muslims living in predominantly Islamic countries. Most see no imminent "clash of civilizations" between the West and the Muslim world and, indeed, are often more satisfied with conditions in their chosen countries than is the average citizen. To the extent that they worry about their situation and future, those concerns focus primarily on the practicalities of jobs and social conditions.

Nor do most Euro-Muslims see adaptation to Western life as incompatible with the tenets of Islam, and few worry about such issues as the role of women in Western societies. Muslims in France, Great Britain, and Spain are, in fact, significantly more likely than the general public in those countries to say that immigrant Muslims want to adopt the customs and way of life of their host country. While many perceive an ongoing struggle between fundamentalists and moderates in their countries, most cast their vote with the moderates. Still, while support for suicide bombings and other Islamic terrorism is negligible among European Muslims, pockets of support persist in all four countries. Indeed, if there is one view that unites European general publics and their Muslim populations, it is a shared concern about extremism in their midst.

Notes

1. The spring 2006 Pew Global Attitudes survey included fifteen countries: China, Egypt, France, Germany, Great Britain, India, Indonesia, Japan, Jordan, Nigeria, Pakistan, Russia, Spain, Turkey, and the United States. All samples are nationwide except for China, India, and Pakistan, which are disproportionately urban. For notes on methodology, see http://pewglobal .org/reports/display.php?PageID=840 (accessed November 22, 2006). The margins of error are 6% for both the British general public and the Muslim population; in France, 4% for the general public and 5% for the Muslim oversample; in Germany, 6% for the general public and 6% for the Muslim oversample; and in Spain, 4% for the general public and 5% for the Muslim oversample.

2. Other related analyses include Allen (2006), Allen and Tyson (2006), and Wike and Horowitz (2006), as well as reports by the Pew Global Attitudes Project released on June 22, July 6, and August 8, 2006.

3. The 2006 GAP surveys, as well as other polls cited in the chapter, were conducted before the outbreak of the military conflict between Israel and Hezbollah in July 2006 and the arrest of terrorists in Great Britain in an alleged plot to blow up multiple transatlantic passenger flights in August 2006. Those events may have hardened views among general publics and minorities in Europe.

4. All interviews cited in this chapter were independently conducted by reporters for the *International Herald Tribune* to illustrate some of the themes cited in the 2006 Pew Global Attitudes reports.

5. In Great Britain and Spain the numbers of Muslims saying that growing Islamic identity is a bad thing are too small to produce statistically reliable distinctions on the primary cause for that concern.

6. See "An Underclass Rebellion: France's Riots." *Economist,* November 12, 2005, 24.

7. Stephen Schwartz, "Radical Roadshow: The British Try to Counter Radical Islam with Slightly Less Radical Islam," *Weekly Standard,* January 31, 2006.

8. For more on the composition of the British Muslim population, see Rex 2002, p. 31.

9. The results of the ICM survey—which was conducted for the *Sunday Telegraph*—were not published all at once; see, for instance, Marcel Berlins, "Writ Large: Sharia Law? Don't Even Think About It," *The Guardian (London),* February 20, 2006, p. 16. The results of the survey are available at http://www.icmresearch.co.uk/pdfs/2006_february_sunday_telegraph_muslims_poll .pdf (accessed April 10, 2008).

References

Allen, Jodie T. August 17, 2006. "The French-Muslim Connection: Is France Doing a Better Job of Integration than Its Critics?" Pew Research Center, Washington, D.C. Available at http:// pewresearch.org/pubs/50/the-french-muslim-connection (accessed February 18, 2008).

Allen, Jodie T., and Alec Tyson. July 19, 2006. "The U.S. Public's Pro-Israel History: In Mid-East Conflicts Americans Consistently Side with Israel." Pew Research Center, Washington, D.C. Available at http://pewresearch.org/pubs/39/the-us-publics-pro-israel-history (accessed February 18, 2008).

Fukuyama, Francis. 2006. "Identity, Immigration, and Liberal Democracy." *Journal of Democracy* 17 (2): 5–20.

GfK NOP Social Research. April 4, 2006. "Attitudes to Living in Britain: A Survey of Muslim Opinion." For Channel 4 (UK). Available at http://www.imaginate.uk.com/MCC01_SURVEY/Site%20Download.pdf (accessed November 22, 2006).

Giry, Stéphanie. 2006. "France and Its Muslims." *Foreign Affairs* 85 (5): 87–104.

Laurence, Jonathan, and Justin Vaisse. 2006. *Integrating Islam: Political and Religious Challenges in Contemporary France.* Washington, D.C.: Brookings Institution Press.

Pew Global Attitudes Project. June 22, 2006. "The Great Divide: How Westerners and Muslims View Each Other: Europe's Muslims More Moderate." Pew Research Center, Washington, D.C. Available at http://pewglobal.org/reports/display.php?ReportID=253 (accessed November 22, 2006).

———. July 6, 2006. "Muslims in Europe: Economic Worries Top Concerns about Religious and Cultural Identity; Few Signs of Backlash from Western Europeans." Pew Research Center, Washington, D.C. Available at http://pewglobal.org/reports/display.php?ReportID=254 (accessed November 22, 2006).

———. August 8, 2006. "In Great Britain, Muslims Worry about Islamic Extremism: Concerns Pre-date Airplane Plot." Pew Research Center, Washington, D.C. Available at http:// pewresearch.org/pubs/48/in-great-britain-muslims-worry-about-islamic-extremism (accessed February 18, 2008).

Rex, John. 2002. "Islam in the United Kingdom." *In* Islam, Europe's Second Religion: The New Social, Cultural, and Political Landscape, ed. Shirleen Hunter, 51–76. Westport, Conn.: Praeger.

Schwartz, Stephen. January 31, 2006. "Radical Roadshow: The British Try to Counter Radical Islam with Slightly Less Radical Islam," *Weekly Standard.*

Walker, Martin. 2006. "Europe's Mosque Hysteria." *The Wilson Quarterly* 30 (2): 14–22.

Wike, Richard, and Juliana Menasce Horowitz. July 26, 2006. "Lebanon's Muslims: Relatively Secular and Pro-Christian, but Support for Terrorism and Anti-Semitism Are Widespread," Pew Research Center, Washington, D.C. Available at http://pewresearch.org/pubs/41/lebanons -muslims-relatively-secular-and-pro-christian (accessed February 18, 2008).

Wike, Richard, and Brian J. Grim. October 30, 2007. "Widespread Negativity: Muslims Distrust Westerners More than Vice Versa." Pew Research Center, Washington, D.C. Available at http://pewresearch.org/pubs/625/widespread-negativity (accessed March 19, 2008).

9

Public Opinion toward Muslim Americans: Civil Liberties and the Role of Religiosity, Ideology, and Media Use

Erik C. Nisbet, Ronald Ostman, and James Shanahan

As Gibson notes (1992), mass political intolerance diminishes and constrains the ability of targeted groups and individuals to fully participate in democratic politics and society. The September 11 attacks, the invasion of and ongoing insurgency in Iraq, and the continuing U.S. War on Terror, have generated debates about restricting the civil and legal rights of Muslim Americans and negative attitudes toward this minority, more so than any other American group since Japanese Americans during World War II. This chapter quantifies and untangles the underpinnings of public opinion toward Islam and Muslims and mass political intolerance towards Islam and Muslim Americans.

We begin by reviewing the public opinion environment toward Islam and Muslims in the United States since 9/11 across several key dimensions: knowledge about Islam, favorability toward Islam, perceptions of Islam's role in terrorism and the U.S. War on Terror, favorability and perceptions of Muslim Americans, and Muslim Americans' civil liberties and legal rights.

Post-9/11 Public Opinion toward Islam and Muslims in the United States

Knowledge about Islam

Polls have used a method for measuring an individual's knowledge about Islam that fits the demands of telephone surveys. It is fast, very simple, and easily coded and tabulated, but it remains debatable how adequately it assesses complex phenomena. This method asks the respondent two fact-based questions. Does the respondent know the name of the Muslim holy book (the Qur'an) and the name used by Muslims for God (Allah)? Using these measures, four surveys taken from March 2002 through July 2005 show that between 42% and 63% of American adults knew that the Qur'an is the correct answer and between 45% and 65% knew that Allah is the correct answer. There is a slight trend toward improvement over time.

American adults have also been asked for assessments of their personal knowledge concerning Islam and Muslims' religious beliefs. Results varied from 25% who felt knowledgeable in November 2000 to 40% in March and September 2006. However, as Table 9.2 demonstrates, the trend is not linear. Generally, these results represent rather modest levels of American public knowledge about Islam and Muslim religious beliefs, which apparently was not much affected by the events of 9/11 in 2001 or the subsequent concerns about terrorism. Cohen (2006)

Table 9.1. Knowledge about Qur'an, Islamic Holy Book, and Allah, the name used for God in Islam. Selected U.S. National Polls, 2002–2005
(Personal telephone interviews; national adult probability samples)

Month(s)/Year	Poll	Pct. Know Qur'an	Pct. Know Allah	Sample Size*
03/02	Pew	43	47	2,002 a
07/03	Pew	42	45	2,002 a
11/04	Cornell	63	65	715 b
07/05	Pew	51	48	2,000 a

Note: Detailed citations found in Reference section.

Cornell 11/04, Pew 03/02, 07/03, 07/05: "Do you happen to know the name of the Islamic equivalent to the Bible? (correct answer "Qur'an")."
Cornell 11/04, Pew 03/02, 07/03, 07/05: "Do you happen to know what name Muslims use to refer to God? (correct answer "Allah")."

* Indicated sample size at the 95% confidence level:
"a" refers to a reported margin of error of +/−2.5%
"b" refers to a reported margin of error of +/−3.6%

Table 9.2. Knowledge about Islamic Religion: Selected U.S. National Polls, 2000–2006 (Personal telephone interviews; national adult probability samples)

Month/Year	Poll	Pct. Knowledgeable of Islamic Religion	Sample Size*
11/00	Public Agenda	33	1,507 b
10/01	ABC/WP	34	1,004 b
11/01	Pew	38	731 c
01/02	ABC/Beliefnet	31	1,023 b
03/02	Pew	34	2,002 a
03/02	Mitofsky	35	2,002 a
10/02	ABC	25	1,018 b
07/03	Pew	31	2,002 a
09/03	ABC	33	1,004 b
07/05	Pew	33	2,002 a
03/06	ABC/WP	40	1,000 b
09/06	ABC	40	1,000 b

Note: Detailed citations found in Reference section.

ABC News 10/01, 01/02, 10/02, 09/03, 03/06: "Do you feel you do or do not have a good basic understanding of the teachings and beliefs of Islam, the Muslim religion?" Percent answer "Do" presented.

Pew question 11/01: "How much would you say you know about the Muslim religion and its practices? A great deal, some, not very much, nothing at all?" "Don't know" and "refused" responses also were tabulated. Percent combines "a great deal" and "some."

Public Agenda Foundation question: "Thinking about the religious beliefs of people who are Muslim, how well do you think you understand the basic ideas of their religion—very well, somewhat well, or not too well?" Percent combines "very well" and "somewhat well."

* Indicated sample size at the 95% confidence level:
"a" refers to a reported margin of error of +/–2.5%
"b" refers to a reported margin of error of +/–3%
"c" refers to a reported margin of error of +/–4%

called these findings "troubling," noting that Islam is the world's second-largest religion, the faith of a fifth of the world's population.

Favorability toward Islam

Favorable opinions of Islam have varied over the last decade. Shortly before the 1993 World Trade Center bombing, a February 1993 poll found only 14% of Americans favorable toward Islam, though a majority of respondents (56%) to the question replied that they "haven't heard enough to say." By comparison, a month after 9/11 the percentage of Americans who had a favorable opinion of Islam was 47%, with only 13% of respondents "unsure" and not expressing an opinion. However, this level of favorability has been the highest since the attacks and was most likely due to a social desire in the immediate aftermath to differentiate between the terrorists and Islam as a whole. Since that period the level of favorable feelings toward Islam among the American public has steadily eroded. The four polls in 2006 demonstrate some variability, possibly due to differences in the wording of the question, with the two sets of ABC News and two CBS News polls approximately 20 points apart from each other (Table 9.3). Averaging the four polls finds only 32% of Americans expressing a favorable opinion toward Islam in 2006. Moreover, *unfavorable* opinion toward Islam has increased since March 2006, with the percentage of Americans expressing an unfavorable opinion of Islam on March, April, and September 2006 polls by both ABC and CBS greater than the number of Americans expressing a favorable opinion for the first time since 2002. This marked increase in unfavorable opinion toward Islam beginning in March 2006 coincided with the increased violence in Iraq and may possibly be a function of increased media attention on sectarian conflict among Muslims.

Lastly, many of the answers to questions about Islam in Table 9.3 were met with large proportions of respondents who stated they were "undecided" or "unsure," usually a mark of high opinion volatility (Bittle and Johnson 2006).

Despite the many laudable values and principles underlying Islam (al-Faruqi 1987; Haneef 1993), since September 11 many Americans have come to see Muslims as dangerous, violent, and hateful fanatics according to several different polls. For example, a national Cornell University poll conducted in November 2004 found that 49% of Americans described Islamic countries and peoples as violent, 47% as dangerous, 45% as fanatical, and 35% as hateful (Nisbet and Shanahan 2004). Likewise, a Pew Global Attitudes Project survey about eighteen months later (May 2006) also found 45% of Americans describing Muslims as violent, 45% as fanatical, and 35% as arrogant. Lastly, a Gallup Organization survey of 1,004 national adults in mid- to late December 2005 found that 33% of the respondents named extremism, radicalism, and close-mindedness as the "least admired" characteristics of Muslims or the Muslim world. Conversely, in the same poll, 52% of the respondents replied "nothing" or "don't know" when asked what they "admire most" about Muslims.

Perceptions of Islam's Role in Current Conflicts and Terrorism

Whatever the intentions and targets of Islamic extremists, there is growing American belief that Islam in general encourages violence against non-believers, even when compared to other religions. Polls conducted for *Newsweek* in the months immediately following 9/11 found from 16% to 19% agreement that Islam itself, rather than Muslim extremists, was responsible for violence such as suicide bombings. Although question wording may account for some variation, there is an increasing trend among Americans to blame the religion, not its fanatical practitioners, for violent behaviors. For example, an ABC/*Washington Post* poll in March 2006 found that 58% of respondents agreed that Islam produces more vio-

Table 9.3. Public Opinion Favorable toward Islam: Selected U.S. National Polls, 1993–2006 (Personal telephone interviews; national adult probability samples)

Month/Year	Poll	Percent Favorable	Sample Size*
02/93	LAT	14	1,273 a
10/01	ABC/WP	47	1,009 b
01/02	ABC	41	1,004 c
02/02	CBS	30	861 d
03/02	Pew	38	2,002 a
03/02	Mitofsky	36	2,002 a
08/02	LAT	28	1,163 c
10/02	ABC/Beliefnet	42	1,018 c
07/03	Pew	40	2,002 a
09/03	ABC	39	1,004 c
09/04	Pew	39	2,009 a
07/05	Pew	39	2,000 a
02/06	CBS	23	1,018 c
03/06	ABC/WP	43	1,000 c
04/06	CBS News	19	899 c
09/06	ABC	41	1,003 c

Note: Detailed citations found in Reference section. Citations include findings from older studies.

ABC/*Washington Post*/Beliefnet question: "Would you say you have a generally favorable or unfavorable opinion of Islam?"

CBS News question: "What is your impression of the religion called Islam? As of today, is it very favorable, somewhat favorable, somewhat unfavorable, very unfavorable, or haven't you heard enough about that to say?" Data combine "very" and "somewhat" favorable solicited by poll questions.

Los Angeles Times Poll question: "What is your impression of the religion of Islam?" (1993); "What is your impression of the Islamic faith? As of today, is it very favorable, somewhat favorable, somewhat unfavorable, very unfavorable or haven't you heard enough about it to say?" (2002). "Don't know" responses coded separately. Data combine "very" and "somewhat" favorable solicited by poll questions.

Mitofsky International and Edison Media Research question, sponsored by *Religion & Ethics Newsweekly, U.S. News & World Report*: "Would you describe your general impression of Islam as . . . very favorable, somewhat favorable, somewhat unfavorable, very unfavorable?" "Don't know," no answer, and refused responses also coded. Data combine "very" and "somewhat" favorable solicited by poll questions.

Pew question: "Would you say you have a generally favorable or unfavorable opinion of Islam?" "No opinion" responses also coded. Data combine "very" and "somewhat" favorable solicited by poll questions.

* Indicated sample size at the 95% confidence level:
"a" refers to a reported margin of error of +/−2.5%
"b" refers to a reported margin of error of +/−2.75%
"c" refers to a reported margin of error of +/−3.0%
"d" refers to a reported margin of error of +/−3.3%

Table 9.4. Public Opinion That Islam Encourages Violence: Selected U.S. National Polls, 2001–2006
(Personal telephone interviews; national adult probability samples)

Month/Day/Year	Poll	Percent Agreement	Sample Size*
12/6–7/01	Princeton/*Newsweek*	18	1,003 b
12/13–14/01	Princeton/*Newsweek*	16	1,002 b
01/02	Princeton/*Newsweek*	19	1,008 b
01/02	ABC/*WP*, quest. a	14	1,023 a
01/02	ABC/*WP*, quest. b	38	1,023 a
03/02	Pew	25	944 b
03/02	Gallup/CNN/USA	35	863 d
10/02	ABC/Beliefnet	23	1,018 a
12/02	Gallup/CNN/USA	39	1,009 b
07/03	Pew	44	1,001 b
09/03	ABC News, quest. a	34	1,004 a
07/04	Pew	46	1.006 b
11/04	Cornell	52	715 c
07/05	Pew	36	1,000 b
02/06	CBS News	39	1,018 b
03/06	Pew	36	1,140 a
03/06	ABC/*WP*, quest. a	33	1,000 a
03/06	ABC/*WP*, quest. b	58	1,000 a
04/06	CBS News	46	899 a
09/06	ABC News, quest. a	33	1,003 a

Note: Detailed citations found in References section. Citations contain findings from older studies.

ABC News/Beliefnet 10/02 question: "Some religious leaders recently have described Islam as a violent religion. Do you think that's a fair comment, or do you think it's an example of anti-Muslim prejudice?" "Both" and "neither" volunteer answers tabulated.

ABC/*Washington Post* 01/02, 03/06, ABC News 09/03, 9/06 question a: "Do you think mainstream Islam encourages violence against non-Muslims, or is it a peaceful religion?"

ABC/*Washington Post* 01/02, 03/06 question b: "Compared to other religions, do you think there are more violent extremists within Islam, fewer, or about the same number as in other religions?" "Unsure" was tabulated for question a and b responses.

CBS News Poll 04/06 question: "Generally speaking, do you think the Islamic religion encourages violence more than other religions around the world, about the same amount, or less than other religions around the world?"

Cornell 11/04 question: See Pew, below.

Gallup/Cable News Network, USA Today 03/02, 12/02 question: "Generally speaking, do you think the Islamic religion encourages violence—more than other religions around the world, about the same amount, or less than other religions around the world?"

Pew 03/02, 07/03, 09/04 question: "The Islamic religion is more likely than others to encourage violence among its believers -OR- The Islamic religion does not encourage violence more than others." "Neither" and "Don't know/Refused" volunteer answers tabulated.

Table 9.4. (*continued*)

Pew 07/05 (reported 09/04) used the same question but added this instruction prior to asking it: "As I read you a pair of statements, tell me whether the FIRST statement or the SECOND statement comes closer to your own views even if neither is exactly right."

Pew 03/06 question: "Tell me whether the first statement or the second statement comes closer to your own views even if neither is exactly right. The Islamic religion is more likely than others to encourage violence among its believers; or, the Islamic religion does not encourage violence more than others."

Princeton Survey Research Associates 12/01, 01/01 question: "From what you know about Islam and its religious teachings, do you think the suicide bombings and other violence by some followers or Islam . . . represent a perversion of Islam by extremists or reflect an important part of Islam's teachings?"

* With indicated sample size at the 95% confidence level:
"a" refers to a reported margin of error of +/–3%
"b" refers to a reported margin of error of +/–3.5%
"c" refers to a reported margin of error of +/–3.6%
"d" not reported

lent extremists than other religions, over three times the percentage that believed the same in January 2002. This trend can be seen in twenty national polls by seven organizations conducted from December 2001 through September 2006.

Several polls since September 11 have also shown that substantial portions of the American public believe that a majority of Muslims are hostile toward the United States. Immediately after the September 11 attacks, an ABC News poll found that 55% of Americans believed that a majority of Arabs and Muslims had a negative opinion of the United States. A Harris poll from the same period found that 50% of Americans believed that Muslims sympathized more with the September 11 terrorists than with the United States. A December 2001 *Newsweek* poll found that these perceptions extended to Muslim-American leaders, with 40% of respondents believing that Muslim-American leaders had not done enough to support the United States and oppose terrorism since the September 11 attacks. According to a March 2002 Gallup poll, 30% percent of Americans also believed that most or all Muslims admired bin Laden.

Beyond 2001, a series of different surveys have asked Americans to estimate what portion of Muslims are hostile to or dislike the United States. In March 2002 the Pew Research Center found that 36% of Americans believed that half or more of all Muslims were anti-American. Pew later found that this number rose to 49% of the public (July 2003) in the wake of the invasion of Iraq, and dropped somewhat to 42% in July 2004. Posing a similar question, the November 2004 Cornell University survey found that 51% of respondents cited half or more of Muslims as hostile toward the United States. Most recently, 49% of respondents to a March 2006 Gallup poll believed that most Muslims had a very unfavorable opinion of the United States.

When respondents were asked in the Cornell poll why they believed Muslims were hostile toward the United States, the two most often cited responses were a fundamental difference between Western and Muslim values/culture (22%) and the United States' policies toward Israel and the Palestinian conflict (22%). However, overall perceptions of responsibility for hostility and dislike toward the United States have evolved since 2002. When asked in a March 2002 Gallup survey whether "unfavorable views Muslims have of the U.S. are based mostly on misinformation provided by their media and government about what the U.S. has done," 78% of Americans agreed. In February 2007, when Gallup asked the same question again, this number had dropped by over 20 percentage points to 57%.

These perceptions of Islamic violence and Muslim hostility may also contribute to a growing sense of a general conflict with Islam and threat among the American population. For example, according to a series of Pew Research Center polls since September 2001, a growing number of Americans (40% in 2006 versus 28% in 2001) view the current situation as "a major conflict between the people of America and Europe versus the people of Islam" rather than a conflict with a "small radical group."

In addition, the percentage of Americans who perceive Islamic fundamentalism or radicalism to be a major threat has increased recently. During the mid-1990s, approximately one-third of Americans viewed Islamic fundamentalism as a major threat. This percentage increased greatly after September 11 to three-fourths of Americans in 2001 and three-fifths of Americans in 2002. Though dipping between 10 and 20 percentage points after 2002, again nearly three-fifths of Americans in September 2006 viewed Islamic fundamentalism as an "extremely important threat."

Favorableness toward Muslim Americans

Prior to 9/11, the lukewarm opinions held toward Muslim Americans and other non-Christian believers presented only "potential tensions" that were "below the surface as few Americans say they are bothered by an increasing number of non-Christians and seculars in American society" (Pew April 2001). After 9/11, however, religion became more prominent in America "to an extraordinary degree." How has increased religious hostility and blame leveled against Islam and foreign Muslims affected relations between Muslim and non-Muslim Americans?

Prior to 9/11, a July 1995 national poll of 1,007 adult participants by Barna Research Group showed that 32% felt Muslims (Islam) had a negative influence on American society. A National Opinion Research Center survey of 2,817 respondents from February through late June 2000 found that 29% felt Muslims who had settled in the U.S. had made "little positive contribution to this country," while 17% said they had made "important" or "one of the most important" contributions. According to a Princeton Survey Research Associate Poll of 2,584 respondents during the early months of 2000, 24% of Americans said they had

Table 9.5. Perceived Threat from Islam: Selected U.S. National Polls, 1988–2006
(Personal telephone interviews; national adult probability samples)

Month/Year	Poll	Percent Threatened	Sample Size*
04/88	AJC	39	1,017 c
02/93	*LAT*	13	1,273 b
10/94	CCFR	33	1,492 b
10/98	CCFR	38	1,507 b
12/01	VVAF	76	1,000 c
06/02	Kaiser/*WP*	61	1,402 b
06/02	CCFR	61	3,262 a
09/03	GMF	44	1,001 c
02/04	Gallup	51	1,002 c
09/04	GMF	51	1,000 c
09/05	GMF	42	1,000 c
09/06	GMF	58	1,000 c

Note: Detailed citations found in References section. Citations include findings from older studies.

American Jewish Congress question: "Now I'm going to read you a list of several different foreign policy issues and developments. Thinking about the next five years or so, please tell me whether you feel each issue I mention poses an extremely serious, very serious, somewhat serious, or not very serious threat to our country's national security interests. Remember, I'm not asking how important the issue is but how serious a threat it is to our national security . . . The spread of Islamic fundamentalism?" Data reported is percentage combined for "extremely serious" and "very serious."

The Chicago Council on Foreign Relations 10/94, 10/98, Gallup 02/04 question: "I am going to read you a list of possible threats to the vital interest of the United States in the next 10 years. For each one, please tell me if you see this as a critical threat, an important but not critical threat, or not an important threat at all . . . Possible expansion of Islamic fundamentalism?" Data reported is percentage "critical threat."

German Marshall Fund 09/03, 09/04, 09/05, 09/06 question: "I am going to read you a list of possible international threats to the U.S. (United States) in the next 10 years. Please tell me if you think each one on the list is an extremely important threat, an important threat, or not an important threat at all . . . Islamic fundamentalism (If needed:) The more radical stream of Islam." Data reported is percentage "extremely important threat."

Henry J. Kaiser Family Foundation, *Washington Post,* Harvard University question: "Now I am going to read you a list of some things people say are potential threats to the quality of life here in the United States. As I read each one, please tell me how serious a threat you think it is to the quality of life here. What about . . . anti-American sentiments in the Muslim world? Is this a very serious threat, somewhat serious, not too serious, or not a serious threat at all to the quality of life here in the United States?" Data reported is percentage "very serious threat."

Los Angeles Times Poll question: "Do you think the religion called Islam poses a threat to the security of the United States and its western allies or not? (If threat, ask:) Is that a major threat or a minor threat?" Data reported is percentage "major threat."

Vietnam Veterans of America Foundation question: "Now, I am going to read you a list of potential threats to U.S. (United States) national security. For each one, please tell me whether it

Table 9.5. (*continued*)

poses a serious threat, a moderate threat, a minor threat, or no threat at all to U.S. national security . . . Uncertain relations with the Muslim world?" Data reported is percentage combined for "serious threat" and "moderate threat."

* Indicated sample size at the 95% confidence level:
"a" refers to a reported margin of error of +/−1.7%
"b" refers to a reported margin of error of +/−2.5%
"c" refers to a reported margin of error of +/−3%

contact with a Muslim person. A September 2000 Pew Research Center poll (Table 9.6) showed that about half of Americans sampled held favorable opinions toward Muslim Americans.

Immediately following 9/11 this percentage actually increased to 59%, the largest favorable percentage recorded (Pew December 2001). Again, as with ratings of Islam, this spike was most likely to due to a strong social desire to differentiate between the terrorists and Muslim Americans as a whole. However, by March 2002 support for Muslim Americans had declined. One in five Americans thought at least half of Muslims living in the U.S. were anti-American. As the March 2002 and July 2003 Pew polls in Table 9.6 demonstrate, Americans differentiate between Muslim Americans and Muslims, with the former generally receiving higher favorableness opinions.

About 38% polled by ABC News/*Washington Post* in early October 2001 said the events of 9/11 had made them more suspicious of people who appear to be "of Arab descent," down slightly from 43% found in a similar poll two days after the attack according to Gary Langer, director of polling for ABC News (Langer 2001a). However, those ABC News/*Washington Post* polls combined the phrase "Arab and Muslim" in many questions (ABC News/*Washington Post* October 2001), leading to ambiguity in interpreting the findings regarding "Arabs" and "Muslims" separately. As Deane and Fears (2006) note, "the two groups are often linked in popular discourse [but] most of the world's Muslims are not of Arab descent." The lowest favorable opinion estimate specific to American Muslims from September 2000 to July 2005 was 39% in an August 2002 *Los Angeles Times* Poll.

However, the most recent surveys regarding opinions toward Muslim Americans show mixed results. Table 9.6 shows a modest rebound toward increased favorability levels in July 2005. However, a Gallup Organization poll conducted in July 2006 found that "substantial minorities of Americans admit having negative feelings or prejudices against people of the Muslim faith" (Saad 2006). For example, 39% of the poll respondents admitted having some feelings of prejudice against Muslims, and 22% also said that they would not like to have a Muslim as a neighbor. In the same poll, large percentages of Americans also reported believing that Muslims living in the United States, including citizens, are too extreme in their religious beliefs (44%), are not loyal to the United States (39%), and are sympathetic to al-Qaeda (34%).

Table 9.6. Public Opinion Favorable toward Muslim Americans and Muslims: Selected U.S. National Polls, 2002–2005
(Personal telephone interviews; national adult probability samples)

Month/Year	Poll	Percent Favorable Muslim Americans	Percent Favorable Muslims	Sample Size*
02/93	Zogby		23	905 d
09/00	Pew	50		2,799 a
03/01	Pew	45		2,041 b
11/01	Pew	59		1,500 c
03/02	Pew	54#		1,058 d
03/02	Pew		47†	944 d
08/02	LAT	39		1.372 c
06/03	Pew		48	2,089 a
07/03	Pew	51#		1,001 c
07/03	Pew		47†	1,001 c
02/04	Pew		48	1,000 c
03/05	Pew		45	1,090 c
05/05	Pew		57	1,001 c
07/05	Pew	55		2,000 b
05/06	Pew		54	1,001 c

Note: Detailed citations found in References section. Citations contain findings from older studies.

Los Angeles Times Poll question: "What is your impression of American Muslims? As of today, is it very favorable, somewhat favorable, somewhat unfavorable, very unfavorable or haven't you heard enough about them to say?" Percent combines "very" and "somewhat" favorable.

Pew 09/00 question: "Now I'd like your opinion of some religious groups. Would you say your overall opinion of Muslim Americans is very favorable, mostly favorable, mostly unfavorable, or very unfavorable?" Interviewers were told to probe to distinguish between "never heard of" and "can't rate," which were included as percents.

Pew 03/01 question: "Now I'd like your views on some groups and organizations. As I read from a list, please tell me which category best describes your overall opinion of what I name. Would you say your overall opinion of Muslim Americans is very favorable, mostly favorable, mostly unfavorable, or very unfavorable?" Interviewers were told to probe to distinguish between "never heard of" and "can't rate," which were included in frequency distributions as percents.

Pew 11/01, 07/05 question: "Now thinking about some specific religious groups. Is your overall opinion of Muslim Americans very favorable, mostly favorable, mostly unfavorable, or very unfavorable? "Never heard of" and "can't rate" responses also were tabulated.

Pew 03/02, 07/03 question: "Now thinking about some specific religious groups. Is your overall opinion of Muslim Americans/Muslims very favorable, mostly favorable, mostly unfavorable, or very unfavorable? Form 1 (#) used term "Muslim American" and Form 2 (†) used "Muslim." Percents of all Pew studies combine "very" and "mostly" favorable.

Zogby 03/93 question: "First, I'm going to name several spiritual groups and as I name each one, please tell me if your overall impression of that group is generally favorable or unfavorable . . . Muslims?" Percent reported is "favorable."

* With indicated sample size at the 95% confidence level:
"a" refers to a reported margin of error of +/–2%
"b" refers to a reported margin of error of +/–2.5%
"c" refers to a reported margin of error of +/–3%
"d" refers to margin of error of +/–3.5%

Public Opinion toward Muslim-American Civil Liberties and Legal Rights

How are these general perceptions and orientations toward Islam and Muslims in the United States translated into public opinion on civil liberties and legal rights for Muslim Americans? In the year following the September 11 attacks, across a variety of national surveys, large portions of the American public expressed a willingness to restrict Muslim and Arab-American civil liberties or legal rights as a means to increase public safety and security.

A 2001 ABC News study found that 42% of respondents supported "giving the police powers to stop and search anyone who appears to be an Arab or Muslim, at random." In addition, some 27% of respondents thought that being Arab or Muslim should be a key factor or component of profiling suspected terrorists (Langer 2001a). In 2002, among the public at large, 58% believed Arabs should pass special security checks before boarding flights, and 49% felt Arabs in the U.S. should carry special identification (Bittle and Johnson 2002). A Fox News poll in June 2002 also found two-thirds (66%) of the public approved of giving the FBI more leeway to attend and conduct surveillance of mosques without first possessing any evidence of wrongdoing. Nearly one-fifth (19%) of Americans also supported fewer legal rights for Muslim-American citizens arrested on suspicion of terrorism than non-Muslim citizens, according to a NPR–Kaiser Family Foundation survey conducted in August 2002.

This climate of public opinion apparently translated into acts of discrimination against Muslim and Arab Americans according to an October 2001 poll of Arab Americans, which disclosed that 20% of those sampled personally had experienced discrimination since 9/11 and 45% knew of another Arab American who had faced discrimination. Not surprised by these poll results, James J. Zogby, president of the Arab American Institute, claimed that politicians, media commentators, and others have "demonized the Arab world" since 9/11, a view shared by many other prominent experts on politics and the media (Deane and Fears 2006).

This experience of the Muslim and Arab-American communities clashes with the perceptions of the general public in the United States. An ABC News poll of November 2001 indicated that a sizable majority of those sampled felt the U.S. had "done enough to protect the rights of Arab-Americans and American Muslims" (73%). The poll also found the following groups' rights had been protected: "average Americans" (81% "yes"), terrorism suspects (71% "yes"), and non-citizen Arabs and Muslims (69% "yes"). However, a breakdown by race showed that whites were 14 to 18 percentage points more likely than non-whites to say the government was protecting civil rights in specific instances (Langer 2001b).

More recent polls have demonstrated that the public's willingness to limit Muslim-American civil and legal rights has not diminished as the events of September 11 have receded. The aforementioned Cornell University poll in November 2004 found substantial percentages of Americans willing to place increased restrictions on Muslim Americans. Twenty-seven percent of poll respondents believed that all Muslim Americans should register their whereabouts with the federal government, 26% agreed that mosques should be closely monitored and surveyed by U.S. law enforcement agencies, 22% agreed that U.S. citizens should be profiled as potential threats based on being Muslim or of Middle Eastern heritage, and 29% agreed that Muslim civic and volunteer organizations should be infiltrated by undercover law enforcement agents to keep watch on their activities and fund-raising. Overall, 45% of respondents to the Cornell poll agreed with at least one of the above statements.

A July 2006 Gallup survey echoed the results of the 2004 Cornell poll. According to the Gallup survey, 39% of Americans favor having Muslims in the United States, *including U.S. citizens,* carry a special identification card, and 41% favor requiring Muslims, again including U.S. citizens, to undergo more intensive security checks at airports.

Beyond civil and legal rights, polls have also disclosed that a sizable portion of the public is uncomfortable with Muslim Americans fully participating in the American political process. For example, 49% of respondents to a January 2003 Fox News poll replied that they would hold a Muslim presidential candidate's religious beliefs against him and would be less likely to vote for him. The Pew Research Center found a similar public opinion trend in a June 2003 survey that disclosed 38% of Americans would not vote for a Muslim candidate for president, even if nominated by their own political party. Most recently, a December 2006 Gallup poll and a February 2007 Pew poll found 45% and 46% of Americans, respectively, stating they would be less likely to vote for a Muslim candidate for U.S. president due to their religion.

The Overall Opinion Climate toward Islam and Muslim Americans

Based on this review of survey research, what are the key conclusions about American public opinion toward Islam and Muslims? First, the large percentages of Americans that have strongly negative stereotypes or perceptions of Islam and Muslims (ranging from 25% to nearly 50% depending on topic and issue), and the level of variability over time, paint a picture of a public that is polarized in its attitudes and opinions toward Islam and Muslims and susceptible to swings in public opinion based on external events. Furthermore, the moderate to low levels of knowledge and familiarity with Islam among the general public (on average, 37% expressed feeling knowledgeable about Islam between July 2005 and March 2006, and only about half of Americans know the most basic facts about Islam) means the public is heavily dependent on media content, heuristic processes employing value or ideological orientations, and elite cues as the bases for making evaluations and judgments regarding Islam and Muslims.

Temporal trends also appear not to favor Islam and Muslims. Basic knowledge and familiarity with Islam has not appreciably increased since 2001, while overall favorability toward Islam has remained low with the occasional severe dip. As the U.S. War on Terror continues, as well as U.S. involvement in Iraq and Afghanistan, the American public is increasingly viewing the situation as a major conflict between Islam as a whole and the United States (40% increase since 2001), rather than between the U.S. and a small radical group. Moreover, on average, about 40% of Americans believe Islam encourages violence more than other religions do, and nearly 60% perceive Islamic fundamentalism as a major threat to the United States. The difference between "mainstream" Islam and Islamic "fundamentalism" is unclear to many Americans: several polls consistently report that approximately two-fifths of the American public describes Muslims generally as "fanatical," "extremist," or "radical."

Low levels of knowledge and/or familiarity may also be one reason that in polls conducted between July 2005 and March 2006, on average 42% of Americans believe that Islam encourages violence more than other religions do. In turn, perceptions of Islamic violence may be an important factor explaining why only 31% of Americans, on average, expressed favorable opinions of Islam on surveys during the same period. Poor knowledge, stereotypes of Muslims, fear, favorability toward Islam and Muslims, hate crimes, and the desire to restrict Muslim civil and political rights might very well be interrelated. After all, the polling trends described above are concomitant both with Gallup's recent poll that found that 39% of Americans support special identification cards for Muslim-American *citizens*, and with the finding of the Council on American-Islamic Relations (CAIR) that the number of assault and other discriminatory complaints filed by Muslims jumped 94% between 2003 and 2005.

The Role of Religiosity, Ideology, and Media Use in Shaping Public Opinion toward Muslim Americans and Their Civil Liberties

What shapes and drives the opinion climate toward Islam, Muslim Americans, and their civil liberties? Scholarly research examining the determinants of public opinion and political tolerance toward minority outgroups has been abundant since Stouffer's (1955) seminal work on support for civil liberties.[1] Summarizing a range of previous research, Sullivan and Transue (1999) note that at the abstract level there is considerable public support and consensus for the general extension and application of civil liberties and political tolerance to minority groups in Western democracies, but that this public consensus quickly evaporates when applied to difficult and specific cases. Though they admit that the variability of public opinion toward civil liberties and political tolerance is somewhat "constrained" by internalized democratic values and culture, within these broad boundaries public opinion may be quite "malleable" depending on two important sets of factors: (a) perceptions of threat stemming from the information environment (i.e., mass media or elite cues), and (b) individual predispositions (i.e., political ideology or religiosity).

Thus, synthesizing different strands of scholarship, we explore how the information environment (such as fear of terrorism and knowledge about Islam), as influenced by the media and individual predispositions, such as ideology and Christian religiosity, combine to directly and indirectly shape stereotypes and perceptions toward Islam and Muslims. We then examine the cumulative impact of these influences on public support for restricting the civil liberties of Muslim Americans.

Mass Media and Information Environment

Sullivan and Transue (1999) argue that the information environment is one of the strongest factors shaping public opinion on restricting civil liberties of particular groups.[2] Previous research also has shown that if the "information environment portrays such groups as violating normative expectations with regard to orderly behavior and proper procedures, many citizens—even those not particularly predisposed toward intolerance—will refuse to tolerate the group and its activities" (Sullivan and Transue 1999, 632). Thus, in the case of Muslim Americans, mass media use may lead to greater public support for restrictions on Muslim Americans by increasing the general fear or perceived threat of terrorist attack and by promoting negative stereotypes or perceptions of Islam and Muslim Americans specifically. At the same time, the mass media also has the potential to ameliorate negative attitudes or debunk stereotypes by increasing familiarity with and knowledge about Islam and Muslim Americans, and thus possibly decreasing support for restrictions.

Cho et al. (2003) and Scheufele, Nisbet, and Ostman (2005) have explored how mass media use may be associated, generally, with threat perceptions after the September 11 attacks, and how these perceptions are more likely to be associated with television media use rather than print media use. Television as a medium provides a more vivid, interactive, stimulating information environment than print, and is therefore more likely to elicit emotional responses from audiences in comparison to print (Cho et al. 2003). This is especially the case for television news coverage of war and terrorism that is live, elicits higher levels of prolonged attention from audience members (Friedlander 1982; Krauthammer 1986), and has strong compelling visuals "including carnage of injury and death, property and environmental wreckage, heightened emotional reactions, and disruption of routine" (Scheufele, Nisbet, and Ostman 2005, 200). Furthermore, Scheufele and his colleagues note that in comparison "print media have limited capacity to depict terrorism visually and no capacity aurally. Print media reports tend to be more static, more expansive, more analytical and logical, more staid, and less immediate than those of broadcast media" (2005, 200).

Beyond differences in form and presentation, Cho et al. (2003) and Scheufele, Nisbet, and Ostman (2005) both note that television and print media tend to have important differences in terms of news framing. "Episodic" framing (event-oriented news reporting that portrays public problems or topics in terms of tangible instances) has been found to be more prevalent in television news than print news and to lead to attributions of individual responsibility for social problems rather than systemic or institutional attributions (Iyengar 1991). Thus, in the case of restrictions on civil liberties, television news that is more episodic may be associated with a tendency to attribute responsibility for actions or threats to specific types of individuals or groups rather than to an overall situation. In addition, previous scholarship has shown that, in times of crisis or war, mass media, particularly television news content and frames, are more likely to generate support for the political regime and expanded government powers, including support for limiting public dissent and other restrictions.[3]

The extent of content analysis and audience surveys regarding the relationship between mass media use, perceptions of threat, and public opinion toward civil liberties since the September 11 attacks is limited. However, findings from Cho et al. (2003), Rosenstiel et al. (2002), and Scheufele, Nisbet, and Ostman (2005) support the general assertions discussed above, especially the differences between television and newspaper content. Cho and his colleagues conducted a content analysis of post–September 11 television and newspaper content and found that the language used in television coverage of the attacks and aftermath was more emotional than newspaper content, especially in terms of "blame" for the attacks. Also, conducting a two-wave survey panel study to examine possible audience responses to these content differences, Cho and his colleagues found that "heavier television news users sustained a higher level of negative emotional reactions to the terrorist attacks than heavier newspaper users" (2003, 322). Rosenstiel et al. (2002) found a similar difference between television and newspaper coverage of the war in Afghanistan, in which print media assertions were 44% more likely to be factual, rather than emotional, compared to television news reporting of the war.

Scheufele and his colleagues (2005) directly examined the association between different forms of mass media use and support for restrictions on civil liberties utilizing a community survey conducted shortly after the September 11 attacks. Their analysis found that television news viewing and time spent watching television were associated with support for expansion of police powers and limits on privacy and information (Scheufele, Nisbet, and Ostman 2005). Conversely, newspaper reading was negatively associated with support for restrictions on civil liberties.

Event-driven news coverage of terrorism or military conflict is not the only manner in which the mass media may influence public opinion toward civil liberties. As Scheufele, Nisbet, and Ostman note, general public opinion toward restricting civil liberties may be "pre-shaped" by previous mass media exposure (2005). For example, previous cultivation research has demonstrated how heavy television exposure is associated with more conservative, authoritarian, and law-and-order attitudes among viewers (Gerbner et al. 1984; Morgan and Shanahan 1991; Shanahan and Morgan 1999). Thus, heavy television viewers may be more apt to support restrictions on civil liberties, especially toward "out groups" in times of crisis or conflict.

Mass Media Portrayals of Islam and Muslim Americans

Beyond general perceptions of threat and fear of a terrorist attack, mass media use may specifically promote political intolerance toward small minority groups (e.g., Muslim Americans) with whom most of the population has little or no first-hand contact. The "television world" is the primary reference point regarding perceptions and beliefs about the group rather than "real world" experience (Gross 1984). In this way news and entertainment media portrayals of Islam and Muslim Americans also may "pre-shape" individual perceptions that increase the likelihood of supporting restrictions on Muslim Americans by promoting negative and threatening stereotypes, symbols, and images of Muslims and Islam. Such a symbolic information environment sets boundaries for political and social discourse and provides a political and cultural schema through which events and news may be interpreted (Shanahan and Jones 1999).

Shaheen (1984; 1997; 2000; 2001) has done extensive research and content analysis on how the American entertainment media has portrayed Arabs, Muslims, and Islam over time. Examining Arab and Muslim characters on television, Shaheen has found that the common qualities that form a standard "tool kit" for entertainment portrayals of Arabs and Muslims include untrustworthiness, a propensity to commit violence and bloodthirstiness, and generalized "dark" and "swarthy" physical traits (Shaheen 1984). Furthermore, reviewing recent television programs and motion pictures from the 1990s, Shaheen found that they "effectively show all Arabs, Muslims, and Arab-Americans as being at war with the United States" (2000, 31). Palestinians, who are often conflated with all Muslims and Arabs, are especially targeted by Hollywood movies and are "characterized by Hollywood as religious fanatics, threatening our freedom, economy, and culture. Producers portray the Palestinian as a demonic creature without compassion for men, women, or children" (Shaheen 2000, 27).

After September 11, Diels (2006) conducted a content analysis of entertainment television's portrayals of Muslims and Arabs since 2001. She found that during the last five years, across both broadcast and cable channels, a "vast majority" of Muslim and Arab characters on American entertainment television "were connected in some way to violence" and featured primarily in plots involving torture or terrorism (Diels 2006, 68).

Said (1997) argues that these stereotypes and clichés found in entertainment media also are representative of a general negative "orientalist" schema employed by journalists when covering Islam and the Middle East. Mortimer echoes this view, writing that this journalistic orientalism promotes the view that Muslims "are inscrutable, irrational savages whose behavior is governed by an arcane but primitive moral code, and who are incapable of feeling normal human emotions" (1981, 495). Mortimer argues that this schema often provides ideological and psychological justification for violence toward and repression of Muslims.

Bajwa (2003), Mousa (1984), and Sheikh, Price, and Oshagan (1995) all conducted content analyses of news media coverage of Arabs, Muslims, and Islam that reaffirmed several stereotypes discussed above. Mousa examined newspaper coverage of Arabs in the *New York Times* from 1917 to 1947 in order to explore how early media coverage may have formed the basis for common journalistic stereotypes and portrayals in contemporary media coverage. His findings demonstrated that most news coverage during the period, especially in later years, was conflict-oriented and episodic, and conflated Palestinians with all Arabs and Muslims.

Sheikh, Price, and Oshagan (1995) conducted a content analysis of newspaper coverage from three newspapers (*Los Angeles Times, New York Times, Detroit Free Press*) from 1988 to 1992. They determined that most news stories involving or mentioning Muslims or Islam primarily focused on foreign affairs rather than domestic matters, focused on crisis events and military conflict, and used the terms "Muslim" or "Islam" "in such a way that it gave the impression that the story referred to all Muslims, when actually referring only to a certain group of Muslims" (Sheikh, Price, and Oshagan 1995, 142). Though the authors did not find a strong negative bias against Islam or Muslims in the news reporting, the significant frequency of such negative terms as "fundamentalist," "militant," "fanatic," and "terrorist" embedded in much of the news content did offer modest support for the conclusion that a majority of news stories portraying Muslims were negative in tone.

Bajwa (2003) replicated Sheikh, Price, and Oshagan's study and examined news coverage of Muslims from 1992 to 2000 across the same three newspapers with similar findings. Most news stories involving Muslims had a foreign, rather than domestic, context. Crises and military conflict dominated the news coverage, and most Muslims were represented collectively rather than as individuals or members of subgroupings. Regarding tone, half the news stories examined by Bajwa were explicitly negative compared to only 24 percent explicitly positive, with the remainder neutral in tone. The most frequent terms used in the news stories examined by Bajwa to describe Muslims were "militants," "terrorists," and "fundamentalists."

Scholarship examining news portrayals of Muslim Americans after September 11 is limited. Weston (2003) and Nacos and Torres-Reyna (2003) both examined newspaper coverage of Muslim and Arab Americans immediately before and after the September 11 attacks. Weston found that pre-attack newspaper stories primarily featured Muslim Americans as struggling against discrimination and stereotypes, while Nacos and Torres-Reyna (2003) observed in their analysis that most pre-attack news stories mentioned Muslim and Arab Americans in terms of domestic politics and campaign finance. However, in the months immediately following September 11, both studies found newspaper coverage of Muslim and Arab Americans substantially differed. Newspaper news attempted to debunk stereotypes, discussed the protection of Muslim-American civil liberties, and projected an overall positive image of Muslims and Arabs in the United States.

Ibrahim (2003) found a similar trend in her analysis of network TV news from the fourteen days following the attacks. According to her study, Muslims within the United States were primarily portrayed as loyal to the United States, inherently peaceful, and the unfortunate victims of hate crimes and discrimination. However, she did note that Muslims living outside the United States were portrayed quite differently by network news during the same time period. They were typically featured as inherently violent, disloyal to the United States, and strongly associated with suicide attacks, jihads, and past global crises.

These findings mirror the trend discussed above of strong, but brief, favorability ratings expressed toward Islam and Muslim Americans immediately after the September 11 attacks. However, content analysis of newspaper and television media news coverage of Islam and Muslim Americans beyond the immediate period following September 11 is not yet available. Therefore, we do not know how media coverage has evolved since the wars in Afghanistan and Iraq, the bombings in Europe, and the continued U.S. War on Terror. Media coverage, like public opinion trends, has likely varied considerably depending on world events and levels of threat: it may have become more negative over time. Moreover, we speculate that many common entertainment and news media practices, stereotypes, "tool kits," and symbols present in media content prior to September 11 have only been amplified in the extensive media coverage that Islam and Muslims have received over the past five years.

Religiosity, Ideology, and Public Opinion toward Islam and Muslim-American Civil Liberties

Beyond the information environment, previous research has demonstrated that individual predispositions such as political ideology and religiosity may be associated with support for restrictions on civil liberties and political intolerance toward specific groups.[4] McClosky and Brill (1983), McClosky and Zaller (1984), Stouffer (1955), Sullivan et al. (1981), and Altemeyer (1996), and, most recently, Davis and Silver (2004) in a post–September 11 survey on civil liberties all found negative associations between conservative ideology and/or dogmatism and support for civil liberties and political tolerance. Furthermore, Merskin's (2004) discourse analysis of Bush's national addresses and rhetoric following the September 11 attacks found Bush's speech employed "historical as well as current popular culture portrayals of people of Arab/Middle Eastern descent" coupled with an ideological and religious rhetoric that served to "revivify, reinforce, and ratify the Arab as terrorist stereotype," and strengthened the perception of "all Arabs as terrorists and all Muslims as Arab terrorists" (Merskin 2004, 172).

More recently, in August 2006, Bush stated in a public news conference that the United States was at war with what he termed "Islamic fascists." The steady diet of inflammatory comments from other political leaders concerning extremists and their activities, usually carried by the news and opinion media, also cannot be discounted as probable influences on public opinion concerning Islam and Muslims (Deane and Fears 2006). Thus, we may surmise that conservatives generally will respond favorably to cues from conservative political elites, and thus will be more likely to be unfavorable toward Islam or Muslims, more likely to possibly perceive Islam as a threat, and thus be more supportive of expanded government powers or restrictions on civil liberties in general, and on Muslim Americans specifically.

Polling data supports this deduction. An October 2002 ABC News poll found that conservatives were more likely to have unfavorable opinions of Muslims (Langer 2002). Pew's July 2005 survey also found substantial differences in opinion based on political ideology. A majority (51%) of Republican conservatives had an unfavorable opinion of Islam, a number 25 and 17 percentage points higher than the numbers for both moderate conservative and liberal Democrats, respectively. A full 37% of Republican conservatives expressed an unfavorable opinion toward Muslim Americans specifically, again almost 20 percentage points higher than conservative/ moderate Democrats, liberal Democrats, *and* liberal/moderate Republicans.

Christian religiosity may also play a central role in shaping public opinion toward Muslim Americans' civil liberties. Scholarship has linked religion and general support for restricting civil liberties or political tolerance across three dimensions of religiosity: denomination, church attendance, and doctrinal belief. Early research by Stouffer (1955) noted a connection between religiosity and political intolerance, and found that Jews were the most tolerant followed by Catholics and then Protestants. Nunn, Crocket, and Williams (1978) demonstrated varied level of support for civil liberties across religious denominations, but later work by Sullivan, Piereson, and Marcus (1982) found that when target groups are accounted for in the analysis, gaps in support between denominations close.

However, Beatty and Walter (1984) found significant differences in political tolerance and support for civil liberties between Catholic, mainline Protestant, and conservative Protestant denominations even after controlling for different "out groups." They also found that a second dimension of religiosity, frequency of church attendance, was significantly associated with increased intolerance across *all religious denominations* (Beatty and Walter 1984). Stouffer (1955) and Filsinger (1976) also found a negative relationship between church attendance and support for civil liberties.

Strength of doctrinal belief, in terms of either biblical literalism or evangelical orthodoxy, also has been found to have a negative association with support for civil liberties. Ellison and Musick (1993) and Wilcox and Jelen (1990) found biblical literalism to be negatively associated with political tolerance and support for civil liberties with the explanation that "Biblical literalism encourages the rejection of, and intolerance for, un-Biblical ideas or lifestyles" (Reimer and Park 2001, 736). Perceived religious dissimilarity leads to political intolerance. Wilcox and Jelen (1990) and Karpov (2002) also found that evangelical doctrinal orthodoxy was a strong predictor of intolerance and support for restriction on civil liberties.

A second reason why Christian religiosity may be linked to negative perceptions of Islam/Muslims and public support for restricting Muslim Americans' civil liberties is that some prominent Christian leaders in the U.S. have framed the September 11 attacks, the invasion of and ongoing insurgency in Iraq, and the continuing U.S. War on Terror as a fundamental religious conflict between Christianity and Islam. For example, popular Christian evangelist Franklin Graham described Islam as "a very evil and wicked religion" (ABC News 2002; Waldman and Caldwell 2001). Also, the Reverend Jerry Falwell, a fundamentalist Christian with a large media-churched following, labeled the Prophet Muhammad a "terrorist . . . a violent man" in early October 2002.

These views expressed by religious leaders are consistent with poll results examining perceptions of Islam and Muslims among highly religious respondents. For example, a July 2005 Pew Research Center poll found white evangelical respondents were 38% more likely than white mainstream Protestants, and 62% more likely than secular respondents, to express unfavorable opinions of Islam generally. They were also 79% and 92% more likely than white Protestants and secular respondents, respectively, to believe Islam promotes violence more than other faiths. Evangelical white conservatives are also most prone to endorse a view that it was a "fair comment" for religious leaders to brand Islam as a violent religion (Langer 2002; see also Cohen 2006). In the November 2004 Cornell University poll, a plurality of evangelical Christians (25%) cited a fundamental clash between Western and Islamic values/culture as the primary reason why Muslims were hostile toward the United States. Overall, several different polls have shown that those who professed no religion, those who were not of a Christian faith, or those who were Catholic were more likely to be favorable to Islam than highly religious Christian Protestants (ABC News poll September 2003; Cohen 2006; Morris 2003b; Pew March 2002; Pew September 2004).

Though previous research has shown general links between religiosity and political intolerance, in the case of the continuing conflict between the United States and global terrorism that is often framed in religious terms by both political and religious leaders, we may expect individuals with high levels of religiosity across denominations—measured in terms of church attendance, biblical literalism, and evangelical self-identification—to be more supportive of restricting civil liberties after September 11, especially those of Muslim Americans.

How Media Use and Predispositions Shape Public Opinion

Theoretically, public opinion has been commonly conceived as a "marriage" between the information environment and individual predisposition (Lippmann 1922; Zaller 1992). Thus, the accessibility or "memory-based" model of opinion formation (Hastie and Park 1986; Iyengar 1990; Moy et al. 2001; Scheufele 2000; Zaller 1992) is a useful theoretical model for explaining how the information environment and predispositions discussed above may influence judgments and evaluations regarding Islam, Muslims, and the restriction of Muslim Americans' civil liberties. Within the "memory-based" model of opinion formation, individuals form judgments and evaluations based upon the overall valence of available and accessible considerations. Thus, individuals will form opinions based upon the range of messages and cues available to them within the information environment (e.g., mass media).

The scholarship reviewed above suggests that the mass media may shape the information environment in several important ways. Both television news and entertainment television may increase fears regarding the likelihood of and danger from terrorist attack, increasing perceptions of threat. Television use, especially entertainment TV, may also generally strengthen authoritarian predispositions and specifically promote negative stereotypes and perceptions of Islam and Muslims. Christian religious media may broadcast cues and messages from prominent Christian leaders that reinforce perceived differences between Islam and Christianity and negative attitudes toward Muslims. Taken together, these information cues may have a strong impact on shaping negative public opinion toward Islam and Muslims and their civil liberties.

On a positive note, the research discussed above also suggests that newspaper use may be associated with less stereotyping of Muslim Americans and increased knowledge and familiarity with Islam. In turn, knowledge of Islam is important, as public opinion polling has suggested that American familiarity with the basic tenets of Islam leads to favorable evaluations of the religion (ABC News poll September 2003; Cohen 2006; Morris 2003b; Waldman and Caldwell 2001). For example, an ABC News analysis asserts that widespread lack of familiarity with Islam affects opinions toward the religion negatively while familiarity with Islam is associated with favorable opinions, a belief that Islam respects other faiths, and that Islam is essentially a peaceful religion (Langer 2002). Thus, newspaper use may provide positive information cues that mediate, or at least ameliorate, negative considerations from other information sources.

Previous research has also portrayed individuals as cognitive misers, using predispositions such as ideology as mental shortcuts or heuristics to process new information, form opinions, and reach decisions (Downs 1957; Popkin 1991). Thus, individuals may use ideology or religiosity as cognitive shortcuts to determine their views and make judgments about an issue, especially in situations where the majority of the public has a low level of knowledge or familiarity about the topic at hand (as Tables 9.1 and 9.2 suggest is the case for Islam).

Furthermore, in the case of strongly held value or ideological orientations, predispositions direct selective exposure or attention toward messages in the media that are consistent with those predispositions. In turn, messages that are consistent with an individual's predisposition or value schema are accepted, while those that are inconsistent are resisted (Zaller 1992). Thus, again employing the "memory-based" model of opinion formation, we can understand how this synthesis between mass media use and individual predispositions can influence an individual's opinions by making certain messages more salient, and therefore more accessible, than others when an individual is asked to make an evaluation or judgment.

Building Models of Opinion Formation toward Islam and Muslim Americans

Based upon the scholarship reviewed thus far, we may hypothesize that value/ideological orientations, such as Christian religiosity and political ideology, and media use, such as television and newspaper news use, may directly or indirectly impact perceptions of threat and the information environment, which in turn may influence public opinion toward Islam/Muslims and public support for restrictions on Muslim-American civil liberties.

Our first hypotheses focus on how media use may impact two key components of the information environment, fear of terrorist attack and knowledge about Islam, as these two constructs may strongly influence perceptions of Islam and Muslims and support for restrictions on civil liberties. We hypothesize that television news will increase public fears about possible terrorist attacks. Also, based on previous research regarding the effects of entertainment television and "mean world syndrome" (Shanahan and Morgan 1999), we hypothesize that entertainment television will also increase fears regarding terrorism. In turn, we hypothesize that newspaper news use will increase factual knowledge about Islam. Formally, we state:

H1a: Television news use and entertainment television will be associated with a higher fear of terrorist attack

H1b: Newspaper news use will be associated with increased knowledge about Islam.

Strongly held predispositions may impact perceptions and knowledge by acting as a "perceptual screen" accepting only those considerations featured in the media that are congenial to their preconceived attitudes (Goidel, Shields, and Peffley 1997; Nisbet 2005; Nisbet et al. 2004). Thus, for value/ideological orientations, we pose a research question (R1), asking: What are the associations between Christian religiosity and political orientations with fear of terrorism and knowledge about Islam?

In addition to fear of terrorism and knowledge, we also wish to explore the associations between value/ideological orientations, media use, fear/knowledge, and public opinion and perceptions of Islam and Muslims generally. Therefore we pose a general research question (R2) asking how these three sets of influences are associated with three key dimensions of public opinion toward Islam/Muslims: negative perceptions or stereotypes of Islam, perceived general threat from Islam, and the perceived degree of dissimilarity between Islam's values and beliefs and Christian or Western values and beliefs.

The last set of hypotheses and research questions focuses on predictors of public support for restrictions on Muslim Americans. Regarding the role of value and ideological orientations, based on the discussion above we hypothesize:

H2: Christian religiosity and conservative political orientations will be associated with increased support for restrictions on Muslim Americans.

As Scheufele, Nisbet, and Ostman (2005) previously found, media use may also impact support for restrictions on civil liberties, with TV use (both news and entertainment) increasing support for restrictions while newspaper use decreased support. Therefore, we hypothesize:

H3a: Television news use and entertainment television will be associated with increased support for restrictions on Muslim Americans.

H3b: Newspaper use will be associated with decreased support for restrictions on Muslim Americans.

The information environment, such as perceptions of threat (e.g., fear of a terrorist attack), or knowledge may also increase or decrease political tolerance and support for restrictions on civil liberties. Thus, we also hypothesize:

H4a: Fear of a terrorist attack will be associated with increased support for restrictions on Muslim Americans.

H4b: Knowledge about Islam will be associated with decreased support for restrictions on Muslim Americans.

Lastly, general attitudes toward Islam and Muslims, such as negative perceptions or stereotypes, perceptions of a generalized threat from Islam, and perceptions of fundamental difference between Islam and Western values may also impact public support for restrictions on Muslim Americans. Therefore, we hypothesize:

H5: Negative perceptions of Islam, perceptions of Islamic threat, and perceived dissimilarity will be associated with increased support for restrictions on Muslim Americans.

Method

The data analyzed for the study are from a national telephone survey conducted between October 25, 2004, and November 30, 2004, conducted by the Survey Research Institute at Cornell University. The sampling frame included U.S. citizens who were at least eighteen years of age from randomly selected households. Within each household, respondents were randomly selected by asking for the household member with the most recent birthday. A total of 715 interviews were completed. The response rate was 25.7% and the cooperation rate 54.5% according to AAPOR standards.

Our analyses are based on a hierarchical ordinary-least-squares (OLS) regression model. In these models, blocks of variables are entered according to their assumed causal order. In other words, exogenous variables, such as demographics, are entered first followed by other antecedent endogenous variables (Cohen et al. 2003). Three different sets of analyses were conducted to address the hypotheses and research questions. The first analysis examined the effects of sociodemographics, religious/ideological orientations, and media use on fear of terrorist attack and knowledge about Islam. In turn, the second analysis examined the impact of the aforementioned influences, as well as fear and knowledge, on three dimensions of public opinion toward Islam/Muslims: negative perceptions, perceived Islamic threat, and perceived Islamic dissimilarity. Lastly, the third analysis examined the cumulative impact of all these influences on public support for restrictions on Muslim-American civil liberties.

Exogenous Variables

The exogenous variables within the models include a set of four socio-demographic characteristics (age, gender, education, and race). *Age* was measured as a continuous variable with a respondent range of 18 to 95 years of age (M=45, SD=17.1). *Gender* was coded with men coded high (48%). *Education* was measured by total number of completed years of schooling, with a respondent range of 0 to 22 years (M=14.7, SD=3.0). *Race* also was coded as a dichotomous variable between white and non-white respondents, with white coded high (69%).

Religious/Ideological Orientations

The two measures of religious and ideological orientations in the analysis were Christian religiosity and political orientation. *Christian religiosity* was tapped by asking respondents three questions measuring church attendance, an individual's level of Christian doctrinal conservatism (i.e., what degree a person subscribes to a literal interpretation of biblical scripture), and whether the respondent self-identified as an evangelical Christian (Ellison and Musick 1995; Nisbet 2005). Church attendance was measured on a six-point scale ranging from "never" to "more than once a week" (M=3.5, SD=1.7). Biblical interpretation was measured utilizing a three-point scale asking respondents whether they believed the Bible was the actual word of God, that the Bible is the word of God but not everything should be taken literally, or that the Bible was written by men/women and is not the word of God, with a more literal level of interpretation coded high (M=2.1, SD=.74). Christian evangelicalism was a self-reported dichotomous measure

(31.4%). All three measures were standardized and added together to form one overall measure of Christian religiosity (a=.71) (Layman 1997).

Political orientation was also a latent variable constructed by combining three different measures. Ideology was measured by asking respondents two questions. The first asked respondents to self-identify on a seven-point scale, ranging from "very liberal" to "very conservative" on economic issues (M=4.6, SD=1.5). The second asked respondents to self-identify on a seven-point scale, ranging from "very liberal" to "very conservative" on social issues (M=4.2, SD=1.8). On both measures conservative ideology was coded high. Political party affiliation was tapped with a single measure asking respondents to self-identify on a five-point scale as a "strongly Democrat," "leaning toward Democrat," "political independent," "leaning toward Republican," or "strongly Republican" (M=3.0, SD=1.4), with Republican affiliation coded high. All three measures were standardized and added together to form one overall measure of political orientation with conservative orientations coded high (a=.77).

Media Use

The measures of media use included assessments of four types of media: newspaper news use, television news use, entertainment television use, and Christian religious media use. *Newspaper news use* was a combined measure of newspaper exposure (days reading the newspaper), attention to news about the U.S. War on Terror, international affairs, and national politics (a=.89). Likewise, *television news use* was a measure that assessed both exposure and attention to TV news. The single measure combined separate indices of exposure to national broadcast network news, exposure to CNN, exposure to Fox News, attention to TV news about the U.S. War on Terror, attention to news about international affairs, and attention to news about national politics (a=.73). *Entertainment TV use* was measured by tapping the level of exposure (in hours) to TV and combining the measure with reported attention to TV dramas and TV comedies (a=.50). Lastly, *religious media use* assessed the level of exposure to Christian religious TV and Christian radio (r=.51)

Fear and Knowledge

Knowledge about Islam was assessed by two measures asking respondents "what name Muslims use to refer to God" (65.2% correct) and the name of the Islamic equivalent of the Bible (63.5% correct). Both measures were dichotomized and added together to form a three-point knowledge scale ranging from zero to two (M=1.3, SD=.84, r=.56). *Fear of terrorist attack* was tapped by combining two separate measures: (a) perceived likelihood of terrorist attack, measured by asking respondents how much they agreed or disagreed on a ten-point scale ranging from strongly disagree to strongly agree with the statement "a future terrorist attack somewhere in the United States is likely within the next 12 months" (M=5.2,

SD=2.8), and (b) perceived personal danger from a terrorist attack, measured by asking respondents how much they agreed or disagreed on the same ten-point scale with the statement "I am personally in danger of being a victim of a terrorist attack" (M=3.1, SD=2.7). Both were combined into one measure ($r=.28$).

Orientations toward Islam

Three variables assessed three general orientations toward Islam and Muslims: negative perceptions/stereotypes, perceived threat from Islam, and perceived dissimilarity. *Negative perceptions of Islam* measured respondents' general perceptions of Islamic countries and peoples. Respondents were asked how much, on a ten-point scale with one being "very little" and ten "a great deal," the following four traits applied to Islamic countries and peoples: hateful, violent, fanatical, and dangerous. The scores for each were combined into an overall additive index (M=23.5, SD=8.7, a=.86).

The *perceived threat from Islam* measure was created by combining two separate survey questions asking respondents to assess the violent potential of Islam and the level of hostility among Muslims toward the United States. The perception of Islam as promoting violence was assessed by asking respondents whether they agreed or disagreed on a ten-point scale with the statement "[T]he Islamic religion is more likely than others to encourage violence among its believers" (M=5.8, SD=3.3). The degree of perceived hostility toward the U.S. within the Muslim world was assessed by asking respondents to provide their estimation of what percentage of overseas Muslims were hostile to the United States ranging from zero to one hundred percent (M=46.0, SD=30.6). Both were standardized and combined into one measure of overall perceived threat ($r=.30$).

Lastly, the third measure, *Islamic dissimilarity*, assessed the perceived dissimilarity between Islamic values and beliefs and Christian/Western values and beliefs using a single item. Respondents were asked whether they agreed or disagreed on a ten-point scale with the statement "[O]verall, Islamic values and beliefs are very similar to Western/Christian values and beliefs," with the measure reverse-coded in the analysis (M=6.7, SD=2.8).

Public Support for Restrictions on Muslim-American Civil Liberties

Public support for restrictions on Muslim Americans was measured by assessing respondents' agreement on a ten-point scale with four statements regarding possible restrictions on Muslim Americans. Specifically, respondents were asked whether all Muslim Americans should be required to register their whereabouts with the federal government, whether mosques should be closely monitored and/or surveyed by U.S. law enforcement agencies, whether U.S. government agencies should profile citizens as potential threats based on being Muslim or having Middle Eastern heritage, and lastly whether Muslim civic and volunteer organizations should be infiltrated by undercover law enforcement agents to keep watch on their activities and fund-raising. The four measures were combined into an additive index scale ranging from four to forty (M=15.5, SD=10.5, a=.86).

Results

We use OLS hierarchical regression with unstandardized partial coefficients, standard error, and final standardized betas reported for each criterion measure to test the hypotheses. The sequence of the blocks of variables as they are entered into the equation is based on their assumed causal priority. In other words, no independent variable or block of independent variables is presumed to be a "cause" of a variable or block of variables that has been entered earlier (Cohen et al. 2003). The contribution of each subsequent block to the variance accounted for by the equation is measured with the incremental R^2 and the sum of the series of incremental R^2 is referred to as the "cumulative R^2" (Cohen et al. 2003).

Analysis One

The first analysis examines the influence of socio-demographics, Christian religiosity/ideology, and media use on fear of terrorist attack and knowledge about Islam. The results demonstrate the power of the media to impact individual perceptions regarding the risk and danger of terrorism. Television news use and entertainment TV use both significantly increase fear of terrorist attack and are the strongest variables in the model ($\beta = .11$ and $\beta = .10$, respectively) accounting for three-fifths of the explained variance, confirming H1a.

The results of the OLS regression examining predictors of knowledge are more complex. Not surprisingly, education plays the strongest role ($\beta = .26$), though gender (male) also makes a significant impact on knowledge ($\beta = .17$). The socio-demographic blocks also account for much of total explained variance. Furthermore, individuals with higher levels of Christian religiosity and strength of belief *are less likely* to possess the most basic knowledge about Islam ($\beta = -.11$). The association of media use with knowledge varies by media type. Newspaper news use significantly increases basic knowledge about Islam ($\beta = .09$), while those who had higher levels of entertainment news use are less likely to be knowledgeable about Islam ($\beta = -.12$), confirming H1b.

Analysis Two

The primary influence associated with negative perceptions of Islam is conservative political orientations ($\beta = .20$); this accounts for over half of the cumulative explained variance. In addition, survey respondents with a higher fear of terrorist attack are also more likely to have negative perceptions of Islam ($b = .10$) while

Table 9.7. OLS Regression: Fear of Terrorist Attack and Knowledge about Islam

	Fear of Terrorist Attack		Knowledge about Islam	
	B (s.e.)	b	B (s.e.)	b
Block One: Demographics				
Age	.02(.01)	.09*	−.00(.00)	−0.03
Gender (male)	.11(.35)	0.01	.08(.01)	.17***
Education	−.06(.06)	−0.04	.08(.01)	.26***
Race (white)	−.72(.47)	−0.06	−.07(.08)	−0.03
Incremental R²		2.0*		15.0***
Block Two: Value/Ideological Orientations				
Christian religiosity	−.00(.09)	−.00	−.04(.02)	−.11*
Political orientation (conservative)	−.08(.08)	−0.04	.00(.01)	.00
Incremental R²		.01		.09***
Block Three: Media Use				
Newspaper news use	.05(.06)	.04	.02(.01)	.09*
Television news use	.12(.05)	.11*	.01(.01)	.06
Entertainment television use	.21(.09)	.10*	−.05(.02)	−.12**
Religious media use	.11(.13)	.04	.01(.02)	.02
Incremental R²		3.0***		2.4***
% Cumulative R²		5.1***		18.2***

Note: ***p≤.001, **p≤.01, *p≤.05. Reported partial coefficients, standard error, and standardized betas.

more educated respondents are less likely to have such perceptions (β=−.10). Likewise, perceptions of Islam as posing a possible threat are also heavily associated with conservative political orientations (β = .13), but higher educated respondents are less likely to perceive Islam to be threatening (β=−.10).

Christian religiosity and religious media use play the most substantial role in the model predicting perceived dissimilarity between Islam and Christian/Western values. The before-entry beta for Christian religiosity is significant with a magnitude of .14, but once Christian religious media use (β=.14) is entered into the model, Christian religiosity becomes completely mediated. These results imply that Christian religious participation and belief lead to higher levels of immersion in the Christian "public sphere" and Christian media use, and in turn Christian media use drives perceptions of Islamic values being fundamentally different from Christian or Western values.

Analysis Three

The third analysis takes the measures from the two previous sets of models and employs them to predict public support for restricting Muslim-American civil

Table 9.8. OLS Regression: Negative Perceptions, Islamic Threat, Islamic Dissimilarity

	Negative Perceptions of Islam		Perceived Islamic Threat		Islamic Dissimilarity	
	B (s.e.)	b	B (s.e.)	b	B (s.e.)	b
Block One: Demographics						
Age	.02(.03)	.03	.00(.00)	.04	.01(.01)	.03
Gender (male)	.75(.89)	.04	.09(.14)	.03	.17(.24)	.03
Education	−.34(.16)	−.10*	−.06(.03)	−.10*	−.07(.04)	−.07#
Race (white)	−.86(1.17)	−.03	−.26(.18)	−.06	.05(.31)	.01
% Incremental R²	1.8*		2.8**		1.2#	
Block Two: Value/Ideological Orientations						
Christian religiosity	−.12(.23)	−.03	.06(.03)	−.08	.08(.06)	.07
Political orientation (conservative)	.85(.19)	.20***	.09(.03)	.13***	.01(.05)	.01
% Incremental R²	4.1***		3.9**		2.3**	
Block Three: Media Use						
Newspaper news use	−.10(.14)	−.03	.02(.02)	.04	−.01(.04)	−.01
Television news use	.19(.12)	.07	.01(.02)	.014	.03(.03)	.05
Entertainment television use	−.15(.22)	−.03	−.02(.03)	−.032	−.06(.06)	−.05
Religious media use	.12(.31)	.02	.04(.05)	.05	.23(.08)	.14**
% Incremental R²	.6		.3		1.6*	
Block Four: Fear and Knowledge						
Fear of terrorist attack	.25(.10)	.10*	.01(.02)	.02	−.02(.03)	−.03
Knowledge about Islam	.33(.56)	.03	−.12(.09)	−.06	−.00(.15)	.00
% Incremental R²	1.0*		.4		.1	
% Cumulative R²	7.5		7.5		5.2	

Note: ***p ≤ .001, **p ≤ .01, *p ≤ .05, #p ≤ .10. Reported partial coefficients, standard error, and standardized betas.

liberties. Five models are presented as each category of variables is individually entered into the OLS regression in causal order to examine progressive mediation and incremental explained variance.

In regards to socio-demographic influences on support for restrictions on civil liberties, education remains a significant predictor across all five models (ranging from β = −.25 to −.11), though its magnitude is progressively mediated, especially by value/ideological orientations and fear and knowledge variables. Age is a significant influence in models one and two (β = .13 and .09, respectively), but is completely mediated in model three when media use is entered into the regression equation.

Conservative political orientations remain a significant predictor of support for restrictions on Muslim-American civil liberties across four of the models (ranging from β = .20 to β = .12), as well as Christian religiosity to a lesser degree

	Model One		Model Two		Model Three		Model Four		Model Five	
	B (s.e.)	β	B (s.e.)	β	B (s.e.)	β	B (s.e.)	β	B (s.e.)	β
Block One: Demographics										
Age	.08(.03)	.13**	.06(.03)	.09*	.05(.03)	.08	.04(.03)	.06	.03(.02)	.05
Gender (male)	.72(.88)	.03	.59(.86)	.03	1.06(.85)	.05	1.56(.85)	.08	1.31(.79)	.06
Education	-.87(.15)	-.25***	-.74(.14)	-.21***	-.67(.15)	-.19***	-.51(.15)	-.14***	-.37(.14)	-.11*
Race (white)	.09(1.15)	.00	-.57(1.12)	-.02	-.20(1.13)	-.00	-.08(1.11)	.00	.47(1.0)	.02
% Incremental R²	7.7		7.7		7.7		7.7		7.7	
Block Two: Value/Ideological Orientations										
Christian religiosity			.57(.19)	.13***	.58(.22)	.13**	.51(.22)	.12*	.45(.20)	.10*
Political orientation (conservative)			.83(.18)	.20***	.75(.18)	.18***	.78(.18)	.19***	.50(.17)	.12**
% Incremental R²			7.0		7.0		7.0		7.0	
Block Three: Media Use										
Newspaper news use					-.07(.13)	-.02	-.07(.13)	-.02	-.08(.12)	-.03
Television news use					.41(.12)	.16***	.40(.12)	.15***	.36(.11)	.14***
Entertainment television use					.47(.21)	.09*	.30(.21)	.06	.36(.19)	.06#
Religious media use					.06(30)	.01	.04(.30)	.00	-.03(.28)	.00
% Incremental R²					3.4		3.4		3.4	
Block Four: Fear and Knowledge										
Fear of terrorist attack							.33(.10)	.14***	.28(.090)	.11***
Knowledge about Islam							-1.89(.53)	-.15***	-.18(.49)	-.14***
% Incremental R²							3.9		3.9	
Block Five: Orientations toward Islam										
Negative perceptions of Islam									.18(.04)	.18***
Perceived Islamic threat									1.49(.27)	.23***
Islamic dissimilarity									-.08(.14)	-.02
% Incremental R²									10.8	
% Cumulative R²	7.7		14.7		18.1		22.0		32.8	

Note: ***p ≤ .001, **p ≤ .01, *p ≤ .05, #p ≤ .10. Reported partial coefficients, standard error, and standardized betas.

(β = .13 to β = .10). These findings confirm *H2*. Furthermore, political orientation is partially mediated by orientations toward Islam once that block of variables is entered into the analysis.

Television news use is the primary media influence on public support for restrictions and remains unmediated by subsequent variables introduced in models four and five (β = .16 to .14), confirming *H3a*. Newspaper news use does not have any significant association, and thus *H3b* is not supported. Entertainment television news use is also significantly associated with support for restrictions (β = .09), as is consistent with *H3a*, but is completely mediated by fear and knowledge once those are entered into the analysis.

Increased fear of terrorist attack leads to greater support for restrictions on Muslim Americans (β = .14), while increased knowledge about Islam is associated with decreased support for restrictions (b = -.15), confirming *H4a* and *H4b*. These influences remain unmediated in model five.

The last model includes three orientations toward Islam: negative perceptions, perceived threat, and perceived dissimilarity. Negative perceptions (β = .18) and perceived threat (β = .23) are both highly predictive of support for restrictions, partially confirming *H5*. However, the before-entry beta for perceived dissimilarity is significant at β = .07, suggesting that the influence of this variable is completely mediated by the other two in the same block. Orientations toward Islam also account for the largest share of incremental variance (10.8%). Overall, the cumulative variance explained is 32.8% once all the variables are entered and the full model is specified.

Discussion

Limitations

Our study has some limitations that must be mentioned before discussing some of its implications and conclusions. First and foremost, a clear understanding and quantification of mass media content is a key component of any analysis of the influence of mass media use on public opinion or perceptions. We have reviewed research that generally addresses mass media content in times of crisis or that addresses reactions to terrorism and charted previous trends in mass media coverage of Islam and Muslim Americans. However, detailed content analysis of mass media coverage of the continuing U.S. War on Terror, and in particular of how Islam and Muslim Americans have been featured in the media coverage of the conflict (especially television news), are not yet widely available. Additional measures would also add to the analysis. They would include (a) religiosity, such as the amount of guidance religion provides in one's life; (b) direct contact and interaction with Muslims; (c) robust measures of knowledge about Islam, and (d) perceived threat directly from Muslim Americans. Lastly, strong causal conclusions drawn from this analysis should be tempered because the data for this study were collected from a cross-sectional survey and we used correlational analysis.

Media and the Information Environment

This paper reinforces and replicates Scheufel, Nisbet, and Ostman's (2005) observations regarding the important role of mass media in influencing public opinion and attitudes toward civil liberties in times of conflict and crisis. Television news and entertainment significantly heightened fears of terrorist attack, which in turn led to negative perceptions of Islam and support for restriction of civil liberties. Television news was also directly associated with support for restrictions. Christian religious media use widened the perceived gap between Islamic and Christian values and beliefs. Newspaper news use was a strong predictor of basic knowledge about Islam, which in turn mitigated support for restrictions on Muslim Americans as compared to the role of television news. However, overall television media played a much stronger role in our analysis than print media, and demonstrates the powerful, and potentially harmful, role of television in our society as an information source in times of conflict. Furthermore, these findings demonstrate the need for journalists, scholars, and policy makers to consider the powerful role that media content plays during times of international conflict in shaping public attitudes not only toward foreign actors or foreign policy, but domestic policies and actors as well.

The Role of Ideology and Christian Religiosity

Ideology, in terms of political conservatism, strongly influences perceptions of Islam (both stereotypes and violence) and support for restricting Muslim-American civil liberties. It was mostly unmediated by media use, fear, or knowledge. This tendency for political conservative individuals to have very negative perceptions of Islamic peoples and countries, and to perceive Islam as a threat due to its presumed violent nature and assumed antagonism toward the United States, may be a reflection of the discourse and cues stemming from conservative political elites and conservative media.

Christian religiosity also plays a substantial role in three different ways. First, it appears to act as a perceptual screen that mitigates the likelihood of highly religious individuals learning about, or being familiar with, basic facts or knowledge about Islam. Other researchers (Nisbet 2005; Scheufele, Nisbet, and Brossard 2003) have likewise found that religiosity mitigates knowledge gain on scientific and political topics. Second, Christian religiosity appears to direct individuals toward religious media use, which in turn appears to expose individuals to messages and cues that reinforce perceived differences between Christian and Islamic beliefs or values. Lastly, Christian religiosity has a direct influence on public opinion about Muslim Americans, with highly religious Christians significantly more willing to restrict Muslim-American civil liberties than moderately religious or secular individuals.

Religion, Media, and International Conflict

The roles that religiosity and television media play in promoting negative views of Islam and Muslims domestically within the United States are also relevant to U.S. conflicts with states and organizations in Muslim countries. Since 9/11, some policy makers and pundits have criticized the role of "fundamentalist" Islam within the Muslim world in amplifying the ongoing conflict that has become known as the "U.S. War on Terror," including the occupations of Iraq and Afghanistan. Some have also accused television news outlets in the Muslim world of directly fostering anti-American attitudes among Muslim and Arab publics, or of indirectly increasing Islamic religiosity (Cherribi 2006; el-Nawawy and Iskandar 2002; Lynch 2006). This study suggests that the processes engendered by Christian fundamentalism, television news, and religious media that produce anti-Muslim attitudes and reduce tolerance within the United States are quite comparable to the role of parallel institutions overseas.

As we stated at the outset, an opinion climate of mass intolerance toward a targeted group results in broad constraints on their political liberties and freedom, which in turn reduces their political and economic opportunities and further socially marginalizes members of that minority. Our findings show the need for policy makers and scholars to pay attention to how Christian religiosity, ideology, and media are shaping public opinion within the United States in a way that contributes to continuing conflict between the United States and the Muslim world overseas and endangers the Muslim-American community.

Notes

1. See for example, Altemeyer (1996); Marcus et al. (1995); Sullivan et al. (1981); Sullivan, Piereson, and Marcus (1982); and Wilson (1994).

2. See Sullivan et al. (1981); Sullivan, Piereson, and Marcus (1982); Gibson (1989); and Marcus et al. (1995)

3. See, for example, Brody (1994); Iyengar and Simon (1993); Reese and Buckalew (1995); and Scheufele, Nisbet, and Ostman (2005)

4. See, for example, Altemeyer (1996); Beatty and Walter (1984); Karpov (2002); McClosky and Brill (1983); McClosky and Zaller (1984); Reimer and Park (2001); Sniderman et al. (1991); Sullivan and Transue (1999); Sullivan et al. (1981); Stouffer (1955); and Wilcox and Jelen (1990).

References

ABC News Poll. January 24, 2002. "Americans Unfamiliar with Islam, but Most Say It's Not Violent." Available at http://abcnews.go.com/sections/us/DailyNews/poll_Islam020124 .html (accessed December 7, 2006).

ABC News Poll. September 7, 2003. "Critical Views of Islam Grow amid Continued Unfamiliarity." Available at http://abcnews.go.com/images/pdf/931a4Islam.pdf (accessed December 7, 2006).

ABC News and Beliefnet. October 2002. Retrieved from the iPOLL Databank, the Roper Center for Public Opinion Research, University of Connecticut. Available at http://www .ropercenter.uconn.edu/ipoll.html (accessed March 20, 2008).

ABC News/*Washington Post*. October 2001. "ABC News/*Washington Post* Afghanistan Attack Poll #2." ICPSR version. Horsham, Pa.: Taylor Nelson Sofres Intersearch [producer], 2001. Ann Arbor, Mich.: Inter-university Consortium for Political and Social Research [distributor], 2001.

ABC News/*Washington Post*. March 2006. Retrieved from the iPOLL Databank, the Roper Center for Public Opinion Research, University of Connecticut. Available at http://www .ropercenter.uconn.edu/ipoll.html (accessed March 20, 2008).

al-Faruqi, Ismail R. 1987. "Introduction." In *The Islamic Theory of International Relations: New Directions for Islamic Methodology and Thought*, ed. AbdulHamid A. AbuSulayman. Herndon, Va.: International Institute of Islamic Thought.

Altemeyer, Bob. 1996. *The Authoritarian Specter*. Cambridge, Mass.: Harvard University Press.

Bajwa, O. S. 2003. "Media Portrayals of Muslims: A Content Analysis of *The Detroit Free Press, The New York Times*, and *The Los Angeles Times*, 1993–2000." Master's thesis, Cornell University, Ithaca, N.Y.

Beatty, Kathleen M., and Oliver Walter. 1984. "Religious Preference and Practice: Reevaluating Their Impact on Political Tolerance." *Public Opinion Quarterly* 48 (1B): 318–329.

Bittle, Scott, and Jean Johnson. 2006. "Public Opinion: Racial Profiling and Islam at Home." Available at http://www.publicagenda.org/specials/terrorism/terror_pubopinion9.htm (accessed February 22, 2008).

Brody, Richard A. 1994. "Crisis, War, and Public Opinion." In *By Storm: The Media, Public Opinion, and U.S. Foreign Policy in the Gulf War*, ed. W. Lance Bennett and David L. Paletz, 210–231. Chicago: University of Chicago Press.

CBS News. February 2002. Retrieved from the iPOLL Databank, the Roper Center for Public Opinion Research, University of Connecticut. Available at http://www.ropercenter.uconn. edu/ipoll.html (accessed March 20, 2008).

CBS News Poll. February 27, 2006. "President Bush, the Ports, and Iraq." Available at http://www .cbsnews.com/htdocs/pdf/poll_bush_022706.pdf (accessed December 7, 2006).

———. April 12, 2006. "Sinking Perceptions of Islam." Available at http://www.cbsnews.com/ stories/2006/04/12/national/printable1494697.shtml (accessed July 12, 2006).

Cherribi, Sam. 2006. "From Baghdad to Paris: Al-Jazeera and the Veil." *Harvard International Journal of Press/Politics* 11 (2): 121–138.

Cho, Jaeho, Micahel P. Boyle, Heejo Keum, Mark D. Shevy, Douglas M. McLeod, Dhavan V. Shah, and Zhongdang Pan. 2003. "Media, Terrorism, and Emotionality: Emotional Differences in Media Content and Public Reactions to the September 11th Terrorist Attacks." *Journal of Broadcasting & Electronic Media* 47 (3): 309–327.

Cohen, Jacob, Patricia Cohen, Stephen G. West, and Leona S. Aiken. 2003. *Applied Multiple Regression/Correlation Analysis for the Behavioral Sciences*, 3rd ed. Mahwah, N.J.: Lawrence Erlbaum Associates.

Cohen, Jon. March 8, 2006. "Americans Skeptical of Islam and Arabs: 9/11 Hardened Americans' Views of Muslims." ABC News/*Washington Post* Poll. Available at http://abcnews.go.com/ US/story?id=1700599 (accessed December 7, 2006).

Davis, Darren W., and Brian D. Silver. 2004. "Civil Liberties vs. Security: Public Opinion in the Context of the Terrorist Attacks on America." *American Journal of Political Science* 48 (1): 28–46.

Deane, Claudia, and Darryl Fears. March 9, 2006. "Negative Perception of Islam Increasing." *Washington Post*, sec. A1.

Diels, J. 2006. "A Cultural Indicators Approach to Understanding the Impact of Media Images of Arab People on Public Opinion Regarding Civil Liberties." Ph.D. diss., Cornell University, Ithaca, N.Y.

Downs, Anthony. 1957. *An Economic Theory of Democracy*. New York: Harper.

el-Nawawy, Mohammed, and Adel Iskandar. 2002. *Al Jazeera: How the Free Arab News Network Scooped the World and Changed the Middle East*. Boulder, Colo.: Westview Press.

Ellison, Christopher G., and Marc A. Musick. 1993. "Southern Intolerance: A Fundamentalist Effect?" *Social Forces* 72 (2): 379–398.

Filsinger, E. 1976. "Tolerance of Non-Believers: A Cross-Tabular and Log-Linear Analysis of Some Religious Correlates." *Review of Religious Research* 17 (3): 232–240.

Friedlander, R. A. 1982. "Iran: The Hostage Seizure, the Media, and International Law." In *Terrorism: The Media and the Law,* ed. Abraham H. Miller, 51–66. Dobbs Ferry, N.Y.: Transnational Publishers.

Gerbner, George, Larry Gross, Michael Morgan, and Nancy Signorelli. 1984. "The Political Correlates of Television Viewing." *Public Opinion Quarterly* 48 (1B): 283–300.

Gibson, James L. 1989. "The Structure of Attitudinal Tolerance in the United States." *British Journal of Political Science* 19 (4): 562–570.

———. 1992. "The Political Consequences of Intolerance: Cultural Conformity and Political Freedom." *American Political Science Review* 86 (2): 338–356.

Goidel, Robert K., Todd G. Shields, and Mark Peffley. 1997. "Priming Theory and RAS Models: Toward an Integrated Perspective of Media Influence." *American Politics Quarterly* 25 (3): 287–318.

Gross, Larry. 1984. "The Cultivation of Intolerance: Television, Blacks and Gays." In *Cultural Indicators: An International Symposium,* ed. Gabriele Melischek, Karle E. Rosengren, and James Stappers, 345–363. Vienna: Verlag der Osterreichischen Akademie der Wissenschaften.

Haneef, Suzanne. 1993. *What Everyone Should Know about Islam and Muslims,* 11th ed. Des Plaines, Ill.: Library of Islam.

Hastie, Reid, and Bernadette Park. 1986. "The Relationship between Memory and Judgment Depends on Whether the Task Is Memory-Based or On-Line." *Psychological Review* 93 (3): 258–268.

Ibrahim, Dina A. 2003. "Framing of Arabs and Muslims after September 11th: A Close Reading of Network News." Ph.D. diss., University of Texas, Austin.

Iyengar, Shanto. 1990. "The Accessibility Bias in Politics: Television News and Public Opinion." *International Journal of Public Opinion Research* 2 (1): 1–15.

———. 1991. *Is Anyone Responsible? How Television Frames Political Issues.* Chicago: Chicago University Press.

Iyengar, Shanto, and Adam Simon. 1993. "News Coverage of the Gulf Crisis and Public Opinion." *Communication Research* 20 (3): 365–383.

Karpov, Vyacheslav. 2002. "Religiosity and Tolerance in the United States and Poland." *Journal for the Scientific Study of Religion* 41 (2): 267–288.

Krauthammer, Charles. 1986. "Terrorism and the Media: A Discussion." In *Terrorism,* ed. Steven Anzovin, 96–108. New York: H. W. Wilson Co.

Langer, Gary. October 10, 2001(a). "Most Favor Broader Police Authority—but Not Targeted at Arabs or Muslims." ABC News Poll. Available at http://abcnews.go.com/images/PollingUnit/868a2%20Stop-Search.pdf (accessed April 11, 2008).

———. November 28, 2001(b). "Majority Supports Military Tribunals." ABC News Poll. Available at http://abcnews.go.com/sections/us/DailyNews/poll_tribunals011128.html (accessed December 7, 2006).

———. October 25, 2002. "More Americans Doubt Islam's Tenets." ABC News. Available at http://abcnews.go.com/US/story?id=90404&page=1 (accessed April 11, 2008).

Layman, Geoffrey C. 1997. "Religion and Political Behavior in the United States: The Impact of Beliefs, Affiliations, and Commitment from 1980 to 1994." *Public Opinion Quarterly* 61 (2): 288–316.

Lippmann, Walter. 1922. *Public Opinion.* New York: Harcourt, Brace and Co.

Los Angeles Times. August 2002. Retrieved from the iPOLL Databank, the Roper Center for Public Opinion Research, University of Connecticut. Available at http://www.ropercenter.uconn.edu/ipoll.html (accessed March 20, 2008).

Lynch, Marc. 2006. *Voices of the New Arab Public: Iraq, al-Jazeera, and Middle East Politics Today.* New York: Columbia University Press.

Marcus, George E., John L. Sullivan, Elizabeth Theiss-Morse, and S. L. Wood. 1995. *With Malice toward Some: How People Make Civil Liberties Judgments.* New York: Cambridge University Press.

McClosky, Herbert, and Alida Brill. 1983. *Dimensions of Tolerance: What Americans Believe about Civil Liberties.* New York: Russell Sage Foundation.

McClosky, Herbert, and John Zaller. 1984. *The American Ethos: Public Attitudes toward Capitalism and Democracy.* Cambridge, Mass.: Harvard University Press.

Merskin, Debra. 2004. "The Construction of Arabs as Enemies: Post–September 11 Discourse of George W. Bush." *Mass Communication & Society* 7 (2): 157–175.

Mitofsky International and Edison Media Research and U.S. News & World Report. March 2002. Retrieved from the iPOLL Databank, the Roper Center for Public Opinion Research, University of Connecticut. Available at http://www.ropercenter.uconn.edu/ipoll.html (accessed March 20, 2008).

Morgan, Michael, and James Shanahan. 1991. "Television and the Cultivation of Political Attitudes in Argentina." *Journal of Communication* 41 (1): 88–103.

Morris, David. September 11, 2003(a). "Critical Views of Muslim Faith Growing among Americans." ABC News Poll: Unease over Islam. Available at http://abcnews.go.com/sections/us/World/sept11_islampoll_030911.html (accessed July 12, 2006).

———. September 11, 2003(b). "Critical Views of Islam Grow amid Continued Unfamiliarity." ABC News Poll: Views of Islam. Available at http://abcnews.go.com/images/pdf/931a4Islam.pdf (accessed December 7, 2006).

Mortimer, Edward. 1981. "Islam and the Western Journalist." *Middle East Journal* 35 (4): 492–505.

Mousa, Issam S. 1984. *The Arab Image in the US Press.* New York: Peter Lang.

Moy, Patricia, Dietram A. Scheufele, William P. Eveland, and Jack M. McLeod. 2001. "Support for the Death Penalty and Rehabilitation: Question Order or Communication Effect?" *Journal of Applied Social Psychology* 31 (11): 2230–2255.

Nacos, Brigitte L., and Oscar Torres-Reyna. 2003. "Framing Muslim-Americans Before and After 9/11." In *Framing Terrorism: Understanding Terrorist Threats and Mass Media,* ed. P. Norris, M. Just, and M. Kern, 135–159. New York: Routledge.

Nisbet, Erik C., and James Shanahan. 2004. "MSRG Special Report: Restrictions on Civil Liberties, Views of Islam, and Muslim Americans." Ithaca, N.Y.: Media and Society Research Group at Cornell University. Available at http://www.comm.cornell.edu/msrg/report1a.pdf (accessed December 7, 2006).

Nisbet, Erik C., Matthew C. Nisbet, Dietram A. Scheufele, and James E. Shanahan. 2004. "Public Diplomacy, Television News, and Muslim Opinion." *Harvard International Journal of Press/Politics* 9 (2): 11–37.

Nisbet, Matthew C. 2005. "The Competition for Worldviews: Values, Information, and Public Support for Stem Cell Research." *International Journal of Public Opinion Research* 17 (1): 90–112.

Nunn, Clyde Z, Harry J. Crockett, and J. Allen Williams. 1978. *Tolerance for Nonconformity.* San Francisco: Jossey-Bass.

Pew Forum on Religion and Public Life. July 24, 2003. "Growing Number of Americans Say Islam Encourages Violence among Followers: Religious Divides on Gay Marriage, Israeli-Palestinian Conflict." Pew Research Center, Washington D.C. Available at http://pewforum.org/press/index.php?ReleaseID=20 (accessed December 7, 2006).

———. July 26, 2005. "Views of Muslim-Americans Hold Steady after London Bombings: Fewer Say Islam Encourages Violence." Pew Research Center, Washington, D.C. Available at http://pewforum.org/docs/index.php?DocID=89 (accessed December 7, 2006).

Pew Research Center for the People and the Press. September 20, 2000. "Religion and Politics: The Ambivalent Majority." Pew Research Center, Washington, D.C. Available at http://people-press.org/reports/display.php3?ReportID=32 (accessed December 7, 2006).

———. April 10, 2001. "Faith-Based Funding Backed, but Church-State Doubts Abound." Pew Research Center, Washington, D.C. Available at http://people-press.org/reports/display.php3?ReportID=15 (accessed December 7, 2006).

———. December 6, 2001. "Post September 11 Attitudes: Religion More Prominent; Muslim-Americans More Accepted." Pew Research Center, Washington, D.C. Available at http://people-press.org/reports/display.php3?ReportID=144 (accessed December 7, 2006).

———. March 20, 2002. "Americans Struggle with Religion's Role at Home and Abroad." Pew Research Center, Washington D.C. Available at http://people-press.org/reports/print.php3?ReportID=150 (accessed December 7, 2006).

———. September 9, 2004. "Views of Islam Remain Sharply Divided: Plurality Sees Islam as More Likely to Encourage Violence." Pew Research Center, Washington, D.C. Available at http://people-press.org/commentary/display.php3?AnalysisID=96 (accessed December 7, 2006).

———. June 22, 2006. "The Great Divide: How Westerners and Muslims View Each Other." Pew Research Center, Washington, D.C. Available at http://pewglobal.org/reports/display.php?ReportID=253 (accessed March 20, 2008).

PollingReport.com. "Religion." Available at http://www.pollingreport.com/religion.htm (accessed December 7, 2006).

Popkin, Samuel. 1991. *The Reasoning Voter: Communication and Persuasion in Presidential Campaigns.* Chicago: University of Chicago Press.

Public Agenda Foundation. January 9, 2001. "It's Wrong to Base Voting on Religion, Say Most Americans." Available at http://www.publicagenda.org/press/press_release_detail.cfm?report_title=For%20Goodness<#213>%20Sake (accessed December 7, 2006).

Reese, Stephen D., and Bob Buckalew. 1995. "The Militarism of Local Television: The Routine Framing of the Persian Gulf War." *Critical Studies in Mass Communication* 12 (1): 40–59.

Reimer, Sam, and Jerry Z. Park. 2001. "Tolerant (In)civility? A Longitudinal Analysis of White Conservative Protestants' Willingness to Grant Civil Liberties." *Journal for the Scientific Study of Religion* 40 (4): 735–745.

Rosenstiel, Tom, Amy Mitchell, Chris Galdieri, Atiba Pertilla, Tom Avila, Wally Dean, Dante Chinni, Nancy Anderson, and Lee Ann Brady. January 28, 2002. "Return to Normalcy? How the Media Have Covered the War on Terrorism." Available at http://www.journalism.org/files/normalcy.pdf (accessed December 7, 2006).

Saad, Lydia. August 10, 2006. "Anti-Muslim Sentiments Fairly Commonplace: Four in Ten Americans Admit Feeling Prejudice against Muslims." Gallup News Service. Available at http://www.gallup.com/poll/24073/AntiMuslim-Sentiments-Fairly-Commonplace.aspx (accessed February 23, 2008).

Said, Edward W. 1997. *Covering Islam: How the Media and Experts Determine How We See the Rest of the World,* New York: Vintage Books. First published 1981 by Pantheon Books.

Scheufele, Dietram A. 2000. "Agenda-Setting, Priming, and Framing Revisited: Another Look at Cognitive Effects of Political Communication." *Mass Communication and Society* 3 (2/3): 297–316.

Scheufele, Dietram A., Matthew C. Nisbet, and Dominique Brossard. 2003. "Pathways to Participation? Religion, Communication Contexts, and Mass Media." *International Journal of Public Opinion Research* 15 (3): 300–324.

Scheufele, Dietram A., Matthew C. Nisbet, and Ronald E. Ostman. 2005. "September 11th News Coverage, Public Opinion, and Support for Civil Liberties." *Mass Communication & Society* 8 (3): 197–218.

Shanahan, James, and Victoria Jones. 1999. *Mass Media, Social Control, and Social Change: A Macrosocial Perspective.* Ames: Iowa State University Press.

Shanahan, James, and Michael Morgan. 1999. *Television and Its Viewers: Cultivation Theory and Research.* New York: Cambridge University Press.

Shaheen, Jack G. 1984. *The TV Arab*. Bowling Green, Ohio: Bowling Green State University Popular Press.

———. 1997. *Arab and Muslim Stereotyping in American Popular Culture*. Washington, D.C.: Center for Muslim-Christian Understanding, Georgetown University.

———. 2000. "Hollywood's Muslim Arabs." *The Muslim World* 90 (1/2): 22–42.

———. 2001. *Reel Bad Arabs: How Hollywood Vilifies a People*. New York: Olive Branch Press.

Sheikh, Kashif Z., Vincent Price, and Hayg Oshagan. 1995. "Press Treatment of Islam: What Kind of Picture Do the Media Paint?" *Gazette* 56 (2): 139–154.

Sniderman, Paul M., Joseph F. Fletcher, Peter H. Russell, Phillip E. Tetlock, and Brian J. Gaines. 1991. "The Fallacy of Democratic Elitism: Elite Competition and Commitment to Civil Liberties." *British Journal of Political Science* 21 (3): 349–370.

Stouffer, Samuel A. 1955. *Communism, Conformity, and Civil Liberties: A Cross Section of the Nation Speaks Its Mind*. Garden City, N.Y.: Doubleday.

Sullivan, John L., George E. Marcus, Stanley Feldman, and James E. Pierson. 1981. "The Sources of Political Tolerance: A Multivariate Analysis." *American Political Science Review* 75 (1): 92–106.

Sullivan, John L., James Pierson, and George E. Marcus. 1982. *Political Tolerance and American Democracy*. Chicago: University of Chicago Press.

Sullivan, John L., and J. E. Transue. 1999. "The Psychological Underpinnings of Democracy: A Selective Review of Research on Political Tolerance, Interpersonal Trust, and Social Capital." *Annual Review of Psychology* 50 (1): 625–650.

Waldman, Steven, and Deborah Caldwell. 2001. "Americans' Surprising Take on Islam: A New Poll Shows That Americans Have Not Turned Anti-Islam." ABC News/Beliefnet Poll. Available at http://www.beliefnet.com/story/97/story_9732_1.html (accessed December 7, 2006).

Weston, Mary A. 2003. "Post 9/11 Arab American Coverage Avoids Stereotypes." *Newspaper Research Journal* 24 (1): 92–113.

Wilcox, Clyde, and Ted G. Jelen. 1990. "Evangelicals and Political Tolerance." *American Politics Quarterly* 18 (1): 25–46.

Wilson, T. C. 1994. "Trends in Tolerance toward Rightist and Leftist Groups, 1976–1988." *Public Opinion Quarterly* 58 (4): 539–556.

Zaller, John. 1992. *The Nature and Origins of Mass Opinion*. New York: Cambridge University Press.

10

The Racialization of Muslim Americans

Amaney Jamal

The state of civil liberties has deteriorated noticeably for all Americans since 9/11. In particular, new legislation passed immediately after 9/11 undermined Muslim and Arab Americans' confidence in their own rights and security. The Patriot Acts 1 and 2 grant the government significant powers to monitor Americans, even allowing the indefinite detention of "non-citizens," and these new powers have been selectively applied—most noticeably to Muslims. In the interests of national security, non-immigrant residents are now required to register under the newly implemented NSEER system (National Security Entry and Exit Registry), and non-compliance constitutes a violation punishable by deportation. Although NSEER initially targeted people from countries of origin in the Muslim world, these provisions have now expanded to include most visitors from around the globe. Yet, in the weeks and months immediately following 9/11 these policies singled out Muslims and created a wave of fear and anxiety among visitors and immigrants from Muslim-majority countries. U.S. government agents have made thousands of "special interest" arrests, and thousands of people who feared arrest because of visa irregularities sought asylum in Canada (Murray 2004). Despite the anti-terrorist rhetoric of this legislation, however, none of those imprisoned were ever directly linked to the September 2001 attacks (see chapter 13, this volume). The vast majority of individuals arrested were eventually cleared of the crimes attributed to them, but many lost months and years of their lives behind bars.

Although the stipulations in the Patriot Acts and other Department of Justice decrees ostensibly apply to all Americans, they effectively single out Arab and Muslim Americans. As Louise Cainkar (2003) comments, "[Attorney General John] Ashcroft has already removed more Arabs and Muslims (who were neither terrorists nor criminals) from the U.S. in the past year than the total number of foreign nationals deported in the infamous Palmer raids of 1919." Expanded secret evidence procedures are used to keep Muslims under arrest, and other provisions for the intelligence community resulted in FBI interrogations at Muslim and Arab community and religious centers across the United States.

A wave of anti-Muslim popular backlash followed post-9/11 government scrutiny. For instance, passengers refused to board airplanes with apparently Muslim individuals on board and many mosques were burned and vandalized. In 2003, the Council on American-Islamic Relations (CAIR) reported that hate crimes against Muslim Americans were up by at least 300% from 2001. By 2005, hate crimes against Muslim Americans had increased by another 50% from 2004 levels. Along these lines, Cainkar reports that "the violence, discrimination, defamation and intolerance now faced by Arabs [and Muslims] in American society have reached a level unparalleled in their 100-year history in the U.S." Recent "anti-terrorism" legislation has caused high levels of fear and anxiety in the Muslim and Arab American communities. My analysis of data collected in a 2001 Zogby poll reveals that 66 percent of all Muslim Americans worry about their future in this country, and 81 percent feel that their community is being profiled.

Exacerbating the sense of Muslim-American vulnerability is mainstream American public opinion. More than 96,000 calls to the FBI were made about "suspicious" Arab and Muslims in the U.S. in the week following the 9/11 attacks alone (Murray 2004, 33). In the immediate days after the attacks, the majority of Americans, according to Gallup polls, were in favor of profiling Muslims.

Figure 10.1 summarizes some findings from the Detroit Arab American Study (DAAS) conducted in 2003 (see below for more details on the study). The study finds that comparable numbers of Arab Americans (56%) and members of the general mainstream population (52%) were willing to support increased surveillance of U.S. citizens in order to ensure security at home. Granting the police more powers to stop and search anyone at random received support from 27% of Arab Americans and 31% of the general population. When asked a general question about giving up some civil liberties to curb terrorism, 55% of the general population and 47% of Arab Americans expressed support. The general population however, is much more likely to support civil rights infringements that

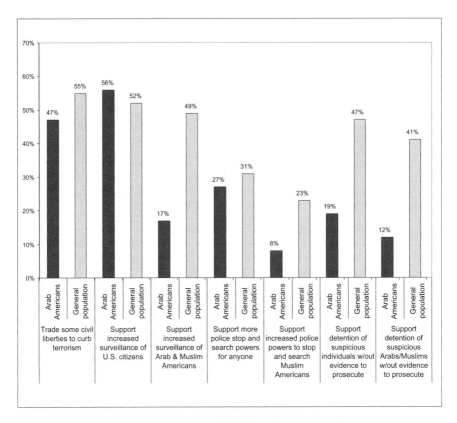

FIGURE 10.1. Restrictions on Civil Liberties to Ensure Security

specifically target Arabs and Muslims. The DAAS found that 49% of the general population would support increasing surveillance of Muslim and Arab Americans, while only 17% of Arab Americans agreed. A full 41% of the general population would uphold the detention of suspicious Arabs and Muslims even without sufficient evidence to prosecute, as compared to only 12% of Arab Americans. Finally, 23% of the general population would support increased police powers to stop and search Muslim and Arab Americans, while only 8% of Arab Americans supported this infringement on their rights. The Detroit findings are in accord with nationwide polls about attitudes toward Muslims, the purported relation between Islam and violence, and toward Muslim Americans (see chapter 9). This backlash granted the U.S. government extended authority and a groundswell of popular support to further promote policies that clash with basic American freedoms and rights.

Why is there so much support for policies so apparently anathematic to basic American values? Several hypotheses can plausibly explain support for taking away the civil rights and liberties of Muslim and Arab Americans. They range from a general sense of vulnerability to more specific anti-Muslim attitudes and predispositions. While the former can be explained away as general fear and worry in the aftermath of the attacks, the latter, I argue, is far more troubling. For if the American population is willing to support infringements on civil liberties by reason of misperceptions that characterize Arabs and Muslims as "Enemy Others," then we must also address the larger phenomenon of the racialization or "otherization" of Arabs and Muslims in mainstream American culture. This racialization process essentially sees Muslims and Arabs as different than and inferior to whites, potentially violent and threatening, and therefore deserving of policies that target them as a distinct group of people and criminalize them without evidence of criminal activity. The binary logic of "us" versus "them," based on a constructed myth of racial difference, permeates U.S. society and provides the lenses through which group differences are organized, imagined, and understood. In the case of the denial of Muslim- and Arab-American civil liberties, unequal access to civil liberties is justified through a racial logic that, while not based on an association between phenotype and backwardness, still follows various historical patterns of racism in the U.S. In addition to the traditional stereotypes, Arab and Muslim minorities are also seen as violent, potentially threatening, and deserving of discrimination.

The single most durable explanation of widespread support for civil liberties infringement, I argue, rests on the racialization of Muslim and Arab Americans as "Enemy Others." I use the term "racialization" to describe the perception and production of an inherent threatening difference between "us" and "them" that provides a scaffold legitimating and supporting the violation of the minority's civil liberties. Although racialization has its roots in domestic politics, the findings of this paper demonstrate that geopolitical realities also shape the ways average Americans construct images of the Arab and Muslim Other in their midst. Both domestic politics and existing geopolitical realities combine to justify the domestic subordination of less tolerated populations, especially when the homelands of those populations are sites of U.S. military campaigns.

The Civil Liberties Debate and Arab and Muslim Americans

The civil liberties debate has raised vital and existential questions. The American public's willingness to give up civil liberties may derive from an intense feeling of individual and collective vulnerability, ideology, religiosity, racism, or media exposure. For Muslim and Arab Americans, however, the debate on civil liberties after 9/11 is of more instrumental and immediate concern. If legislation that singles out Muslim Americans continues to be passed with widespread acceptance, then there may be no end in sight for discrimination. Therefore, it is crucial to understand the sources of support for such infringements on civil rights and liberties.

One set of explanations for support on infringements on civil liberties draws from party identification as "Democrat" or "Republican," and ideological commitment as "liberal" or "conservative." It has been argued that liberal ideologues tend to hold civil liberties to be inalienable rights for all. Conservative ideologues, on the other hand, tend to view civil liberties as rescindable because of the value placed on "security," respect for authority, obedience, and the law (McClosky and Brill 1983; McClosky 1964).

Perceptions of threat are another crucial factor explaining support for civil liberties infringements. A wealth of literature demonstrates that those individuals who feel most personally threatened are most likely to protect themselves. As Davis indicates, the response to such perceived threats may become "overwhelmingly intolerant" (Davis 1995; Davis and Silver 2004). Further, others find that those who perceive future threat are more likely to support even extreme anti-terrorism policies domestically (Huddy et al. 2005; Herrmann et al. 1999; Jentleson 1992). This sense of threat not only leads to an increased toleration for civil liberties violations, it also increases prejudice against the suspected group (Bettencourt et al. 2001; LeVine and Campbell 1972; Struch and Schwartz 1989). Anxiety and threat are powerful tools in the way the "War on Terror" is fought.

An alternative explanation focuses on racial motivations. According to this logic, Americans in favor of infringing on Muslim and Arab Americans' civil liberties do so because they hold negative views about an entire "people." These negative views are fed by a variety of misperceptions and stereotypes. The Muslim and Arab American has been popularly constructed as an irrational, terror-supporting, and fanatical "Enemy Other" since long before 9/11. American foreign policy has consistently justified intervention in the Muslim world along similar lines. When United States leaders characterize the Arab and Muslim world as inherently undemocratic due to fundamental value differences between "us" and "them," they promote an environment of intolerance at home. Thus, the racialization of Arab and Muslim Americans, a process decades in the making, also explains the overwhelming support for the infringement of Arab and Muslim civil liberties (Moallem 2005).

This paper moves beyond the narrow phenotypical definition of racialization, wherein race relations are strictly structured by biological differences. Rather, this paper adopts a larger definition of racialization that incorporates the process of "othering." This process of othering is based on assumptions about culture and religion instead of phenotype. The racialization of Arabs and Muslims stems from two intertwined processes.

First, in a society that is already constructed along racial lines, any perceived difference between the dominant mainstream and a minority Other tends to conform to the racist framework. This othering process lends itself to the *already existing* paradigm of defining oneself vis-à-vis other groups along the lines of racial categories. This form of racism is not contingent only on differences in appearance but also on differences in cultural attributes. More problematic for Arabs and Muslims is that these differences are exacerbated by popular and government discourses that deem them an Enemy Other, especially after 9/11.

The loyalties of the Arab and Muslim communities have consistently been questioned since the attacks. Only 38% of Americans in the Detroit metro area believe that Arabs and Muslims are doing all that they can to fight the War on Terror. Muslims and Arabs across the U.S. are consistently asked to apologize for 9/11, as if they were behind the attacks. And yet, ironically, the numerous and countless condemnations emanating from mosques and organizations in the U.S. that emphatically denounce the attacks have received little media attention. Americans remain suspicious of Arabs and Muslims. When asked whether Arabs and Muslims could be trusted, Americans in the Detroit metro area ranked them as the least trustworthy subpopulation. Specifically, 20% of Americans have little or no trust for whites; 24% have little or no trust for blacks, and 30% have little or no trust for Muslims and Arabs. Not only are Arabs and Muslims different, they are also perceived as a threat treated with great suspicion because they are assumed to originate from the Middle East. They are presumed to be operating "against us."

The binary construction of "us" versus "them" is not new to American social relations in the U.S. or abroad. Racial relations in the U.S. have been constructed through the binary lens of the dominant and the subordinate, a legacy of the history of race relations in this country. Likewise, the lens through which America sees the rest of the world is tinted with this dichotomy: "we," whoever and wherever "we" are, enjoy both cultural and moral superiority. Such interactions with Others abroad translate into a racial logic in a U.S. context that views group differences through racial lenses at home. The process of othering, be it based on phenotype or cultural difference, therefore lends itself to racialization, particularly when it involves the attribution of essentializing characteristics to the *entire* group. The racialization of Arabs and Muslims, however, draws on yet another element of difference. Not only are they different at home, but their difference is exacerbated by geopolitical realities wherein the U.S. has utilized the construction of the Other as enemy-terrorist to justify its campaigns abroad.

The second process of racialization involves the direct subordination of the minority Other. The very process of rendering the Other inferior to white Americans, or some imagined group of acceptable Americans, is at the heart of racialization. In the case of Muslim and Arab Americans, the way that Otherness is determined is through a process by which the dominant social group claims moral and cultural superiority in the process of producing an essentialized, homogeneous image of Muslim and Arab Americans as non-whites who are naturally, morally, and culturally inferior to whites. Terrorism, according to this logic, is not the modus operandi of a few radical individuals, but a by-product of a larger cultural and civilizational heritage: the Islamic Other.

In Omi and Winant's words, racialization is "a matter of both social structure and cultural representation" (1994, 56). Cultural representations of Muslims and Arabs derive from an American media regime that has vilified this population for decades, and from a social structure that adopts and resorts to the rhetoric of moral superiority to justify its intervention in the Middle East and discrimination against Arab and Muslim Americans.[1] Racialization is not static but is produced, reproduced, and solidified in a variety of forums: family networks, religious institutions, government offices, and even schools (Coates 2004). Since "immigrant America" is a conglomeration of these "subordinate" minority groups, these perceptions of Other manifest themselves in the daily interactions that govern the incorporation of minority groups into the mainstream. In this regard, the incorporation of minority groups is not only about the acquisition of necessary language tools and specific technical labor skills; it is also about confronting one's place in the context of U.S. racial hierarchies.

The racialization of Arabs and Muslims has involved a process of juxtaposing the Other with and separating the Other from dominant mainstream culture. This process did not begin with 9/11, though those events galvanized it. Susan Akram discovers this process in the "deliberate mythmaking" tactics of film and media, in the polemical stereotyping strategies of "experts" on the Middle East, in the selling of foreign policy agendas, and in "a public susceptible to images identifying the unwelcome 'other' in its midst" (Akram 2002, 61). A long history of misrepresentation and promotion of violent stereotypes marks the popular American media; Arab and Muslim Americans were portrayed as terrorists long before 9/11.[2] Muslims and Arabs are consistently absent from that desirable group of "ordinary people, families with social interactions, or outstanding members of communities such as scholars or writers or scientists." This process of demonization, Akram goes on to say, "has been so complete and so successful that film critics, most Americans and social commentators have barely noticed" (Akram 2002, 66). In fact, since the 1960s large segments of U.S. culture have unofficially classified Arabs and Muslim as terrorists and perceived them as threats to national security (Hassan 2003).

The racialization of Arab and Muslim Americans captures the ways in which the dominant social structure of this country has positioned itself vis-à-vis this subpopulation. Americans have come to know and learn about Islam and Arabs through the prisms of terrorism and barbarism. It is no surprise that 42% of Americans in the Detroit metro area believe that 9/11 was a result of a deeply rooted disrespect for democracy, freedom, and the rights of women. A large percentage of Americans clearly believe that there is a fundamental clash of values between "us" and "them." Simply put, the U.S. was attacked because it is fundamentally "good," while the Other is fundamentally "evil." These perceptions of the Other have shaped post-9/11 discussions and introspective deliberations. Even in our attempts to understand, we still claim moral superiority. Hence we ask the question, "Why do they hate us?" Seldom has the question been asked, "Why do *we* hate *them*?" Nor have we seriously considered why we have always perceived Arabs and Muslims as a threat to our values. These perceptions of Other, I argue, are a by-product of the racialization patterns of Muslims and Arabs in the U.S. This pattern of racialization, I posit, explains why large sections of the general American population are willing to do away with the civil liberties of Muslims and Arabs in the United States. Racialization occurs as Arab- and Muslim-American civil rights are removed; in such infringements, we are witnessing the continual characterization of *Arab* and *Muslim* as a violent race. In what follows, I test this hypothesis on survey data from the Detroit area.

Data and Test

I use data gathered in 2003 as part of the Detroit Arab American Study (DAAS). The DAAS was produced through an intensive collaboration between the University of Michigan, the University of Michigan–Dearborn, and an advisory panel of community representatives from over twenty secular, religious, and social service organizations. The DAAS is a representative survey of all adults (eighteen years and older) of Arab or Chaldean descent who resided in households in Wayne, Oakland, and Macomb counties during the six-month survey period, July to December 2003. A total of 1,016 face-to-face interviews were conducted between July and November 2003. Seventy-three percent of those who were asked to participate in the survey did so. All references to "Arabs and Chaldeans" in this report refer to that population. In addition, 508 members of the general adult population in these three counties were interviewed during roughly the same period through the Detroit Area Study (DAS). This is a representative sample of the Detroit area population, referred to in this study as the "general population." About 85 percent of the questionnaire items are common to both surveys, permitting extensive comparison of the two populations. Analysis performed in this part of the chapter relies on the DAS data.

In order to test my argument, I construct two ordered logit models. The first model examines the factors associated with Americans who support the infringement of civil liberties for members of the *general* population. The dependent variable reflects the answers of respondents to questions about whether they are willing to infringe on the rights of the *general* population. It is an index variable based on answers to three questions. The first question asks whether the respondent supports an increase of surveillance of the general population by the U.S. government. The second question asks whether the respondent would support giving the police more power to search anyone at random. The last question asks whether the interviewee supports detaining suspicious individuals even if there is insufficient evidence to prosecute. The second dependent variable asks specifically about the respondent's willingness to infringe on the civil liberties of Arab and Muslim Americans. This, too, is an index variable consisting of three questions. The first question asks whether a respondent would support the increased surveillance of Arab and Muslim Americans; the second question, whether he or she would support giving the police more powers to stop and search anyone who looks Arab or Muslim; and the third, whether those surveyed support the detention of suspicious Muslims and Arabs even when there is insufficient evidence to prosecute. The scores were aggregated such that one affirmative response placed the individual in the first category, two affirmative responses were assigned to the second category, and three affirmative responses placed individuals in the third category. Respondents who disagreed with all three statements were assigned to the zero category.

Several independent variables are included in the equation to test the overall hypotheses I discuss in the previous section. To capture anxiety and perceptions of threat, I include a variable that gauges individual levels of security after the attacks. The questions are "How much—if any—have the events of 9/11 shaken your own personal sense of safety and security? Have they shaken it a great deal, a good amount, not too much, or not at all?" To capture ideological inclinations, I include measures of party identification: whether a respondent identifies as Democrat or Republican. I also include a measure of conservative/liberal leanings. The question asks: "Thinking politically and socially, how would you describe your own general outlook—as being very conservative, moderately conservative, middle-of-the-road, moderately liberal, or very liberal?" Finally, I include a set of variables that serve as plausible explanations for the 9/11 attacks. Two of the explanations describe the results as related to either U.S. foreign policy in the region or to the acts of a few extremists. The other two measures address the "clash of civilizations" hypothesis. The first of these questions asks whether there is a religious conflict between Islam, on the one side, and Christianity and Judaism, on the other. The second of these asks whether respondents believe that the attacks occurred because the U.S. supports democracy, freedom, and the rights of women. I also include several demographic variables to gauge whether basic demographic patterns explain support for civil liberties infringements. In the model are controls for religion; Catholics and Protestants are included as dummy variables. The reference group includes Jews, other Christians, and those who did not designate a religion. Education, income, age, and gender are also included. Finally, I include a measure of exposure to the news in the aftermath of 9/11 to gauge whether media consumption is associated with a willingness to infringe on the civil liberties of the general population as well as of Arab and Muslim Americans. Table 10.1 presents the logit coefficients, and the appendix provides a complete coding sheet.

The most interesting finding that emerges from the regressions is that the segments of the population supporting civil liberties infringements in general

Table 10.1. Ordered Logit Regressions on Support for Civil Liberties Infringements for the
General Population and for Muslim/Arab Americans (Robust Standard Errors)

| | | Supports Civil Liberties Infringements for | |
		General Population	Arab and Muslim Populations
DEMOGRAPHICS	Gender	**.763*** **(.207)**	.054 (.215)
	Education	−.094 (.089)	−.136 (.090)
	Income	−.008 (.053)	−.022 (.051)
	Age	.281 (.167)	−.023 (.162)
IDEOLOGY	Liberal/Conservative	**−.218*** **(.112)**	−.111 (.119)
	Republican	**.557*** **(.277)**	−.443 (.300)
	Democrat	**−.459*** **(.229)**	−.353 (.228)
	Religious Conflict	.048 (.203)	.199 (.195)
REASONS FOR 9/11	Clash of Values	.366 (.200)	**.366*** **(.200)**
	U.S. Intervention	−.053 (.204)	−.133 (.199)
	A Few Extremists	**.637*** **(.287)**	.296 (.269)
SAFETY/SECURITY	Personal Sense of Security Shaken	**.454*** **(.233)**	.104 (.269)
RELIGION AND ATTENDANCE	Protestant	−.128 (.254)	**.575*** **(.273)**
	Catholic	.235 (.261)	.273 (.269)
NEWS EXPOSURE	Follow News	.035 (.049)	−.014 (.051)
		N = 365	N = 369

*Significant at the .05 level
**Significant at the .01 level

and those supporting them for Arab and Muslim Americans only are quite different. Women are more likely than men to support reducing the civil liberties of the
general population in the hope of achieving greater security. This is a phenomenon
well documented after 9/11; the term "security moms" has become part of our

cultural jargon.[3] Some have even speculated that George Bush won a significant number of 2004 votes from women who were concerned about security issues. The model also finds that conservatives, as expected, are more likely than liberals to support the civil liberties infringements of the general population. Personal security, measured by whether respondents were shaken by the events of 9/11, is also significant in this model. Those who felt most vulnerable after the attacks were also most likely to express support for a reduction in civil liberties. Finally, respondents who believe that the attacks of 9/11 were committed by a few extremists also support a reduction in civil liberties. The clash of civilization indicators (religious conflict and clash of values) are not pertinent here. Perhaps they believe that decreased liberties are a good way to guarantee security from those extremist elements.

The characteristics of individuals supporting infringements on the civil liberties of Arab and Muslim Americans are different. Those Americans willing to support reduced rights for Arabs and Muslims are more likely to be Protestant, and they are more likely to attribute 9/11 to an inherent clash of values between the U.S. and the Muslim world. Ideology, gender, and personal security are not statistically significant in this model. While the first model supports conventional wisdom—women, conservatives, and Republicans are all more likely than men, liberals, and Democrats, respectively, to do away with civil liberties—the findings on Arabs and Muslims are more troubling. It appears that those people who believe that the U.S. was attacked because of a clash of values are more likely to encourage reduced rights for Arab and Muslim Americans. These respondents, who seem most comfortable with constructions of "us" and "them," are willing to do away with the civil liberties of Arabs and Muslims. That Protestants are more likely to be willing to curb Arab and Muslim civil liberties further illustrates that perceived differences explain this pattern of support. Religious denomination was not at all significant in the model that gauged support for civil liberties infringements of the general population. Yet, when the target group is Arab and Muslim, Protestants (who constitute about 40% of the DAS sample) are more willing to reduce their civil liberties. This likelihood of support for civil liberties infringements among those who believe that a clash of value exists between Americans and Muslims while controlling for Protestant denomination and pinning all other variables at their means is captured in Figure 10.2 below.

In general, those who believe that the U.S. was not attacked because of a clash of values between the U.S. and Muslim world are 25–30% more likely to reject infringements on the rights of Arab and Muslim Americans than those who do. Non-Protestants are 43–52% more likely than Protestants to reject infringements on these rights. The starkest probability difference is between those who are non-Protestant and do not believe in a clash of values, and those who are Protes-

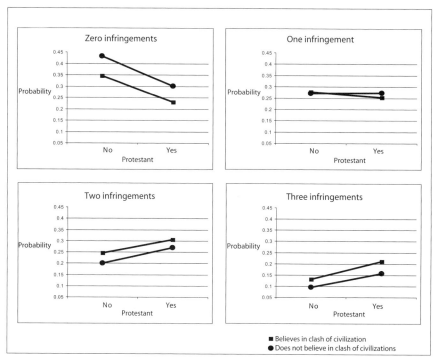

FIGURE 10.2.
Predicted Probabilities of Support for Civil Liberties Infringements

tant and do believe in a clash of values. Protestants who do believe that a clash of values explains 9/11 are almost twice as likely as non-Protestants who do not believe in a clash to support three civil liberties infringements on the civil rights of Arab and Muslim Americans (22% versus 12%).

These worrisome numbers raise the most concern among members of the U.S. Arab and Muslim minorities. My analysis of data from a Zogby survey (2001) reveals that 66 percent of Muslim Americans worry about their future in the U.S. If the dominant culture sees them not only as different but also as a threat, as adhering to a value system that opposes "American values," then it is all the more acceptable to do away with their civil rights. Since the attacks of 9/11, hate crimes against Arabs and Muslims in the U.S. have consistently been on the rise year after year. The racialization of Arabs and Muslims by the mainstream, decades in the making, has manifested itself since 9/11 in support of discriminatory legislation and law enforcement. The media have long portrayed this minority as a population to guard against. The general population, these results show, is following suit.

212 · Amaney Jamal

The Racialization of Tolerance

The disturbing reality reflected in the findings above has also paved the way for an opportunity. While worrying about the presence of the Other in their midst, Americans are also attempting to learn more about this population. Since 9/11, copies of the Qur'an have been selling quickly at bookstores across the country. Interfaith dialogue and mosque open houses, which strive to educate Americans about Islam, became more common after the attacks. In fact, a third of the DAAS respondents reported that they received an act of solidarity or kindness from a member of the general population. Though many Americans remain wary, they also seek tolerance for the Arab and Muslim Other.

Yet, tolerance and the discourse on tolerance are not void of the context in which tolerance is either granted or withdrawn. The very fact that Muslims and Arabs are rallying Americans to be more tolerant illustrates a conundrum surrounding the issue of toleration itself. Some Arabs and Muslims have accepted racial profiling, claim to understand lengthy interrogations as their children stand by at airports, and apologize over and over for 9/11 because they feel this self-subjugation will win tolerance from the mainstream. However, tolerance assumes equality and good faith in interactions. It also assumes that dominant institutions—media, churches, government, and so on—are not operating to espouse intolerance against a certain population. In the end, tolerance is granted by elite members of a dominant mainstream that is united in its culture and values toward a subordinate Other. In the words of Herbert Marcuse, tolerance is "determined and defined by the institutionalized inequality (which is certainly compatible with constitutional equality). . . . In such a society, tolerance is de facto limited on the dual ground of legalized violence or suppression (police, armed forces, guards of all sorts) and of the privileged position held by the predominant interest and their connections" ([1965] 1969a: 84–85). He goes on to say, "[I]n the United States, this tendency goes hand in hand with the monopolistic or oligopolistic concentration of capital in the formation of public opinion, i.e. of the majority" ([1965] 1969b: 118). Essentially, tolerance is a tool of racialization.

Whether tolerated or rejected, the construction of the Other is similar. We can take great pride in our toleration of those who do not share our values, or we can take great pride in resisting accommodation because others do not share our values. In the end, the construction of the Other is the same. Whether tolerated or resisted, the Other is, for the general population, always that which is different. This element of difference—and the ways it is constructed and manifested—defines how tolerant we are. The process of racialization is inherent to our toleration of the Other. Rather than look for the commonalities that unite all humankind, we erect differences and either applaud our tolerance or justify our intolerance. Thus, the debate on whether Arab and Muslims are worthy of civil liberties protections is the wrong one to have. The racialized symptomatology of constructing Arabs and Muslims as enemy Others itself needs to be scrutinized and fixed. As Rodney Coates reminds us, one does not treat the symptoms of smoking by curing the cough (Coates 2004, 874). Unfortunately, Arabs and Muslims possess neither the resources, nor the power, nor the media necessary to alter mainstream public opinion. The tides of public opinion continue to operate against them.

Survey

1. Gender:
   Coding: 1: Male; 2: Female
2. Education:
   Coding: 1: Less than High School; 2: High School; 3: Some College; 4: BA; 5: Professional Degree
3. Age:
   Coding: 1: 18–24; 2: 25–57; 3: 58+
4. Household Income:
   Coding: 1: $19,999; 2: 20,000–49,999; 3: 50,000–74,999; 4: 75,000+
5. Republican: Generally, speaking, do you usually think of yourself as a Republican, Democrat, Independent, or what?
   Coding: 1: Republican; 0: All Else
6. Democrat: Generally speaking, do you usually think of yourself as a Republican, Democrat, Independent, or what?
   Coding: 1 Democrat; 0: All Else
7. Liberal/Conservative: Thinking *politically and socially,* how would you describe your own general outlook—are you very conservative, moderately conservative, middle-of-the-road, moderately liberal, or very liberal?
   Coding: 1: Very Conservative; 2: Moderately Conservative; 3: Middle of Road; 4: Moderately Liberal; 5: Very Liberal
8. Protestant: Are you Protestant, Catholic, or Orthodox Christian?
   Coding: 1: Protestant; 0: Other
9. Catholic: Are you Protestant, Catholic, or Orthodox Christian?
   Coding: 1: Catholic; 0: Other
10. Follow 9/11 events/Media:
    Since 9/11, how closely have you been following the news about the "war on terrorism"—very closely, somewhat closely, a little, or not much at all?
    Coding: 1: Very Closely; 2: Somewhat Closely; 3: A Little; 4: Not Much at All
11. Explanations for 9/11:
    Now I'll read you some possible explanations for the terrorist attacks on 9/11.
    For each one, please tell me whether you think this is a possible explanation or not.
    Just answer yes or no.
    a. *U.S. Intervention:* It's because of the U.S. intervention in the Persian Gulf.
    b. *Extremist Beliefs:* It's because of the extremist beliefs of a few terrorists.
    c. *Religious Conflict:* It's because of the conflict between Christianity and Judaism on one side and Islam on the other.
    d. *Clash of Values:* It's because the U.S. believes in democracy, freedom, and equal rights for women.
    Coding: 1: Yes; 0: No

12. Personal security shaken by events of 9/11:
   How much—if any—have the events of 9/11 shaken your own personal sense of safety and security? Have they shaken it a great deal, a good amount, not too much, or not at all?
   Coding: 1: A Great Deal; 2: A Good Amount; 3: Not Too Much; 4: Not at All
13. Civil Liberties: General Population
   a. Do you support increasing surveillance of U.S. citizens by the government? [Response Options: Yes or No]
   b. Do you support giving the police powers to stop and search anyone at random? [Response Options: Yes or No]
   c. Do you support detaining some suspicious individuals even if there is not sufficient evidence to prosecute them in the courts? [Response Options: Yes or No]
14. Willingness to Give Up Civil Liberties of Arab Americans
   Index variable consisting of the following three questions:
   a. Do you support increasing surveillance of Arab Americans by the government? [Response Options: Yes or No]
   b. Do you support: Giving the police powers to stop and search anyone who appears to be Arab or Muslim, at random? [Response Options: Yes or No]
   c. Do you support detaining some suspicious Arabs and/or Muslims even if there is not sufficient evidence to prosecute them in the courts? [Response Options: Yes or No]

Notes

1. As Rodney Coates notes, these depictions of "other" entire subgroups are commonplace in American popular culture (2004). Moreover, evidence seems to support the vilification of racial non-elites. Blacks and Hispanics, for example, are more likely to be presented as criminals than as victims or more positively (Chiricos and Eschholz 2002). These types of perceptual biases have dire consequences when racialized minorities confront the legal system (Berger 2002).
2. See Suleiman (2002); Mandel (2001); Tessler and Corstange (2002); Shaheen (2003); Gerges (2003).
3. Jill Lawrence, "Parties' Issues Coincide with Parents' Issues," *USA Today*, May 31, 2005, sec. Washington/Politics.

References

Akram, Susan. 2002. "The Aftermath of September 11, 2001: The Targeting of Arabs and Muslims in America." *Arab Studies Quarterly* 24 (2/3): 61–118.

Bettencourt, B. Ann, Kelly Charlton, Nancy Dorr, and Deborah L. Hume. 2001. "Status Differences and In-group Bias: A Meta-analytic Examination of the Effects of Status Stability, Status Legitimacy, and Group Permeability." *Psychological Bulletin* 127 (4): 520–542.

Berger, Vivian. 2002. "A Legacy of Racism." *National Law Journal* 24 (55). Available at http://www.law.com/jsp/article.jsp?id=1032128694425 (accessed December 13, 2006).

Cainkar, Louise. 2002. "No Longer Invisible: Arab and Muslim Exclusion after September 11," *Middle East Report* 224 (Fall). Available at http://www.merip.org/mer/mer224/224_cainkar.html (accessed December 13, 2006).

———. 2003. "Targeting Muslims, at Ashcroft's Discretion," *Middle East Report Online* (March 14). Available at http://www.merip.org/mero/mero031403.html (accessed December 13, 2006).

Chiricos, T., and S. Eschholz. 2002. "The Racial and Ethnic Typification of Crime and the

Criminal Typification of Race and Ethnicity in Local Television News." *Journal of Research in Crime and Delinquency* 39 (4): 400–420.

Coates, Rodney. 2004. "Critical and Ethnic Studies: Profiling and Reparations." *American Behavioral Scientist* 47 (7): 873–878.

Davis, Darren. 1995. "Exploring Black Political Intolerance." *Political Behavior* 17 (1): 1–22.

Davis, Darren, and Brian Silver. 2004. "Civil Liberties vs. Security: Public Opinion in the Context of the Terrorist Attacks on America." *American Journal of Political Science* 48 (1): 28–46.

Gerges, Fawaz. 2003. "Islam and Muslims in the Mind of America." *Annals of the American Academy of Political and Social Science* 588 (1): 73–89.

Hassan, Salah D. 2003. "Enemy Arabs." *Socialism and Democracy* 17 (1). Available at http://www.sdonline.org/33/salah_d_hassan.htm (accessed December 13, 2006).

Herrmann, Richard K., Philip E. Tetlock, and Penny S. Visser. 1999. "Mass Public Decisions to Go to War: A Cognitive-Interactionist Framework." *American Political Science Review* 93 (3): 553–573.

Huddy, Leonie, Stanley Feldman, Charles Taber, and Gallya Lahav. 2005. "Threat, Anxiety, and Support of Antiterrorism Policies." *American Journal of Political Science* 49 (3): 593–608.

Jentleson, Bruce W. 1992. "The Pretty Prudent Public: Post-Vietnam American Opinion on the Use of Force." *International Studies Quarterly* 36 (1): 49–74.

LeVine, Robert A., and Donald T. Campbell. 1972. *Ethnocentrism: Theories of Conflict, Ethnic Attitudes, and Group Behavior.* New York: Wiley.

Mandel, Daniel. 2001. "Muslims on the Silver Screen." *Middle East Quarterly* 8 (2). Available at http://www.meforum.org/article/26 (accessed December 13, 2006).

Marcuse, Herbert. [1965] 1969a. "Repressive Tolerance." In *A Critique of Pure Tolerance,* 2nd ed., ed. Robert P. Wolff, Barrington Moore Jr., and Herbert Marcuse, 81–117. Boston: Beacon Press.

———. [1965] 1969b. "Postscript." In *A Critique of Pure Tolerance,* 2nd ed., ed. Robert P. Wolff, Barrington Moore Jr., and Herbert Marcuse, 117–123. Boston: Beacon Press.

McClosky, Herbert. 1964. "Consensus and Ideology in American Politics." *American Political Science Review* 58 (2): 361–382.

McClosky, Herbert, and Alida Brill 1983. *Dimensions of Tolerance: What Americans Believe about Civil Liberties.* New York: Russell Sage Foundation.

Moallem, Minoo. 2005. *Between Warrior Brother and Veiled Sister: Islamic Fundamentalism and the Politics of Patriarchy in Iran.* Berkeley: University of California Press.

Murray, Nancy. 2004. "Profiled: Arabs, Muslims, and the Post-9/11 Hunt for the 'Enemy Within.'" In *Civil Rights in Peril: The Targeting of Arabs and Muslims,* ed. Elaine Hagopian, 27–68. Ann Arbor, Mich.: Pluto Press.

Omi, Michael, and Howard Winant. 1994. *Racial Formation in the United States: From the 1960s to the 1990s.* New York: Routledge and Kegan Paul.

Struch, Naomi, and Shalom H. Schwartz. 1989. "Intergroup Aggression: Its Predictors and Distinctness from In-Group Bias." *Journal of Personality and Social Psychology* 56 (3): 364–373.

Shaheen, Jack. 2003. "Reel Bad Arabs: How Hollywood Vilifies a People." *Annals of the American Academy of Political and Social Science* 588 (1): 171–193.

Suleiman, Michael. 2002. "Stereotypes, Public Opinion and Foreign Policy: The Impact on Arab-American Relations." *Journal of Arab Affairs* 1 (4l): 147–166.

Tessler, Mark, and Daniel Corstange. 2002. "How Should Americans Understand Arab Political Attitudes? Combating Stereotypes with Public Opinion Data from the Middle East." *Journal of Social Affairs* 19 (Winter): 13–34.

Zogby International and Project MAPS. December 19, 2001. "American Muslim Poll." Zogby International, Utica N.Y. Summary available at http://www.zogby.com/americanmuslims2001.pdf (accessed April 13, 2008).

PART FOUR

WESTERN MUSLIMS, CIVIL RIGHTS,
AND LEGAL INSTITUTIONS

Canadian National Security Policy and Canadian Muslim Communities

Kent Roach

Canada has a somewhat better reputation as a welcoming place for Muslims and for respect for civil liberties than the United States and many European countries, such as the United Kingdom or France. After the terrorist attacks of September 11, 2001, Canada did not derogate from its constitutional bill of rights, the Canadian Charter of Rights and Freedoms, as the United Kingdom did. Unlike the United States, it had a relatively robust political debate about its immediate legislative response to 9/11, and Muslim voices were heard during that debate. Canada's reputation is also affected by the sometimes harsh criticism it has received for its comparatively liberal immigration policies and its refusal to join the invasion of Iraq. Canada has demonstrated official concern for the treatment received by its citizens abroad who are suspected of terrorism by calling an expensive and unprecedented public inquiry to examine the actions of Canadian officials relating to the extraordinary rendition of Maher Arar, a Syrian-born Canadian citizen, from the United States to Syria. Building on its official recognition and promotion of multiculturalism, Canada has created a new cross-cultural round-table on national security issues and made efforts to engage with the Muslim communities on security issues.

In this chapter, I critically examine Canada's post-9/11 national security policy with special attention to its effects on Canadian Muslims and their engagement in its development. I suggest that while, in some respects, Canada's reputation for respect for civil liberties and a welcoming multiculturalism is deserved, especially in comparative perspective, Canada can, and should, do more to ensure greater respect for equality, multiculturalism, and international law in its anti-terrorism activities. Such improvements might not only result in moral and normative gains, but also be instrumental in combating terrorism. Better relations between Canadian governments and the Muslim minority, a strong condemnation of racial and religious profiling, the deletion of the religious or political motive requirement from Canada's definition of terrorism, and better review of Canada's national security activities may actually help make Canada more secure from terrorism. It may also contribute to social cohesion and avoid the type of cross-cultural conflict that has recently taken place in the Netherlands, France, and Australia.

Canada's Muslim Communities

Between 1991 and 2001 Canada's Muslim population more than doubled, growing from 1% to 2% of Canada's total population: there were 579,640 Muslims in the 2001 Canada census, up from 253,000 in 1991 and 98,165 in 1981. The Muslim minority in Canada is larger than other non-Christian religious communities, including the Jewish, Hindu, Buddhist, and Sikh (Statistics Canada 2005). The Muslim minority will likely continue to grow both because of high fertility rates and continued immigration: Canada continues to facilitate more immigration than most other Western countries. For example, the percentage of Canadians who are foreign-born is twice that of Americans (Kymlicka 1998, 1).

Canada's Muslim minority is heavily urbanized with large numbers in Toronto, Ottawa, and Montreal, and there are ten federal ridings in those cities whose Muslim population is over 10 percent. Especially since 9/11 there have been signs of a growing political awareness and activism within Canadian Muslim communities. For example, the Canadian Islamic Congress has prepared report cards for all federal members of Parliament and urged Muslims to become active and engaged on a variety of public issues, including security issues (Canadian Islamic Congress 2004). During Canada's 2006 election campaign the leaders of the major parties made it a point to visit and be photographed in mosques.

An important feature of the Canadian Muslim minority is its diversity, with large numbers of immigrants coming from South and Southeast Asia and the Middle East. The majority of Canadian Muslims are Sunni, but there are also significant Shia, Ismaili, and Ahmadi populations. Even within sects, there are important differences of nationality, with some mosques housing populations from

Southeast Asia, and others host Muslims from Arab countries, Africa, or Bosnia. The diversity of the Canadian Muslim community in terms of national origin, sect, and political and religious orientation may affect its political engagement in Canada. There are also a number of different groups that compete to represent Muslims in Canadian political life. All these factors, along with the small size of the community and its newness, suggest that the road to political clout for Muslims in Canada will be a tumultuous one for the foreseeable future.

The Anti-Terrorism Act, 2001

Canada's main initial response to 9/11 was the introduction of a massive new anti-terrorism bill on October 15, 2001. The bill, known as Bill C-36, created many new crimes relating to financing of and preparation to commit terrorist activities which were, for the first time, defined in Canada's Criminal Code. It also provided for increased powers of preventive arrests, listing of terrorist groups and individuals by the executive, enhanced provisions for protecting national security confidentiality, and a new procedure for the deregistration of charities on the basis of involvement with terrorism in Canada or abroad.

The political engagement of Muslims in Canada against the anti-terrorism bill may, in some respects, be as important as its legal details. Representations against the bill were made by various Muslim groups, including the Council on American-Islamic Relations, the Muslim Lawyers Association, and the Canadian Muslim Civil Liberties Association. Riad Saloojee, the executive director of the Canadian branch of the Council on American-Islamic Relations (CAIR-CAN), has commented that "the public advocacy of Canadian Muslims against Bill C-36 represented a departure from previous insularity regarding public policy and marked a re-assertion of their agency in a climate where they were victims of anti-Muslim hate" (Saloojee 2003). The lobby against Bill C-36 was also striking because it saw a broad alliance of civil society groups, including civil liberties groups, groups of lawyers including the Canadian Bar Association, Aboriginal groups, unions, the refugee community, charities, faith communities, and elements of the anti-globalization movement, who, each for their own reasons, feared aspects of the bill (Roach 2003).

The Coalition of Muslim Organizations, comprising more than 140 Muslim organizations in Canada, made lengthy submissions to both parliamentary committees that reviewed Bill C-36. The coalition argued that the bill violated the Canadian Charter of Rights and Freedoms and made use of legal analysis offered by the mainstream Canadian Bar Association (Mia 2002). At the same time, the coalition argued from the experience of Canadian Muslims that

> xenophobia, fear and a general state of tension, coupled with the vague and
> overly broad powers in the Bill will contribute to many innocent Canadians

being subject to unwarranted invasions of privacy, humiliating investigations and possible loss of liberty and privacy. ... Those who will be wrongfully charged, arrested and imprisoned may be vindicated in the fullness of time, but at incalculable cost: the stigma, shame and humiliation that will have devastating effects on families, reputations, friendships, businesses and jobs. (Coalition of Muslim Organizations 2001, 25–26)

The broad-based opposition to the bill in civil society caused the government to amend the bill in November 2001. The amendments included a five-year renewable sunset for new police powers of preventive arrest and a clause that permits detention for up to seventy-two hours on the basis of reasonable suspicion and for investigative hearings that allow judges to require those with information about terrorism to answer questions and produce documents without regard to the right against self-incrimination. In addition, annual reports were statutorily required on the use of these two new investigative powers. Other important amendments introduced in November 2001 include judicial review of executive certificates designed to protect national security information, the deletion of a requirement that protests and strikes must be lawful to be exempted from a broad definition of terrorism that includes intentional disruption of essential public or private services, and a statement that the expression of religious or political opinion or belief will not normally in itself be considered a terrorist activity. This latter amendment demonstrates the Canadian government's sensitivity to fears of religious or political persecution and is unique among countries that have followed the British model of requiring proof of political or religious motive for crimes of terrorism (Roach 2007).

The November 2001 amendments also included a requirement that both the law and its operation be subject to a three-year review by a parliamentary committee. This parliamentary review will provide an opportunity for a remobilization of the civil society coalitions that initially opposed the bill. At the same time, Canada will also face pressures to enact new laws relating to the incitement of terrorism and other forms of extremist speech as advocated by the United Nations Security Council Resolution 1624. Although Canada already has hate speech laws that have been found to be reasonable limits on freedom of expression, prosecutions based on other forms of extremist speech that attempt to glorify or justify terrorism may prove to be both difficult and divisive. They may also not be particularly effective as a strategy to prevent terrorism (Roach 2006).

The November 2001 amendments made to Bill C-36 improved the bill from both normative and instrumental perspectives. It is important for a democracy that the public be informed of the extent to which extraordinary police powers are used. Although some, including some Muslim groups, argued in favor of a sunset for the entire bill, both the sunset provisions and the three-year review allow some opportunity for reflection about both the necessity of the law and its impact on specific communities. The expanded exemption for even unlawful protests and strikes from the act's broad definition of terrorism recognizes the important role that protests and strikes, including civil disobedience, can play in a democracy. The narrower definition of terrorism can also be defended in instrumental terms: police and security intelligence should not devote limited resources for terrorist investigations to the activities of even the radical wings of the labor, Aboriginal, animal rights, or anti-globalization movements.

Despite the amendments, the bill still contains several features that may have harmful effects on Muslims in Canada. Terrorism is still legally defined in very broad terms; it includes a large variety of activities committed both inside and outside of Canada. Section 83.01(b) of Canada's Criminal Code, as amended by the 2001 Anti-Terrorism Act (ATA), now defines a terrorist activity as follows:

an act or omission, in or outside Canada,

(i) that is committed
   (A) in whole or in part for a political, religious or ideological purpose, objective or cause, and
   (B) in whole or in part with the intention of intimidating the public, or a segment of the public, with regard to its security, including its economic security, or compelling a person, a government or a domestic or an international organization inside or outside Canada, and
(ii) that intentionally
   (A) causes death or serious bodily harm to a person by the use of violence
   (B) endangers a person's life
   (C) causes a serious risk to the health or safety of the public or any segment of the public
   (D) causes substantial property damage, whether to public or private property, if causing such damage is likely to result in the conduct or harm referred to in any of clauses (A) to (C) or,
   (E) causes serious interference with or serious disruption of an essential service, facility or system, whether public or private, other than as a result of advocacy, protest, dissent or stoppage of work that is not intended to result in the conduct or harm referred to in any of clauses (A) to (C) and includes a conspiracy, attempt or threat to commit any such act or omission, or being an accessory after the fact or counseling in relation to any such act or omission, but, for greater certainty, does not include an act or omission that is committed during an armed conflict and that, at the time and in the place of its commission, is in accordance with customary international law or conventional international law applicable to the conflict, or the activities undertaken by military forces of a state in the exercise of their official duties, to the extent that those activities are governed by other rules of international law.
   Amendment 1.1: For greater certainty, the expression of a political, religious or ideological thought, belief or opinion does not come within

paragraph (b) of the definition 'terrorist activity' in subsection 1 unless it constitutes an act or omission that satisfies the criteria of that paragraph.[1]

This definition of terrorism is broader than those found in many international law instruments.[2]

One problematic aspect of the above definition is that terrorism is defined, in part, by reference to the commission of acts with a religious or political motive. In this respect Canada followed the British as opposed to the American example. This requirement was opposed by various Muslim groups, as well as civil liberties groups, on the basis that it would require the police to collect evidence about a terrorist suspect's religion and politics and could encourage a process of guilt by association based on religion and politics. There have indeed been complaints subsequent to the enactment of the law that police and security intelligence officials have asked Canadian Muslims questions regarding, for example, the frequency of their prayers and their opinions about Osama bin Laden. The political or religious motive requirement can be seen as a denunciation of political and religious extremism that, especially after 9/11, is often associated with Islam in the West. It is significant in this regard that Indonesia, Pakistan, and most Arab states have specifically rejected the political and religious motive requirement in their new anti-terrorism laws (Roach 2004; Ramraj, Hor, and Roach 2005).

In Canada's trial of two Sikhs charged with conspiracy to commit murder in relation to the 1985 Air India bombing that killed 329 people, evidence of religious and political motive relating to support for Sikh independence and opposition to India was allowed under the regular criminal law relating to murder, but the trial judge ultimately held that many others in the Sikh community would have similar motives to commit acts of terrorism against Indian targets in 1985.[3] In this respect, evidence of motive did not substantially advance the prosecutor's case. There is, however, a danger that police, prosecutors, and juries might give political and religious motive evidence a disproportionate weight and use such evidence to bolster a weak case. A public opinion poll after the trial indicated that 68 percent of respondents with an opinion disagreed with a trial judge's 2005 acquittal of the two Sikhs and thought the men should have been convicted.[4] This poll suggests that the accused in the Air India trial may have been wise to waive their right to a jury trial and submit to trial by judge alone.

Both the United Nations and the Commonwealth Secretariat have expressed reservations about the political and religious motive requirement on the basis that it may make it more difficult to obtain convictions. Ziyaad Mia, a lawyer representing the Coalition of Muslim Organizations, put the point well when, in November 2001, he argued that the motive requirements "do nothing to further the government's objective and will only result in targeting vulnerable communities and individuals. . . . If people fly a plane into BCE Place in downtown Toronto simply because they are crazy, they will receive a lesser criminal sanction than if they do it in the name of God or Buddha. Why is that distinction made?" (Canada 2001). Mia returned to these themes during the three-year review when he told the same committee that the motive requirement needs to be removed "because it is inefficient in terms of prosecutions and because it feeds profiling" (Canada 2005b).

In response to criticisms of the religious or political motive requirements from Muslim, legal, and civil liberties groups, the Canadian government added section 83.01 (1.1) as part of the November 2001 amendments. This section provides that the expression of religious and political belief will not constitute a terrorist activity unless it falls under the other components of Canada's broad definition of terrorism. The legal effect of this amendment is dubious; indeed, it may open the possibility that some expressions of religious and political belief could be defined as a terrorist activity on the basis that they constitute threats to commit terrorism that are included as part of the definition of terrorism in section 83.01. Nevertheless, the amendment is also a testament to the Canadian government's sensitivity to claims that its anti-terrorism efforts were directed against particular religions. This provision is not found in British, Australian, or South African anti-terrorism laws, which also define terrorism in part as acts committed with religious or political motive. Canada's statement that expressions of religious belief will not generally constitute acts of terrorism may be related to Canada's official embrace of multiculturalism (Roach 2007).

There were also calls during the debates over Bill C-36 for the enactment of anti-discrimination and anti-profiling laws as part of the ATA. Irwin Cotler, then a backbencher and subsequently the federal minister of justice, called for the enactment of an anti-discrimination provision patterned after the prohibition of detention or internment on the basis of race, national or ethnic origin, color, religion, sex, age, or mental or physical disability found in section 4(b) of Canada's Emergencies Act (Cotler 2001). This clause was included in recognition of the injustice suffered by people of Japanese origin interned during World War II and the mistreatment of people of Ukrainian origin during World War I. Others called for more robust restrictions on the use of race or religion to justify a broader range of investigative activities (Choudhry and Roach 2003). A private members' bill, Bill C-296, was subsequently introduced to prohibit the use of stereotypes, rather than reasonable suspicion, in singling out individuals for greater scrutiny or differential law enforcement treatment. It was introduced by a member of Canada's third political party, the social democratic New Democratic Party, which has been particularly active in matters involving discrimination against Muslims since September 11. Canada's multiparty system, which may only become more robust should current Canadian interest in proportional representation be realized, may increase the opportunities for Muslims to find allies and gain greater representation within the Canadian political system.

Representation, however, does not guarantee success, and it is significant that the government did not amend the ATA to include an anti-discrimination or anti-profiling provision despite Cotler's recommendations and attempts to present the bill as not only consistent with but also protective of rights. It will be interesting to see if an anti-discrimination or anti-profiling amendment is proposed or adopted as part of the ongoing three-year parliamentary review of the act. At the same time, an anti-discrimination or anti-profiling provision is not a panacea; it would not be self-executing and could prove to be mainly symbolic.

The ATA included a new offense of hate-motivated mischief against religious property and expanded powers to remove hate literature from the internet. These provisions were defended on the basis of the connection between racial and religious hatred and terrorism and responded to an increase in reported hate crimes in Canada after September 11. The Canadian government was prepared to proclaim its commitment to principles of anti-discrimination by extending the criminal law, but it was not prepared to introduce an anti-discrimination clause that would bind state officials. This state of affairs also indicates how Muslims in Canada may be both drawn toward the state for protection against hate crimes and fearful that the state will target or investigate them as potential terrorists because of their religion or ethnicity. It is noteworthy that the Muslim groups that appeared before parliamentary committees were more concerned with possible state abuse of new powers than with the ability of the state to defend them against hate speech and hate crimes.

Another important feature of the ATA is that it applies to a broad range of acts committed inside or outside Canada. People can be prosecuted in Canada for sending financial and other support to struggles fought in foreign lands. In recognizing the difficulty of defining terrorism, the Supreme Court of Canada has noted that "Nelson Mandela's African National Congress was, during the apartheid era, routinely labeled as a terrorist organization, not only by the South African government but by much of the international community" (*Suresh v. Canada* 2002, par. 95).[5] The only exemptions from the scope of international terrorism targeted by the law are for armed conflict conducted according to customary or conventional international law or the official activities of a state military force to the extent that those activities are governed by other rules of international law. This would not necessarily apply to all resistance efforts against repressive regimes. The extraterritorial application of various terrorism crimes, including those of financing terrorism, as well as the provision for the deregistration of charities, will have a disproportionate effect on Canada's Muslim population because of its close and recent connections to the Middle East and the religious requirement to contribute to charities. This was a point made by the Coalition of Muslim Organizations, which argued that "the charities are suffering. Innocent people in Somalia, Ethiopia, Afghanistan and Chechnya are not getting funds to enable them to feed themselves and keep themselves warm this winter because

money is not being sent overseas due to the palpable fear in the community"
(Canada 2001).

The ATA also recognized and extended the powers of Canada's signal intelligence agency, the Communications Security Establishment (CSE), to intercept
communications from the global information infrastructure including international phone calls and e-mails for the purpose of collecting intelligence about foreign individuals, states, organizations, or terrorist groups related to international
affairs, defense, or security. The minister of defense now has statutory powers to
authorize the CSE to intercept private communications for the sole purpose of collecting foreign intelligence. Although the intercepts must be directed at foreign
entities and must include satisfactory measures to protect the privacy of Canadians, the intercepts can include information with a connection to Canada. There is
no provision for judicial warrants but the CSE is reviewed by a retired judge to
ensure that its activities are in compliance with the law. Intercepts of foreign communications might well have a disproportionate effect on newcomer communities
such as Muslims who frequently use the global information infrastructure.

Despite the fears of Muslim groups and others such as trade unions and civil
liberties groups, Canada's use of its new ATA has so far been quite sparing. The
first charges under the new law were laid by the Royal Canadian Mounted Police
(RCMP) on March 31, 2004. Charges of knowingly participating in the activities
of a terrorist group and facilitating a terrorist activity were laid against Mohammad Momin Khawaja. The twenty-five-year-old Canadian-born citizen, whose
parents emigrated from Pakistan, is alleged to have participated in the activities
of a terrorist group and facilitated terrorist activity in and around Ottawa and
London in late 2003 and early 2004. He has also been charged with terrorist financing and offenses relating to explosives. Officials have linked his arrest with
nine men in the London area and the seizure of a large amount of ammonium
nitrate stored near Heathrow Airport. The fact that Mr. Khawaja is a Canadian
citizen precluded the use of immigration law procedures, to be examined below,
against him. Khawaja's father was temporarily detained by Saudi authorities at
the time of his son's arrest, and there have been claims that Canadian officials
were involved in the Saudi detention. Media reports subsequent to the arrest focused on the political and religious beliefs of the Khawaja family, but the RCMP
also issued a press release stating that its focus was on individuals and not on
Ottawa's large Muslim community.[6]

Annual reports on the use of new powers of investigative hearings and preventive arrests are required by law, and they indicate that these new powers were
not used in Canada between the enactment of the law in late 2001 and the end of
2004. An attempt was made to use an investigative hearing to examine a reluctant
witness under oath in connection with the Air India trial. The Supreme Court of
Canada held that the new procedure was constitutional, but extended immunity
provisions in the law to ensure that evidence compiled at an investigative hearing

could not be used in subsequent immigration or extradition proceedings. The Court also indicated that there was a rebuttable presumption that the hearings be held in open court.[7] The investigative hearing was never used in the Air India prosecution, and it is doubtful that it would have led to a different outcome. The eventual acquittals in that case were based on the many credibility problems that the trial judge found with the prosecution's witnesses. It should not be assumed that restricting rights will necessarily produce more convictions or prevent terrorism.

So far thirty-eight groups have been listed by the federal cabinet of elected ministers as terrorist groups. Hamas was listed in late November 2002, and Hezbollah was listed one month later after lobbying and threats of litigation by B'nai Brith. Lebanon complained about the listing, and the National Council on Canada-Arab relations called for some Jewish settler groups to be listed (Roach 2003, 37–38). Kahane Chai (Kach), a group of right-wing anti-Arab Jews, was listed as a terrorist group by the federal cabinet in June 2004. In addition, over 450 groups and individuals have been listed as terrorists under regulations enacted under the United Nations Act.

There have been mistakes: for instance, Liban Hussein, an Ottawa Muslim from Somalia who ran a money exchange business, was wrongfully listed as a terrorist. The list was prepared by the United States, but accepted by both Canada and the United Nations. Canada also attempted to extradite Hussein to the United States, before concluding, after seven months, that an error had been made in listing him as a financier of terrorism (Dosman 2004). A civil suit brought by Hussein was subsequently settled out of court and subject to a confidentiality agreement. Hussein's brother, however, was convicted in the United States of running a money transfer business without a license and sentenced to eighteen months in jail even though no links to terrorism were proven.[8] Canada has followed the United Nations and many other countries in compiling lists of terrorists and terrorist groups. Although listing decisions can be challenged in court after they have been made, they cannot be challenged before they are made, and errors have been made. A person challenging a listing decision can also be denied access to most of the government's information on the grounds of national security confidentiality.

The Use of Immigration Law as Anti-Terrorism Law

One of the reasons Canada has been relatively restrained in its use of the new ATA is that it has made more extensive use of its immigration laws as anti-terrorism law. Although Canada's Immigration and Refugee Protection Act (IRPA) has been subject to criticism in both Canada and the United States for being too liberal, it contains many powers that are much less restrained than Canada's enhanced criminal law. For example, under section 34 of the IRPA "engaging in terrorism," being "a danger to the security of Canada," or "being a member of an organization that there are reasonable grounds to believe engages, has engaged or will engage" in acts of terrorism are grounds to make a non-citizen inadmissible to Canada. Under Canadian immigration law membership in a terrorist organization can be "proven" at a standard well below proof beyond a reasonable doubt. Under Canadian criminal law membership in a terrorist group is not a crime, and participation, instruction, or facilitation with regard to terrorism all require proof of various forms of blameworthy intent beyond a reasonable doubt. Although the Supreme Court of Canada has held, in a landmark equality rights case, that non-citizens are a "discrete and insular minority" vulnerable to discrimination by the majority, it has also accepted that non-citizens do not have a right to remain in Canada and can be treated more harshly under immigration law than under the criminal law.[9] The IRPA subjects non-citizens to considerably lower standards of adjudicative fairness than under even the enhanced criminal law of the ATA (Mia 2005). It is in this context that the Canadian government has chosen to rely more on immigration law than the new criminal law to deal with suspected international terrorists. As Audrey Macklin suggests, "laws that arouse deep concerns about civil liberties when applied to citizens are standard fare in the immigration context" (Macklin 2001, 393). Such use of immigration law as anti-terrorism law has important repercussions for newcomer communities such as Muslims and makes them vulnerable to burdens, including the risk of wrongful identification as a terrorist, that are not imposed on citizens (Cole 2003).

Project Thread

Procedures used under Canadian immigration law for preventive or investigative detention are more draconian than those available under the criminal law, even as enhanced by the ATA. The ATA provides for preventive arrest for a seventy-two-hour period, but with the possibility of peace bonds being imposed for a longer period. In contrast, the IRPA authorizes a much broader form of preventive detention on reasonable grounds that a non-citizen, including a permanent resident, is inadmissible and a danger to the public. As under the ATA, there would be review within forty-eight hours by an official within the Immigration Division, but not by a judge. Continued detention can be authorized on the basis that "the Minister is taking necessary steps to inquire into a reasonable suspicion that they are inadmissible on grounds of security or for violating human or international rights" (Canada 2004b, 3–4). This is a form of investigative detention not contemplated under the ATA. There is no limit on this period of detention, but the reasons for the detention must be reviewed every thirty days.

The above powers of investigative detention were used in Canada in August 2003 with respect to Project Thread, in which twenty-one non-citizens from Pakistan were arrested for typical immigration act violations relating to a fraudulent school being used to obtain student visas. Nevertheless, the arrests were headline news in Canada in large part because of a sensational "backgrounder" prepared by a Public Service and Anti-Terrorism Unit, composed of Mounties and immigration officials. The news release stated that the young men were "from, or have connections to, the Punjab province in Pakistan that is noted for Sunni extremism."[10] This led an aunt of one of the detained men to comment, "Pakistan only has four provinces. I don't see how being from one of them makes you a terrorist. Whatever happened to innocent until proven guilty? They're holding them because they're from one country and they're Muslim so therefore they have to be terrorists. I'm Canadian-born Pakistani and I never thought something like this would happen in Canada."[11]

The backgrounder went on to state that the men arrested "appear to reside in clusters of 4 or 5 young males and appear to change residences in clusters and/or interchange addresses with other clusters. . . . All targets were in Canada prior to September 5, 2001. . . . A confirmed associate of the group . . . provided an offer of employment from Global Relief Foundation . . . [which] has been identified by the United Nations as a fundraising group that provides financial support to terrorist groups, including al-Qaeda. . . . One of the targeted apartments is reported to have aeroplane schematics posted on the wall, as well as pictures of guns." And then the allegation that was the lead in the newspapers: "One of the subjects is currently enrolled in flight school to qualify as a multi-engine commercial pilot. His flight path for training purposes flies over the Pickering Nuclear Plant" (Bell and Stafford 2003).

Not surprisingly given the dramatic nature of this extraordinary press release, the initial detention of these nineteen men (the same number involved in the 9/11 attacks) was highly publicized and initially raised many security concerns in Canada. The men were entitled to prompt administrative hearings, but most of them were detained under section 58(1)(c) of IRPA on the grounds that "the Minister is taking necessary steps to inquire into a reasonable suspicion that they are inadmissible on grounds of security or for violating human and international rights" (Canada 2004b, 3–4).

The aftermath of these detentions suggest that the front-page news about a suspected al-Qaeda cell with designs on a nuclear plant was grossly unfair. Both the RCMP and immigration officials subsequently retracted the claims of a security threat with one official stating: "I can comfortably say there is no known threat; what is being investigated is a reasonable suspicion. It's taken the spin that it has taken in the media for whatever reason."[12] One of the reasons for the media spin, of course, was the sensational backgrounder prepared by the government.

Many of the men have been released since adjudicators determined that they were not a security threat and the widely publicized reference to flying over a nuclear plant turned out to be a routine flight path for those learning to fly. The men reported being asked questions about their religious and political beliefs, and some claimed that they were also threatened during their periods of detention. Those who have been deported or detained have also been found not to be security threats. Ten of the men made refugee applications on the basis that the publicity surrounding the case has made them liable to detention under Pakistan's harsh anti-terrorism laws. One of the men, Muhammad Naeem, subsequently described how his medical studies in Canada had been disrupted by his arrest and detention. He commented: "People try to avoid me. I can no longer sit in social circles. I feel like I live in some sort of a cage. I can't return to Pakistan because I could be arrested and tortured. I can't travel to the United States because I will be under constant suspicion. But if I stay here, I won't be free either. People here no longer trust me. Canada can seem like hell sometimes."[13] The body charged with hearing complaints against the RCMP has subsequently complained that their investigation of Project Thread has been hampered by the RCMP's refusal to disclose to them all of the evidence in the case, including information for search warrant applications (Heafey and the Commission for Public Complaints 2005, 35). The complaints body, however, subsequently rejected a complaint of discriminatory profiling on the basis that the RCMP members were not motivated by racism and had used criteria other than country of origin to select the targets of their investigation (Commission for Public Complaints 2006).

The whole incident has caused widespread resentment among Canada's Muslim communities, with some criticizing the apprehension of the men as the actions of a police state, and others suggesting that it is an example of profiling that victimizes the innocent. On the other hand, Canada's leading national newspaper refused to condemn the operation. It argued that the proceedings, unlike post-9/11 immigration proceedings in the United States, were conducted in public and that "preventive detention may be necessary in some cases."[14] It defended the double standards between immigration and criminal law by recognizing that the case against the men in the Project Thread detentions "would be laughed out of a criminal-court bail hearing, smacking of preventive detention and guilt by association."[15] These comments raise a recurring theme in post-9/11 security policies: namely, how Muslim communities are particularly vulnerable to harsh anti-terrorism laws that would not be accepted for citizens.

Security Certificates

Security certificates are an extraordinary procedure introduced in Canadian immigration law in the early 1990s and confirmed in a 2001 redraft of the law. They involve two elected ministers of the Crown and the ministers of immigration and public safety certifying that a non-citizen is a risk to the security of Canada. Since their enactment, security certificates have only been used in twenty-seven cases. This procedure preempts other immigration procedures, including applications for refugee status. Once a security certificate is signed it is subject to judicial review by one judge of the Federal Court of Canada, a court that specializes in judicial review of immigration and other administrative law matters involving the federal government. The law provides for reviews of detention, often at six-month intervals. If the security certificate is upheld as reasonable, the non-citizen is then subject to deportation.

The procedure for reviewing security certificates is extraordinary because the judge is required to hear the evidence in the absence of the person named in the certificate and their counsel if, in the judge's opinion, the disclosure of information would be injurious to national security or the safety of any person. Such information can be used by the judge in determining the reasonableness of the certificate, but it cannot even be included in a summary of evidence that can be provided to the person. The Supreme Court of Canada upheld a somewhat similar procedure in 1992, but stressed the importance of providing at least a summary of the evidence to the person named in the certificate.[16] The Court in that case also sidestepped the question of unequal treatment of citizens under the criminal law and non-citizens under immigration law by stressing that non-citizens do not have an absolute right to remain in Canada.

In 2004 the Federal Court of Appeal upheld the constitutionality of security certificates in the case of Adil Charkaoui who had been detained on the basis of a security certificate since May 2003. The Court of Appeal recognized that security certificates "derogate in a significant way from the adversarial process normally adhered to in criminal and civil matters," but stressed the government's duty to make full disclosure of the facts in its possession and the judge's "pro-active role in the interest of ensuring fairness" (*Charkaoui v. Canada* 2004, par. 75 and 80, respectively).[17] The Court of Appeal stressed the state's interest in national security:

> [T]he threat of terrorism or a threat to national security does not represent or reflect a situation of normality, at least not in our country . . . If we were to accept the appellant's position that national security cannot justify any derogations from the rules governing adversarial proceedings we would be reading into the Constitution of Canada an abandonment by the community as a whole of its right to survival in the name of a blind absolutism of the individual rights enshrined in that Constitution. We fail to discern any legislative intention along those lines, quite the contrary. (*Charkaoui v. Canada* 2004, par. 84 and 100, respectively)[18]

The Federal Court of Appeal stressed the public's interest in indefinitely incapacitating non-citizen terrorist suspects over the need to ensure that such suspects receive fair treatment. Key to such fair treatment is the suspects' right to mount an adversarial challenge to the government's case against them; a case that may be based on faulty intelligence from either Canada's own security intelligence agency, those of other governments, or persons who are being held under extreme conditions. Miscarriages of justice in past terrorism cases resulted in large part because the state did not disclose all the evidence to the accused (Roach and Trotter 2005). If such miscarriages can occur in criminal trials and appeals, they can certainly occur under the truncated security certificate procedures of the immigration law. The Federal Court of Appeal also failed to engage with the inequality of treatment of non-citizens under security certificates, as opposed to citizens who must be charged with criminal offenses. The sister of a thirty-one-year-old Moroccan alleged to have received training in an al-Qaeda camp and subject to a security certificate has argued that "all I want for him is to be judged with the same fairness, in open court, as pedophiles and serial killers. They told us Canada was a land of democracy and respect for ethnic minorities. I can't believe Canada would treat us this way."[19]

The Federal Court of Appeal's decision can be unfavorably compared to that made by the House of Lords one week later in its landmark case dealing with the Belmarsh detainees. In an 8–1 decision, the House of Lords found that derogation of fair trial rights to allow the indefinite detention of non-citizens suspected of terrorism who cannot be deported because of concerns that they would be tortured was a disproportionate and arbitrary response to the terrorist threat and one that discriminated against non-citizens.[20] Although non-citizenship has been recognized as a prohibited ground of discrimination under the Canadian constitution, the Canadian courts have not seriously considered the case that security certificates subject non-citizens to departures from fair procedures that would not be tolerated for citizens. Canada has relied on security certificates more than criminal charges with respect to suspected al-Qaeda terrorist suspects even though, as the House of Lords noted in the Belmarsh case, deportation may not be the best way to combat international terrorism. The Supreme Court subsequently allowed the detainees to appeal on the basis that the security certificate procedure denied them a fair opportunity to know the case against them.[21] The Court did not release the detainees but gave the government a year to devise a fairer system. A new system has been introduced to allow security-cleared special advocates to see and challenge the secret evidence. Concerns have been raised, however, that special advocates may not be able to communicate with detainees after the special advocates have seen the secret evidence and that lawyers for the detainees may not be able to act as special advocates.

Security certificates are currently being used against five Muslim men in Canada who are suspected of involvement with terrorism. Mahmoud Jaballah, alleged to have terrorist ties with the Egyptian al-Jihad, has been detained since August 2001 on a security certificate ordering his deportation to Egypt. Hassan Almrei, from Syria, has been detained since October 19, 2001. In 2005, he staged a hunger strike of over sixty days to protest his conditions of confinement in a remand center designed for prisoners awaiting trial. Mohamed Harkat has been detained since December 10, 2002, with allegations that he has ties to the Algerian Islamic Army Group. Mohammad Mahjoub, a forty-five-year-old Egyptian, has been detained the longest. He has been detained since June 26, 2000, and is alleged to have worked for bin Laden and to have worked with the Vanguards of Conquest, a group that wishes to overthrow the Egyptian government. Adil

Charkaoui was detained in May 2003, but was released in February 2005 on strict conditions on his fourth detention review.

Many prominent Canadians, including award-winning filmmaker Denys Arcand, came forward to post bail bonds for Charkaoui. The same occurred in June 2005 when Alexandre Trudeau, a filmmaker and son of former prime minister Pierre Trudeau, supported an unsuccessful attempt by Hassan Almrei to obtain bail. He argued that he was acting out of patriotism and because of his shame that people could be held in Canada without charge, but many articles in the mainstream media were skeptical about his support for a person who had already been determined a security threat by a judge in part on the basis of secret evidence. Although "the security certificate five" are not nearly as high profile as Maher Arar, they have received growing support from refugee advocates and civil libertarians and growing attention from the Canadian media.

One factor in the long-term detention of the above suspects on security certificates is uncertainty about whether Canada would deport a person to a risk of torture. In a 2002 case involving a member of the Tamil Tigers, the Supreme Court of Canada ruled that the Canadian Charter of Rights and Freedoms would, in most cases, prohibit the deportation of a person to a country where there is a substantial risk of torture. Interestingly, however, the Court did not articulate an absolute rule or indicate what exceptional circumstances might justify deportation to torture. The Court also did not address the situation of those who may be subject to continued detention because their removal from Canada would expose them to a risk of death or torture and hence be unconstitutional. The government is arguing in at least one case that a person detained under a security certificate should be deported to Egypt even if that results in torture or, alternatively, that "the threat to national security is so great that this man can never be released."[22] The Canadian courts have also refused to stay deportations to allow United Nations committees such as the Human Rights Committee and the Committee against Torture to hear complaints that non-citizens will be tortured if deported from Canada to Iran (Roach 2005). Another factor is that Canadian immigration law places no limits on the time that a person subject to a security certificate may be detained.

The Safe Third Country Agreement

In December 2001 Canada and the United States agreed to implement a "safe third country agreement" as part of border agreements to increase security and ensure the flow of goods and people at the border. This agreement will preclude most refugees who reach the United States from making a refugee application to Canada. Unless other measures are taken to increase refugee applications, this may significantly reduce the number of refugees Canada considers in any year. The agreement responds to perceptions that Canada's refugee policy is too liberal and generous, and reflects a desire among some in Canada to minimize border irritants between Canada and the United States given Canada's reliance on trade with the United States (Roach 2003).

A poll conducted in Canada in November 2002 indicated that 44 percent of respondents agreed with the proposition that the government might want to respond to terrorism by "restricting the number of immigrants that come to Canada from Muslim countries." This number was only marginally down from 49 percent who supported such immigration restrictions a year earlier. At the same time an almost equal number of respondents in 2002 (42 percent) opposed such restrictions.[23] Security issues may assist in the further politicization of immigration policy in Canada and be used as a vehicle for debate about multiculturalism in Canada.

Reliance on immigration law in an attempt to prevent terrorism is both radically over- and underinclusive (Roach 2006). Policies such as the Safe Third Country Agreement will turn away many more legitimate refugees than it will deflect terrorists. The type of long-term and preventive detention that is allowed with security certificates issued under Canadian immigration law may be successful in incapacitating suspected terrorists, albeit without a clear finding of guilt and at a cost of creating fear and resentment in newcomer communities. Most of those detained will eventually be deported from Canada. Given the international nature of terrorism, it is not clear that deflection or deportation of suspected terrorists to other countries will actually increase security. It may simply displace the problem of global terrorism. In addition, the immigration law approach that Canada has relied upon cannot be used against terrorist suspects who are Canadian citizens. A failure to use Canada's criminal anti-terrorism laws may result in inexperience that could threaten the ability of Canada to secure criminal convictions in terrorism cases. There was much public disillusionment in Canada over the recent acquittal of two Sikh Canadian citizens charged under the pre-9/11 criminal law with the 1985 bombing on an Air India flight that departed from Canada. There is a danger that police and prosecutors will not live up to the high standards of proof demanded by the criminal law so long as they can rely on the shortcut of using immigration law with its broader liability rules, lower standards of proof, and its ability to rely on secret evidence.

Maher Arar

One of the more dramatic examples of abuse of immigration law powers and procedures is the practice of extraordinary rendition of non-citizens. In Canada, a major, multimillion-dollar public inquiry, the Royal Commission of Inquiry, headed by a respected judge, was appointed by the federal government to examine the actions of Canadian officials in relation to the extraordinary rendition of Maher Arar, a Canadian citizen born in Syria, from the United States to Syria. Arar was returning to Canada when he was detained in the United States and transported to Jordan and then on to Syria, where he was detained for almost a year. He says he was tortured and signed a false confession about involvement with terrorism. An independent fact finder appointed by the Royal Commission of Inquiry has confirmed Mr. Arar's claims that he was tortured while he was in Syria and has also found that three other Canadians of Arab origin were tortured while detained in Syria on suspicion of involvement with terrorism (Canada 2005c). The government has not expanded the mandate of the Arar inquiry into the actions of these three men, but an extensive report on the Arar case was made public in 2006.

At first, Arar's treatment did not spark widespread concern in Canada, but public pressure mounted until the government decided to appoint the inquiry in early 2004. The inquiry has a factual mandate to investigate and report the actions of Canadian officials in relation to Arar's detention in the United States, his deportation to Syria, his treatment in Syria, and his return to Canada. The governments of both Syria and the United States have declined invitations to participate in the inquiry, which many see as extraordinary because of its examination of information concerning national security matters. Large portions of the inquiry have been conducted in private without Mr. Arar, his lawyers, or the media being present because of concerns about national security confidentiality. Many of the witnesses from the RCMP, the Canadian Security Intelligence Service (CSIS), and Canada's Department of Foreign Affairs have also been called to give public testimony. The very fact that such a large-scale inquiry was called by the government suggests an enhanced awareness in Canada of the dangers faced by Canadians with origins in the Middle East when they travel abroad and when they may have associations with those who may be the subject of security intelligence or police investigations relating to national security.

The Royal Commission of Inquiry also has a policy mandate to make recommendations on an independent, arm's-length review mechanism for the national security activities of the RCMP. This aspect of the inquiry recognizes that the RCMP has more tools at hand in the national security area with the enactment of the 2001 Anti-Terrorism Act. Unlike the Patriot Act and subsequent American legislation in relation to national security, Canada's ATA did not enhance review powers over national security activities. At present, the Commission for Public Complaints has only limited powers to oversee how the RCMP handles complaints, and it has no power to monitor the legality and propriety of RCMP activity in the absence of a complaint. Representatives of Canadian Muslim communities have argued before the Arar commission that many Muslims in Canada are fearful and reluctant to make complaints, and that the RCMP should be subject to regular independent reviews even in the absence of a complaint. They also point to the Arar case as an example of the need for an integrated review mechanism because Mr. Arar was affected by the actions of not only the RCMP, but by Canada's civilian security intelligence agency, CSIS, and other departments of government including the Department of Foreign Affairs.

Review and audit of national security activities are of particular importance to Canadian Muslim communities who may suspect, but not know for sure, that they are subject to surreptitious scrutiny from the state and who may, for various reasons relating to employment, social stigma, and lack of citizenship, be reluctant to complain about the treatment they receive from police, security intelligence, or customs agents.

Enhanced and integrated review of national security activities will focus on the propriety of state action, but it also has a potential to improve the effectiveness of the state's actions (Roach 2006). There is also an ongoing inquiry into the 1985 Air India bombing that will examine matters such as sharing of information and cooperation between the RCMP and CSIS, as well as the adequacy of aviation security. There have also been proposals for a committee of parliamentarians whose purpose will be to review all of the state's national security activities; to facilitate this, they would have access to classified information. The auditor general in Canada has already made reports about the inefficiencies of information sharing and watch lists in Canada. Inefficiencies in watch lists mean that the wrong people may be targeted and that legitimate suspects may be left off the list. Moreover, watch lists should be subject to both internal and external review to ensure that they are accurate and that people are not misidentified or wrongly placed on them. The targeting of the wrong people not only threatens civil liberties and human rights, but also wastes limited resources. Similarly, the alienation of Muslim communities by insensitive or heavy-handed tactics that inspire fear and distrust may dry up sources of information and cooperation. As suggested at the outset, the dichotomy between rights and security is often based on false premises. The use of harsh state tactics, such as racial and religious profiling, not only offends equality values, but is also frequently counterproductive to the task of identifying potential terrorist plots.

The Khadr Family

Although Maher Arar has become an object of considerable public sympathy in Canada, the same cannot be said of the Khadr family. The family was led by Ahmed Khadr, who was imprisoned in Pakistan in 1995 and 1996 and was eventually released after Canadian Prime Minister Jean Chrétien intervened on his behalf. Subsequently, it came to light that Khadr was associated with Osama bin Laden and al-Qaeda. Some Canadian officials testified at the Arar inquiry of the "Khadr effect" in which there were lingering concerns about the loyalty of Canadians held abroad on suspicion of involvement with terrorism. Ahmed Khadr was killed in fighting with Pakistani soldiers in 2003 and was eulogized by some as a founding member of al-Qaeda (Bell 2004, 186).

One of Khadr's sons, Omar Khadr, has been detained at Guantanamo Bay since late October 2001. He has now been charged with the killing of a U.S. Army soldier in combat on the Afghanistan-Pakistan border. His trial has been delayed

by a challenge in American courts to the constitutionality of trial by military tribunals. American officials have decided not to seek the death penalty against
Omar Khadr in part because he was fifteen years old at the time of the alleged offense. In addition to litigation in the United States, Omar Khadr is suing the
Canadian government alleging a failure to provide consular access, and he has
obtained an interlocutory injunction enjoining Canadian officials from continuing to question him at Guantanamo Bay on the basis that there was a serious
question whether such questioning violated Khadr's rights under the Canadian
Charter.[24]

Another son, Abdullah Khadr, is presently under arrest in Canada pending
proceedings for extradition to the United States on charges of procuring weapons
for use against American forces. Upon his return to Canada and before his arrest,
Abdullah Khadr was quoted as saying that "every Muslim dreams of being a
shaheed [martyr] for Islam . . . like you die for your religion. Everybody dreams of
this, even a Christian would like to die for their religion."[25] Another son,
Abdurahman Khadr, was also detained at Guantanamo; he has been released and
has returned to Canada. He has described his family as "an al-Qaeda family."[26]
The youngest son, Abdulkarim Khadr, was paralyzed in Pakistan in the fighting
that killed his father and now lives with his mother in Toronto. A sister, Zaynab
Khadr, was the subject of a publicized search warrant upon her return to Canada,
and the RCMP has stated that the search of a laptop computer in her possession
has provided "time and place information regarding activities of key al-Qaeda
and Taliban personalities who are presently at large and operating against coalition troops."[27]

The Khadr family is, to say the least, unpopular in Canada and provides a
counternarrative to that of Maher Arar. For example, Canada's domestic intelligence agency responded to a court decision prohibiting it from continuing to
question Omar Khadr at Guantanamo with the statement that "the Khadr family
has made no secret of its affiliation to al-Qaeda or its loyalty to Osama bin Laden"
and stated that its questioning of Khadr was shared with the United States as part
of its investigation of "Sunni Islamic extremism."[28] At the same time, the court's
order and subsequent American charges against Khadr have renewed some public
interest in Omar Khadr's case. For example, Canada's national newspaper has
editorialized that "the Canadian government has acted scandalously" both by
interrogating the teenager and by failing to lobby as effectively as the United
Kingdom and Australia, which have been able to secure the release of their citizens held at Guantanamo. It stated that "there is not and may never be a groundswell of opinion that Omar Khadr's rights need protection. But they do. The
Canadian government's eagerness to exploit Guantanamo in the case of a Canadian teenager incarcerated since he was 15 is shameful."[29]

Although the Khadr family and Maher Arar have generally been presented
as competing narratives of guilt and innocence, respectively, in terms of public

discourse about Muslims in Canada, this dichotomy can break down. The independent fact finder who examined and confirmed Maher Arar's claims of torture reported that Arar feels isolated from the Muslim community, has stopped attending the mosque, and believes that some Muslims are unwilling to support him or associate with him (Canada 2005c, 22). Arar was unable to obtain employment after his return to Canada in 2003 despite his skills as a university-educated expert in computers. This suggests that the so-called Khadr effect (lingering suspicions about the loyalty of Muslims who have come to the attention of authorities at home and abroad) may have a harmful impact throughout Canadian society, particularly within Canada's Muslim communities, whose members may fear being associated with anyone who may attract suspicions.

Cross-Cultural Roundtables and Outreach to Muslim Communities

In 2004, as part of a new all-risk national security policy, the government of Canada committed itself to the creation of a "[C]ross-Cultural Roundtable on Security . . . comprised of members of ethno-cultural and religious communities from across Canada." The roundtable will "engage in a long-term dialogue to improve understanding on how to manage security interests in a diverse society" (Canada 2004a, 2). The roundtable has subsequently been established and is chaired by Zaheer Lakhani, a medical doctor who has been honored for his outreach work with the Ismaili community. Its fifteen members include others who have worked with Canada's diverse Muslim communities, as well as other ethno-cultural communities in Canada. On the occasion of its first meeting, Anne McLellan, then minister of public safety, stated that the roundtable was "an excellent opportunity for two-way dialogue between those who make national security policy and Canadians who are particularly concerned with the consequences of these policies" (Canada 2005a).

It remains to be seen whether the Cross-Cultural Roundtable on Security will yield dividends in terms of social solidarity, and eventually security, but there are some promising signs of increased engagement between Canada's Muslim community and the Canadian government. The minister of public safety held private meetings with about a hundred Muslims in the wake of the London bombings in the summer of 2005. The president of the Coalition of Muslim Organizations called the meeting "a sign of respect," and 120 imams in Canada issued a statement in late July 2005 after the London bombings stating in part that Canadian Muslims

> have journeyed from six continents to make Canada our home. Our life in Canada has been of positive contribution and near seamless integration. It has not been a clash of cultures or of civilizations. . . . We have opposed, and will

continue to oppose, all extremism, hate and terrorism. Anyone who claims to be a Muslim and participates in any way in the taking of innocent life is betraying the very spirit and letter of Islam. We will confront and challenge the extremist mindset that produces this perversion of our faith. (CAIR-CAN 2005)

This important statement received media attention in Canada, and the then prime minister of Canada, Paul Martin, subsequently met for an hour with nineteen imams who signed this statement. The public was not unaware of the potential security benefits of greater trust and dialogue with the Muslim community; along these lines, an article in a national newspaper was entitled "Imams Vow to Report Extremists."[30] At the same time, however, divisions in Canada's diverse Muslim community were also apparent with one secular Muslim organization criticizing the prime minister for meeting with the imams[31] and another imam from Toronto refusing to sign the statement and claiming that Canada's security intelligence agency had harassed him, his mosque, and others in the community.[32] The security intelligence agency responded that it had investigated the allegations and found them to be unfounded, with the media reporting that the imam in question has been associated with Ahmed Khadr, a man with known al-Qaeda connections.[33] It is difficult to predict whether the attempts to build bridges between Muslim communities and the Canadian government with respect to security issues will be successful or how Canada might react to the strains of an act of terrorism within its borders.

The Future of Multiculturalism in Post-9/11 Canada

Since 1971, Canada has had an official policy of multiculturalism, and section 27 of the 1982 Canadian Charter of Rights and Freedoms provides that Charter rights should be interpreted in a manner consistent with Canada's multicultural heritage. Multiculturalism is nevertheless controversial in Canada, with some critics arguing that it encourages immigrants to remain rooted in the culture, language, and politics of their homeland. Such critics point to the Khadr family as a symptom of the ills of multiculturalism. Others, however, defend Canadian multiculturalism as a means of allowing Canada's diverse population to integrate and point to Canada's comparative lack of ethnic strife and high levels of integration as measured by citizenship, political participation, use of its two official languages, and intermarriage (Kymlicka 1998). Defenders of multiculturalism point to the Royal Commission of Inquiry's scrutiny of the activities of Canadian officials in relation to Maher Arar as an example of the Canadian state's recognition of the vulnerable position of many foreign-born citizens and as a sign of its concern and respect for such citizens. Others dispute that the Canadian state is truly committed to multiculturalism and non-discrimination and cite Canada's refusal to extend the Arar inquiry to examine the detention in Syria of other foreign-born

Canadian citizens on the basis of suspicions of involvement in terrorism as evidence for their claims. In December 2006, the government appointed an internal inquiry chaired by a former justice of the Supreme Court of Canada to examine the actions of Canadian officials in relation to three Canadian citizens held in Syria on suspicions of terrorism.

Future relations between Canadian governments and Canada's diverse Muslim communities are uncertain, but the creation of the Cross-Cultural Roundtable, the inquiry into the activities of Canadian officials in relation to Maher Arar, the three-year review of the ATA, and meetings between senior members of the Muslim community and senior ministers and the prime minister are all positive signs. The fact that the roundtable was included as an important part of Canada's new national security policy, along with a commitment to independent review of the RCMP's national security activities, suggests some awareness that better relations with Muslim communities and closer review of national security activities could improve security rather than detract from it. Canada's Muslim communities have condemned terrorism, and they stand to lose the most from terrorism and the state's reaction to it. Their leaders have been actively involved in the political process and have been trying to alleviate societal fears. Nevertheless, such progress is fragile, and could be seriously disrupted by either a terrorist act or an act of state abuse in a terrorism-related investigation.

Notes

The author thanks Anver Emon and Ziyaad Mia for helpful comments on an earlier draft and Malcolm Katz for research assistance, and accepts full responsibility for errors and misunderstandings.

1. The entire Criminal Code is available at http://laws.justice.gc.ca/en/C-46/text.html (accessed December 13, 2006).

2. *Suresh v. Canada (Minister of Citizenship and Immigration)*, [2002] 1 S.C.R. 3.

3. *R. v. Malik and Bagri*, [2005] B.C.S.C. 350.

4. Robert Matas and Campbell Clark, "Poll Finds Most in B.C. Reject Air-India Verdict: Almost Half of Those Who Followed the Trial Say Their View of the System Has Worsened," *Globe and Mail*, March 31, 2005, sec. A7.

5. *Suresh v. Canada (Minister of Citizenship and Immigration)*, [2002] 1 S.C.R. 3.

6. Colin Freeze and Kim Lunman, "Khawaja Family Absent from Mosque: Congregation Wonders about Fate of Fellow Members," *Globe and Mail*, April 3, 2004, sec. A7.

7. *Application under section 83.28 of the Criminal Code* (Re), [2004] 2 S.C.R. 248. See also *Vancouver Sun (Re)*, [2004] 2 S.C.R. 332.

8. Jake Rupert, "The End of the Sordid Hussein Tale," *Ottawa Citizen*, October 2, 2003, sec. A1.

9. *Andrews v. Law Society of British Columbia*, [1989] 1 S.C.R. 143; see also *Chiarelli v. Canada (Minister of Employment and Immigration)*, [1992] 1 S.C.R. 711.

10. Michelle Shephard and Betsy Powell, "Police Arrest 19 in Terror Probe: Citizenship Officer Triggered Alarm, One Man Enrolled in Flight School," *Toronto Star*, August 22. 2003, sec. A1.

11. Ibid.

12. Marina Jimenez, Colin Freeze, and Victoria Burnett, "Case of 19 Starts to Unravel: RCMP, Immigration Say No Evidence National Security Is at Clear Risk," *Globe and Mail*, August 30, 2003, sec. A5.

13. "No Hope in a Land of Dreams," *Toronto Star,* November 30, 2003, sec. A7.

14. Editorial, "The Arguments Made in Protection's Name," *Globe and Mail,* August 29, 2003, sec. A16.

15. Ibid.

16. *Chiarelli v. Canada (Minister of Employment and Immigration),* [1992] 1 S.C.R. 711.

17. *Charkaoui v. Canada (Minister of Citizenship and Immigration and the Solicitor General of Canada),* [2004] F.C.A. 421.

18. Ibid.

19. Ann Carroll, "Charkaoui Challenges Security Certificate Case Goes to Federal Court of Appeal: Held Without Bail Since May 2003, Face Possible Deportation to Morocco," *Montreal Gazette,* November 7, 2004, sec. A2.

20. *A (FC) and Others (FC) v. Secretary of State for the Home Department,* 2004 UKHL 56.

21. *Charkaoui v. Canada (Minister of Employment and Immigration),* [2007] 1 S.C.R. 350.

22. Harold Levy, "Must Deport Jaballah, Court Told," *Toronto Star,* August 17. 2004, sec. A16.

23. Mike Blanchfield, "Canadian Attitudes on Immigration Hardening against Muslims," *Ottawa Citizen,* December 24, 2002, sec. A1.

24. *Khadr v. Canada (Her Majesty the Queen),* 2005 F.C. 1076.

25. Unnati Gandhi, "Khadr Son Allegedly Admitted Father's Role: Terror Suspect Confessed Senior Khadr Organized Attacks, Documents Maintain," *Globe and Mail,* December 20, 2005, sec. A15.

26. Ibid.

27. Michelle Shephard, "Mounties Uncover 'Al Qaeda' Cache," *Toronto Star,* June 14, 2005, sec. A1.

28. Colin Freeze, "Judge Orders Canada to Stop Quizzing Teen in Guantanamo," *Globe and Mail,* August 10, 2005, sec. A1.

29. Editorial, "Omar Khadr's Limbo," *Globe and Mail,* August 11, 2005. sec. A14.

30. Unnati Gandhi, "Imams Vow to Report Extremists: Working with Authorities 'A Religious Duty,' Canadian Muslim Leaders Announce," *Globe and Mail,* July 22, 2005, sec. A7.

31. Mohammed Adam, "Muslims Search for a Common Voice: Canadian Muslims Are Grappling with How to Protect Their Faith and Preserve Their Diversity," *Ottawa Citizen,* August 14, 2005, sec. A1.

32. Colin Freeze, "Imam Warns Ottawa to Back Off Muslims," *Globe and Mail,* July 25, 2005, sec. A10.

33. Colin Freeze, "Imam's Accusations Unfounded, CSIS Says," *Globe and Mail,* July 27, 2005, sec. A4.

References

Bell, Stewart. 2004. *Cold Terror: How Canada Nurtures and Exports Terrorism around the World.* Etobicoke, Ontario: John Wiley and Sons.

Bell, W., and L. Stafford. August 19, 2003. *Project Thread Backgrounder: Reasons for Detention Pursuant to 58(1)(c).* Available at http://www.threadbare.tyo.ca/modules.php?op=modload&name=News&file=article&sid=222&mode=thread&order=0&thold=0&POSTNUKESID=d36565ca95bc55cbff5e77ef535d42dd (accessed December 13, 2006).

Canada. Senate. December 5, 2001. *Special Committee on Bill C-36: Transcripts of the Testimony by the Coalition of Muslim Organizations.* Available at http://www.law.utoronto.ca/c-36/December4.pdf (accessed December 14, 2006).

Canada. Privy Council Office. April 2004(a). *Securing an Open Society: Canada's National Security Policy.* Available at http://www.pco-bcp.gc.ca/index.asp?lang=eng&page=information&sub=publications&doc=natsec-secnat/natsec-secnat_e.htm (accessed February 28, 2008).

Canada. Department of Citizenship, Department of Justice, and the Solicitor General Canada. 2004(b). *Sixth Annual Report: Canada's Crimes against Humanity and War Crimes Program 2002–2003.* Available at http://canada-justice.ca/en/dept/pub/cca/report0203/pdf/war -crimes-e.pdf (accessed December 13, 2006).

Canada. March 7, 2005(a). "Inaugural Meeting of Cross-Cultural Roundtable on Security." Available at http://ww2.ps-sp.gc.ca/publications/news/2005/20050307_e.asp (accessed December 13, 2006).

Canada. Senate. May 2, 2005(b). *Special Committee on Bill C-36 Transcripts of the Testimony by the Coalition of Muslim Organizations.*

Canada. Commission of Inquiry into the Actions of Canadian Officials in Relation to Maher Arar. October 14, 2005(c). *Report of Professor Stephen J. Toope, Fact Finder.* Available at http://www.ararcommission.ca/eng/ToopeReport_final.pdf (accessed December 14, 2006).

Canadian Islamic Congress. April 13, 2004. *Towards Informed and Committed Voting: A Research Report on Grading Federal MPs—2000–2004.* Available at http://www.canadianislamiccon-gress.com/election2004/Election2004.pdf (accessed December 13, 2006).

Choudhry, Sujit, and Kent Roach. 2003. "Racial and Ethnic Profiling: Statutory Discretion, Constitutional Remedies and Democratic Accountability." *Osgoode Hall Law Journal* 41 (1): 1–36.

Coalition of Muslim Organizations. November 8, 2001. *Standing Committee on Justice and Human Rights: Submission on Bill C-36: Anti-Terrorism Act.* Available at http://www.muslimlaw.org/MLA.c36.pdf (accessed December 13, 2006).

Cole, David. 2003. *Enemy Aliens: Double Standards and Constitutional Freedoms in the War on Terrorism.* New York: New Press.

Commission for Public Complaints. February 28, 2006. *Chair's Final Report.* File PC-2003-2070.

Cotler, Irwin. 2001. "Thinking Outside the Box: Foundational Principles for a Counter-Terrorism Law and Policy." In *The Security of Freedom: Essays on Canada's Anti-Terrorism Bill,* ed. Ronald Daniels, Patrick Macklem, and Kent Roach, 111–129. Toronto: University of Toronto Press.

Council on American-Islamic Relations Canada [CAIR-CAN], July 21, 2005. "Canadian Imams Denounce Terrorism, Call on Muslims to Challenge and Confront Terrorism." Available at http://www.caircan.ca/itn_more.php?id=1789_0_2_0_C (accessed December 13, 2006).

Dosman, E. Alexandra. 2004. "For the Record: Designating 'Listed Entities' for the Purposes of Terrorist Financing Offences at Canadian Law." *University of Toronto Faculty Law Review* 62 (1): 1–28.

Heafey, Shirley, and Commission for Public Complaints against the RCMP. June 2005. *Review: Annual Report 2004/2005.* Ottawa: Minister of Public Works and Government Services. Available at http://www.cpc-cpp.gc.ca/app/DocRepository/1/PDF/AR0405_e.pdf (accessed December 13, 2006).

Kymlicka, Will. 1998. *Finding Our Way: Rethinking Ethnocultural Relations in Canada.* Toronto: Oxford University Press.

Macklin, Audrey. 2001. "Borderline Security." In *The Security of Freedom: Essays on Canada's Anti-Terrorism Bill,* ed. Ronald Daniels, Patrick Macklem, and Kent Roach, 383–404. Toronto: University of Toronto Press.

Mia, Ziyaad. 2002. "Terrorizing the Rule of Law." *National Journal of Constitutional Law* 14 (1): 125–152.

———. 2005. "The End of Law: Canada's National Security Legislation and the Principle of Shared Humanity." LLM thesis, University of Toronto.

Ramraj, Victor V., Michael Hor, and Kent Roach, eds. 2005. *Global Anti-Terrorism Law and Policy.* New York: Cambridge University Press.

Roach, Kent. 2003. *September 11: Consequences for Canada.* Montreal: McGill-Queens University Press.

———. 2004. "Anti-Terrorism and Militant Democracy: Some Western and Eastern Responses." In *Militant Democracy,* ed. Andras Sajo, 171–207. Amsterdam: Eleven International Publishing.

———. 2005. "Constitutional, Remedial and Institutional Dialogues about Rights: The Canadian Experience." *Texas International Law Journal* 40 (3): 577–584.

———. 2006. "Must We Trade Rights for Security: The Choice between Smart, Harsh or Proportionate Security Strategies in Canada and Britain." *Cardozo Law Review* 27: 2151–2221.

———. 2007. "The Post 9-11 Migration of the Terrorism Act, 2000." In *The Migration of Constitutional Ideas,* ed. Sujit Choudhry. Cambridge: Cambridge University Press.

Roach, Kent, and Gary Trotter. 2005. "Miscarriages of Justice in the War against Terror." *Penn State Law Review* 109 (4): 967–1041.

Saloojee, Riad. September 9–11, 2003. "Life for Canadian Muslims the Morning After: A 911 Wake-Up Call." Paper presented at the Seventh Annual Metropolis Conference, Oslo, Norway.

Statistics Canada. May 26, 2005. *Ecumenical Canada.* Available at http://www43.statcan.ca/02/02a/02a_008_e.htm (accessed December 14, 2006).

12

Counterterrorism and the Civil Rights of Muslim Minorities in the European Union

Anja Dalgaard-Nielsen

"Let no-one be in any doubt, the rules of the game are changing," announced Prime Minister Tony Blair in the wake of the terrorist attacks on London's subway in July 2005. Among the new measures proposed by his government in response to the bombings were: easier procedures to deport persons "fostering hatred" and "advocating violence," criminalizing "condoning or glorifying terrorism," granting the police authority to detain terrorist suspects for a longer period (up to three months) before raising charges, granting the foreign secretary the right to issue so-called control orders restricting the liberty of terrorist suspects, and the compilation of an international database of persons engaging in "unacceptable behavior" to be denied entry into the UK.[1]

The UK initiatives are not unique. Since 9/11, a number of European countries have gradually tightened their legislation and expanded the powers of law enforcement and security agencies. Terrorist crimes now earn tougher penalties. Law enforcement and intelligence services gained enhanced powers to monitor, search, detain, and prosecute terrorist suspects in most European countries.[2]

Moreover, the European Union has taken major steps toward coordinating and integrating the counterterrorism efforts of member states. EU member states

246 · Anja Dalgaard-Nielsen

are gradually developing a common legal framework for combating terrorism that includes a common definition of terrorism, common minimum sentences, and a common arrest warrant. They are also attempting to enhance information sharing and coordinated collection of intelligence through a number of EU working groups focusing specifically on counterterrorism.

Proponents of these measures claim that they represent crucial steps in the effort to protect civilians against threats by terrorists who operate across unguarded inner European borders. The right of European citizens to live in freedom from fear of random and indiscriminate terrorist attacks against soft civilian targets, they claim, must take precedence over the rights of terrorist suspects slated for deportation or placed under surveillance. Critics, however, argue that the broad scope of some of these measures imperils basic civil liberties, particularly for European minorities. They point out that the discursive coupling of problems like illegal immigration, organized crime, and terrorism might cause increasing stigmatization of Muslims in Europe, and that the EU's expanding role in fighting terrorism is problematic because of an absence of established channels for democratic control and oversight of EU initiatives, agencies, and working groups.[3]

This chapter outlines and evaluates the main new anti-terrorism initiatives of the European Union in the areas of intelligence and law enforcement, and makes recommendations for counteracting their negative effects on civil rights, particularly those of Muslim minorities in Europe.

Counterterrorism in the European Union

The European Union reacted to the emergence of al-Qaeda-inspired terrorism with a broad range of initiatives spanning from efforts against the presumed root causes of terrorism to enhanced judicial cooperation and civil protection inside the Union. The many initiatives are summarized in the EU Plan of Action on Combating Terrorism, which is complemented by a host of other plans, programs, and communications.[4]

The action plan identifies the EU's "seven strategic objectives":

1. To deepen the international consensus and enhance international efforts to combat terrorism;
2. To reduce the access of terrorists to financial resources;
3. To maximize the capacity within the EU bodies and Member States to detect, investigate and prosecute terrorists and to prevent terrorist attacks;
4. To protect the security of international transport and ensure effective systems of border control;

5. To enhance the capability of the European Union and of [M]ember States to deal with the consequences of a terrorist attack;
6. To address the factors which contribute to support for, and recruitment into, terrorism;
7. To target actions under EU external relations towards priority Third Countries where counter-terrorist capacity or commitment to combating terrorism needs to be enhanced. (Council of the European Union 2004b, 2)

The most significant new initiatives following 9/11 have been in the areas of intelligence, law enforcement, and legal cooperation—notably in the effort to detect, intercept, investigate, and prosecute terrorists. Systematic efforts to coordinate and exchange information between European secret services and police agencies date back to the 1970s. In 1976 the so-called Trevi group, consisting of the home affairs or justice ministers of the member states of the then European Community was set up with the goal of strengthening cooperation on internal security in Europe. A decade later Belgium, France, Germany, Luxembourg, and the Netherlands strengthened practical collaboration and the exchange of information among national police authorities with the 1985 Schengen Agreement. The agreement envisaged the gradual abolition of checks at the five signatories' borders, but made entry into these countries more difficult to outsiders. The agreement included such measures as access by all Schengen countries to the Schengen Information System providing personal identity and other data throughout the Schengen area, close police and judicial cooperation, and joint efforts to combat drug-related crimes. In May 1999 the Schengen Protocol to the Treaty of Amsterdam of October 2, 1997, incorporated Schengen cooperation into the framework of the EU judicial cooperation that had been included as an EU objective with the 1992 Treaty of Maastricht, leading, in part, to the establishment of Europol (the European Police Office) with the objective of improving member state cooperation in combating terrorism and organized crime.[5]

The 9/11 attacks on the U.S. gave a boost to ongoing EU efforts to intensify police, intelligence, and legal cooperation. Just one week after the attacks, the European Commission presented a proposal for a common definition of terrorism, which was later adopted with slight alterations. It included the following:

[I]ntentional acts . . . which, given their nature or context, may seriously damage a country or an international organization where committed with the aim of:

. . . (i) seriously intimidating a population, or (ii) unduly compelling a Government or international organization to perform or abstain from performing any act, or (iii) seriously destabilizing or destroying the

> fundamental political, constitutional, economic or social structures of a
> country or an international organization:
> (a) attacks upon a person's life which may cause death;
> (b) attacks upon the physical integrity of a person;
> (c) kidnapping or hostage taking; ...
> (e) causing extensive destruction to a Government or public facility, a trans-
> port system, an infrastructure facility, including an information system, a
> fixed platform located on the continental shelf, a public place or private
> property likely to endanger human life or result in major economic loss. ...
> (Official Journal of the European Communities 2002, 4)

This agreement was accompanied by the establishment of common minimum penalties and sanctions relating to terrorist offenses (Commission of the European Communities 2004a). Moreover, the EU Council drew up a common list of individuals and organizations linked to terrorist activities, which the member countries pledged to investigate and prosecute through close collaboration among law enforcement authorities (Council of the European Union 2001b; Commission of the European Union 2004b, 1–3).

The definitional agreement helped pave the way to the adoption of the EU warrant of arrest, which is a radical departure from traditional interpretations of transborder law enforcement. The warrant applies when the maximum period of the penalty for the crime is at least a year in prison and the charge is related to terrorism or other serious crimes such as murder, corruption, or illicit drug trafficking (Commission of the European Communities 2005b). The warrant, based on the principle of mutual recognition of decisions by EU judiciaries, had been discussed since the 1999 EU summit in Tampere, Finland, but only entered into force in January 2004. It had gained political traction only after al-Qaeda's 2001 attacks on the U.S. The warrant effectively allows any member state to enforce a sentence or obtain an individual's arrest and extradition from any other EU state with minimal formalities and within sixty days from the extradition request (Wouters and Naert 2003, 14).

The implementation of the warrant has not been smooth. When Madrid was hit by simultaneous bombs in March 2004, two major EU members, Germany and Italy, had still not integrated the warrant into national law. Moreover, only three months after Italy implemented the warrant (the last country to do so), in July 2005, the German Constitutional Court ruled that the warrant was unconstitutional. The court argued that the law did not adequately exploit the opportunities for securing the rights of the defendant laid out in the EU framework decision on the arrest warrant.[6] Still, the common warrant is considered a success by the EU because it is widely used and has shortened the average extradition time from about nine months to about forty days (Commission of the European Communities 2005a, 5).

Box 12.1. EU Counterterrorism Coordination Organizations

EU Council: Legislates, updates Plan of Action on Combating Terrorism every six months, compiles and updates list of terrorist organizations, persons, entities.

Europol: Collects, analyzes, shares information about international terrorism.

Eurojust: Forum for magistrates and prosecutors that coordinates and supports member state investigations.

Police Chief Task Force (PCTF): Operational coordination, exchange of information and experience.

Terrorism Working Group (TWG): Representatives from national interior or justice ministries; develops common threat assessment, cooperation between EU bodies.

Working Party on Terrorism (COTER): Representatives from foreign affairs ministries; develops threat assessment and policy recommendations regarding third countries.

SitCen: Merges internal and external threat information to provide a comprehensive threat assessment.

Counter-Terrorism Group: Representatives from EU national intelligence agencies plus Norway and Switzerland.

Also in reaction to the 9/11 attacks, the EU allocated an increased budget to Europol, the European police cooperation agency that began operating in 1999. It also established Eurojust, an agency formed of prosecutors, judges, and police officers to promote coordination among national authorities in investigating and prosecuting serious crime concerning two or more member states (Wouters and Naert 2003, 23).

To further promote coordination and exchange of information and experience, a number of new agencies and working groups have been established or have refocused on counterterrorism. Box 12.1 provides an overview of some of the major organizations.[7]

The amount of intelligence and information sharing is frequently criticized for being insufficient because of the transnational character of the threat and the relative ease of movement inside the Schengen area. Among the challenges are an alleged lack of trust between different countries and services, divergent threat perceptions across the different EU member states, turf wars, and excessively complicated institutional structures. A number of member states still prefer to cooperate bilaterally or in smaller informal groupings, like the so-called Group of Five (Germany, France, Italy, Spain, and the United Kingdom). Those limitations reduce the ability of the various EU coordination groups to support proactive investigations to intercept plots and disable terrorist cells. They are mainly limited to analyzing past experiences to develop common threat assessments.[8]

Still, it is reasonable to assume that the amount of information being shared is on the rise. Cooperation will continue to increase as more terrorist attacks cause threat perceptions to converge and as the necessary trust gradually builds up as it tends to do over time in such ventures. In spite of current challenges, the EU is gradually creating a common legal framework for combating terrorism and the member states are sharing a growing volume of information through the EU.

Advantages and Limitations of the New Measures

Anti-terror measures, legislative changes, and the increased international cooperation have intensified divisions in Europe and North America. Those supporting the new laws and improved international cooperation typically indicate three factors that make these changes imperative: the extreme violence of "new" terrorism, the threat's transnational character, and its use of the newest technology for communication and organizational purposes.

First, these advocates argue, the new terrorism is different from both common criminal activities and the kind of political terrorism that ravaged Europe in the 1970s and 1980s. The "old" terrorism used violence selectively to bring attention to a political cause, or to obtain political concessions. Extreme violence was regarded as counterproductive because it might provoke a public backlash and a crackdown by state authorities. In contrast, the new terrorism aims at maximizing casualties. The strikes against the U.S. that killed 2,986 people in New York, Pennsylvania, and Washington, D.C., have left no one in doubt of the terrorists' indiscriminate strategy. Attacks against soft, unprotected, and arguably non-protectable targets like the public transportation systems of Madrid and London require strategies that increase the chance of detecting and foiling plots before they are realized or quickly dismantling terrorist networks before they can strike again, the argument goes.[9]

Furthermore, advocates claim, technological developments have overtaken existing law. The exploitation of mobile phones and the internet by increasingly sophisticated al-Qaeda operatives and sympathizers necessitates an update of the legal instruments available to monitor suspects and detect or investigate plots. These instruments include roving wiretaps to keep track of mobile communications, the authority to monitor and seize electronic correspondence and records of internet logs, and charting e-mail and short message service (SMS) communication patterns (who has been in contact with whom, when, and from where?).

Finally, supporters argue, terrorists operate transnationally and must be countered in part through intensified international cooperation in law enforcement, intelligence, and justice; particularly in the European Union where internal border controls among Schengen countries have been abolished. EU countries are more interdependent than ever because they have to defend a common external frontier to ensure border security and must rely on mutual cooperation to counter organized crime and terrorist cells which, unlike security services and police forces, can operate more or less freely across internal Schengen borders.[10] The transnational nature of terrorism in a borderless Europe thus calls for information sharing and operational cooperation. It also, the argument continues, increases the need to harmonize sanctions and investigative methods to prevent terrorists from exploiting discrepancies among EU member states by establishing bases in the countries with the weakest law enforcement regimes in the hope of targeting other Schengen member states (Townsend 2003, 1).

Critics of the new measures maintain that authorities have gone too far in their attempt to shore up security at the expenses of basic civil rights. To be sure, they argue, responses to the new and more violent terrorism require that extra resources be allocated to prevent or investigate attacks and that international cooperation be strengthened. However, new national laws that expand the opportunities to monitor, detain, and deport suspects, as well as EU-coordinated efforts to compile and share information about citizens, compromise individual liberty, due process guarantees, the right to a speedy and fair trial, the protection of private spaces, and the secrecy of mail and telecommunication services.[11]

Critics also disagree with the broad scope of the common EU definition of terrorism and with measures adopted by individual EU member states because of concerns over the broad criminalization of indirect support for terrorist activities and the creation of new categories of illegal activities. For example, critics note that it might be difficult to judge whether support for humanitarian activities and organizations in the West Bank and Gaza should be regarded as financing terrorism. Moreover, due process guarantees and the presumption of innocence are compromised by measures such as the automatic freezing of assets belonging to persons or entities on the EU Council's terrorism list, which is drawn up based on secret intelligence.[12]

Impact on Muslim Minorities and
Social Cohesion of European Societies

All democratic states face challenges when they attempt to fashion a counterterrorism system that does not sacrifice fundamental rights. Yet, arguably, the European states face a greater challenge than the U.S. and Canada because rights
protection, security, and the cohesion of societies depend on creating measures
that do not appear arbitrary and do not appear discriminatory to restive and vulnerable Muslim minorities. The challenges are greater for European countries
because of the nature of the threats currently facing them and because of the
composition of European societies. Terrorism in Europe is "homegrown," and
relations between European minorities and majorities are already strained in a
number of states over issues like welfare, discrimination, and crime.

Whereas the U.S. could, at least initially, focus its response on a foreign terrorist organization with a physical base in a foreign country, the most immediate
threat to European security does not emanate from the Afghan mountains or
foreign universities and cities. Instead, it emanates from Europe's own suburbs,
from extremists on the fringes of Muslim groups, such as the individuals who
formed the cells that attacked Madrid and London. This sort of homegrown terrorism has given a boost to preexisting xenophobia and mistrust toward Muslim
minorities in Europe (Allen and Nielsen 2002, 7). In this context, the potential for
terrorism to corrode the social fabric of European societies is high, as al-Qaeda-
inspired violence provokes counterviolence from rightist extremists, which, in
turn, hardens lines between communities. We witnessed such vicious cycles both
in the Netherlands after the murder of the filmmaker Theo van Gogh and in the
UK after the bombings in London. Moreover, homegrown terrorism also increases the risk that authorities, eager to intercept or disrupt further plots, will be
tempted to use dragnet measures and therefore broadly target members of specific ethnic or religious groups.

There are indeed indications that new national powers are being used in a
way that is discriminatory, or at least is perceived as such. The UK Institute of
Race Relations has published a study that scrutinized the application of the British 2000 and 2001 Terrorism Acts during the three years following 9/11. The
study, which analyzed about half the number of total arrests and detentions made
under these laws (the cases in which the necessary information was available),
indicates that the vast majority of those arrested were Muslims of Middle Eastern
or North African origin. Moreover, it finds a large gap between the number of arrests (609) and the number of convictions secured in open court (15), indicating
that a large number of innocent people have been adversely affected by the Terrorism Acts.[13] Though official Scotland Yard statistics show only a slight increase
in the percentage of Asians (mainly Muslims) being stopped and searched from

2000 to 2004 (from about 10 percent to about 12 percent of all those being stopped and searched by the London Metropolitan Police) the total number of stop-and-search actions have increased significantly since 2000–2001.[14]

Whereas such dragnet measures might have some disruptive and deterrent effects, they also infringe upon the rights of a large number of innocent people. Such individuals get caught up in humiliating investigations which frequently do not lead to convictions in open courts. Such rights violations are likely to contribute to the perception among Europe's Muslim minorities of being unjustly targeted, and therefore decrease their willingness to cooperate with authorities' counterterrorism efforts.

The responsibility to avoid discrimination and alienation as a result of the application of new powers is primarily a member state's responsibility because the European Union does not have operational counterterrorism capabilities. Yet, the Union is an important actor that influences member state actions through its legislative and coordinating role. Critics have specifically expressed concern about a November 2002 recommendation by the European Council that member states cooperate through Europol to develop terrorist profiles on the basis of characteristics such as nationality, age, education, and family situation to help identify terrorists seeking entry to or who are already present on the territory of member states. Such profiles, critics argue, are likely to lead to widespread discrimination.[15]

Fighting Terrorism without Sacrificing the Civil Rights of Muslim Minorities

To avoid discriminatory infringements on the civil liberties of minority groups, security measures should ideally be either precisely targeted, affecting only a very narrow group of suspects, or, if that is impossible, universal and therefore nondiscriminatory. Nondiscriminatory measures ensure that all citizens have a stake in upholding a proper balance between rights and security needs and make it more likely that the political process will lead to a reasonable balance over time. Airport screening, which affects most citizens in the U.S. and Europe, is an example of a nondiscriminatory measure, even though a certain amount of profiling might take place in the selection of passengers for extended security checks.

An alternative to discriminatory measures that directly target individuals in ways that violate their civil liberties is to rely on protective measures at airports, and to firmly protect and control sites and materials of interest to terrorists (Cole 2005). Still, the open, complex, and interdependent Western societies have countless vulnerable points. It is practically and economically impossible to protect all potential targets against all types of attack at all times. An intensified and internationally coordinated effort by intelligence services and law enforcement agencies is arguably indispensable to protect civilians from terrorist strikes, as shown by the experiences of a number of countries engaged in a long-term fight against faith-inspired terrorism and suicide attacks.[16]

Furthermore, the new prominence of self-motivated and self-recruited terrorist cells composed of persons from Muslim minorities with no previous criminal record or contact with known al-Qaeda members is a unique challenge to European counterterrorism. It might be practically impossible to rely only on very narrow targeting because the information needed to preempt an attack is likely to be sparse or nonexistent. Thus, it is to be expected that proactive intelligence and law enforcement efforts will remain key to European efforts against terrorism, and that these efforts will not always be as precisely targeted as they should be to avoid breeding resentment.

Two things need to be done to minimize the negative impact of these measures on civil rights in general and on the civil rights of Muslim minorities in particular. First, the application of these measures should be subject to procedural safeguards and democratic oversight. Second, the use of exceptional measures and their impact on liberties should be documented, reviewed, and evaluated at regular intervals.

Safeguards and Democratic Oversight

Whereas national governments have frequently succeeded in rushing new anti-terrorism measures through national parliaments in the wake of serious terrorist attacks, the EU system is typically slower because of the higher number of actors involved and the complicated power-sharing and decision-making mechanisms. The speedy adoption of the Framework Decision on the European arrest warrant represents an exception to this norm. Some have noted that while the EU may pose a potential threat to basic rights through its expanding counterterrorism role, it also provides crucial protection of these rights. The cumbersome decision-making process decreases the danger that comprehensive new measures will be passed quickly and without review (Brimmer 2006, 164). Moreover, respect for human rights is among the founding principles of the European Union, as stated in the EU treaty and the treaties of Amsterdam and Nice. In principle, this means that the obligation to protect fundamental rights takes precedence over the obligation to cooperate in the fight against terrorism.[17]

Among EU actors and institutions which provide oversight and safeguards are the EU Parliament, which has established itself as a defender of civil and human rights and has frequently managed to moderate European Council or European Commission proposals in ways favoring the protection of these rights; the European Court of Justice, which provides legal recourse; and the EU Network of Independent Experts on Fundamental Rights (CFR-CDF), which advises the commission and reports annually on the state of rights protection in the Union.

In addition, a new independent European Union Agency for Fundamental Rights is being established, with a mandate to monitor developments in the Union and provide expertise and advice to EU agencies on how best to protect these rights in the formulation and implementation of EU initiatives (Commission of the European Communities 2005c).

In reality, democratic oversight and rights protection in the EU are not as straightforward as it might appear. The court and the parliament have either limited or no power over a number of counterterrorism measures that were adopted by the Union under its second pillar (external relations) or its third pillar (cooperation in judicial and home affairs).

The common list of persons and organizations affiliated with terrorism, for example, is drawn up by the council under the second pillar, where the European Court of Justice has no jurisdiction. The common list, moreover, is adopted as a so-called "Common Position" by written procedure with no parliamentary scrutiny on either the national or the EU level. The European Court and Parliament, likewise, have limited scope to review and influence counterterrorism cooperation that falls under the third pillar—as does much of what the EU has done to counter cross-border crime and terrorism.[18]

Finally, it might be difficult to ensure oversight and accountability of the activities of new EU agencies and the various EU-level working groups because national representatives work behind closed doors. The new anti-terrorism powers of U.S. authorities are frequently challenged in courts, and a series of alleged abuses of new powers by the executive have made U.S. politicians demand increased oversight over the Department of Justice. Direct and systematic control and oversight of Europol, for example, will probably prove more complicated (U.S. Department of Justice 2003). An individual may, of course, complain of an alleged violation of his or her rights through national courts, but this would be a rather long and cumbersome way to proceed (Grabbe 2002, 4). This problem might become more significant if Europol begins to develop a practical and operational role in cross-border counterterrorism efforts, as recommended by the UK presidency.[19]

Ideally, a strengthening of measures to ensure democratic oversight and accountability ought to go hand in hand with expanded powers for counterterrorism agencies at both the national and the EU level. Thus, arguably, the right of the European Parliament to produce counterterrorism legislation and of the European Court of Justice to review it should be expanded as the EU develops a common legal framework and expands the exchange of information and intelligence.

Review and Evaluation

When policy makers debate "the right balance" between liberty and security in the effort against terrorism, the tacit assumption is that various law enforcement measures, while infringing on liberty, do actually enhance security. This might be so, but it is not necessarily the case.

Europe's previous experience with separatist and leftist terrorism certainly provides valuable lessons for organizing and conducting effective counterterrorism campaigns. However, both the threat and the societal context of terrorism have changed markedly. The current challenge is from a transnational network of persons held together by a common ideology and common perceived grievances. Self-starting cells of self-recruited individuals might conduct planning, fund-raising, training, and target selection locally, or they may receive support from the remnants of al-Qaeda's leadership. Attackers might have a previous criminal record, or they may be apparently well integrated in European societies. In the new context, counterterrorist measures targeting minority groups may increase radicalization and increase the risk that al-Qaeda-inspired terrorism can corrode the social fabric of European societies.

Today's terrorism raises a number of new challenges that require the assessment and evaluation of new measures and their impact on both liberties and security at regular intervals. A more widespread European use of sunset clauses—clauses by which legislation automatically expires at a certain date unless reenacted by national legislatures—might be a way of ensuring that such evaluations are carried out even in busy and future-oriented legislative environments.

The U.S. Congress included a sunset provision in the Patriot Act that caused parts of the legislation to expire by 2005 unless they were reenacted. Similarly, the extended arrest and detention powers granted to Canadian police in the wake of 9/11 are set to expire after five years unless reenacted (see chapter 11). Such sunset provisions are not unknown in Europe—the French anti-terrorism legislation and part of the German legislation passed in the wake of the attacks on the U.S. were set to expire in 2003 and 2007, respectively. Sunset clauses, however, are not systematically used across Europe: the Danish "anti-terror package," for example, has no expiration date.[20]

An expiration date provides an opportunity for civil society organizations and civil rights groups to mobilize and for politicians to reengage in debate over measures that are frequently passed under pressure in the wake of a dramatic terrorist attack. Approaching expiration dates could also serve as a trigger for systematic efforts to evaluate the pros and cons of different measures. The European Union Agency for Fundamental Rights, which is expected to monitor respect for fundamental rights, could help inform such debates by evaluating the costs of new measures in terms of civil rights infringements. In order to make informed decisions, policy makers will also need to be able to evaluate the benefits of new legislation in terms of improved security.

The U.S. Department of Justice, prompted by congressional and broad public resistance to the Patriot Act and an upcoming expiration date, attempted to document the effectiveness of the new powers it was granted after 9/11 in *Report from the Field: The USA PATRIOT Act at Work*. This report outlines the department's arguments in favor of the legislation and describes specific cases in which the new powers were important to foil plots or secure convictions (U.S. Department of Justice 2004).

Ideally, such reviews of the security benefits and effectiveness of new powers should be independent, not carried out by the agencies which originally lobbied for them. Moreover, it is clearly difficult to identify good indicators of effectiveness in an area where non-events (the absence of attacks) are the ultimate measure of success. The deterrent effect of anti-terrorism efforts is difficult to measure because the absence of attacks might indicate either successful deterrence and disruption or simply the absence of actual attempts to target a given country. Likewise, a high number of foiled plots and convictions might indicate that counterterrorism efforts are effective or, alternatively, it might merely reflect an overall increase in terrorist activity.

Yet, despite these difficulties, an attempt to gauge the effectiveness of expanded powers and surveillance, even if it has to rely on crude measures and estimates, is a necessary prerequisite for an informed debate over new laws and powers. Annual reports summarizing the use of various measures and powers as well as outcomes of investigations might be a useful starting point because they would provide greater transparency and possibly also dissipate misunderstandings and unfounded fears. The Canadian anti-terrorism bill, for example, explicitly calls for such annual reports (see chapter 11). An attempt to account for the usefulness and use of various measures would also be helpful to explain these laws and measures to minorities who feel unjustly targeted. The UK Home Office, in a leaked report about radicalization and relations with Muslim communities in the UK, emphasized the need to provide such information on arrests and searches (UK Home Office 2004).

Finally, periodic reviews would decrease the risk that exceptional measures quietly become permanent practices of European internal security, independent of the evolution of threat levels. There are historical examples of how civil rights have been temporarily limited during a national security crisis, such as the internment of Japanese Americans after the attack on Pearl Harbor in 1941. These rights were fully restored with the cessation of hostilities. The open-ended nature of the effort against terrorism, however, casts a long shadow over the future of civil rights. Terrorism has been around for hundreds of years, and most likely there will always be groups of people who, rightly or wrongly, feel unfairly treated to such an extent that they resort to the use of extreme violence against civilian populations to further their cause. According to the rationale of curbing civil rights in the name of internal security, current tougher provisions could, in principle, be upheld indefinitely. If the United Kingdom's Prevention of Terrorism Act of 1974, originally introduced as exceptional and temporary, teaches us anything, it is that anti-terrorism measures tend to stick. The act eventually became accepted as a permanent part of the legal and law enforcement framework of the UK (Haubrich 2005, 302). Sunset clauses would ensure that changes affecting both security and civil liberties are at least regularly debated.

Conclusion

Several European countries have already been targets of al-Qaeda-inspired terrorism. Further attacks have been intercepted, cell members arrested, and convictions handed down in open courts. Many governments across the continent feel the pressure to act. As a result, national laws have been tightened, counterterrorism agencies have been furnished with more resources and new powers, and EU-level legal and law enforcement cooperation has intensified.

There are good reasons to assume that effective international coordination of intelligence-gathering and law enforcement efforts help counter the threat of al-Qaeda-inspired terrorism. But there is also much evidence that intensified counterterrorism efforts have already negatively impacted the protection of the civil rights of European minorities, or have the potential to do so in the future. This, in turn, is likely to have a negative impact on security as key minority groups become less inclined to cooperate with authorities in the effort to protect against terrorism. Counterterrorism measures might thus have a negative impact both on liberties and, indirectly, on security. Europe, therefore, needs strong democratic control and accountability and regular evaluation of new measures.

The European Union attempts to protect basic rights by various means, but measures for democratic control and independent oversight have not kept up with the new developments in the area of cooperation on internal security. And while Europe has seen lively debates in the European Parliament and elsewhere about tradeoffs between security and liberty in the age of al-Qaeda-inspired terrorism, there have been few attempts to document and evaluate how, and to what extent, different measures actually add to security. Such attempts, possibly involving Muslim minorities, would enhance transparency, make it easier to explain various measures to the targeted minorities, and permit an informed democratic debate over the merits of new laws and powers. While time-consuming and difficult, evaluation, debate, and dialogue are necessary prerequisites for fighting terrorism without sacrificing the social cohesion of European societies and the civil liberties of vulnerable Muslim minorities.

Notes

1. Tony Blair, "PM's Press Conference—5 August 2005." Available at http://www.number10 .gov.uk/output/Page8041.asp (accessed December 17, 2006). See also British Irish Rights Watch, "Briefing on the Prevention of Terrorism Bill 2005," available at http://www.birw.org/BIRW

%20Briefing.html (accessed December 17, 2006). See also EurActiv.com, "Is Europe Putting Up the Barricades?" July 29, 2005, available at http://www.euractiv.com/en/justice/europe-putting -barricades/article-143101 (accessed December 17, 2006).

2. Haubrich (2005); Lepsius (2002, 85); van de Linde et al. (2002); Shapiro and Suzan (2003, 75–77).

3. For examples of the views of both proponents and opponents, see Lucy Sherriff, "Clarke: Europe Must Trade Civil Liberties for Security; 2-for-1 Special?" *The Register,* September 7, 2005. Available at http://www.theregister.co.uk/2005/09/07/lib_security_trade/ (accessed December 17, 2006).

4. Commission of the European Communities (2004b; 2004c); Council of the European Union (2002; 2004b); House of Lords, European Union Committee (2005, 7 and 11); Euractiv.com, October 8, 2004, "Hague Programme—JHA Programme 2005–10." Available at http://www .euractiv.com/en/justice/hague-programme-jha-programme-2005-10/article-130657 (accessed December 17, 2006).

5. See Official Journal of the European Communities (2000); Anderson and Appap (2002, 4); Wouters and Naert (2003, 20).

6. The Framework Decision stipulates a number of instances in which a country is not obliged to extradite and expressly stipulates the inviolability of rights of the detainee following the European Convention on Human Rights—rights which might be brought into question by the arrest warrant (right to information, interpretation, counsel, assistance).

7. For a fuller overview, see Council of the European Union (2004a).

8. International Institute for Strategic Studies (2005); Balzacq and Carrera (2005, sec. 4).

9. For examples of the arguments of proponents see Dinh (2001); Clarke (2005); Andrew Kramer, "Case against Five Suspected Members of Terrorist Cell Tests Government's New Spy Powers," *Associated Press,* February 25, 2003; Bloomberg, "U.K. Urges Human Right Curbs in EU Terrorism Fight," Bloomberg.com, August 13, 2003. Available at http://www.bloomberg.com/ apps/news?pid=10000102&sid=aoRHRj3qBvKY&refer=uk (accessed December 16, 2006).

10. Currently the Schengen Group consists of most EU members plus Norway and Iceland. The ten newer members, the United Kingdom, and Ireland have not joined the agreement.

11. We find these rights laid down, for example, in the European Convention on Human Rights (available at http://conventions.coe.int/treaty/en/Treaties/Html/005.htm [accessed December 16, 2006]), the Danish constitution Grundloven, sections 71 and 72 (available at http:// www.folketinget.dk/pdf/constitution.pdf [accessed December 16, 2006]), and the United Nations Universal Declaration of Human Rights, articles 9 and 12 (available at http://www.un.org/ Overview/rights.html [accessed December 16, 2006]).

12. See EU Network of Independent Experts in Fundamental Rights (CFR-CDF) (2003); Robinson, Schwimmer, and Stoudmann (2001); Lepsius (2002, 86); Alan Travis, "Police to Get Extra Week to Question Terror Suspects," *The Guardian,* May 12, 2003, sec. 4.

13. Ironically, though most of those detained were Muslims, the majority of the convicted were white rightist extremists. This might be because it is generally easier to prove membership in a rightist organization than in a loose terrorist network. See "New Study Highlights Discrimination in Use of Anti-Terror Laws," *Institute of Race Relations,* September 2, 2004. Available at http://www.irr.org.uk/2004/september/ak000004.html (accessed December 16, 2006).

14. Rosie Cowan and Alan Travis, "Muslims: We Are the New Victims of Stop and Search: Police Accused of Misusing Anti-Terror Powers," *The Guardian,* March 29, 2004, sec. 1. This corresponds to the development in the U.S., where surveys indicate that Arab Americans perceive an increased degree of discrimination and profiling after September 11, 2001 (Arab American Institute Foundation 2002).

15. Commission of the European Communities (2004a); EU Network of Independent Experts in Fundamental Rights (CFR-CDF) (2003, 21).

16. Davis and Jenkins (2002, 37); Delpech (2002, 7); Jenkins (2002, 28); Shapiro and Suzan (2003, 77); Tucker (2003, 3).

17. The EU Treaty states the Union shall respect the fundamental freedoms guaranteed by the European Convention on Human Rights of 1950. These include the right to liberty and security, the right to habeas corpus, the right to a speedy trial, the right to a fair and public hearing, the presumption of innocence, and the right to respect for privacy as laid out in Articles 5, 6, and 8 of the European Convention on Human Rights. Available at http://conventions.coe .int/treaty/en/Treaties/Html/005.htm (accessed December 16, 2006).

18. For an overview of democratic control and accountability mechanisms in the EU's legal cooperation, see Grabbe (2002). See also Hayes (2005, 4) and Wouters and Naert (2003, 40).

19. SAIS Center for Transatlantic Relations, Cooperative Security Program. June 2003. *Shoulder to Shoulder: Views from Governments and Civil Society on Cooperative Security,* 1, no. 1, Washington, D.C. Available at http://www.iansa.org/documents/2003/shouldertoshoulder_ june2003.pdf (accessed December 16, 2006).

20. As noted previously, this "package" includes changes in the criminal code, the Administration of Justice Act, law on competition and consumers' conditions on the market for telecommunications, law on arms, law on the release of and extradition of criminals to Finland, Iceland, Norway, and Sweden, Law no. 378, 06/06/2002 (currently in force). For the French and German legislation see Haubrich (2005, 291).

References

Allen, Christopher, and Jorgen Nielsen. May 2002. *Summary Report on Islamophobia in the EU after 11 September 2001.* On behalf of the European Monitoring Centre on Racism and Xenophobia, Vienna. Available at http://eumc.europa.eu/eumc/material/pub/anti-islam/ Synthesis-report_en.pdf (accessed December 16, 2006).

Anderson, Malcolm, and Joanna Apap. October 2002. *Changing Conceptions of Security and Their Implications for EU Justice and Home Affairs Cooperation.* Centre for European Policy Studies, Policy Brief 26. Available at http://aei.pitt.edu/1984/01/PB26.PDF (accessed December 16, 2006).

Arab American Institute Foundation. July 2002. *Profiling and Pride: Arab American Attitudes and Behavior since September 11.* Available at http://aai.3cdn.net/d7083bd00cf4ce3240_wfm6ii8b7 .pdf (accessed December 16, 2006).

Balzacq, Thierry, and Sergio Carrera. July 2005. *The EU's Fight against International Terrorism: Security Problems, Insecure Solutions.* Centre for European Policy Studies, Policy Brief 80. Available at http://merln.ndu.edu/merln/mipal/reports/CEPS.pdf (accessed December 16, 2006).

Brimmer, Esther. 2006. "Safeguarding Civil Liberties in an Era of Insecurity." In *Transatlantic Homeland Security: Protecting Society against Catastrophic Terrorism,* ed. Anja Dalgaard-Nielsen and Daniel S. Hamilton, 147–171. London: Routledge.

Clarke, Charles. September 7, 2005. Speech to European Parliament. Strasbourg, France. Available at http://www.eu2005.gov.uk/servlet/Front?pagename=OpenMarket/Xcelerate/ ShowPage&c=Page&cid=1107293561746&a=KArticle&aid=1125559979691&date=2005-09 -07 (accessed December 16, 2006).

Cole, David. September 23, 2005. "Paradigms of Prevention: The Rule of Law and the War on Terror," Paper presented at Muslims in Western Politics symposium, Indiana University, Bloomington, Indiana.

Commission of the European Communities. March 24–25, 2004(a). "Freedom, Security and Justice: Information Dossiers—Terrorism 2004." Available at http://ec.europa.eu/justice_ home/news/information_dossiers/terrorism_2004/documents_en.htm (accessed December 16, 2006).

———. October 20, 2004(b). *Communication from the Commission to the Council and the European Parliament: Critical Infrastructure Protection in the Fight against Terrorism.* Brussels. Available at http://ec.europa.eu/councils/bx20041216/com_2004_702_en.pdf (accessed December 16, 2006).

———. October 20, 2004(c). *Communication from the Commission to the Council and the European Parliament: Preparedness and Consequence Management in the Fight against Terrorism.* Brussels. Available at http://ec.europa.eu/justice_home/doc_centre/criminal/terrorism/doc/com_2004_701_en.pdf (accessed December 16, 2006).

———. February 23, 2005(a). *Report from the Commission, Based on Article 34 of the Council Framework Decision of 13 June 2002 on the European Arrest Warrant and the Surrender Procedures between Member States.* Brussels. Available at http://ec.europa.eu/justice_home/doc_centre/criminal/doc/com_2005_063_en.pdf (accessed December 16, 2006).

———. May 2005(b). "European Arrest Warrant Replaces Extradition between EU Member States." Available at http://ec.europa.eu/justice_home/fsj/criminal/extradition/fsj_criminal_extradition_en.htm (accessed December 16, 2006).

———. June 30, 2005(c). *Proposal for a Council Regulation Establishing a European Union Agency for Fundamental Rights. Proposal for a Council Decision Empowering the European Union Agency for Fundamental Rights to Pursue Its Activities in Areas Referred To in Title VI of the Treaty on European Union.* Brussels. Available at http://eur-lex.europa.eu/LexUriServ/site/en/com/2005/com2005_0280en01.pdf (accessed December 16, 2006).

Council of the European Union. October 19, 2001(a). "Declaration by the Heads of State or Government of the European Union and the President of the Commission." Available at http://www.dpt.gov.tr/abigm/abtb/Zirveler/2001%20Gant%2019%20Ekim%20(Informal).pdf (accessed December 16, 2006).

———. 2001(b). "Conclusion and Plan of Action of the Extraordinary European Council Meeting on 21 September 2001." Available at http://ue.eu.int/ueDocs/cms_Data/docs/pressData/en/ec/140.en.pdf (accessed December 16, 2006).

———. June 5, 2002. *Draft Programme to Improve the Cooperation in the European Union for Protecting the Population against Bacteriological, Chemical, Radiological or Nuclear Terrorist Threats.* Document 13320/02. Brussels. Available at http://europapoort.eerstekamer.nl/9345000/1/j9vvgy6i0ydh7th/vgbwr4k8ocw2/f=/vg6ojq9p7lya.doc (accessed December 16, 2006).

———. May 25, 2004(a). *Working Structures of the Council in Terrorism Matters—Options Paper.* Brussels. Available at http://www.statewatch.org/news/2004/jun/eu-plan-terr-options.pdf (accessed December 16, 2006).

———. November 29, 2004(b). *EU Plan of Action on Combating Terrorism—Update.* Brussels. Available at http://www.statewatch.org/news/2004/nov/terr-action-plan-14330-rev1.pdf (accessed December 16, 2006).

Davis, Paul K., and Brian M. Jenkins. 2002. *Deterrence & Influence in Counterterrorism: A Component in the War on al-Qaeda.* Santa Monica, Calif.: Rand.

Delpech, Thérèse. December 2002. *International Terrorism and Europe.* Institute for Security Studies: Chaillot Papers (no. 56). Available at http://aei.pitt.edu/518/01/chai56e.pdf (accessed December 16, 2006).

Dinh, Viet D. December 4, 2001. Statement before the Committee on the Judiciary, U.S. Senate. Available at http://judiciary.senate.gov/testimony.cfm?id=128&wit_id=78 (accessed April 12, 2008).

EU Network of Independent Experts in Fundamental Rights (CFR-CDF). March 31, 2003. *The Balance between Freedom and Security in the Response by the European Union and Its Member States to the Terrorist Threats.* Available at http://ec.europa.eu/justice_home/cfr_cdf/doc/obs_thematique_en.pdf (accessed December 16, 2006).

Grabbe, Heather. October 2002. *Justice and Home Affairs: Faster Decisions, Secure Rights.* Centre for European Reform Policy Brief. Available at http://www.cer.org.uk/pdf/policybrief_jha.pdf (accessed December 16, 2006).

Haubrich, Dirk. 2005. "Anti-Terrorismusgesetze und Freiheitsrechte nach dem 11. September: Grobbritannien, Frakreich und Deutschland im Vergleich." In *Transatlantische Beziehungen,* ed. Thomas Jäger, Alexander Höse, and Kai Oppermann, 267–285. Wiesbaden: VS Verlag für Sozialwissenschaften.

Hayes, Ben. 2005. *Terrorising the Rule of Law: The Policy and Practice of Proscription.* Statewatch. Available at http://www.statewatch.org/terrorlists/terrorlists.pdf (accessed December 16, 2006).

House of Lords, European Union Committee. March 8, 2005. *After Madrid: The EUs Response to Terrorism,* 5th Report of Session 2004–05. London: Stationery Office Limited. Available at http://www.publications.parliament.uk/pa/ld200405/ldselect/ldeucom/53/53.pdf (accessed December 16, 2006).

International Institute for Strategic Studies. 2005. "The EU's Role in Counterterrorism: Coordination and Action." *Strategic Comments* 11 (2).

Jenkins, Brian M. 2002. *Countering Al Qaeda: An Appreciation of the Situation and Suggestions for Strategy.* Santa Monica, Calif.: Rand.

Lepsius, Oliver. 2002. "The Relationship between Security and Civil Liberties in the Federal Republic of Germany after September 11." In *Fighting Terror: How September 11 Is Transforming German-American Relations.* Washington, D.C.: American Institute for Contemporary German Studies. Available at http://www.aicgs.org/documents/lepsiusenglish.pdf (accessed December 16, 2006).

Official Journal of the European Communities. September 2000. *The Schengen* Acquis. Available at http://europa.eu.int/eur-lex/pri/en/oj/dat/2000/l_239/l_23920000922en00010473.pdf (accessed December 16, 2006).

———. June 2002. *Council Framework Decision of 13 June 2002 on Combating Terrorism.* Available at http://europa.eu.int/eur-lex/pri/en/oj/dat/2002/l_164/l_16420020622en00030007.pdf (accessed December 16, 2006).

Robinson, Mary, Walter Schwimmer, and Gerard Stoudmann. November 29, 2001. "Action against Terrorism Must Not Undermine Human Rights." Press Release [United Nations Commission for Human Rights; Council of Europe and Organization for Security and Co-operation in Europe]." Geneva/Strasbourg/Warsaw. Available at http://www.osce.org/press_rel/documents/2001-775-odihr.pdf (accessed December 16, 2006).

Shapiro, Jeremy, and Benedicte Suzan. 2003. "The French Experience of Counterterrorism." *Survival* 45 (1): 67–98.

Townsend, Adam. May 2003. *Guarding Europe.* Centre for European Reform Working Paper. Available at http://www.cer.org.uk/pdf/wp440_borders.pdf (accessed December 16, 2006).

Tucker, Jonathan B. March 2003. "Strategies for Countering Terrorism: Lessons from the Israeli Experience." *Journal of Homeland Security.* Available at http://www.homelandsecurity.org/journal/Articles/tucker-israel.html (accessed December 16, 2006).

UK Foreign and Commonwealth Office/Home Office. April 6, 2004. *Draft Report on Young Muslims and Extremism: Relations with the Muslim Community.* London. Available at http://www.globalsecurity.org/security/library/report/2004/muslimext-uk.htm (accessed December 16, 2006).

U.S. Department of Justice. Office of the Inspector General. April 2003. *The September 11 Detainees: A Review of the Treatment of Aliens Held on Immigration Charges in Connection with the Investigation of the September 11 Attacks.* Available at http://www.fas.org/irp/agency/doj/oig/detainees.pdf (accessed December 16, 2006).

———. July 2004. *Report from the Field: The USA PATRIOT Act at Work.* Available at http://www.lifeandliberty.gov/docs/071304_report_from_the_field.pdf (accessed December 16, 2006).

van de Linde, Erik, Kevin O'Brien, Gustav Lindstrom, Stephan de Spiegeleire, Mikko Vayrynen, and Han de Vries. 2002. *Quick Scan of Post 9/11 National Counter Terrorism Policymaking and Implementation in Selected European Countries.* Santa Monica, Calif.: Rand Europe.

Wouters, Jan, and Frederik Naert. March 2003. *The European Union and "September 11."* Institute for International Law Working Paper No. 40. University of Leuven. Available at http://www.law.kuleuven.be/iir/nl/wp/WP/WP40ed2e.pdf (accessed December 16, 2006).

13

The Preventive Paradigm and the Rule of Law: How Not to Fight Terrorism

David Cole

According to a Bush administration Justice Department website, www.lifeandliberty.gov, we are "winning the war on terrorism with unrelenting focus and unprecedented cooperation." We have captured or killed some 3,000 al-Qaeda "operatives," including two-thirds of its leadership. We have disrupted terrorist plots all over the world—the website claims 150, although President Bush in a recent speech claimed only 10. The Justice Department has prosecuted over 400 individuals in "terrorism-related cases" since 9/11, and obtained convictions or guilty pleas in more than 200 of these cases. It claims to have broken up terrorist cells in Buffalo, Detroit, Seattle, Portland (Oregon), and Northern Virginia. Over 515 foreign nationals linked to the investigation of 9/11 have been deported. Most important, and most salient for Americans, there has not been another terrorist attack on U.S. soil in the more than six years since 9/11.

Of course, on May 1, 2003, President Bush also infamously proclaimed victory in Iraq, in bomber jacket regalia aboard the aircraft carrier USS *Abraham Lincoln;* shortly thereafter, he announced that "we found the weapons of mass destruction." Since then, almost 4,000 American servicemen and servicewomen and at least twenty times as many Iraqis have died in Iraq, and we still have not found any weapons of mass destruction. So victory proclamations from this administration deserve a dose of skepticism.

How does one measure victory in the "global war on terrorism"? In April 2004, the State Department reported that terrorist incidents worldwide had dropped in the previous year, a fact Deputy Secretary of State Richard L. Armitage promptly cited as "clear evidence that we are prevailing in the fight" against terrorism. Two months later, a chagrined Colin Powell acknowledged that the department had miscounted, and that in fact terrorism worldwide had increased. Where the initial report stated that the number of injuries resulting from international terrorist incidents had fallen from 2,013 in 2002 to 1,593 in 2003, the new report conceded that, in fact, terrorist-related injuries had actually risen to 3,646. In 2005, the State Department eliminated numbers from its annual terrorism report, saying they were too difficult to track accurately, but soon thereafter a leak suggested another reason for the omission: government analysts had found that terrorist incidents worldwide had jumped threefold from 2003 levels, with 651 attacks in 2004 resulting in 1,907 deaths. This can hardly be interpreted as progress in the global war on terror.

The administration insists that "everything changed" after 9/11 and that we must operate within a new paradigm of prevention. When suicide bombers threaten to attack us, prosecution after the fact is a patently insufficient response: we must stop them before they act. Citing the need to prevent terrorist attacks, the administration has invoked the "preventive paradigm" at home and abroad as a justification for abandoning traditional limits on the use of coercive state power. This has freed the state to use force not merely reactively, to defend against attacks or to punish wrongdoers, but proactively, to prevent terrorist attacks before they are launched. Thus, the Pentagon's 2002 National Security Strategy advanced a new and controversial "preventive" justification for going to war, arguing that in light of the threats now posed by weapons of mass destruction, war is justified not only when the nation is under attack or the threat of imminent attack—the only justifications recognized by international law—but also when we face a more speculative, but potentially catastrophic, future threat. This was the asserted theory behind attacking Iraq. No one argued that an attack by Iraq on the United States was imminent, but the administration contended that the potential for attack with weapons of mass destruction at some undetermined time in the future and by some undetermined terrorist group that might obtain the weapons from Iraq was sufficient to justify war now.

The administration has similarly defended the use of cruel, inhuman, and degrading treatment to interrogate al-Qaeda suspects on the ground that the information so obtained may help prevent future attacks.[1] It has cited a "new paradigm" to argue that the Geneva Conventions and other rules of war do not apply to the conflict with al-Qaeda. It claimed that the Geneva Conventions apply only to wars between nations and internal civil wars and, therefore, that its rules, including the obligation to treat detainees humanely, are inapplicable at Guantánamo and at secret CIA "black sites" where al-Qaeda detainees are held. Here, too, the motive for denying Geneva Conventions protection was precisely to allow interrogators to use coercive means to extract intelligence from suspects.

At home, Attorney General John Ashcroft repeatedly trumpeted a parallel new "paradigm of prevention" in law enforcement and intelligence gathering. Asserting that it would help prevent the next attack, the administration subjected 82,000 Arab and Muslim immigrant men to fingerprinting and registration, subjected 8,000 Arab and Muslim men to FBI interviews, and preventively detained over 5,000 foreign nationals, nearly all of them Arabs and Muslims. As part of its preventive paradigm, the government adopted an aggressive strategy of pretextual arrest and prosecution, holding people on minor charges—such as immigration violations, credit card fraud, or false statements—or on no charges at all, as "material witnesses," when it suspected them of terrorist ties but lacked the evidence to try them for terrorism. On a similar preventive rationale, the administration pushed for expansive new powers in the USA Patriot Act, and since then the FBI reportedly has used the act to issue tens of thousands of "national security letters" annually—administrative subpoenas that demand the secret production of information on customers from telephone and internet companies and financial institutions without any court review.[2] And the preventive rationale has been advanced to justify the National Security Agency's warrantless wiretapping of countless persons in the United States, without congressional or judicial approval, pursuant to an executive order adopted in secret and in contravention of a criminal prohibition on such surveillance.

As these examples illustrate, the preventive paradigm puts tremendous pressure on the rule of law. Designed to place enforceable constraints on state power, the rule of law generally reserves detention, punishment, and military force for those who have been shown, on the basis of sound evidence and fair procedures, to have committed some wrongful act in the past that warrants the government's response. The police can invade privacy by tapping phones or searching homes, but only upon a showing of probable cause that evidence of crime is likely to be found. Individuals can be arrested, but only where there is probable cause that they have committed a crime. They can be preventively detained, but only where there is both probable cause of past wrongdoing and evidence of danger to the community or a risk of flight. Punishment requires proof of guilt beyond a reasonable doubt. Nations may use military force only when subject to attack or imminent attack. The administration's preventive paradigm, by contrast, justifies coercive action—from detention to torture to bombing—on the basis of speculation about future contingencies, without either the evidence or the fair processes that have generally been considered necessary before the state imposes coercive measures on human beings.

When the state begins to direct highly coercive measures at individuals and other states based on necessarily speculative predictions about future behavior, it inevitably leads to substantial compromises on the values associated with the rule of law—such as equality, transparency, fair procedures, and checks and balances. The administration's "War on Terror" has been characterized by radical departures from each of these values.

Equality

Equality is the linchpin of the rule of law. Unless everyone is treated equally, a legal system is unjust. Yet equality is often one of the first values to go when a nation adopts a preventive approach to law enforcement. This is because the sacrifices that a preventive approach entails might well be unacceptable if imposed generally on the citizenry, but are much easier for the majority to accept if the sacrifices are exacted only or predominantly from a disempowered minority. After a series of terrorist bombings in 1919, for example, the federal government responded with the "Palmer Raids," a nationwide roundup of foreign nationals, based not on their involvement in the bombings, but on charges of association with communist organizations. Writing about the raids, Louis Post observed that "the delirium caused by the bombings turned in the direction of a deportation crusade with the spontaneity of water seeking out the course of least resistance" (1923, 307). Foreign nationals were targeted not because they were the bombers, but because the government could get away with targeting foreigners for their associations. At the time, Congress repeatedly refused to extend similar guilt-by-association laws to citizens.

The Bush administration has similarly followed the "course of least resistance." It employed immigration laws to round up thousands of foreign nationals for preventive detention in the first two years after 9/11, arresting many without charges, detaining them in secret, denying them hearings, and then refusing to release them even when some admitted that they had violated immigration laws and agreed to leave the country. As in 1919, such broad sweeps and abusive practices would not have been acceptable if applied to U.S. citizens but they were tolerated because they were targeted at "them," not us.

The administration has argued that detainees at Guantánamo deserve no rights because they are foreign nationals outside our borders. It secretly adopted the position that an international treaty prohibition on cruel, inhuman, and degrading treatment did not apply to foreign nationals held outside the United States, thereby freeing federal interrogators to employ such tactics as waterboarding, threatening attacks with dogs, application of extreme heat and cold, and other abuse in CIA "black sites."

The administration's initial military tribunal rules, promulgated by President Bush in November 2001, permitted defendants to be tried and executed on the basis of secret evidence that neither they nor their chosen civilian lawyer has any opportunity to confront or rebut. The rules apply only to foreign nationals accused of terrorist crimes, not U.S. citizens. When the Supreme Court declared those rules unlawful in 2006, Congress responded by enacting the Military Commissions Act, which, among other things, eliminates habeas corpus review for foreign nationals deemed to be "enemy combatants." And when Michael Chertoff, then a Justice Department official, was questioned about charges of ethnic profiling, he categorically denied that the administration engaged in this practice, explaining that what it did was target "foreign nationals based on their country of origin."

Thus, time and time again, the administration's preventive paradigm has treated foreign nationals as if they do not deserve the same basic respect and humane treatment that U.S. citizens would insist upon—and that international human rights treaties demand. The preventive paradigm, it turns out, is much easier to sell to the American public if the American public is assured that they will not be its targets.

Transparency

The rule of law also demands transparency. Especially where the government is employing harshly coercive measures, it is critical that its actions be subject to public scrutiny and that its evidence be subject to adversarial testing. Yet the preventive paradigm relies heavily on secrecy, which is justified on the ground that if we are to prevent the terrorists from acting, we cannot let them know what we know. So the foreign nationals rounded up on pretextual immigration charges in the wake of 9/11 were arrested in secret and tried in closed hearings. Their names remain secret to this day, even though none turned out to be terrorists. Until a court ordered their identities disclosed in 2006, the hundreds of "enemy combatants" imprisoned at Guantánamo were also held in secret.[3] In fact, the Guantánamo detainees were held virtually incommunicado until a federal court ordered that they be granted access to attorneys in January 2004.[4] The United States would grant access to Guantánamo to the United Nations Human Rights Committee only on the condition that its representatives speak to no prisoners—a condition the Human Rights Committee rejected.

In addition to secret detentions and secret processes, the government has resorted to secret evidence as part of its preventive paradigm, denying those locked up or charged in the War on Terror any opportunity to see or confront the evidence against them. Thus, when the Supreme Court ruled that the Guantánamo detainees could challenge the legality of their detentions in federal court, the administration began to provide hearings for them to challenge the government's determination that they were "enemy combatants," but the decision makers often based their allegations on secret evidence that the detainee could not see. As noted above, President Bush's military tribunal order permitted defendants to be tried and convicted of war crimes on the basis of secret evidence. And the administration has relied on secret evidence to designate groups and individuals as "terrorists" in order to freeze their assets and bar all transactions with them.

Perhaps the most dramatic assertions of preventive secrecy have come in the form of the "state secrets" privilege. This privilege is a judicially created doctrine designed to shield truly important secrets from disclosure through litigation. It is typically invoked in employment disputes regarding the termination of CIA employees, where disclosure of the reasons behind the termination would reveal secret investigations or tactics. However, unlike most privileges, which simply protect information from disclosure, the state secrets privilege can lead to wholesale dismissal of a lawsuit when the government argues that it needs the secret information to defend itself but cannot use it without revealing national security secrets.

The administration has resorted to this defense in an attempt to block all judicial inquiry into two of the most dubious practices of the preventive paradigm: the rendition of suspects to third countries for torture and the warrantless wiretapping of Americans. Regarding the wiretapping, the administration has acknowledged that the surveillance program exists, described its basic contours in public, and submitted a forty-two-page single-spaced memorandum to Congress defending the program's legality by asserting a sweeping theory of absolute presidential power in wartime. But when faced with lawsuits the would test this theory in the courts, the administration invoked the "state secrets" privilege and argued that because the NSA program was officially a secret, the administration's claim of unchecked power could not be reviewed by the courts. Thus far, the lower courts are divided on whether the privilege demands dismissal of the NSA cases. But, if the administration succeeds, it will obtain through a claim of secrecy the very unchecked power it seeks.

Fair Procedures

A third foundational element of the rule of law is the notion that before the government takes a person's liberty, it must afford that person "due process." This has long been understood to demand at a minimum notice of the charges and evidence against one, a meaningful opportunity to defend oneself, and a neutral arbiter. The point of such process is to avoid error by requiring the state to establish, through an adversarial process, that the individual has engaged in conduct that warrants the deprivation of liberty.

When the goal of detention is preventive, not punitive, and when the basis for suspicion is not objective evidence of wrongdoing but vague suspicions based on speculations and stereotypes, fair hearings are an impediment to detention. So the administration has sought to do away with fair hearings. In some instances, the executive has sought to deny any hearings at all. Thus, until the Supreme Court ruled against it in the "enemy combatant" cases of June 2004, the administration insisted that the Guantánamo detainees deserved no hearings whatsoever. It similarly sought to do all it could to delay and deny hearings to the immigrants rounded up as "suspect terrorists" in the wake of 9/11, largely because it realized that it lacked any evidence to show that the individuals were in fact suspected of terrorism or in any other way a danger to the community (U.S. Department of Justice 2003; Cole 2003, 21). And as the discussion of secret evidence above suggests, where the executive has provided hearings it has often rendered them meaningless by permitting the outcome to be predicated on secret evidence not subject to any adversarial testing.

Checks and Balances

Finally, the rule of law requires a commitment to checks and balances. Without a system of divided powers, who will hold the state to its obligation to obey the rules? In our constitutional system, federal power is divided three ways: Congress is assigned the power to make laws, the executive is given the responsibility of enforcing the laws, and the judiciary's obligation is to ensure that the rule of law is maintained. Divided power, however, while less susceptible to abuse, is also less efficient. In periods of crisis, when prevention becomes the priority, power almost inevitably shifts to the executive branch, which has the ability to take initiative, act swiftly, and preserve confidence. Precisely because executive power is likely to be increased during periods of crisis, it is all the more important to maintain the checking functions of the other branches.

Yet the Bush administration has repeatedly advanced a view of executive power that would literally eviscerate the checking functions of the other branches. In the administration's view, the president as commander in chief has unilateral authority to select "the means and methods of engaging the enemy," and the other branches have no say in the matter. That authority, it has argued, gave the president the power to order warrantless wiretapping by the NSA, despite a statute that expressly criminalizes such conduct. That authority, the Justice Department argued in an August 2002 memo, empowered the president to order torture as a means of interrogation, despite a federal criminal statute and an international treaty that prohibit torture under all circumstances. And that authority, the administration argued, meant that neither Congress nor the courts could exercise any oversight of the administration's detention of "enemy combatants."

The administration's argument has not fared well in the courts. In *Rasul v. Bush*, concerning whether Guantánamo detainees could challenge the legality of their detention in federal courts, the Supreme Court in June 2004 unanimously rejected the administration's contention. The administration argued that permitting judicial review of the detention of enemy combatants would raise "grave constitutional problems" because it would "directly interfere with the Executive's conduct of the military campaign against al-Qaeda and its supporters."[5] Six justices, writing for the majority, ruled that courts could review the detainees' claims. Justice Scalia dissented, joined by Chief Justice Rehnquist and Justice Thomas. The dissenting judges agreed, however, that as a constitutional matter, Congress could have extended habeas jurisdiction to the Guantánamo detainees; they simply concluded that Congress had not, in fact, chosen to do so.[6] Thus, not a single justice accepted the Bush administration's contention that the president's role as commander in chief could not be limited by congressional and judicial oversight.

The administration similarly argued in *Hamdi v. Rumsfeld,* involving the detention of Yaser Hamdi, a U.S. citizen captured in Afghanistan and detained as an "enemy combatant," that the Court could not review the factual basis for Hamdi's detention because that would impermissibly interfere with the president's power. The Court again rejected the assertion. As Justice O'Connor wrote for the plurality, "Whatever power the United States Constitution envisions for the Executive in its exchanges with other nations or with enemy organizations in times of conflict, it most assuredly envisions a role for all three branches when individual liberties are at stake."[7]

In *Hamdan v. Rumsfeld,* which ruled that the military tribunals created by the president were illegal, the Court again rebuffed an assertion of unilateral executive power. The administration argued that "the detention and trial of petitioners—ordered by the President in the declared exercise of the President's powers as Commander in Chief of the Army in time of war and of grave public danger—are not to be set aside by the courts without the clear conviction that they are in conflict with the Constitution or laws of Congress."[8] Yet, without any deference to the president, the Court went out of its way to rule that the president had violated both domestic military law—the Uniform Code of Military Justice (UCMJ)—and the Geneva Conventions, international treaties governing the treatment of prisoners during wartime. As the Court stated, even assuming the president has "independent power, absent congressional authorization, to convene military commissions, he may not disregard limitations that Congress has, in proper exercise of its own war powers, placed on his powers."[9]

Are We Safer?

The rejoinder to such criticisms is that in the preventive paradigm, the balance between liberty and security must be struck differently in order to prevent catastrophic attacks. But even if one accepts such a utilitarian approach to first principles, there is very little evidence that the preventive paradigm has made us safer, and substantial reason to believe that it has made us more vulnerable to another attack.

There is nothing wrong with prevention, of course: the question is how one goes about it. The bipartisan 9/11 Commission identified dozens of sensible preventive measures that we should be taking, but are not.[10] These are not dramatic or aggressive "shock and awe" initiatives, but the slow and painstaking work of assessing vulnerabilities, collecting and analyzing information, shoring up defenses, building coalitions, and working to reduce the social factors that contribute to the dangerous transition from fundamentalist beliefs to terrorist action. They don't make for photo ops wearing bomber jackets or sound bites pulled from old Westerns, but they would make us safer.

Coercion and military action are sometimes necessary and appropriate. Using military force to destroy al-Qaeda's training camps and infrastructure in Afghanistan after the 9/11 attacks was widely viewed as legitimate; the United States had the support of a wide-ranging coalition, and both NATO and the United Nations recognized the acts of 9/11 as an "armed attack" that triggered the right of self-defense. The Afghanistan offensive initially succeeded in capturing or killing many al-Qaeda leaders, closing their training camps, and capturing documents and computers from their headquarters that helped to locate still other al-Qaeda operatives. By contrast, using military force in Iraq, where we faced no imminent threat, had not been attacked, and acted against the wishes of the UN Security Council and most of the world, has inadvertently helped to inspire, recruit, build, and train a terrorist network. The difference is that in Afghanistan we acted in a context that existing law and the world acknowledged was legitimate—self-defense—while in attacking Iraq our actions are widely viewed as deeply illegitimate.

At the end of the day, the administration's trump card in any debate on national security is the fact—for which we are all grateful—that apart from the anthrax mailings of 2001, there has not been another terrorist attack on U.S. soil since 9/11. When the first secretary of homeland security, Tom Ridge, announced that he was stepping down in December 2004, he actually knocked on wood on the podium while noting this absence. The gesture was fitting, because it is difficult to see how many of the administration's most heralded preventive initiatives have contributed to the absence of a terrorist attack.

The military offensive against al-Qaeda in Afghanistan certainly deserves credit for hampering al-Qaeda's effectiveness. The war in Iraq, however, has erased those gains and then some: it has created the world's leading training ground for terrorists, while inciting others as well to turn to violence against the United States. And according to the National Intelligence Estimate, al-Qaeda has reconstituted itself in Pakistan while we were focused on Iraq.

Meanwhile, despite the claims of the lifeandliberty.gov website, the administration has little to show for its preventive campaign at home. Of the 82,000 Arab and Muslim foreign nationals subjected to special registration, 8,000 called in for FBI interviews, and over 5,000 locked up in preventive detention, not one stands convicted of a terrorist crime today. The government's record here, in what is surely the most aggressive national ethnic profiling campaign since World War II, is 0 for 95,000. As for the 515 deportations, most were carried out under a policy that barred deportation unless an individual was first cleared by the FBI of any connection to terrorism. These deportations, therefore, are misses, not hits, in terms of identifying actual terrorists.

The vast majority of the more than four hundred criminal indictments and over two hundred convictions in "terrorism-related" cases identified on the Justice Department's website are for minor nonviolent crimes, *not* terrorism. In 2005, the *Washington Post* examined these cases in detail and found that only thirty-nine involved any convictions on charges related to terrorism.[11] And of those thirty-nine, nearly all involved charges of material support for terrorist groups, not actual terrorism or even conspiracy to engage in terrorism. Under the material support statute, the government argues that it need not show that an individual's support had anything to do with furthering a terrorist act. In one case I am handling, the government has argued that the law prohibits a U.S. human rights group from offering human rights advocacy training to a Turkish organization, even though the government does not dispute that the intent of the training is to *discourage* terrorism and encourage peaceful resolution of disputes.[12]

A Syracuse University research institute using Justice Department records found that the median sentence actually handed down in cases labeled "terrorist" by the Justice Department in the first two years after 9/11 was only fourteen days, not the kind of sentence that will incapacitate or deter a committed terrorist (Transactional Records Access Clearinghouse 2003). In 2005, New York University's Center on Law and Security reviewed the prosecutions in "terror-related" cases and concluded that "the legal war on terror has yielded few visible results. There have been . . . almost no convictions on charges reflecting dangerous crimes" (2005, 1).

Some of the convictions the administration has obtained seem to have more to do with inflating the numbers for its "lifeandliberty" website than with any actual threat to national security. Consider the prosecution of Lynne Stewart, a sixty-five-year-old criminal defense lawyer in New York City. In June 2000, while representing Sheikh Omar Abdel-Rahman, who is serving multiple life sentences for conspiring to bomb the bridges and tunnels around Manhattan, Stewart issued a statement from the sheikh to the press, and thereby contravened an administrative restriction that barred her from assisting the sheikh in having contact with the outside world. Before 9/11, the government responded, appropriately, by revoking Stewart's visitation privileges and insisting that she sign a more restrictive agreement before visiting the sheikh again.

After 9/11 the government resurrected the matter and charged Stewart with the crime of providing material support for terrorism. She was convicted in February 2005 after a trial tainted by highly prejudicial and largely irrelevant evidence—including a tape from Osama bin Laden played for the New York jury around the anniversary of the 9/11 attacks, even though neither Stewart nor her co-defendants were alleged to have had any ties to al-Qaeda. Stewart, who was being treated for cancer, faced the possibility of spending the rest of her life in jail, but was ultimately sentenced to twenty-eight months in prison. Her conviction provides another statistic in the Justice Department's effort to show results in the "war on terrorism," but does not make us one iota safer.

Several of the government's most prominent cases have disintegrated under close scrutiny. Attorney General John Ashcroft repeatedly heralded the prosecution of Sami Al-Arian, a computer science professor at the University of South Florida, as Exhibit A in why the Patriot Act was essential. Yet after hearing the prosecution present eighty witnesses and hundreds of hours of taped surveillance over six months of trial, Al-Arian's lawyers rested without calling a single witness, and a jury in Tampa found Al-Arian not guilty of the most serious charges against him, including conspiracy to murder and to aid a terrorist organization. It deadlocked 10–2 in favor of acquittal on all the rest. *Time* magazine quoted a former FBI official who stated that in late 2002 the FBI was pressured to make a case against Al-Arian despite weak evidence: "'We were in shock, but those were our marching orders,' sa[id] the supervisor, who felt that the Justice Department was rushing to indict before it had really appraised the evidence."[13]

The administration had earlier claimed to have uncovered an espionage ring at Guantánamo Bay, consisting of a Muslim chaplain and three translators. It charged Captain James Yee, the chaplain, with taking classified information off base, but then dismissed all charges when it could not establish that any of the information was even classified. It brought thirty charges against Ahmed Al-Halabi, a twenty-four-year-old translator, some carrying the death penalty, but after ten months dropped all the serious charges and accepted a guilty plea for time served. A third man, Ahmed Fathy Mehalba, also pleaded guilty to minor crimes, again essentially for time served. And the government dropped all charges against a fourth man, Jack Farr.

The government prosecuted Sami Al-Hussayen, a Saudi Arabian student at the University of Idaho, for material support to a terrorist group, but when the evidence showed only that he ran a website with links to other websites—pure speech—a jury acquitted him of all terrorism charges. And the administration's first jury conviction for material support to terrorism in a post-9/11 case, in Detroit, was thrown out in September 2004 when the government admitted that the prosecutor had failed to disclose that its principal witness had lied on the stand.

Perhaps most prominently, the administration abandoned its efforts to hold U.S. citizens Jose Padilla and Yaser Hamdi in military custody as "enemy combatants" when faced with the possibility that it might have to justify its actions in an open hearing. After the Supreme Court held that the government had to provide Hamdi a hearing to show why he was detained, the administration simply let him go, on the condition that he return to Saudi Arabia and renounce his citizenship. When Jose Padilla's lawyers sought Supreme Court review of his detention, the administration suddenly transferred him to civilian criminal custody, where he faces charges, not of being a "dirty bomber," but of playing a marginal role in a nebulous conspiracy to support unnamed terrorist groups. Although Padilla was ultimately convicted, the case against him was very weak, and the government made no effort to prove that he planned any terrorist conduct in the United States or elsewhere.

Despite its aggressively preventive tactics, the administration has yet to identify a single al-Qaeda cell in the U.S. The "lifeandliberty" website claims that terror cells in "Buffalo, Detroit, Seattle, Portland (Oregon), and Northern Virginia" have been disrupted, but does not claim that any of these groups were al-Qaeda cells. The Virginians were convicted of playing paintball and attending training camps to fight in the Kashmir conflict between Pakistan and India. The Portland group attempted to go to Afghanistan to fight alongside the Taliban—treason, perhaps, but not terrorism. The "Buffalo cell" consisted of six young men, actually from Lackawanna, a small town near Buffalo, who followed a charismatic religious leader to an al-Qaeda training camp in Afghanistan before 9/11, but returned home and undertook no activity whatsoever in furtherance of any illegal, much less terrorist, conduct. The reference to Seattle presumably refers to James Ujaama, a black activist held as a material witness, then charged with conspiracy to run a terrorist training camp, but ultimately convicted only of making a donation to the Taliban in contravention of an economic embargo before 9/11. The only "cell" identified in Detroit is the one noted above, in which all charges were dismissed.

Meanwhile, the only criminal conviction of an Islamic fundamentalist for an actual attempted terrorist attack since 9/11 is that of shoe bomber Richard Reid, and he was captured not through any preventive initiative of the government, but because an alert airline employee noticed a strange-looking man trying to light his shoe. Three people have been convicted of conspiracy to engage in terrorist conduct, but there is little evidence that the preventive paradigm played an important role in the convictions. Zacarias Moussaoui pleaded guilty to conspiracy to engage in terrorism, but he was arrested *before* 9/11, and thus before the preventive paradigm was in place. Iyman Faris, an Ohio truck driver, pleaded guilty to providing material support for researching how to bring down the Brooklyn Bridge with an acetylene torch, but that plot raises more questions about Faris's sanity than about our national security. Finally, Ahmed Abu Ali was convicted of conspiring to kill President Bush while Abu Ali was studying abroad in Saudi Arabia. The only person with whom he allegedly discussed the plot was killed by the Saudis, and Abu Ali's conviction rested solely on a confession that he claims was false and extracted by Saudi security services through torture, a practice for which the United States has long criticized the Saudis.

So at the end of the day, the "preventive paradigm" at home has netted few actual terrorists. In Iraq the War on Terror has, in all likelihood, created and trained more terrorists than have been captured or killed. It is possible, of course, that some of these measures have produced valuable intelligence that allowed us to disrupt terrorist plots, although if that were so one would expect to see more successful terrorism prosecutions. It is also possible that these measures have deterred some terrorists from coming here to attack us, but that is ultimately unknowable.

What can be known is that the administration's tactics have spawned unprecedented levels of distrust toward law enforcement within the Arab and Muslim communities in the United States, and toxic levels of anti-Americanism abroad. The perception and reality that the administration has unfairly targeted innocent Arabs and Muslims, used coercion against them preemptively and without a solid case, and disregarded fundamental principles of the rule of law and human rights has fueled resentment around the globe. In the long run, that resentment is the greatest threat to our national security and the most likely source of the next attack.

Notes

Some of the material in this chapter originally appeared in a review of Daniel Benjamin and Steven Simon's *The Next Attack*, in the *New York Review of Books*, David Cole, "Are We Safer?" *New York Review of Books* 53 (4) (March 9, 2006). Available at http://www.nybooks.com/articles/18752 (accessed December 19, 2006). The argument sketched here is developed in more detail in Daniel Cole and Jules Lobel, *Less Safe, Less Free: Why America Is Losing the War on Terror* (New York: New Press, 2007).

1. No one defends torture or coercive interrogation as a way of solving past crimes or punishing perpetrators. The only justification offered is the forward-looking one of preventing future harms.

2. See Dan Eggen, "FBI Sought Data on Thousands in '05," *Washington Post,* May 2, 2006, sec. A4.

3. *Associated Press v. United States Department of Defense,* [2006] 410 F. Supp. 2d 147 (S.D. NY 2006); see also Thom Shanker, "Pentagon Plans to Tell Names of Detainees," *New York Times,* Feb. 26, 2006, sec. 1, p. 20.

4. *Al Odah v. United States,* [2004] 346 F. Supp. 2d 1, 5 (D. DC 2004).

5. Brief for Respondents at 42, 44, *Rasul v. Bush,* [2004] 542 U.S. 466.

6. *Rasul v. Bush,* 542 U.S. at 506 (Scalia, J., dissenting).

7. U.S. 507 at 536 (Breyer, J., concurring).

8. Brief for Respondents at 23, *Hamdan v. Rumsfeld,* No. 05-184 (U.S., filed February 23, 2006) (quoting *Ex parte Quirin,* 317 U.S. 1, 25 [1942]).

9. *Hamdan v. Rumsfeld,* 126 S. Ct. 2749, 2774 n.23 (2006) (citing the "lowest ebb" passage of Justice Jackson's concurrence in *Youngstown Sheet & Tube Co. v. Sawyer,* 343 U.S. 579, 637 [1952] [Jackson, J., concurring]). In a concurring opinion, Justice Kennedy explained that in creating military tribunals, the president was acting at the lowest ebb of presidential power because he had acted "in a field with a history of congressional participation and regulation," where the

Uniform Code of Military Justice had established "an intricate system of military justice." 126 S. Ct. at 2800–2801 (Kennedy, J., concurring, joined by Souter, Ginsburg, and Breyer, JJ.).

10. The full report is available at http://www.9-11commission.gov/ (accessed December 16, 2006).

11. See Dan Eggen and Julie Tate, "U.S. Campaign Produces Few Convictions on Terrorism Charges; Statistics Often Count Lesser Crimes," *Washington Post,* June 12, 2005, sec. A1.

12. *Humanitarian Law Project v. Mukajey,* 509 F.3d 1122 (9th Cir. 2007).

13. See Tim Padgett and Wendy Malloy, "When Terror Charges Just Won't Stick," *Time,* December 19, 2005, 46–67.

References

Center on Law and Security at NYU Law School. February 2005. *Terrorist Trials: A Report Card.* Available at http://www.lawandsecurity.org/publications/terroristtrialreportcard.pdf (accessed December 16, 2006).

Cole, David. 2003. *Enemy Aliens.* New York: New Press.

Post, Louis. 1923. *The Deportations Delirium of Nineteen-Twenty: A Personal Narrative of an Historic Official Experience.* New York: Da Capo Press.

Transactional Records Access Clearinghouse. December 8, 2003. *Special Report: Criminal Terrorism Enforcement after the 9/11/01 Attacks.* Available at http://trac.syr.edu/tracreports/terrorism/report031208.html (accessed December 16, 2006).

U.S. Department of Justice. Office of the Inspector General. April 2003. *The September 11 Detainees: A Review of the Treatment of Aliens Held on Immigration Charges in Connection with the Investigation of the September 11 Attacks.* Available at http://www.fas.org/irp/agency/doj/oig/detainees.pdf (accessed December 16, 2006).

14

Recommendations for Western Policy Makers and Muslim Organizations

Abdulkader H. Sinno

It is good to understand key linkages between institutions and policies, but what do the leaders of these institutions need to do to promote equality, security, justice, and liberal values in Western democracies? I make suggestions for both Western policy makers and Muslim organizations based on the collective findings of the contributors to this book, in the hope of improving prospects for members of Western Muslim minorities and for the democratic institutions of their countries.

What Should Western States and Elites Do?

The situation for most Western liberal democracies and their minorities is far from ideal. In this section, I provide policy recommendations for Western states in the hope of encouraging best practices that would consolidate Western liberal democracies and provide a fair and equal treatment to their Muslim minorities. Western political, media, and religious elites are largely responsible for managing the process of mutual adjustment between their countries' institutions and the new Muslim minorities. They may want to do the following:

Avoid creating unnecessary grievances. Some of the words and actions of Western elites that damage relations between Western Muslims and their states are unnecessary and should be responsibly avoided. Examples include statements by U.S. religious and military leaders denigrating the religion and the Prophet Muhammad (see Haddad and Ricks, this volume). They also include statements by European politicians trying to seem tough on immigration in countries where Muslims are perceived negatively by a large section of the electorate. The short-term benefits of such behavior are far outweighed by the costs: elite discourse makes Islamophobia appear to be legitimate, and rival politicians could up the ante in coming elections. The consequences can also be felt on the street: Nicolas Sarkozy's words comparing minority youths to scum to be cleaned by high-powered hoses were still resonating in the French polity two years later. Western politicians should realize that Muslims are an integral part of society and refrain from capitalizing on Islamophobia, unless they wish their societies to become terminally segregated along ethnic lines. If at all possible, European political leaders should openly and clearly encourage inclusion, moderation, and tolerance along the line of Canadian and, to a lesser degree, American and British leaders.

Avoid generalization based on isolated incidents. Political elites should avoid irresponsibly making generalizations about Muslim minorities in the wake of high-profile crimes. The murder of Dutch moviemaker Theo Van Gogh, who had produced with the former Dutch parliamentarian Ayaan Hirsi Ali a provocative short movie that offended the sensitivities of some Muslims, by a Moroccan fanatic with little support in 2004 was a terrible crime but should not have been made into an iconic event by politicians across Europe. French politicians and Jewish leaders are also misguided and quite unfair when they broadly speak of French Muslim anti-Semitism in the wake of particular hate crimes perpetuated by some Muslim youths. As Allen and Wike show in this volume, 71 percent of French Muslims have a favorable opinion of Jews; this is much higher than the proportions of the public in most Western countries that hold favorable opinions of Muslims. Every hate crime should be prosecuted and condemned, but to keep hammering French Muslims collectively with false accusations of anti-Semitism may increase their isolation, stoke resentment, make them the target of hate and discrimination, and lead to a self-fulfilled prophecy. Precise thinking and language by political and communal leaders will go a long way to reduce tensions.

Refrain from attempts to "change" Islam or manipulate Muslim organizations. Talk or initiatives by Western leaders about "changing" Islam produce defensiveness and perceptions of threat among Western Muslim minorities whose members generally and rightly perceive non-Muslim politicians to have superficial and distorted knowledge of their beliefs and communities (Klausen; Haddad and Ricks). The Bush administration has tried to engage in such manipulation.[1] Other measures, such as training a new generation of European imams, are sensible and necessary, but they must be implemented in collaboration with local Muslims (as in Britain, under the leadership of Muslim peer Nazir Ahmed), not in spite of them (as in France). Experiments to impose Muslim organizations by the state have proven to be a failure in France (Klausen). Picking and choosing Muslim interlocutors among many legitimate ones has also shown to be counterproductive in the United States (the co-optation of the largely unpopular Shaykh Hisham Kabbani) and Britain (Klausen).

Seek the advice of bona fide experts. The Bush administration's use of "experts" whom many Muslims perceive to be Islamophobic or ideological nemeses of Islam has added to tensions between it and the American Muslim community. One such incident was the nomination and recess appointment (after opposition in Congress) of Daniel Pipes, who is perceived by many Muslim Americans to advocate their disenfranchisement in the hope of serving right-wing Israeli interests, to the board of the United States Institute of Peace on April 1, 2003. Instead, Western governments should wisely consult and cooperate with non-ideological academic experts who have precise and meaningful knowledge of Western Muslims. Many among them are Western Muslims who can function as facilitators and mediators in case of conflict. Seeking their input would also put Western Muslims at ease and facilitate their cooperation with law enforcement, encourage their integration, and promote their civic involvement.

Make foreign and domestic policies consistent. It would be hard to convince Western Muslims that their governments respect Islam and Muslims if they do not do so in their foreign policies. As many Pew Research Center surveys have shown, Muslims around the world, including Western Muslims, strongly disapprove of the Bush administration's treatment of Muslim POWs in the Guantánamo Bay prison and elsewhere, as well as the treatment of Iraqis and Afghans under occupation.[2] They hold no illusions that this administration respects the lives, dignity, and welfare of Muslims overseas, and its transgressions against Muslim-American civil rights seem to confirm views that its attitudes toward Muslims do not stop at the border. British association with the policies of the Bush administration also stoked resentment among British Muslims (Sinno and Tatari). Western governments can only benefit from adopting domestic and foreign policies that respect the tenets of international law and the dignity, lives, and welfare of all without exception. One benefit would be Muslim minorities whose members have more confidence in the goodwill of their own governments and who do not avoid public service out of concern that they may some day be used to enforce inhumane policies toward their co-religionists or co-ethnics at home and abroad.

Avoid relying on transnational ties to deal with domestic Muslims. European governments must recognize that their Muslim citizens and residents form communities that are independent of their countries of origin. French policies that leverage North African states to increase control over French Muslims have led to the fragmentation of the French Muslim community, a loss of legitimacy for its leaders, and poor results overall (Klausen). The same could be said of the German effort to leverage relations with Turkey. It cannot be otherwise. Even if French and German Muslims are not completely European, they are not subjects of Algeria or Turkey anymore. For a European government to leverage ties to a foreign government in dealing with its own Muslims is derogatory because it implies that it cannot deal with Muslims directly, the way it deals with other citizens, because they are different. It is also counterproductive because it slows integration. European leaders must clearly accept that Muslims are integral and permanent members of their societies who have complete rights and must be treated with dignity. Western states must allow legitimate Western Muslim organizations to develop independently and accept their legitimacy.

Increase both the efficiency of law enforcement and guarantees to preserve the civil rights and liberties of Muslim minorities. The prevention of al-Qaeda-style terrorism is more effective with the collaboration and input of Muslim communities. But such communities are not likely to provide their support if they feel harassed, profiled, abused, or discriminated against by their own governments and law enforcement agencies. The strengthening of law enforcement mandates must therefore be accompanied by institutional checks, grievance procedures, periodic review by independent commissions, and a strengthening of non-discrimination laws (Dalgaard-Nielsen; Roach; Cole). Such measures would make Western Muslims even more comfortable cooperating with their countries' law enforcement agencies. In spite of some limitations, the Canadian model (Roach) of strengthening law enforcement while establishing checks and sunset clauses on new legislation, seeking cyclical reports on their effectiveness from independent parties, requesting input from Muslim organizations, and actively countering discrimination is clearly more effective and just than the United States and United Kingdom models of mostly increasing the powers given to law enforcement. Lessons from the Canadian experience should be considered across the West.

Develop consistent hate speech and freedom of expression laws. Hate speech and blasphemy laws need to be consistent and equitable. They must be extended to protect Muslims if they exist on the books to protect other religions. It is hard to expect Muslims in Germany to accept that it is legitimate for non-Muslims to ridicule their prophet and beliefs when strict laws limit speech that denies the Holocaust. Both types of attacks are distasteful and are often driven by malice, whether Islamophobic or anti-Semitic. The same applies to blasphemy laws in a number of European countries: they should be equitably formulated where they exist or scrapped for the equal benefit or annoyance of all (Soper and Fetzer). Free speech ought to be either absolute or restricted equitably, preferably the former.

Promote responsible behavior by media outlets. Western media must develop an ethos of fairness and a respectful language when addressing Muslim minorities. While national American newspapers generally tend to not promote negative stereotypes of Muslims in the post-9/11 era, tabloids, Fox News, European magazines like *Paris Match,* and many Christian media do.[3] Nisbet et al. in this volume show how coverage by such media outlets promotes negative attitudes toward Muslim Americans and a willingness to restrict their civil liberties. How can a devout Muslim feel at home in France when French magazines use phrases like "*fous d'Allah*" (madmen of Allah) in their descriptions of people like him?[4] And while freedom of expression should be protected, it should be promoted along with a culture of respect for the rights and sensitivities of minorities. Publishing the derogatory cartoons of the Prophet Muhammad was not perceived by most Muslims as an act in defense of free speech but as an act of spite and intimidation toward a vulnerable minority. All this is not new for Western media; they have dealt with similar issues in regards to other minorities. They should extend lessons learned and reasonable courtesy to the Muslim minority as well, perhaps along the lines of the "Jew test" (a directive to journalists to consider whether they would use the same words in an article if "Muslim" were replaced by "Jew") practiced by the editor of a Danish newspaper (Nielsen). Media behavior shapes societal attitudes, including those of targeted minorities. Some Hollywood outfits understood their responsibility after 9/11 and stopped portraying Muslims as repulsively one-dimensional murderers and villains. Others must catch up quickly.

Avoid discrimination or the appearance of discrimination in immigration and citizenship laws. Discrimination in citizenship and immigration laws weakens integration by sending the message that Muslims have been defined as a separate community to be kept from growing and to be collectively targeted based on imputed identity. Extended American checks on immigration applications from Muslim countries and requirements that Muslim immigrants register before others, restrictive German naturalization laws, and recent Dutch regulations that ask immigrants to watch videos that include men kissing to screen out those who do not share Dutch values are perceived by Muslims to be such discriminatory laws. Such laws are counterproductive: they increase resentment among Muslim minorities, making them less likely to adopt the dominant culture of the country, and may push a few toward extremism.

Avoid discrimination in employment and education. European countries would benefit more from having highly educated and professionally accomplished Muslims instead of marginalized and desperate Muslim youths. There is no doubt that discrimination in both spheres exists in the West. Anti-discrimination laws are stricter and better enforced in North America than in Europe. Europeans will need to do the same if they want to help their disadvantaged Muslims feel that they can succeed by integrating and playing by the rules of the game. The alternative is that dissatisfied Muslim youths will look elsewhere for fulfillment: crime, drugs, and perhaps even radical politics. Laws that fight discrimination against some minorities (such as the Race Relations Act of 1976 and the Public Order Act of 1986 in Britain) should be expanded to protect Muslims as well if they don't already. States, like France, that do not have clear and comprehensive laws to protect all minorities, including members of religious minorities, from discrimination should develop them and enforce them on a regular basis.[5]

Avoid religious discrimination. This is not much of a problem in North America and in the UK. Other west European countries are beginning to move in the right direction, but much remains to be done: elevating Islam to the status of Christianity and Judaism in Germany and French Alsace in regards to religious tax distribution; not discriminating against religious schools and the building of mosques in Greece, Spain, and elsewhere; allowing Islamic garb in public schools in France, and so on.[6]

Encourage effective representation to institutionalize conflict resolution. Western societies and Muslim minorities need Muslims in elected office and in the hallways of power who are empowered to speak frankly on issues affecting Muslims. Muslim representation should not reek of tokenism as it does in the case of many European Muslim parliamentarians who are restricted by their own parties (Sinno; Sinno and Tatari). Token representatives are likely to incur the scorn of members of Muslim minorities and increase the sense of the futility of civic participation among them. Disenchanted Muslims would look elsewhere for leadership and representation in the public sphere. The leaders of even the most disciplined European parties should show flexibility in allowing Muslim elected officials to express minority grievances and to be involved in genuine and meaningful conflict resolution. This would serve them electorally by drawing the Muslim vote and would help integrate Muslim minorities in the political process. It would also help move conflict from the streets to a more benign institutional setting in countries like Britain, France, and Belgium. It may also help develop an appropriate vocabulary and norms for managing conflict and grievances because Muslim representatives would be interacting with government officials on a regular basis.

What Should Western Muslim Organizations and Leaders Do?

Muslim leaders and organizations must recognize that they need to address serious and sometimes legitimate concerns among Western publics and groups that impede their own integration and prospects. They may want to do the following:

Develop a sense of belonging and ownership. Western Muslims must fully accept and clearly assert that they are full stakeholders in their countries' political systems, security, economies, and futures. They must fully realize that what affects their countries—terrorism, war, crime, bad policies—affects them as well. Muslim organizations should be explicit about asserting that Western Muslims' future and lives are in their countries and about promoting a sense of belonging and ownership. They should continue to develop a vocabulary and language that genuinely reflects their pride in being Muslim citizens of their countries. Of course, with belonging comes the right and obligation to engage society and advocate for their positions in all spheres. They must accept that their countries' institutions are legitimate even if they are flawed. Only then can they work to reform these institutions through legal means to gain their rights, remedy transgressions, and make policies more equitable.

Focus on leadership, outreach, and coalition building. Americans who do not know much about Islam and Muslims are more likely to hold very unfavorable opinions of Muslims and Islam, and to want to restrict their civil rights.[7] This presents a serious risk for American Muslims because no more than 40 percent of the general public feels knowledgeable about Islam (Nisbet et al.). The same may apply to other Western countries as well, which bodes ill because a 2002 survey found that 73 percent of the British public knows "nothing" or "not very much" about Britain's Muslim community.[8] To effectively engage society and state institutions, Western Muslim organizations must encourage civic engagement from within their communities, reach out to other social, religious, and political groups and build solid coalitions with others who share their concerns. Doing so would remove fears that they cannot function effectively within the context of Western liberal democracies and will make others familiar and comfortable with their presence in the public sphere.

Increase transparency and avoid the appearance of double-talk. The detractors of Western Muslims often make use of accusations of double-talk that evoke the anti-Semitic canard of double loyalty. Such accusations have been used by those trying to undermine Western Muslim academics such as Tariq Ramadan and leaders of American Muslim organizations. Western Muslim leaders and organizations must diffuse such attacks by increasing the transparency of their institutions. They must develop a clear and consistent agenda to promote within their communities and to the broader public. They should deal courageously themselves with any contradictions in this agenda until they feel comfortable sharing it with all audiences. Being consistent, transparent, and principled increases the ability to dissent and to advocate.

Rethink the fiqh (jurisprudence) of minorities. Western Muslim organizations should encourage and build on the efforts of innovative Muslim theologians by reconsidering the premises of the theology of being a Muslim in a non-Muslim country for the long term. It is an empirical fact that members of Muslim minorities cannot prosper and live fulfilling lives if they do not accept, or are perceived not to accept, some basic principles of life in liberal democracies. These include accepting the freedom of others to act according to their own beliefs in the public sphere so long as they do not cause direct harm, unfettered freedom of speech so long as it is allowed for everyone, and acceptance of the legitimacy of government institutions.

Redress attitudes toward the gay community and Jews in their own countries. Western Muslim organizations must face directly, honestly, and conclusively some thorny issues that cause concerns among some non-Muslim Westerners. Those include attitudes toward gay rights in countries like the Netherlands and toward Western Jews in countries like France. A generally tolerant society is a society that would be good for Muslims. Conversely, Muslims must fear for their own rights in Western societies the moment gay rights are curtailed or anti-Semitism raises its ugly head because they would be next in line. In no way should Muslim organizations promote intolerance against members of the GLBT community, Jews, or anyone else. In fact, they are well advised to fight intolerance alongside other like-minded groups. Muslim organizations should be quick to condemn and preempt hate crimes perpetuated by youths of Muslim background. Theological sanctions against homosexuality should be understood to be a matter of personal belief that does not have to translate into a political position. Jewish attitudes on the Arab-Israeli conflict should not color how Muslim and Jewish compatriots should treat each other. More importantly, gay people and Jews are members of fellow minorities that share the concern of Western Muslims with civil rights, civil liberties, hate crime, media transgressions, and protections under the law. They are natural allies to be respected and dealt with in spite of disagreements on lifestyle and foreign policy. One illustration of the potential of such cooperation is the coalition that backed Keith Ellison, the first successful Muslim candidate for Congress. It included, among others, Jews, Muslims, and gays from Minnesota's Fifth Congressional District (Sinno). Muslims should be on the front line of the fight for minority rights for all and actively learn from the American Jewish experience how to do this effectively. Respect, of course, does not preclude potential disagreement on issues like gay marriage or some Israeli policies, but disagreement should be voiced in a respectful and reasoned way that does not undermine broader common interests.

Develop a culture of open exchange within Muslim communities. Muslim organizations must encourage open debate and discussion within Muslim communities to avoid alienating segments of these communities, to reflect their broader attitudes toward societal inclusiveness, and to make the Western Muslim experience a richer and more meaningful one. Western Muslim communities are very diverse in every respect, and to restrict internal debates by proclaiming anyone outside the fold would necessarily exclude certain segments of the Muslim population and create conflict within the community. Western Muslims, if they are to truly embrace societal diversity and a consistent discourse, will then also have to both accept and even encourage such diversity within the community. This may raise difficult challenges such as integrating gay Muslims and dealing with generational differences, historical sectarian divisions, and some generally unpopular Muslim feminist demands. Such issues, and many others, have confounded other Western religious communities as well. Addressing these challenges may be difficult, but avoiding them may exact a higher price: rejecting diversity could lead to irreconcilable divisions similar to the ones that splintered Judaism and many Protestant denominations in the United States.

Effectively debate gender issues. Western Muslims should openly, clearly, and proactively address gender issues. Honor killings, forced marriages, and genital mutilations performed by some traditional European Muslim families are flagrant violations of women's rights under both the laws of Islam and those of the countries of residence. Western Muslim organizations should be at the forefront of educating immigrant populations on the illegality and harm caused by such practices to Muslim women. To do so would also diffuse Islamophobic attacks that try to associate such practices with Islam and Western Muslims in general.

Address security fears. Western Muslims must understand that the security fears of Western publics (Wike and Allen) and states are very real and legitimate. They must further understand that terrorist attacks by Western Muslim individuals could produce once unthinkable devastating restrictions on their collective civil rights and prospects in volatile times. Western Muslim organizations must therefore (1) make it clear that they understand that this is the case, (2) clearly declare their support for security measures that do not discriminate against Muslims or cause harm to society at large, and (3) educate Western Muslims about the importance of preventing any act of terrorism by members of Muslim minorities. They should also consistently engage elected officials to provide them with a Muslim perspective on issues of security and civil rights and to seek institutional means of representation on this issue (for instance, congressional committees in the U.S. and the Canadian Cross-Cultural Roundtable on national security issues).

Engage media organizations. Western Muslims should actively engage the editors, producers, and managers of media outfits to educate them about Muslim sensitivities. Results could be surprisingly effective. For example, in 2006 a group of Indiana Muslims met with the editors of a small midwestern town's newspaper to explain to them that some letters they published were either Islamophobic or anti-Semitic. The editors learned from the discussion, apologized for not being able to identify the hate speech, promised to be more vigilant, and invited members of the Muslim community to contribute op-eds to the religion section. At the time of this writing, only one Islamophobic letter had been published in this newspaper since the meeting, and in that case the editors promptly contacted members of the Muslim community requesting a response. While not all newspaper editors could be expected to be as gracious as these Indiana ones were, engagement can raise awareness and promote understanding. Muslim-American organizations should also promote letter and op-ed writing among Western Muslims to help expose the public and politicians to their views.

Develop effective imam training programs. Western Muslim leadership on the local level is often provided by mosque leaders. Communities would therefore benefit immensely from an infusion of skilled imams (Klausen). Imam training programs must equip their graduates with critical skills beyond theological knowledge. They must train imams to become good communicators in the national language who are comfortable addressing Muslims and non-Muslims, to effectively engage in interfaith and intercultural projects, to address local legal and political issues affecting the community, to effectively run mosques, to deal with the media, and to counsel diverse, sometimes troubled, but often sophisticated populations of Western Muslims. Imams should also develop networks of continuing education and exchange with similar professionals. Such imams would make the mosque a more relevant institution for many Muslims and reduce local tensions.

Participate in established institutions. Muslim Americans should actively engage and participate in established civic and political institutions—join political parties, support political campaigns, run for elected office, form political action committees, lobby, volunteer, and so on. Until they do, their views and positions will not be considered in the hallways of power. Politicians need to feel the presence of Muslims in their communities and to understand that they matter. It is incumbent upon Western Muslims to make their presence known.

Conclusion

The venture of researching the politics of Western Muslims is in its infancy. There is still much to be learned and understood. Cutting-edge research will likely take the shape of more sophisticated and more comprehensive analyses of institutions, public opinion, minority attitudes, media content, religious and political discourse by Western Muslims and their detractors, elite behavior, identity formation, and legal developments. Cumulative and expanded knowledge is important because the situation of Western Muslims will likely evolve in dramatic ways in coming years. Western politicians and elites, as well as Western Muslim leaders, may want to track this research closely—the stakes are high. They must behave wisely if they wish to preserve the human rights, dignity, and security of their populations while preserving, even refining, their liberal and democratic institutions.

Notes

1. "Hearts, Minds, and Dollars: In an Unseen Front in the War on Terrorism, America is Spending Millions . . . to Change the Very Face of Islam," David E. Kaplan, *U.S. News and World Report,* April 25, 2005.

2. See the different reports of the Pew Global Attitudes Project, available at http://pewglobal.org/.

3. There are exceptions, among them occasionally Islamophobic columns by conservative syndicated columnists such as Cal Thomas and Ann Coulter.

4. Incidentally, *Paris Match* also uses "*fous de Yahweh*" to describe religious Jews.

5. On the vestigial state of laws protecting against discrimination in France, see "Anti-discrimination Legislation in EU Member States: France," a report prepared by Sophie Recht, European Monitoring Center on Racism and Xenophobia, 2002. Online at http://www.migpolgroup.com/multiattachments/2394/DocumentName/ART13_France-en.pdf (accessed April 16, 2007).

6. See the chapters in part 1 and chapters 6 and 7 of this volume for more details.

7. "Views of Muslim-Americans Hold Steady after London Bombings," Pew Research Center, July 26, 2005, p. 6.

8. "Attitudes towards British Muslims," November 4, 2002, a survey commissioned for Islam Awareness Week 2002 by the Islamic Society of Britain and conducted by YouGov. Online at www.isb.org.uk/iaw/docs/SurveyIAW2002.pdf (accessed April 16, 2007).

Contributors

Jodie T. Allen is Senior Editor at the Pew Research Center. She was previously managing editor and columnist for *U.S. News & World Report,* Washington bureau chief for *Slate Magazine,* and editor of Outlook, the Sunday commentary section of the *Washington Post,* where she was also an editorial writer and business columnist. She has held positions in government and in private research organizations and is a member of the Council on Foreign Relations and the National Academy of Social Insurance.

David Cole is a law professor at Georgetown University Law Center, a volunteer attorney with the Center for Constitutional Rights, and the legal affairs editor for *The Nation.* He is author of *Enemy Aliens: Double Standards and Constitutional Freedoms in the War on Terrorism; Terrorism and the Constitution: Sacrificing Civil Liberties in the Name of National Security;* and *No Equal Justice: Race and Class in the American Criminal Justice System.*

Anja Dalgaard-Nielsen is Senior Research Fellow at the Danish Institute for International Studies (DIIS) and Program Director for DIIS Studies in Terrorism and Counterterrorism. She is a non-resident Fellow at the Center for Transatlantic Relations, Johns Hopkins University School of Advanced International Studies (SAIS), Washington, D.C., and holds a Ph.D. from Johns Hopkins University SAIS.

Joel S. Fetzer is Associate Professor of Political Science at Pepperdine University. He specializes in comparative immigration politics and is author of *Public Attitudes toward Immigration in the United States, France, and Germany* and co-author of *Muslims and the State in Britain, France, and Germany.*

Yvonne Yazbeck Haddad is Professor of History of Islam and Christian-Muslim Relations at the Edmond B. Walsh School of Foreign Service at Georgetown University. She is past president of the Middle East Studies Association and a former editor of *Muslim World*. Her published works include *Contemporary Islam and the Challenge of History* and *Not Quite American? The Shaping of Arab and Muslim Identity in the United States*.

Amaney Jamal is Assistant Professor of Politics at Princeton University. She is principal investigator of "Mosques and Civic Incorporation of Muslim Americans"; co–principal investigator of the Detroit Arab American Study, a sister survey to the Detroit Area Study; and Senior Advisor on the Pew Research Center Project on Islam in America. In 2005, Jamal was named a Carnegie Scholar.

Jytte Klausen is Professor of Comparative Politics at Brandeis University and an affiliate at the Center for European Studies, Harvard University. Her most recent book is *The Islamic Challenge: Politics and Religion in Western Europe*. Klausen received the Carnegie Scholars Award in 2007.

Jorgen S. Nielsen is Danish National Research Foundation Professor of Islamic Studies and Director of the Centre for European Islamic Thought, Faculty of Theology, University of Copenhagen. He has been active in research on Muslims in Europe, previously at the University of Birmingham, UK, since the late 1970s and is chief editor of the series *Muslim Minorities*, published by Brill, Leiden.

Erik C. Nisbet is Assistant Professor of Communication at the Ohio State University. He specializes in comparative political communication and opinion formation, with a special focus on the role of mass media and public opinion in international conflict.

Ronald Ostman is Professor Emeritus of Communication and former Department Chair at Cornell University, where he has taught and conducted research since 1979. He was a Visiting Fellow at the New Zealand Council for Educational Research in 1986, a Fulbright Scholar at the University of Pune, India, in 1988–1989, and a consultant on Information Dissemination for the World Health Organization, Geneva, in 1996.

Robert Stephen Ricks is a Ph.D. student in Arabic and Islamic Studies at Georgetown University. He received his M.A. in Arab Studies from Georgetown and his B.A. from Brigham Young University. During the 2003–2004 year, he was a fellow at the Center for Arabic Study Abroad in Cairo.

Kent Roach is Professor of Law at the University of Toronto where he holds the Prichard-Wilson Chair in Law and Public Policy and cross appointments in criminology and political science. He is the author of eight books, including *September 11: Consequences for Canada,* and the co-editor of six books, including *Global Anti-Terrorism Law and Policy.* He served on the research advisory commission for the Commission of Inquiry into the Activities of Canadian Officials in Relation to Maher Arar.

James Shanahan is Associate Professor in and Chair of the Department of Communication at Fairfield University. He is co-author of *Television and Its Viewers*.

Abdulkader H. Sinno is Assistant Professor of Political Science and Middle Eastern Studies at Indiana University, Bloomington. He is author of *Organizations at War in Afghanistan and Beyond*. He specializes in the study of Middle Eastern politics, the politics of Western Muslims, and conflict processes and state building. He is working on a new manuscript on Muslim representation in Western democracies.

J. Christopher Soper is Professor of Political Science at Pepperdine University. He is co-author of *The Challenge of Pluralism: Church and State in Five Democracies; Faith, Hope, and Jobs: Welfare-to-Work in Los Angeles;* and *Muslims and the State in Britain, France, and Germany*.

Eren Tatari is a doctoral student in the Political Science Department at Indiana University. She teaches and writes on Muslims in the West with a focus on local politics and gender issues. Her dissertation work explores Muslim local representation in the UK.

Richard Wike is Associate Director of the Pew Global Attitudes Project. He received his Ph.D. in political science from Emory University and has published articles in a variety of publications, including the *Journal of Politics, Social Science Quarterly,* and *Polity,* as well as the Pew Research Center's online publication, Pewresearch.org.

Index